Unsung Courage

Arthur Bishop

Unsung Courage

20 Stories of Canadian Valour and Sacrifice

HarperCollins*PublishersLtd*

Acknowledgements

The largest contributor to this book was Dennis Joyes of the Main Reference Centre of the Metropolitan Reference Centre. Dennis steered me to the main sources of information I needed in my research. I am also grateful to him for catering to my frequent requests and for his recommendations and suggestions. I should also like to thank Lesley Bell, the Team Leader of that division of the MTRL for her assistance and guidance.

Many of my old buddies from 401, the Ram Squadron, RCAF came to my aid in the preparation of the chapter "They Kept Coming Back." I am much obliged to the following ex-Rams: Gib Coons, Hap Kennedy, Scotty Murray, Rod Smith, Ray Sherk and Ken Woodhouse.

Thanks to Carolyn Gossage who was of great help in preparing the "One in a Million" and "Soldier of the Queen's" chapters.

As always, I am grateful to my printer, Wesley Douglas of Reprodux, for his help with photocopying and other collateral printing chores.

It was also great to be working again with my old friend, editor Don Loney, who did such a magnificent job in whipping this manuscript into shape. By the same token I want to thank Rodney Rawlings, who copy-edited the m/s, for his close attention to detail.

Finally I am indebted to my agent Frances Hanna for her perseverance in finding the right home for this book, my new publisher HarperCollins.

Arthur Bishop

Unsung Courage:
20 Stories of Canadian Valour and Sacrifice
Copyright © 2001 by Arthur Bishop
All rights reserved. No part of this book may be used or reproduced in any manner whatsoever without prior written permission except in the case of brief quotations embodied in reviews. For information address
HarperCollins Publishers Ltd,
55 Avenue Road, Suite 2900,
Toronto, Ontario, Canada M5R 3L2

www.harpercanada.com

HarperCollins books may be purchased for educational, business, or sales promotional use. For information please write:
Special Markets Department,
HarperCollins Canada,
55 Avenue Road, Suite 2900,
Toronto, Ontario, Canada M5R 3L2

First edition

Canadian Cataloguing in Publication Data

Bishop, William Arthur, 1923–
Unsung courage : 20 stories of Canadian valour and sacrifice.

ISBN 0-00-200076-8

1. World War, 1939–1945 – Personal narratives, Canadian.
I. Title.

D811.A2B57 2001   940.54'8171   C2001-9301421-1

HC 6 5 4 3 2 1

Printed and bound in the United States
Set in FF Scala and Scala Sans

Contents

Introduction

I have long felt that a representative survey of some of the thousands of Canadians whose feats of bravery and sacrifice during World War II remain largely unknown was long overdue and needed to be told. To pay them proper tribute presented its own difficulties. A suitable selection had to be made to provide as broad a cross-section of experiences as possible.

Those choices are mine and they include the stories of:

- Wally Reyburn, an unarmed war correspondent, one of the first men to land on the beaches at Dieppe and, after being wounded during that bloody nine-hour battle, one of the last to leave
- Ralph Manning, a torpedo bomber pilot, who sank the German tanker *Proserpina*, robbing Rommel of his oil supply and ensuring the British victory at El Alamein
- Espionage agent Guy Bieler, for whom the Gestapo provided a guard of honour at his execution in recognition of his courage under interrogation and torture
- George Evans, who ran away from home when he was 15 years old to join the merchant marine and serve as a stoker in the convoys on the dreaded Murmansk run
- 18-year-old rifleman Ken Cambon, who survived four-and-a-half years of captivity at the most notorious of all the Japanese "slave" prisoner-of-war camps, Niigata, where 80 Canadians were brutally murdered and many more subjected to continuous torture

These stories bring together my own experiences as a fighter pilot in World War II, recollections of conversations, interviews, and shared events, as well as study and research through a variety of sources: biographies, autobiographies, histories, official documents, citations, and correspondence. Some of the material is first-hand and unaltered.

In publishing this book, I hope I have succeeded in bringing these gallant Canadians out of the wings and into the spotlight to receive the recognition and respect they so richly deserve.

ARTHUR BISHOP

TORONTO

In the Air

Chapter 1

They Kept Coming Back

"Mind if I borrow your kite? Mine's U/S."

What could I say? Sure! Be my guest! With all the low cloud and drizzle dangling over Biggin Hill fighter field in Kent that wet, soppy, mid-winter morning, who needed it? If Tex Davenport was gung-ho or crazy enough to want to risk a "Rhubarb"—those dubious two-plane low-level raids against the enemy coastal defences in France—he was welcome to take my freshly overhauled Spitfire YOK as a substitute for his own unserviceable aircraft. As he climbed into the cockpit I waved him goodbye and silently wished him luck. That was the last I would see of him for another five months—and the very last I would ever see of my precious fighter.

I am reminded of a remark Tex had made to me earlier that very day, that in the event he was captured he'd say to the Germans: "Y'all stop hitting me over the balls with a wet shoelace and I'll tell you anything you want to know."

Shortly before 1100 hours on 9 January 1944, Tex, with Bill Klersy as his number two, took off at low level for random targets in the Pas de Calais. Tex had charted a course southeast to Folkestone on the coast, then a turn to starboard to cross the English Channel in a direction that would take them to a point between Boulogne and Calais. It was dicey enough just getting there. With Tex navigating and Bill tucked in closely alongside, they flew partly on instruments through a soup of drizzle and snow squalls, and partly on ground contact.

Around noon I was getting ready to walk from the pilots' dispersal hut to the officers' mess for lunch, when out of the overcast a single Spitfire wallowed in for a landing—but the squadron letters on the side of the fuselage were not YOK! A downcast Bill Klersy climbed out of his aircraft and shook his head. I didn't need to ask what happened; he was only too anxious to get it off his chest.

"It was rough," he blurted out as we strolled back to dispersal. As soon as he and Tex had hit the coast, flak had erupted all around them. As they crossed in over land, the cloud was right down on the deck and they lost visual contact but there was no letup from the enemy fire. "Stuff was bursting all around, heavy and light. It was hairy. Tex radioed he was pancaking and I got the hell out of there as quick as I could." Incredibly, Bill's aircraft didn't have a single hole in it.

Later, over a drink in the mess, Bill began to wind down. His main concern was how Tex had made out. "I hope he's all right," he said, and, symptomatically of the comradeship we shared in those days, added, "I loved that little guy."

In fact, that "little guy" was in good shape, which is more than could be said for my poor old YOK: Tex would later tell me that it had been so riddled with gunfire it was beyond saving. ("You wouldn't've wanted it back, Bish.")

Tex had landed in an open field wheels up and climbed out of the battered Spitfire. Because it was raining, there was no one about, though the landscape was thick with gun emplacements. Had the weather been clear, his downed plane would have been easily spotted and the Germans would have picked him up. (But that's academic; on a clear day he wouldn't have been on a Rhubarb anyway.) Shedding his battle-dress jacket and cutting off the tops of his flying boots (designed to resemble ordinary shoes after so doing), he made for nearby bushes, where he hid until nightfall. By this time it had stopped raining and he was able to move slowly in a southerly direction, guided by the North Star. He had been shot down near Boulogne.

At first light, Davenport stumbled into a concrete structure that—as he discovered much later—was a V-1 flying bomb launch-pad site. Though there were several German soldiers and French workmen about, no one paid him the slightest attention. He realized the danger of walking about in broad daylight, however, and found a hiding place among some trees.

Sheltering by day and wandering south by night, sustained by the rations from his escape kit—malt tablets, chocolate, and Benzedrine pills—he finally reached Amiens, where he found his way to the railway station. He seems to have been blessed with luck. Though his appearance by this time was scruffy—he hadn't shaved for several days and his clothes had become quite soiled from lying on the ground—no one stopped him, not even several uniformed Germans whom he passed along the way. Davenport ordered a ticket *sud*, which he paid for in French currency out of his escape kit.

The trainmaster, a member of the Resistance, recognized Tex as the Allied airman who had been shot down some days ago; word had been passed through the Underground that an individual wearing blue (air force) clothing was a downed flyer. He issued the ticket without comment. Tex sat down on a bench, picked up a newspaper that lay there, and pretended to read it as two German soldiers plunked themselves down beside him. "I buried my face in the paper and thumbed my nose at them," he told me later with a smirk.

Davenport intended to stay on the train and let it take him as far south as it went. He was fortunate that the Germans had rerouted some of the trains. "I breathed a sigh of relief," he said, "when we kept on going straight through Paris after only a brief stop. Some Germans boarded the train, looked around but asked no questions. Then, satisfied everything was okay, they got off."

For the next day and a half he sat in the cold, uncomfortable train with its wooden seats, alternately dozing and staring out the window, trying to stay inconspicuous and avoid any conversation with the other passengers. However, one kindly Frenchman seated across from him insisted on befriending his fellow traveller and generously sharing his loaf of bread. Then for Davenport the trip suddenly came to an abrupt end. At a stop in which the train sat idle for over half an hour he was unexpectedly and rudely jostled by the conductor, who grabbed him by the shoulder, pulled him from his seat, and propelled him toward the door shouting: "*Allez! Allez vite!*" Davenport had no choice but to submit, but he was totally unprepared for what happened next. As he stumbled onto the wooden platform a smiling couple rushed forward to greet him like a long-lost relative, and with the words "*Pressez! Pressez!*" he was hustled into the back of a truck.

He was driven to the house where the couple lived, which abutted a small mill, outside a tiny hamlet near Toulouse in the south of France some 60 miles from the border with Spain. Convinced he was among friends and at this point having nothing to lose anyway, Davenport showed them his dog tags, identified himself, and admitted he was the pilot of the Spitfire shot down in France on January 9 in case they wanted to check up on him. They simply nodded and smiled. What did *that* mean? After several glasses of cognac and some food, the husband (Tex never did reveal his hosts' names to me and, as far as I know, to anyone else except, probably, the air force authorities) acknowledged that, yes, they knew he was the downed British pilot. In fact, he had been shadowed ever since the trainmaster had recognized him at Amiens. At every stop along the way members of the Underground had been on hand in case he detrained, ready to shelter him. It had been no accident that he had finally been "apprehended" and turned over to the French couple for safekeeping.

He was to lie doggo until arrangements could be made with the Maquis Resistance fighters to take him across the Pyrenees into neutral Spain. Meanwhile he could, if he wished, help turn out printed forms such as registration sheets and other clerical documents for the German army. That explained the mill adjacent to the house. But work for the German army? It was the turn of the lady of the house to explain, "*Une opération couverte*." Just a cover-up. The printing press was also used to produce counterfeit money to help undermine the enemy-run economy. Davenport readily agreed to participate; the idea appealed to his devilish nature. He was also drilled in the location of factories and German installations in the area that the French wanted targeted by the Royal Air Force (RAF).

After two months of relative comfort, Davenport was turned over to the Maquis and taken to a cabin sheltered in some woods at the foot of the Pyrenees where, with half a dozen others, he was told to wait for a suitable time for them to be escorted across the mountains into Spain. Conditions and timing had to be just right before any trek to freedom could be attempted or even contemplated, taking into account such factors as weather—winter blizzards—and constantly changing and rotating German border patrols as well as regular aerial surveillance flights over the area by the Luftwaffe.

For the evaders, time hung heavily on their hands; the waiting was an exercise in self-discipline. Exercise was one answer to boredom—pushups, running on the spot, and knee bends—but due to the meagre rations meted out to them, they became easily exhausted. "I would strip down to the waist and rub myself all over with snow," Tex told me. "It invigorated me but I was still hungry all the time." They became increasingly withdrawn, sleeping the days and nights away.

By April, the snowstorms had eased, and one night the men were escorted by experienced mountain climbers across the Pyrenees, plodding slowly and in single file through snowdrifts, a journey that took four days in which one of the men slipped off a precipice and was lost. Once across the border they were turned over to the Spanish border guards and thrown in jail, an unpleasant finale to a venture that had left them malnourished and weak. Finally the British embassy in Madrid arranged for their release. Davenport was sent to Gibraltar and from there flown to England.

On 18 May 1944, three weeks before the invasion of Europe, Tex turned up in our officers' mess tent at Tangmere airfield on the coast of Surrey, during the evening drinking hour, to be welcomed by Klersy, me, and the others, to whom he told his story. Pulling a wad of pound notes from his pocket, he bragged with a wink and a twinkle in his eye that it represented repayment by British intelligence for the "gold watch, gold cigarette case, gold lighter, and my mother's pearl brooch keepsake that I had to throw away while dodging the Germans." Same old Davenport. Next day he returned to Ops (operations) with us.

Ironically, earlier that spring of 1944, Johnnie Johnson, the top Allied Ace in the Eastern Theatre, who had been taken off operations for a rest as a staff officer at Group Headquarters, successfully persuaded the chiefs at Fighter Command to put a halt to the Rhubarb forays—purportedly Churchill's idea in the first place—which accomplished very little and had cost the lives of many of our best fighter pilots.

Our chief nemesis that winter of 1943–44 was the "air lock." That bloody air lock!

In early January we were issued extra-range drop-tanks, which were affixed to the bellies of our new Spitfire Mark-1 X-Bs. When we switched over to the disposable tanks from the main fuel tanks after takeoff, and vice versa while over enemy territory when the disposable tanks ran dry, an air lock would often occur and result in a total loss of engine power. Planes would crash on takeoff, injuring and killing pilots.

Orders were issued to pilots forthwith to climb to 1000 feet and circle the field before switching the tanks. This didn't solve the problem of the air lock, but it saved a few pilots who were able to land wheels down on the runway when their engine quit. The other vexation, engine failure when switching back to the main tanks, could sometimes be solved by pumping the hand primer to inject fuel into the carburetor and re-firing the engine.

That didn't always work. If the engine refused to start, a pilot was left with two options: (1) make for the English Channel if it was within gliding distance, bail out as far as possible from the enemy coast, and be picked up by the Air-Sea Rescue Service or (2) keep heading inland—the closer to the Spanish border, the better the chance of evading capture. If the engine still hadn't caught by the time the plane was down to 10,000 feet, the pilot had to hit the silk and hope for the best.

When my engine packed up at 20,000 feet over the Crecy Forest— "Creaky" Forest—in northern France, which bristled with flak guns, I decided on exactly that course of action, chancing my way through the ugly black bursts of antiaircraft shells, all the while pumping the primer like crazy and losing height fast. When I hit the coast I was down to 6000 feet, but mercifully the faithful Merlin roared back to life and I made a beeline back to base.

In mid-March 1944, two of our pilots, Ray Sherk and Ken Woodhouse, both fell victim to the air lock—one day after the other.

The morning of March 15 marked the second time Ray Sherk had gone missing. Eighteen months earlier he had been shot down in the North African Desert near El Alamein. Taken prisoner, he and another Hurricane pilot, Don McLarty, were flown in an Italian Savoia Marchetti 82 Italian transport from Derna across the Mediterranean to Brindisi on the Adriatic heel of Italy. En route they were seated behind two enemy officers, who were wearing holstered revolvers. Sherk was tempted to grab the pistols and hijack the plane. But then what? Where to? He thought better of the idea.

Sherk and McLarty ended up in an Italian prisoner-of-war camp at Sulmona, 60 miles east of Rome. But the POW camp couldn't hold them. Their escape involved a number of close calls, not helped by Sherk's persistent mania for fighting his own mini-war by sabotaging German trucks whenever the chance presented itself. By November of 1943 they reached the Canadian lines near the Sangro River.

Now, on this March Sunday morning in 1944, only a month after joining our squadron, Ray Sherk was about to face a similar adventure. South of Arras his engine suddenly went, as he said, "deader than King Henry the Eighth." Sherk lost a lot of height while he pumped the primer like mad before taking to his parachute. But he managed to land safely at the edge of the Newfoundland War Graves cemetery at Beaumont Hamel—scene of a World War I battle on 1 July 1916, in which 800 out of 900 Newfoundlanders were killed in a matter of hours. "Helmets and rifles from that battle were still scattered about everywhere," Sherk reported.

He was greeted by a farmer, Louis Serre, and several youngsters who had been waiting in some nearby woods. Having identified himself by pointing to the Canada shoulder badges on his battle-dress jacket, Sherk was taken to Serre's house a half-mile away where the Frenchman's family offered the Canadian a very welcome glass of wine. Having hastily shed his battle dress and assumed the role of one of the family, Sherk felt an overwhelming sense of relief. It didn't last long. Some time later the roar of motorcycles signalled the arrival of the Gestapo. Calmly and matter-of-factly the Serres shepherded their ward to a haystack behind the house where they hid him. The Germans did not discover the downed airman.

That day had been a banner one for 401 Squadron. A few miles from where Ray went down, four of our pilots accounted for as many Focke-Wulf 190 German fighters destroyed. That afternoon, celebrating the victorious outing, we toasted Ray in absentia and wished him luck. He later recalled, "Here I was, hiding out in a bloody haystack with visions of you guys back at Biggin Hill enjoying your usual evening thrash. You couldn't feel much lonelier than that."

That night the Serres, taking no chances of a return visit by the Gestapo, moved Sherk to Mademoiselle Louisette Bouchez's house. Later he was moved to Elaine Mapleaux's house in the village of Herbuterne until she found a safe place for him to stay with Leo Roussel, a school teacher, and his wife Renée in the adjacent village of Maily-Mailett. Leo, who was active with the Underground, was a master forger and provided Sherk with a false identity card under the name of Raymond Fournier; occupation *charron*—blacksmith.

For two weeks, Sherk waited patiently for the time when he could proceed south to eventually cross the French border into neutral Spain, "enjoying good food and wine on the way." On one occasion, he said, "I even went pheasant hunting with Leo, who, qualifying as the owner of a farm, was allowed to keep firearms."

Later Sherk was joined by an American, a downed B17 Flying Fortress American bombardier, Roy Carpenter. Both men decided the time had come to push on south. Leo Roussel introduced them to another member of the Underground, Leo Deflandre, who agreed to guide them by rail to Paris, then on to Bordeaux. But at the outset, things did not go quite according to plan.

On the platform of the Amiens railway station, Sherk was immediately recognized for who he was—an Allied airman—by an alert pair of German soldiers who promptly arrested him. But when the train arrived, in the ensuing confusion of passengers arriving and departing, he was able to break loose from his captors, lose himself in the crowd, and board the train just as it pulled out of the station. He soon found his two companions, who were astounded that he had been able to escape so easily.

The trip to Paris and then, after changing trains, to Bordeaux was uneventful. "We slept most of the way—or pretended to, to avoid drawing attention to ourselves." At the southeastern French port,

Leo Deflandre turned them over to another Underground guide, Guy Mazet, who took them by bus to Dax, 100 miles north of the Pyrenees, the route to freedom. Now they were left on their own, to make the rest of the journey on foot, sustained by bread and root vegetables their escort had provided them.

When they reached the border they approached a French peasant who introduced them to a local smuggler who agreed—for a price—to take them through the mountains, a day's trek. Once across the border they were immediately arrested by the Spanish police, not what they expected from a "neutral" republic. Yelling and screaming at the top of their lungs, the airmen demanded to see the proper authorities. Their outrage paid off quickly. They were taken before a Spanish army officer who, to their surprise, invited them to the mess to lunch. Afterwards they were driven to the British consulate in Pamplona, the city famed for the annual "Running of the Bulls." Then on to Madrid, Gibraltar, and England.

Before Sherk left Herbuterne in France, Leo Roussel had asked him to, when he made it back to England, request the BBC in one of their nightly transmissions to radio a message, "The sky is blue," so that the French Underground would know their efforts had succeeded. Sherk passed the request on to MI-9 who quickly processed it. He learned later that when the French Resistance received the message they were jubilant; it served as a great tonic for all the risks they had taken and were still taking. (Sadly, he also later learned that both Leo Roussel and Leo Deflandre, who had done so much to make his and his American comrade Roy Carpenter's escape possible, were subsequently arrested by the Gestapo and executed.)

Ray was the third homing pigeon to return to 401 Squadron during my tenure there. He had high hopes of continuing his tour of operations, cut so short in March, but the powers that be ruled otherwise. To his chagrin he concluded the war as an instructor back in Canada. In fact the garrulous Ray Sherk—the superb evader—had experienced and done more than his share.

Ken Woodhouse would always remember Thursday, 16 May 1944—the day after Ray Sherk went down—as "a turning point where a 20-year-old kid was tested and became a man ... the beginning of an adventure where I saw the worst and the best in people." Looking back on that date, to the rest of us with the squadron at the time, it seemed a miracle that the same Woody, who'd gone missing just over a week earlier, suddenly reappeared in the doorway of our dispersal hut after escaping from France in only eight days. Eight days!

Those eight days started out as a fighter sweep over France. At 20,000 feet somewhere south of Amiens, undisturbed by enemy fighters who were too busy defending the Fatherland to bother with the likes of us, we switched over from the auxiliary tanks to the main fuel supply. Woody's voice crackled over the radio-transmitter (R/T), giving his call sign to identify him and telling us he was turning back with engine trouble. That was for the benefit of the German interceptor stations. When his engine refused to restart, thanks to that damned air lock, he headed inland before bailing out.

Drifting in his parachute, he heard a muffled impact as his Spitfire crashed into some woods near the village of Remerangles. Looking west, he noticed a small truck kicking up a cloud of dust heading in the direction where he would likely land—Germans on their way to pick him up. "They sure don't give a guy much of a head start," he thought and hoped to beat them to the ground and hide in some woods nearby.

Woody came down heavily in a shallow, bowl-shaped field and in the process injured his left knee. He immediately began burying his parachute, intending to make a dash for it into the woods. He'd no sooner finished hiding it than the truck pulled up smartly about a hundred feet away. The driver climbed out and began frantically waving at him. Friend or foe? No way of telling, really. He wore blue overalls and no uniform, and seemed to be unarmed. Still, he had an angry, authoritative look. After only minutes in a hostile environment, Woody's instincts told him to get the hell away—fast. But with his injured leg he didn't get far, and all the while the driver was shouting at him. Woody didn't understand the language, but the words sounded suspiciously like, "Stop or I'll shoot!" in German.

With a bum leg he quickly realized his predicament was hopeless and he could hardly expect to outrace a truck. Win or lose, he succumbed to the inevitable and abjectly surrendered to the driver who kept yelling and motioned him to get into the back of the vehicle and stay hidden under some burlap sacks.

Woody's concerns and apprehensions were understandable. "The escape lectures our intelligence officers put us through made us suspicious of most everyone in occupied France. But I conceded that this fellow seemed to be sticking his neck out for me so I decided to play it by ear." He'd come to the correct conclusion, as he was soon to discover. The driver, a French farmer named Maurice Rendu, had been active for many years with the French Underground, helping Allied flyers evade capture.

The truck had barely got started when it suddenly ground to a stop. Then to Woody's alarm he heard the driver's voice. Though he couldn't understand what was being said, there was no mistaking the guttural tone of the voice of a second person. Later he learned that the German soldier had asked the driver if he had seen a parachutist. "Yes," was the reply. "The parachute landed over there!" Rendu had pointed in the direction where the Spitfire had crashed. That satisfied the German soldier and Rendu was allowed to continue on his way. About half a mile further on, he backed his truck against a hay shed and told Woody to burrow into the hay, to stay put and keep quiet until he returned.

Woody whiled away the time hiding any evidence that could identify him as an escaper. With the knife he'd pocketed inside his flying boots, he cut the tops off, making them into ordinary shoes. With a razorblade from his escape kit, he stripped the pilot's wings from his battle-dress jacket and put them in his shoe as insurance that if captured he could convince the Germans that he was an Allied pilot and not a spy. In the same vein he taped his dog tags onto the back of one leg. He also pocketed his expensive Rolex wristwatch, a gift from his parents when he joined the air force, which would be a dead giveaway.

While he was waiting he heard a car drive up and then German voices. The enemy was searching for him. Thankfully they did not search for long, and inexplicably they never came anywhere near the hay shed. Probably Rendu's earlier explanation that a parachutist had landed some distance away had satisfied them, for they soon left. Afterwards Rendu arrived with his wife and son and offered Woody a loaf of bread and a bottle of cider, then promptly left after telling him they would be back at dusk.

As promised, they returned and took him further away from the search area to Rendu's parents' house in the village of Fay St. Quentin. There Woody was introduced to two rough-looking characters in typical French work clothes who were actually downed members of an American bomber crew. He had been inducted into an escape operation! Next day he was grilled by an interrogator for the Resistance who spoke perfect English to make sure he was not a German "plant." Once he got past "name, rank, and serial number," Woody was asked questions unrelated to military matters but which would reveal whether he was a genuine Allied airman. He passed muster, but not without some difficulty. Questions about baseball stumped him. "Being a Western Canadian, I was a hockey fan, not a baseball fan," he told me.

Two days later before dawn, all three men were herded into the back of a truck driven by Rendu's father, Wilfred, and accompanied by a French *gendarme*, the chief of police of the area and a member of the Resistance, to begin a journey to Paris. En route they were joined by four more airmen, one of whom, an American air gunner, had been attended to by a French surgeon. It seemed to Woody that "The country must be full of airmen in hiding." They drove as far as Beauvais, where they were turned over to other members of the French Resistance and provided with identity cards as well as travel documents for the train journey to the French capital.

At the station, one of their Resistance guides bought the tickets, while the seven evaders, as instructed, stood about looking as casual as possible, avoiding even eye contact with one another. ("If you must smoke, make sure the cigarette stays in your mouth.")

The train coach was tailor-made for the evaders. Divided into sections like a loaf of sliced bread, the only entrance to the compartments was on either side; once the train got rolling, each compartment was isolated from the others so that there was no way a German or French railway official could check them.

But there was a snag. As they neared Paris, the Resistance men examined the identity cards the evaders had been issued at Beauvais. The cards were so badly put together that they would never pass the most cursory inspection; some of them didn't even have photographs. In effect they were useless. The guides tore them up and threw the pieces out the window. Better to have no I.D. at all than be caught with counterfeit papers and have to explain them. "With no identity cards at all, we could at least pretend we were escaping unaided," Woody remembered.

It had been a little over two days since he'd parachuted into France, and here he was debarking onto the platform of the Gare du Nord in Paris to play "follow the leader" behind a Resistance guide with six other escapers. It all seemed so simple and yet unreal—almost dreamlike. Then three things took place in succession that scared him out of his wits and snapped him back to reality.

At the same moment that their train pulled into the station, so did a German troop train. Soldiers detrained at the rail line next to them, less than 20 feet away. "Our plans for complete indifference to our surroundings ended right there," Woody recalled. How could you maintain your composure with hundreds of enemy soldiers all around you?

Worse still, as they approached the gate at the end of the platform, a tall, severe-looking Gestapo officer stood squarely in their path and seemed to be glaring suspiciously at all passengers. Woody was sure he'd been singled out. Yet all seven seemed to have escaped detection until a voice rang out, "Hey guys, wait for me!" in plain English! It was the wounded American airman who was falling behind. Stunned, the other six had the good sense and presence of mind to ignore him. "I was trying to make myself invisible," Woody said. "But I felt as big and obvious as a bus in a bicycle race. I was sure the Germans could read 'Made in Canada' stamped all over me." Once again luck was with the evaders for no one paid any attention—the shout must have gone unheard in the noisy station.

Outside the station, as instructed, they split up into pairs, circling the building while waiting to be approached by new guides. Wistfully, Woody recalled seeing a sign over an office door: Canadian National Railways. "Sort of gave me a twinge of homesickness!" he said. They were met by a tall man and an older lady who led them to an apartment where they were given food. From there Woody found himself in the care of a young woman who took him to her apartment across from the Luxembourg Gardens via the Metro. En route, he was witness to just how the conquerors treated the conquered.

At one station stop, a dozen German soldiers, well under the influence, crowded their way onto the subway car in which Woody and his escort were riding and began roughly pushing the passengers standing by the doorway out onto the platform. Then they shoved others out of their seats to make room for themselves. Fortunately, Woody and his companion were at the other end of the car.

He spent the night at the apartment across from the Luxembourg Gardens. From there Woody was taken by another guide, a male, to various locations, ending up, on his fifth day as an evader, at Lycée St. Louis, a high school in the heart of Paris and the apartment home of Maurice and Marguerite Cavalier, who were harbouring two Canadian airmen. Maurice claimed to have lived in Medicine Hat, Alberta, close to Woody's home in Prince Albert, Saskatchewan, and his wife said she had a sister still living there. It occurred to Woody that they had probably never lived there at all but were testing him for authenticity. "I sure fell for that one," Woody told me. "It was just as well, though. I had heard stories of evaders being shot by the Resistance when their identity was in doubt. Who could blame them?"

Woody was given a false identity card as well as a pass for travelling in the restricted 15-mile zone along the northern coast of France and a train ticket leaving Paris that night for St. Brieux in Brittany. He was also given a special travel pass and finally a train ticket to his destination. After bidding his hosts farewell, Woody and his guide set off for the railway station. They had not gone 150 feet when they encountered two burly *gendarmes*, one of whom said something Woody couldn't understand. He knew that one peep out of him in his poor French would buy him a one-way ticket to a prisoner-of-war camp—or worse. He did the only thing he could; he reached into his pocket and produced his newly issued identity card. Unsmiling, the *gendarme* looked at it and returned it. Woody walked on, not daring to look behind. When he reached his guide, the Frenchman, fearful that the *gendarmes* might be suspicious, told him to run for it. Together they hightailed it for several blocks before reaching a cafe where the guide was well known and they were served a stiff drink.

When Woody reached the station, he noticed several familiar faces in the crowd, among them the two Canadians he had met at the Cavaliers'—six in all making up an "escaping team" of seven under the charge of a new guide, a young woman who proved to be very feisty. Although all the evaders, as well as their guide, had been given reserved seats with "Coach 27" stamped on them, the aisle was crowded with people, some sitting, others standing, all carrying parcels. Undaunted, the young female led the way cursing and shouting, pushing and shoving, fighting her way to their compartment, No. 68. But it too was full of people who steadfastly refused to leave their seats even when she presented the reserved tickets. Angrily she ordered the evaders to get off the train. Once again they had to shove and push their way back through the crowded coach to get back onto the platform, where she told them to wait.

She soon returned with a protesting railway official in tow, whom she berated loudly, waving the reservation tickets in his face. Once more, the group had to bump and push their way through the protesting passengers to their assigned compartment, where, after much ranting on the part of the French railway man, the "squatters" were forced to reluctantly give up their seats. This wasn't popular with the other passengers; as the journey progressed, they became increasingly restless and then hostile, thinking the contingent must be made up of important German civilians.

At dawn the train stopped at St. Brieux in Brittany, and a new Resistance guide took over and they transferred to another train. A far cry from the mainliner in which they'd spent the night, it resembled an old streetcar, with standing room only at either end. That didn't bother Woody; after sleeping all night, he was glad to stand for a change. But it was mingling shoulder to shoulder with German soldiers that gave him the creeps. He kept moving about, facing the other way from any of them who looked likely to engage him in a conversation.

After several hours the train arrived at the village of Guingamp, an entry point into the restricted 15-mile zone. For the escapers this was as the crossing of the Rubicon. When they had to walk through the station gate, they knew German security would be at its tightest. If they could get past the gate, they would probably make good their escape.

Woody pondered the alternative. If caught, because they were dressed in civilian clothes and carried forged documents, they could hardly expect the Germans to respect the Geneva Convention as it pertained to prisoners of war. They would likely be shot as spies. "Far worse," Woody recalled with a shudder, "we had knowledge of escape routes, names of people who'd helped us, places where we'd hidden out, even German military installations."

But their worst fears were never realized. Incredibly, no one stopped them as they filed through the gate past their guide, who nodded in the direction of a house down the end of the street for them to enter. They split into two groups on either side of the street, but foolishly arrived at the house at the same moment. This made their guide, who was already twitchy because they had not been asked for passes and suspected that they might be under surveillance, even more jittery. His apprehension extended to the owner of the house who wanted them out of there just as quickly as possible. "We were just too hot for his comfort," Woody said. The guide calmed him down before setting off to look for other houses that would take them in.

A short while later another member of the Resistance arrived and took Woody and another evader to a large house nearby, owned by Francine St. Laurent, who fed them, gave them soap and water to wash, and showed them a bedroom where they could spend the night. Sheltering airmen was nothing new to Mme St. Laurent; by war's end, 32 would have passed through the house.

Next day toward dusk, Woody and his companion were loaded into the back of a truck in which there were six other airmen, and driven through the countryside. The truck stopped periodically to let one or two evaders off, an escort appearing out of the shadows by the side of the road. Woody and two others were led away by a young French girl to her house and then later to a farmhand's cabin, where they spent the night. Next morning before dark, she brought them back to the house where they waited until nightfall to be joined by others, and were then led through minefields and heavily fortified and patrolled areas along the coast. They still had no idea, nor would the girl tell them, how they would be taken to England.

They had been following a wooded trail when, to their horror, they stumbled onto a German army post. Soldiers were walking to and fro between the buildings, which emitted enough light through the doors and windows to make them—as well as the group—visible. Everyone stopped dead. Then some evaders dove into the woods, while others milled about. Woody decided to walk right through. The guide and another airman joined him. "I know without doubt we were seen," he told me, and then explained that he learned many years later that the "German" soldiers they had encountered were actually White Russians captured on the Eastern Front who agreed to fight for the German army. That night, he was later told, the soldiers had been drinking heavily and one of them had accidentally shot and killed a fellow soldier. That was the confused scene the evaders had walked into—and away from.

Finally the group reached its destination, a stone brick building known as the House of Alphonse, they were to await the code message from the BBC: "Good evening the House of Alphonse"— a signal that the Royal Navy was preparing a pickup that night. There were some 30 in the group gathered, who were briefed on the extreme dangers of the operation and how to conduct themselves as they were led from the house to the cliffs overlooking the beach at Anse Cochat.

Now came the most difficult, terrifying part of the entire exercise: silently climbing down the cliffs to hide in the caves below. One dislodged rock could clatter down the cliff and alert the German patrols. The leaders of the operation who preceded them down the cliffs silently walked into a natural cave facing the sea to signal intermittently with a flashlight attached to a long tube so the signal could not be seen by the Germans.

After what seemed an interminable wait, one of the guides indicated to the evaders to follow. "To my great surprise," Woody reported, "two rowboats had pulled up on the shore almost right in front of us, unseen and unheard. Two Royal Navy sailors were in each boat manning muffled oars. It didn't take us long to climb aboard.

"After some minutes of rowing silently in the pitch blackness at sea we found ourselves at the side of motor gunboat #503. Our escape had been a success!" For the first time in seven days, Woody was safe from the Germans.

On March 26, only 10 days after he had gone down, to our utter surprise Woody casually walked into our dispersal hut at Biggin Hill. He could offer no details about his escape, having been sworn to secrecy to protect the Underground who had made his rescue possible. He did admit, however, that he had been in Paris and had been damned scared with so many Germans around.

Following the Allied invasion of France on 6 June 1944, by mid-month our squadron had moved from Tangmere airfield on the Sussex coast in England to a landing strip at Beny-sur-Mer just over three miles inland from the Normandy beach designated "Juno." Because we were chiefly engaged in a ground support role—attacking convoy transports, troops, tanks, and gun installations at low level—the German antiaircraft fire in the vicinity immediately south of the bridgehead was fierce. The Spitfire was lamentably unsuitable for a ground support role. It had a liquid-cooled engine, as opposed to an air-cooled engine, which made it highly vulnerable to ground flak or even a rifle bullet. As Hap Kennedy (about whom more later) said, "We had a lot of casualties. ... It made for fast promotion." At times, very occasionally, we did encounter enemy fighters as well. This did not bother us like the flak did. In fact, we looked upon it as an opportunity—none more so than Scotty Murray, one of our flight commanders.

On the late afternoon of June 28 as we idled the time away on readiness chewing the fat, Scotty was preaching the merits of being the flight leader. "I'm safe as number one," he opined. "The Huns always pick out the number-four guy because he's at the tail end. Number three maybe. Even number two. But never number one!" But an hour later, it was his number two, Cliff Wyman, who called the break, and it was Scotty, the leader, who was shot down when a dozen Focke-Wulf 190s bounced us 10 miles east of Domfront.

Though he bailed out at 14,000 feet, he tumbled 12,000 feet before pulling the ripcord of his parachute. On landing he buried the silk, then "started running like hell across fields and over fences," to get as far from the scene as possible. In the distance he could see some German soldiers, so he hid under some leaves to wait until dark and then try his luck getting through the front lines. A little later he heard people speaking French. Having attended school in Montreal he knew enough French to communicate. He spoke with the Frenchmen, who recognized him as a downed British flyer (he still had on his battle-dress jacket). Scotty was taken to a barn where he spent the night.

Next morning Scotty was taken to a farmhouse where he had breakfast with a family, including the children who were getting ready to go to school. He was served a cup of "white stuff." Puzzled at what it might be, he learned as soon as he took a mouthful. Calvados, that hearty local Norman brew which "at seven-thirty in the morning hit me with a wallop."

For the next two-and-a-half months he was moved from one house to another. At one point he was hidden in the basement of a house in which two German officers were billeted. Finally, he was led to members of the French Resistance who took him to some woods where a group of English, American, and Polish evaders was being sheltered. They were being kept there waiting for the Allies to advance. With the fall of Caen, the capital of Normandy, on July 9, a breakout from the bridgehead now seemed a certainty.

But Scotty didn't care to wait. He was impatient to get back to the squadron. To a couple of Americans he had befriended—one a pilot, the other a paratrooper—he said, "I don't know about you guys but I'm not going to hang around any longer. I'm going to make a break for it." The trio left the woods and scouted the area south of Falaise. But there was such a heavy concentration of German troops to the north that they decided to try their luck to the west. There the Germans were in full retreat, stringing wire across the roads in their wake to impede the American advance after the breakout at Avranches on July 30. Scotty and the two Americans kept out of sight until one day at last they saw American soldiers. By various means of transport, Scotty returned to Beny-sur-Mer a week later.

On July 3, 401 Squadron took off before daybreak. The Germans brought up their troop reinforcements and supplies by transport at night to avoid being harassed by our aircraft. Our purpose was to surprise them. We were north of Falaise and it was barely getting light when we spotted a line of vehicles turning north. Lorne "Cam" Cameron—our commanding officer (CO)—led the squadron down the length of the column head on. Flak was frightful, coming at us from vehicles in the column and guns positioned along the road. Cam was hit almost immediately and lost his engine. He made a U-turn south and landed wheels up in a muddy field. Hap Kennedy called over the R/T to ask, "Are you okay, Red One?" Back came the gruff reply: "Get the hell away from here!" Red One didn't want us drawing attention to him.

It was still fairly dark, so Cam was able to abandon his aircraft and hide in a haystack until nightfall. He trudged north, hopeful of sneaking through the lines in the dark. But he soon realized that with the concentration of troops and gun emplacements, transport, and tanks, he faced the impossible. He hid out in some woods that next day and the following night started walking south.

Two days later he came to a farmhouse. Deciding to take his chances, he went inside and identified himself as a Canadian pilot to the farm family who promptly led him into the hayloft where he came face to face with Scotty Murray.

After comparing notes, Cam decided to keep going south rather than wait for the Allied advance, while Scotty chose to try the direct route through the lines. The farm family provided Cam with workers' clothes and he set off.

Cam kept moving south, taking his chances in going up to farmhouses asking for food and shelter. To his surprise he found himself most welcome. The news was that the Americans had broken out and France would soon be free again. He was greeted almost as an advance liberator. He travelled for some weeks, always at night, sometimes putting as many as 20 miles behind him. He calculated that he was near Poitiers—some one hundred miles from where he had been shot down—when he was led into a barn where he met three others in the same boat: British paratroopers who, cut off from their unit, had been on the run since the night before the Allied landings. The four held a council of war, the other three deferring to Cam, who held the senior rank among them. They agreed that their best bet would be to contact the French Resistance.

They inquired of their host how and where the Underground could be contacted. They were taken through several villages, and from one person to another, until they met a Frenchman who refused to give his name or identify himself, but who agreed to drive them to Bordeaux, where they could board a ship or take a train to Spain. "I'll never forget that bastard as long as I live," Cam said to me. "He had a nasty fat face and two middle fingers missing from his right hand."

When they reached the French port, the driver pulled into a circle and stopped in front of a building. He then stepped out of the car whereupon two Gestapo officers stepped forward and arrested the four passengers. They were handcuffed and thrown into a cell. They rattled their chains and demanded to be treated as prisoners of war. Their protestations were ignored and they were accused of espionage. Periodically, they were dragged before a panel of Gestapo officials and interrogated.

But their imprisonment in the Bordeaux jail did not last long. The Allies were quickly overrunning France. The Gestapo unchained the prisoners and turned them over to the German army. They were shoved into the back of a wood-burning truck, which headed east.

That night the truck pulled off the side of the road, and the driver and two guards sat down by the ditch and opened several bottles of Schnapps. Cam and the paratroopers bided their time, waiting until the Germans were drunk enough to be overcome. By dark, two of them were dead drunk, the other half asleep, when their "prisoners" made their move. They throttled them, commandeered the truck, which they drove some miles on, then abandoned it and ran into some woods distancing themselves as fast and as far as possible from the soldiers. It probably wouldn't have mattered; everywhere, the Germans were in rout—much too busy to concern themselves with hunting down a few fugitives.

It wasn't long before Cam and the paratroopers met up with French partisans who guided them to the advancing Americans. Cam made his way back to our squadron, which had moved north and east to Poix behind the British-Canadian advance. He persuaded Charlie Trainer, the CO, to allow him one more flight for "one last crack at those rotten bastards" before being flown back to England and then home to Canada.

Meanwhile, in July 1944, Tex Davenport had been shot down again by ground fire and belly-landed his aircraft east of the Orne, just south of the mouth of the river. There were few German troops in the area now that the Allied breakout had begun south of Caen, so Tex made himself scarce in the nearby woods until it got dark, then swam across the river to the Allied side.

After being shot down twice, he was ready to pack it in. But next day he shot down a Messerschmitt 109 and, as he put it, "That li'l ole adrenaline just started flowing all over again." He stayed on to complete his tour.

*

Shortly before lunch on the beautifully clear day of July 26, my Ops tour with 401 Squadron having ended, I said goodbye to my CO, Irving "Hap" Kennedy, and my other comrades, parting with the "family" I had lived and flown with for more than a year and a half, and hopped into a Jeep to be driven to a nearby airstrip from which to board an Anson transport that would take me back to England and—eventually—home to Canada. I didn't see Hap again until three months later, when he arrived home in his native Cumberland, Ontario, near Ottawa for a hero's welcome, shortly after which he related the following story to me.

At about the time I was airborne as a passenger in the Anson over Cherbourg—by then in American hands—on our way to cross the English Channel, Hap's Spitfire, YOD, was hit by heavy flak at 9000 feet near Dreux and caught fire, forcing him to bail out. As he drifted down, the wind blew him right over a German car in which he counted four soldiers. The driver began turning off one road and onto another to follow his descent. Kennedy landed safely in a farm field, and as he began unbuckling his parachute harness, a French woman rushed over, scooped up the white silk, put it under her skirt and beckoned him to hide in the nearby barn. He decided that would be the first place the Germans would look for him, so he dove into some woods just as the car pulled into the lane that led to the farm. The soldiers accosted the woman, who yelled back at them, and they quickly confiscated the parachute. They knew that the downed pilot couldn't be far away.

Kennedy dashed through the woods and into a field where he hid, face down, in chest-high hay. He could see the Germans, who had swung their vehicle to the edge of the field and were firing wildly into the air with their rifles as well as over the top of the hay. Hap couldn't suppress a smile.

By evening the Germans finally gave up and drove off. Shortly afterwards, three small French boys wandered over to him. They had been searching for him, to bring him some bread and a tin of cherries which he hungrily devoured. They left but soon returned with a change of clothing. Kennedy knew he had to move. Our intelligence had warned us that the Germans would make an extensive search for three days of the area in which an Allied airman was shot down. (However, that was all the time they could afford, and they would then call off the hunt.)

Kennedy made for some dense woods a mile away. As he walked cautiously along a dirt road, a German soldier approached, but Kennedy kept walking and the German passed right by, paying no attention to him. Hap's tattered clothing had passed the acid test. On reaching the woods, he made a bed for himself out of leaves under a large beech tree just as it began to rain. That was a relief; it meant that any scent would be washed away, making it impossible for dogs, which the Germans were bound to use, to track him down. Consoled by this fact, he slept soundly.

Next day Kennedy lay doggo. At the edge of the woods he could see a farmhouse and people moving about. All day, he kept careful watch and that evening, convinced there were no Germans around, he decided to chance it. He walked up to the house and knocked on the door. The family, which had just sat down to dinner around the kitchen table, let him in. He introduced himself as an Allied pilot who had been shot down. They had seen his Spitfire crash and they made him welcome. But although they fed him, they refused to shelter him. It was too risky. He thanked them for their hospitality, then returned to the refuge of the woods where he decided to wait until an opportunity presented itself to make his move.

Meanwhile, the French family contacted the Maquis, who approached him and interrogated him severely for fear that he might be an imposter. He gave them his name, serial number, date of birth, and, since they'd seen the Spitfire with squadron markings painted on it, squadron number as well. When British intelligence confirmed his identity, they sheltered him in a hayloft, planning to have him flown out at night by one of the Lysander aircraft that carried out these missions, landing and taking off from small fields in the darkness.

However, with the American breakout at St. Lô, the Germans had poured so many troops into the area that these operations had to be curtailed. Instead, the Maquis would provide Kennedy with a false passport so that he could make his way across the front lines on foot by himself. In the meantime he was told to stay put. While he waited and fretted, he had a few close calls and anxious moments when Germans visited the farm to pick fruit and drink from the cider barrels. He dared not risk a confrontation without proper identification. On one occasion he hid under the straw, on another he feigned sleep.

When, after some weeks, he was provided with a passport under the name of Jacques Michel Kattchix, a Belgian farm labourer, along with a hoe to support the masquerade, the Maquis wished him luck, told him to travel west, and sent him on his way.

With the breakout at St. Lô, he had no idea where the front line would be and decided not to take any chances; he planned to avoid all towns and main roads, and stick to the back dirt roads and fields. Even so, German troops seemed to be everywhere. Then one night he heard the sound of heavy artillery which he gauged to be about 15 miles away. Next morning there was a marked increase in the number of German troops on the road marching eastward. Kennedy took to the fields and that evening heard the rattle of machine guns. Sometime later, the noise of machine guns petered out to be replaced by the sound of rifle fire. This told him that resistance had diminished, so he decided to sit and wait it out.

Early next morning a Jeep with two American soldiers in it pulled up beside Kennedy as he waited by the side of the road. He walked up to the Americans and told them who he was. The Americans told him they'd drive him to their HQ. When Hap asked if he could bring the hoe—which he now regarded as something of a trophy—the Americans laughed and took Kennedy aboard, hoe and all.

Postscript

While I was writing this chapter, Ken Woodhouse made this very moving statement to me about the French people who helped him and our other pilots escape:

> The question still troubles me, "Could I have done the same thing if our roles had been reversed?" It is one thing to fight a war as an airman when you only have concern for yourself, but it is quite another thing to fight as a civilian where not only your life, but those of your family, friends, and neighbours are forfeited if you are caught.

Chapter 2

The High Cost
of Delivery

March 1945—Nassau, the Bahamas

My introduction to the Royal Air Force Ferry Command came late in the game. Just as the war in Europe was winding down, I bummed a lift from Montreal in a Liberator as far as Nassau on my way to spend my month's discharge leave from the RCAF with friends in Miami, Florida. Before hopping aboard a United States Air Force DC-3 transport for the last leg of the journey, I stayed over at the Royal Victoria Hotel where the ferry aircrews were billeted. In aggregate they formed a cosmopolitan collection of civilians and military airmen who came from the United States, Canada, Australia, Great Britain, New Zealand, and France.

This association, brief though it was, gave me new insight and perspective on their aerial operations during World War II, which most people either took for granted (as I did) or knew little if anything about. The role of these aircrews did not attract the same, if any, attention as that of their comrades-in-arms in battle. But their contribution was no less important, and, though they did not face the same dangers as combat aircrews, their risks were no less formidable. While there is no definitive listing and statistical summary available, according to Carl Christie, former senior research officer of the Directorate of History and author of Ocean Bridge: The History of RAF Ferry Command, *it has*

generally been accepted that up to 300 men were lost in ferrying opera-
tions, among them 176 Canadians. Although the service came under the
administration and jurisdiction of the Royal Air Force, it was head-
quartered in Montreal and was very much a Canadian contribution,
one vital to achieving air supremacy in the war.

And it was a Canadian who thought of the idea of ferrying aircraft
from North America to the United Kingdom across the Atlantic and sent
it off the deck in the first place.

June 1946: 21 Peel Street, Montreal, Quebec

After the war, when my parents left Ottawa to move back to
Montreal, one of their close neighbours was Sir William Hildred,
director of the newly formed International Air Transport
Association (IATA). At the time I was a reporter with the *Windsor
Star*. While on a weekend visit with my parents, my father arranged
for me to interview him. It so happened Air Marshal Sir Frederick
"Ginger" Bowhill, the former head of RAF Ferry Command, was in
Montreal at that same time. Both he and Sir William were invited
to cocktails at Peel Street the evening after I had interviewed the
former in his offices at Place d'Armes Square that morning.

Old home week! Harking back to 19 July 1941 when Air Marshal
Bowhill arrived in Montreal to take over what next day officially
became RAF Ferry Command, accompanied by Sir William
Hildred from the British Ministry of Aircraft Production (MAP) to
act as his financial advisor, my father led off the discussion by chid-
ing: "Ginger, I don't know how in hell you ever got that job."

Bowhill smiled, but before he could reply, Hildred broke in: "I can
answer that. He was the logical fellow to take it on. Up until then
he'd been head of Coastal Command and knew more about marine
aviation than anyone else in the air force." In fact, in World War I,
he had been a squadron commander in the Royal Naval Air Service.

BISHOP: I know that. But he had been so adamantly opposed to
ferrying aircraft from Canada to Great Britain.

BOWHILL: That was at the beginning of the war. Transatlantic flight was something relatively new. It was still a gamble.

BISHOP: But look at Lindbergh, Amelia Earhart, Amy Mollison—even Wrong-way Corrigan. They made it okay.

BOWHILL: Individuals for fame, glory—and money. There were many who didn't. I thought the odds of getting numbers of aircraft across was too much of a gamble. In winter, suicidal.

BISHOP: You mean the diehards at the Air Ministry didn't want to risk it.

BOWHILL: Partly. At the time, Britain was pressed for money in so many directions the Air Council felt that setting up a ferry service would be much too expensive.

BISHOP: So the alternative was to crate the aircraft and send them over by ship. Wasn't that costly—and time-consuming?

BOWHILL: So it turned out. But it seemed like the only alternative back then. However, many of the ships carrying the American-built Lockheed Hudsons being sent over to replace our aged Avro Ansons were being sunk by the very menace they were needed to combat—the German U-boats.

HILDRED: After Dunkirk in June 1940, the situation changed dramatically. Winston [Churchill] appointed Max [Canadian-born Lord Beaverbrook] as Minister of Aircraft Production working independently of the Air Ministry.

BISHOP: How did that go down?

HILDRED: Not very well. The Air Ministry didn't like civilians taking on what they considered their responsibilities. They called him the Great Disorganizer, accused him of flying by the seat of his pants. But he got things done.

BISHOP: I remember him telling me when I was [in] England that he was determined to get this ferrying service off the ground.

HILDRED: In a sense he already had. In August [1940], only three months after taking office, he engineered the signing of a joint agreement between Morris Wilson, Edward Beatty, and George Humphrey, who represented our organization [MAP] in

Canada, creating the Canadian Pacific Railway Air Services Department [ASD].

Quite a conversation—and quite a story.

The groundwork had been laid. The nucleus of an organization had been formed. Aircraft had been on order from Lockheed in Burbank, California, from the beginning of the war. It was now a question of finding aircrews to deliver them. The RAF, fighting for its life, could hardly be expected to contribute. The RCAF, in the early stages of developing the British Commonwealth Air Training Plan (BCATP), was desperate for instructors and aircrew recruits. Count them out. So, where to turn?

The Ministry of Aircraft Production agreed to release 25 of its flyers, mostly test pilots. British Overseas Airways Corporation made available some of its crews—navigators as well as pilots—but there was a limit to the number that could be spared. There was, however, another market and a lucrative one from this standpoint: the United States, which was still neutral.

In 1938 my father had recruited two former Great War flyers, Clayton Knight, a cartoonist from New York, and Homer Smith, a Canadian financier living in the United States, in a scheme to lure American pilots to join the RCAF as soon as war broke out. When the ferrying service got under way, the Clayton Knight Committee, as it was called, with the agreement of the RCAF began to divert some of these recruits to the Air Services Department (ASD). By September 1940 there were 44 of these pilots in various stages of training and, with a guarantee of up to $600 per transatlantic trip, very well paid in comparison to their military counterparts, but without family or disability benefits. The Canadian Department of Transport supplied the need for radio operators by sending out a signal to its radio stations across Canada, asking for volunteers to be trained in flight procedures. At the very start, then, the job of flying planes from Canada to Great Britain rested solely with civilian aircrews.

But none of those recruited by the ASD so far were among those who made the first jump across the pond, a flight unofficially credited to the newly formed ferry scheme, even though it had no part in it.

Sunday, 25 October 1940: Stranraer, Scotland

Ian Ross, the Scots-Canadian pilot of the flying boat *Guba,* was so outraged by the discourteous reception he and his crew received on arrival from the local officials of the Wigtown port that he threatened to refuel the aged Catalina and fly the bloody plane back to Botwood Bay, Newfoundland, where they had taken off 12 hours earlier. After the rigorous flight they'd been through, they thought they deserved better.

It had been a hairy trip—and a damned cold one. The *Guba* had no oxygen or cabin heat, so that the crew's hands were numbed by the cold. Worse still, there was no de-icing equipment. Seven hours into the flight, ice began to build up on the aircraft. A chunk of ice was thrown off a propeller and broke a window, adding to their discomfort. Finally, Ross was able to climb the flying boat above the clouds. Five hours later, when they descended through cloud, they could see a pillar of smoke rising from what they learned later was the *Empress of Britain* sinking after being torpedoed. When they landed, thoroughly chilled and exhausted, they were treated with complete indifference. They had not been expected and were made to feel anything but welcome. Ross did not carry out his threat, however. In the end, the crew returned to the new world by ship.

It had been a stalwart effort which, if it accomplished nothing else, had at least served to satisfy Beaverbrook's impatience to get the show in the air despite the fact that plans to implement the ASD ferrying service were already well under way. In fact, the impetuous Beaver had less than three weeks to wait for the official inaugural transatlantic flight attempt by the ASD team—organized and trained under Don Bennett, a former senior captain with Imperial Airways and a pioneer of the North Atlantic air route.

Armistice Day, 11 November 1940: Gander, Newfoundland

Back in August, Bennett and one of his assistants had brought home two Hudson Mark-IIs from the Lockheed factory in Burbank, California, to Montreal for training and testing while others, Mark-IIIs, were being modified for transatlantic flight. The two 1100-horsepower Cyclone engines had been replaced with more powerful 1200-horsepower engines and overload fuel tanks were added to increase the range. The first of the Hudson Mark-IIIs arrived at St. Hubert airport across from Montreal on the south shore of the St. Lawrence on October 8, followed by others later in the month. On October 29, the first of the seven Hudsons scheduled for the Atlantic hop was flown to Gander airport in Newfoundland. The others followed on successive days. Bennett, who would lead the flight, arrived November 9, but weather for the next two days prevented takeoff.

The seven crews each consisted of a pilot, a copilot who in the absence of available navigators would chart the course if need be to their destination—Aldergrove on the northern coast of Ireland near Belfast—and a radio operator; six of the latter were Canadians. The pilots were a mixture of British BOAC veterans and Americans. The procedure laid down—presumably by the Air Ministry, Lord Beaverbrook, or both—was for the aircraft to fly in a loose Vic (Vee) formation maintaining contact visually and by radio. (This would prove impractical; as soon as the aircraft encountered heavy cloud, the formation would break up and everyone would be on their own anyway.)

The historic occasion—the first transatlantic flight ever attempted in wintertime—began at 2000 hours on that cold November 11. The seven Hudsons took off in quick succession.

Kirsten T.o.S.

Edward Smith, one of the American pilots, recalled: "Visibility was good, we easily located the running lights of the other planes and were soon in position on the port side of the Vee in the formation." This was not the case with pilot Ralph Adams' crew. His Canadian radio operator, Curly Tripp, later recorded: "For the first hour there seemed to be planes all around us, and which one was the leader was the question." It was the start of troubles that were to beset the crew throughout the trip.

To take advantage of the prevailing wind, for the first leg of the flight Bennett led the formation at an altitude of 9000 feet in bright moonlight over a thick layer of cloud. The air was calm and clear; it was smooth going so far. But aboard Ralph Adams' Hudson, which had finally found its place in the formation, there was trouble.

Adams had turned over the controls to his copilot to make a routine check of the aircraft with his flashlight when he discovered an oil leak. This was somewhat disconcerting, and they had the option of turning back to Gander; but after radio operator Tripp signalled the condition to Bennett, Adams, while keeping a close watch on the oil gauges, was satisfied the leak was not severe enough to abort, and decided to press on.

His problems were only starting, however. An electrical short-circuit occurred in the radio transmitter; sparks were spitting in all directions accompanied by loud static. "Shut that fucking thing off," Adams shouted to Tripp, who needed no such instruction. With the fear of fire breaking out in such a heavily gassed-up aircraft, he had already done so.

Adams climbed the Hudson to 16,000 and had just levelled out when the engines started to cut out. He and his copilot hastily reached for the hand pumps and gas valves. But there was no real cause for alarm; it was simply the bomb bay tank running dry, though it came at an unexpected moment.

After being airborne for 45 minutes, the seven Hudsons ran into a front that they had been warned about, but much sooner and thicker than had been anticipated, encountering heavy icing.

Breaking formation, they climbed to between 18,000 and 22,000 feet to get above it, but they were still in the soup. At this height the crews needed oxygen, which they sucked through a rubber hose connected to an oxygen tank.

To make matters worse for Adams and his crew, the compass went on the blink, leaving them without navigational aid *or* radio. Tripp finally got the radio transmitter working again, but it was of little use. Due to the German bombing, the control stations in the British Isles had been shut down. There was only one beacon operating—on Storrey Island off the north coast of Ireland. But it only flashed for two minutes at a time and then only at intervals of 20 minutes, making homing in on it absolutely impossible.

Nevertheless, despite such trials, all of the Hudsons landed safely and without incident at Aldergrove. Bennett in the lead plane was the first to land, his flying time 10 hours and 17 minutes. His aircraft had 250 gallons of fuel left out of the 878 at time of takeoff—an average consumption of 61.1 gallons per hour. Historically, it is worth noting that, as Sholto Watt wrote in his book *I'll Take The High Road*, "If this flight had not been successful, the whole ferrying project might have been abandoned."

Despite the success of the mission, Bennett had hoped to convince Beaverbrook of the shortcomings of flying in formation and persuade him to give him more navigators so that each plane could fly solo. But he realized this was not the time to raise the issue. All seven Hudsons had made it across, and that was that, as far as the Beaver was concerned.

As it turned out, there were only three more formation flights anyway. The second and third were carried out without incident. On the second flight on the night of November 28/29, one of the seven Hudsons, flown by Pat Eves, landed at Prestwick in Scotland due to navigational error, though it was widely believed it was because Eves had left his golf clubs there—not to mention that his copilot's wife lived at nearby Crier.

On the third flight on December 17, a new record was established of 10 hours and 10 minutes' flying time and, once again, one of the aircraft ended up in Prestwick. In just over a month, 21 Hudsons had made it safely across the Atlantic. Quite an achievement—something for the skeptics to chew on. The fourth attempt, on December 29, led by Don Bennett—who, having arrived back from England, flew *The Spirit of Lockheed and Vega,* a Hudson donated by the 18,000 Lockheed and Vega plant employees to the people of England as a Christmas gift—was plagued with problems, none serious enough to down the aircraft.

Only four of the seven aircraft made it across the ocean. One crashed on takeoff, blocking the runway for the seventh in line. Another had to turn back with engine trouble. One of the four that did make it never found Aldergrove but ended up at Speke aerodrome near Liverpool instead. In one way, however, the abortive flight was fortuitous. Bennett was now able to convince Beaverbrook of the futility of formations. At the same time, the Minister of Aircraft Production agreed to arrange for navigators graduating from the BCATP to make one ferrying flight on their way to operational training schools in Great Britain.

The first non-formation ferry flight took place on 15 February 1941 from Gander to Prestwick, which by this time had become the designated terminus for the ferry flights, in 10 hours and 43 minutes. Others took place in rapid succession, and as the frequency and reliability became recognized, they attracted VIPs and senior service personnel who wanted to reach the British Isles in the shortest possible time rather than the long—and very dangerous—surface trip by ship. Ironically, it was one of the first passenger ferry flights that saw the service's first fatality.

25 February 1941: Musgrave Harbour, Newfoundland

On February 17, the noted Canadian physician, Sir Frederick Banting, co-discoverer of insulin who at the time was working with the National Research Council, took off from St. Hubert as a passenger in a Hudson captained by Joe Mackey, an American veteran of the second formation flight. Mackey's crew was made up of a Canadian radio operator, Bill Snailham, and a copilot/navigator from England, William Bird. By the time the aircraft touched down at Gander a couple of hours later, the weather had already begun closing in and it snowed steadily for the next two days, scrubbing all flying.

On Thursday, February 20, although snow continued to fall throughout the day, clear flying conditions across the Atlantic were forecast and at approximately 2100 hours Mackey's Hudson was on its way. He was 25 miles and as many minutes into the flight when the starboard engine began to fail, then quit cold. He had no alternative but to turn around and head back to the field. Snailham requested a radio bearing from Gander. He had no sooner received it when smoke started to pour from the pilot's control box. Mackey ordered his passenger and crew to dump out all the baggage and put on their parachutes. He had lost height, down to 5000 feet, when the starboard engine started to lose power. At 2500 feet he told the others to jump but, fighting the controls, even though he was not strapped into his seat, he was unable to leave it to get his parachute, so he decided to ride his ship down for a crash. In the darkness dead ahead he could make out a snow-covered lake (near Musgrave Harbour, Newfoundland). What he couldn't see were some rocks directly in his path. The Hudson struck the rocks and smashed into trees on the lake shore. Mackey managed to shut down the starboard engine before the plane hit the rocks. He was knocked unconscious when his head banged into the instrument panel.

It had all happened so fast that none of the other three had been able to bail out; both Snailham and Bird were killed and Banting was severely injured. Mackey came to an hour later, his left leg badly bruised and with lacerations to his head and forehead. Bandaging his head, he tried to help Banting, who had a broken arm and a gash in his head that was bleeding profusely. Banting was utterly delirious, completely unaware that he had been in an aircraft accident. Taking off his flying suit and boots, he made for the door, announcing that it was time he went to bed. Only fast action on Mackey's part prevented the doctor from falling and injuring himself further. Mackey caught him, then helped him to the bunk and bundled him in parachute silk and a couple of overcoats. By noon he was able to put him to sleep and start out to search for help.

Although RCAF Douglas Digby planes scanned an area 50 miles out to sea parallel to the coast, they were looking in the wrong direction. And in any case, poor visibility caused by snow and light rain made detection virtually impossible. When Mackey, who had trudged through the snow two miles to the south in a vain attempt to find help, returned to the aircraft six hours later, he was utterly exhausted. He discovered that Banting had left the aircraft. After resting for an hour, Mackey went outside to search for Banting, and found him in some brush 25 feet from the doorway of the plane in a half-sitting position with one of his shoes off. "He had obviously been dead for some time," Mackey later reported. Two days later, a search plane finally spotted the stranded pilot, and provisions were dropped to sustain him until he could be reached by a ground rescue party.

By December 1940, 674 Hudsons, 91 PBY Catalina flying boats, 58 Liberators, and 20 Flying Fortresses were ready for delivery over the next six months. Except for the PBYs, these American-built aircraft were now reaching St. Hubert on a regular basis, flown in by the factory crews. After servicing and modifications, they were flown to Gander for the trip across the Atlantic.

The PBYs were flown to Boucherville on the St. Lawrence River near Montreal for servicing. Due to their extended endurance, they were eagerly awaited by RAF Coastal Command, and were flown to Bermuda as the jumping-off point. At this time the name of the organization was changed to ATFERO, an acronym for Atlantic Ferry Organization.

The main problem ATFERO faced was a shortage of aircrews. The cart was getting ahead of the horse. A crisis was rapidly developing with the increase in aircraft production and a severe shortage of pilots to deliver them.

It became patently obvious to the RAF, all things considered, that if the number of pilots required to do the job—which it estimated to be in the neighbourhood of 1000—were to be enlisted, it would have to assume this manning responsibility itself. Meanwhile, the RCAF opened an Operational Training Unit at Debert, Nova Scotia, to provide ferrying training for selected BCATP graduates— pilots, navigators, and wireless operators. The RAF would provide the instructors and maintenance staff, while administration would come under RCAF control. At the same time the ATFERO training organization had been expanded and the Return Ferry Service (RFS) inaugurated, the first east-west flight was taking place aboard a Hudson on May 3. From this time forward, full loads of aircrews were returned to the starting point and this helped somewhat to alleviate the aircrew shortage.

For the passengers, these turnaround trips, usually lasting as long as 14 hours, were anything but comfortable. They were squeezed into a freezing bomb bay, wearing the heaviest flying clothing available or stuffing themselves into sleeping bags, often having to suck on oxygen tubes for hours at a time. The flights served their purpose, but as each month went by the backlog of American planes unferried to Britain had been growing; by the end of June it amounted to 133 aircraft. Concern was mounting over this delay and the drain the ferrying service was imposing on RAF operations.

Sir Archibald Sinclair, British secretary of state for air, approached the U.S. ambassador to Britain, John Winant, with the suggestion that "the Americans might themselves help us by ferrying aircraft across." Franklin Roosevelt and his advisors took it from there. The U.S. president proposed to Winston Churchill that the United States Army Air Corps (USAAC) pilots fly all the aircraft from the American factories to Montreal, thus freeing those already engaged in this role for transatlantic duties. In addition, looking to the future, American military pilots would gain experience in long-range flying in various kinds of aircraft.

The British prime minister wasted no time in assenting to the arrangement—"I am deeply grateful to you for your proposal of May 29 which we at once accept in principle"—and putting it into operation from the British end. RAF Ferry Command officially came into being on July 20 with Air Chief Marshal Sir Frederick "Ginger" Bowhill, who had originally turned thumbs down on a transatlantic ferrying service, in command and headquarters in Montreal. From ATFERO it inherited an organization of 400 aircrew, 207 American and Canadian civilians, and 33 pilots on loan from the airline company BOAC, 36 from the Air Transport Auxiliary, 118 RAF, 18 RCAF—mostly flying boat pilots—and 3 from the Royal New Zealand Air Force (RNZAF). In addition a number of Canadian Pacific personnel, chiefly in an administrative capacity, remained on loan to the new organization.

The creation of Ferry Command had an almost immediate effect on aircrew strength. The crews flying back from the United Kingdom via the RFS helped on that score. More American civilians were available now that the USAAC had assumed the job of aircraft delivery. BCATP graduates were soon to join the pool. Pilots completing their operational training made two or three ferrying trips before joining Coastal Command squadrons. Navigators and wireless operators, however, usually made only a single trip on their way to an operational squadron posting. Other one-trip pilots included RCAF staff officers and senior instructors such as Paul Davoud and Keith Hodson, who took command of 410 and 401 Squadrons respectively, as well as Jack Godfrey ("I saved the government a thousand bucks") who was posted to 402 Squadron. Since its inception, beginning with the first flight in November the previous year, by July 1941, 200 aircraft had been delivered overseas by the ferrying service with the loss of only one.

But there was a downside. Within 10 days of each other, two Hudsons crashed, killing all aboard, among them two Canadian civilian radio operators, Wilfred Bratherton and Frank Godfrey. The first crash took place on July 25 at the Mull of Kintyre on the approach to Prestwick, the other on August 3 near Moncton, New Brunswick. A week later, on August 10, an RFS four-engine Liberator crashed into a mountain on the Isle of Arran at the mouth of the Clyde. All 21 civilian airmen lost their lives, including eight Canadians, among them the pilot, Josiah James, the copilot, Francis Bradbrooke, and the radio operator, Ralph Brammer. Other Canadian fatalities were returning radio operators John Drake, Wilfred Kennedy, George Laing, Hugh McIntosh, and William Marks.

At first it was thought that the plane had been lost somewhere over the Atlantic. But next morning, Monday, August 11, a farmer on the Isle of Arran tending his sheep came across the wreckage near the top of Goat Hill. It was a horrible scene. Wreckage was scattered over a wide area and it took two days for rescue teams to recover the bodies.

Four days later a second fatal RFS accident took place when another Liberator crashed taking off from Ayr aerodrome in Scotland. Nine Canadian civilians were killed in the crash, one that was fraught with irony.

According to his best friend, Henry Flory, a Liberator navigator with Ferry Command, the pilot of the ill-fated aircraft, BOAC captain Richard Stafford, had been under severe stress from his day-and-night job of instructing the new arrivals at St. Hubert. Added to this was his distress and frustration at being unable to obtain permission to bring his wife to Canada from Great Britain. Finally in August, after a year's separation from her, he had been told he could make the next round trip to Scotland and bring his wife back with him along with his aircrew passengers.

Then, at the last minute, room had to be made aboard the Liberator for Sir Arthur Purvis, Scots-born Canadian head of the

British Purchasing Commission in the United States, who had been summoned to an emergency meeting (possibly linked to the Churchill-Roosevelt shipboard meeting off the Grand Banks of Newfoundland to which Beaverbrook had been ferried four days earlier). The RAF Traffic Officer on duty at Ayr that night perfunctorily and unhesitatingly bumped Stafford's wife. According to Flory: "It was a dreadful mistake! Stafford pleaded with this bureaucratic cretin to have his wife put back on the flight but to no avail."

Flory believed that the anguish and rage Stafford must have felt over this inconsiderate treatment by an officious "pigeon" was responsible for what happened next on that dark, rainy night. To the astonishment of those watching, Stafford taxied his Liberator onto the shortest runway without even bothering to turn right to get to the end of it, and began revving up the four engines for takeoff into a slipping crosswind, something that defied all the basic fundamentals of flying. Onlookers gasped as the aircraft picked up speed, then, before it had gone 100 yards, suddenly veered off the runway onto the grass. Then, in violation of his own golden rule instruction to his flight students—"If the bloody thing starts to swing on takeoff, stop it and start again"—Stafford made no attempt to brake the aircraft, which bounced over the slight rise where the two runways intersected and at 150 miles an hour began careening headlong straight toward a six-foot embankment at the end of the field. Stafford pulled the nose up but not soon enough to avoid crashing into the barrier, breaking the aircraft in two and sending the nose hurtling 60 feet into the air and finally collapsing across a railway track. To the horror of those watching, flames shot up into the sky.

All 22 people aboard were killed, although one of the passengers lived for a few hours before succumbing to his injuries. Canadian fatalities including Purvis were a pilot, James Moffat, and seven radio operators: Richard Coates, Robert Duncan, Wesley Goddard, Donald Hannant, John MacDonald, Glenwood McKay, and Albert Tamblin.

Before the end of 1941, five other Ferry Command flights took the lives of seven more Canadian aircrews. On the night of August 31/September 1, a Liberator en route to Prestwick crashed at Chamberlain near Kintyre—the second crash at the Mull—killing all 10 aboard, among them the Canadian radio operator Samuel Sydenham.

On September 1, a Hudson was lost out of Gander with the first all-Canadian Ferry Command crew, two of whom were the first RCAF aircrew to make a ferry flight. Lost and presumed dead were the pilot flight Lieutenant Robert Leavitt, the navigator, Sergeant Edwood McFall, and Robert Anderson, a Canadian civilian.

On September 27, one Hudson crashed at Dundalk in Ireland, killing the three crewmen: Flight Lieutenant Louis Dubuc of the RCAF, Canadian civilian radio operator Samuel Kenny, and an RAF navigator. That same night another Hudson disappeared over the Atlantic, carrying an RCAF pilot, Flight Lieutenant Harold Oldham, and navigator Sergeant Ronald Law, as well as a civilian radio operator, Cyril Small from Newfoundland. Then on October 11 a Canadian civilian radio operator was part of the crew of a Hudson presumed lost after taking off from Gander.

During the year, 29 Canadian airmen and six civilians had lost their lives on ferry flights and one other Canadian airman was killed on a training flight. Tragic though these fatalities were and serious though the loss of aircraft was, it was a small price to pay in relation to what had been achieved. Over that same period, 593 aircraft had been delivered at a critical time in the war. Included in that total were 404 Hudsons, 89 Catalina flying boats, 78 Liberators, 20 Flying Fortresses, and two Lockheed Lodestars. Most of the Hudsons, Liberators, and flying boats went into service with RAF Coastal Command to combat the growing German U-boat menace to the flow of supplies from North America to Great Britain.

But, during 1941, this success had early on begun to lead to problems. The rapid acceleration of traffic overloaded the jump-off and delivery points, whose facilities were already stretched to the limit.

At St. Hubert, deliveries crowded the RCAF elementary flying school training program while Gander was hard pressed, coping with the needs of Eastern Air Command and Ferry Command at the same time.

These problems had been anticipated as early as 1940 when Air Vice-Marshal Jack Slessor, head of the Air Ministry planning section, had urged that "the organization of the Greenland-Iceland route be tackled vigorously and soon."

Early in 1941, the USAAC began surveying Greenland as well as Labrador for suitable airfield sites. In the latter case a Canadian surveyor, Eric Fry, came upon a sandy plateau on the shore of Goose Bay which both the Americans and the RCAF agreed would serve as an excellent connecting point with Greenland. It now fell to the Canadians to build it. That this was accomplished in record time under polar conditions prompted one historian to bill it as "one of Canada's remarkable wartime engineering feats."

At the same time, the Americans had been building bases in Greenland (for the defence of which the U.S. government agreed to accept full responsibility). The base at Narsarssuak was known by its code name, "Blueie West 1"; the base at Sondre Stromfjord was "Blueie West 8"; and the base near Angmagssalik was "Blueie East 2." These facilities bridged the gap between Goose Bay and Reykjavik and Karldaharness in Iceland, which the British had occupied after the German invasion of Denmark in April 1940. Montreal remained the principal Ferry Command western terminus, but headquarters had been moved to Dorval, a new airfield west of the city.

By the end of March 1942, the second air route to Great Britain, which the noted historian Carl Christie called the "Ocean Bridge," was finally in place. But it still had to be scouted. That job was entrusted to a team headed up by Louis Bisson, a well-known Canadian bush pilot, Don McVicar, an experienced civilian pilot who had joined Ferry Command in November, and George Evans, an American. All three were well qualified for the assignment, having just completed a feasibility study of a route through the Canadian Arctic in two ski-equipped single-engine Norsemans and a Hudson.

The plan called for Bisson and his crew to fly a Liberator, the mother ship which would make the turnaround journey, accompanied by McVicar and Evans with their crews in Canso amphibians, the Canadian-built version of the Catalina (PBY). On April 7, the trio took off from Goose Bay for Blue West 8 in Greenland.

There was too much cloud cover for a star shot; they had to settle for navigating by dead reckoning. After flying across Davis Strait—which seemed like an endless journey—they were relieved to see the Greenland icecap ahead of them. Even that inhospitable, massive, two-mile-thick ice slab was a welcome sight. Their problem was finding Blue West 8. They had been unable to make contact by radio, a common problem when flying in the north. Pinpointing proved difficult; along the indented coastline all fjords looked pretty much alike. Having identified what he thought to be the Sondrestrom inlet, McVicar suddenly spotted what he took to be the shadow of his own plane below him. It turned out to be the other Canso. McVicar followed Evans' airplane onto the long gravel runway. Both amphibian pilots had parked their aircraft when the Liberator came barrelling in, kicking up a cloud of dust and gravel.

The next leg was to the RAF station at Reykjavik, Iceland. Because Bernt Balchen, the noted Norwegian pilot-explorer who commanded the U.S. Army Air Force (its name changed from Army Air Corps the previous June) base, advised Bisson that his station had as yet had no radio communication with Iceland, Bisson opted for a night takeoff, which would put the flight over Iceland at noon in broad daylight.

Shortly after takeoff McVicar's aircraft lost its heat. The crew shivered in the severe minus-40-degree cold that caused the window in the navigator's hatch to frost over. McVicar's fingers were so paralyzed that he couldn't hold a sextant, and his eyes were running with tears so that he could hardly see, making it impossible for him to take a star shot. He had to rely on dead reckoning, without a clue as to what the wind factor might be. Then a small fire broke out in the electrical system, robbing the Canso of its electric power. For the crew, without radio, almost freezing and unsure of their position, it was frightening. Acting purely by guesswork, McVicar let down to 300 feet, then to 100. With a limited visibility of less than a mile it was scary; he ran the risk of flying into an iceberg. To his relief he finally spotted some seagulls, then a fishing trawler and straight ahead the coast of Iceland and Reykjavik. Bisson followed a short time later in the Liberator. But there was no sign of Evans.

The RAF control tower fired off rockets to help the missing Canso pilot find the field. McVicar knew that Evans was an expert pilot, but he worried about his lack of experience and unfamiliarity with British and Canadian radio ranges and procedures so different from the beam-flying the American flyer was used to. But that was not the problem. Far from it. Evans' crew had no radio; it had failed. Flying through snow and fog, Evans had descended too soon. His first sight of land was a mountain and only a violent swerve away from it saved his life and that of his crew. He then followed the ragged coastline all the way round until he found Reykjavik. McVicar would later write: "It had been a tough flight for both of us. Evans said if he never saw another Cat [Canso] for the rest of his life it would [be] OK with him."

The final leg to Prestwick was anticlimactic by comparison. But overall, the northeast passage survey proved the route to be thoroughly viable. The point having been made, by May the new route was put to heavy use, climaxed in July by the mass movement of the USAAF Eighth Air Force as part of the Bolero plan to build up American Forces in Great Britain. On one occasion there were 91 planes on the ground at Goose Bay in a single day.

Five hundred miles south of Goose Bay, the staging area for ferrying Catalina flying boats across the Atlantic from Bermuda had been set up by a seasoned flying-boat pilot, Group Captain

Taffy Powell, a former captain with Imperial Airways and later chief navigation officer of RCAF Eastern Command.

Powell commandeered the Imperial Airways base on Darrel's Island and took over the Belmont Manor Hotel on the south shore of Warwick Parish for living quarters. With a golf course, tennis courts, swimming pool, and the beach, there was none of the frustration during waiting periods that the aircrews experienced at Gander.

This lap of luxury contrasted sharply with the job of crossing the ocean in flying boats cruising at an average speed of 100 miles an hour or less during trips that lasted as long as 24 hours. The first crossing took off on 29 January 1941, with two veteran Canadian radio operators, Robert Hodgson and Frank Eyre.

Six hours into the flight, in pitch-black darkness, the automatic pilot jammed and the starboard aileron dropped fully down. This sent the Catalina into a spiral dive. As a result, both ailerons began to flutter due to the steep angle. The chief pilot instructed the radio operators to signal an SOS, but that was impossible. The aerials broke off in the dive and wound themselves around the ship.

The aircraft dove from 20,000 to 1000 feet. As the pilot and copilot struggled with the controls, the crew jettisoned everything that could be spared: flares, spare parts, and toolkits. Finally, a mere 100 feet over the water, the pilots were able to level the plane. But in the process the ailerons had been torn right off.

By daylight the aircraft was flying without any lateral control. To stay airborne the pilot had to fly straight ahead and hope for the best, since any attempt to use the rudder would put the machine into a flat spin. There was one saving grace, but it proved to be of no help. The radio was working; one of the aerials had worked itself free and was trailing the ship. Hodgson got off a signal: "Both ailerons gone." It was received all right, but no one believed it. How could a Catalina weighing 15 tons possibly stay in the air under such conditions?

In fact it took all the strength the pilot and copilot had to keep the machine flying. They dared not take their hands off the controls for even a second. To make matters worse, they had to fly through a storm. But hang on they did, miraculously able to land their flying boat on the water at Milford Haven on the southeastern tip of Wales after flying for a total of 28 hours and 50 minutes. The water was rough and after the ordeal the crew had already been through, they couldn't face the prospect of seasickness. So the pilots took off again and flew for another three miles to bring the plane nearer to the moorings.

That first flight from Bermuda underscored the main concern of Catalina crews—the ever-present danger of engine and mechanical failure. Also, the belief was widely held that the PBY could only fly on one engine when the fuel tanks were half empty. Notwithstanding these problems, by mid-1941 the ferry service from Bermuda had been firmly established.

In 1942 a Ferry Command detachment had been posted to Elizabeth City, North Carolina, where the crews picked up the Catalinas and flew them to Bermuda. Enter Don McVicar, one of the trio to pioneer the northeast "Ocean Bridge" route. On November 27, he flew a PBY off Pasquotanic Bay to Great Sound, Bermuda. But he had to wait until December 15 for suitable weather conditions to make one of his most memorable Atlantic crossings.

McVicar and his flight engineer, Bill Baker, had had plenty of time to study the most feasible method of getting the Catalina across the drink. He was far from satisfied with what he had learned from the other pilots. Most of them advised that the most economical speed was 80 knots. That meant they might have to stay in the air for as long as 30 hours. McVicar disagreed. He had calculated that the best miles-per-gallon speed was 105 knots. On that basis, he filed a flight plan of 23 hours and 35 minutes.

When the crew climbed into the flying boat shortly after noon, their biggest problem at the outset was to get the heavily loaded Catalina—37,000 pounds—into the air. On the takeoff run, the boat rode so low in the sea that the water splashed up over the cockpit, and took two minutes to get airborne at full power and another

15 minutes to reach 3000 feet. McVicar maintained that altitude until the weight decreased from fuel consumption.

Thus lightened, to improve flying conditions he climbed the PBY to 7000 feet, which ate up 20 minutes, and levelled off, maintaining a flying speed of 105 knots (125 knots ground speed). After three hours in the air, they had flown 380 miles of the 3000-mile flight to Greenock. At the four-hour mark it was time to move the gas from the overhead fuselage tanks to the wings. But after several minutes, Baker reported that there was no suction from the fuel transfer pump. The immediate reaction was "Sabotage!" McVicar quickly calculated that they could continue on for another hour before they would have to turn back, a prospect he far from relished; he had no experience or training in night water landings, a limitation he kept secret from his crew. Then the flight engineer found the culprit—sand was clogging the pump.

McVicar reckoned that they could cover the next 2000 miles and still have a reserve of fuel. But because of increased cloud cover that ruled out astro navigation, they would have to rely on radio and dead reckoning for bearings. With weather a constant consideration, now came the decision every ferry captain had to face at one time or another, one that was his responsibility and his alone to make: whether to turn back or continue.

McVicar estimated that in the nine hours they had been airborne they had flown 1197 miles with an 18-knot tailwind. Turning around would mean flying into a headwind at a reduced ground speed of 98 knots. Total time airborne would be 21.3 hours, leaving plenty of fuel in reserve in case the Bermuda weather soured. "But after we returned," McVicar wrote later, "we'd be facing another long, monotonous wait for the good forecast. The loss of astro was very serious but I decided to press on."

In this case McVicar's concern about the weather turned out to be well founded. A forecast deep low-pressure area with an associated cold front off the tip of Greenland that McVicar had hoped to fly around hit them sooner than expected. Around midnight, the

Catalina was bounced about and a slight coating of frost formed on the wings. McVicar was unable to climb above the storm as ice began to pile up on the outside of the aircraft. Baker backfired the engines to prevent the carburetors from icing.

Using the Aldis lamp as a flashlight, the crew could see a coating of ice on the bottom of the wings that resembled stalactites. Then suddenly the aircraft shuddered, on the verge of a stall. Over the roar of the engines they could hear a rattling that sounded like someone was pelting the aircraft with ice cubes—a mixture of sleet and hail.

The radar antennas were vibrating violently, so coated with ice that they looked like solid blocks. Then the wire antennas broke away from the wing roots with a loud crack. McVicar realized he had waited too long to try and climb above the front and was left with only one course of action—dive out of it into the warmer weather. Flashes of lightning erupted all around. Baker continued to backfire the engines. The turbulence was so rough it pushed the crew members against their safety belts. With the altimeter out of commission, McVicar had to judge his altitude by pure guesswork. It was good enough to get the aircraft safely out of the storm with enough height to spare. His quick action paid off. Ice began sliding off the wings and the engines started to run smoothly. That incredibly frightening affair had lasted only 20 minutes, but it was 20 minutes the crew would never forget. As McVicar wrote: "If that wasn't hell it was a pretty good imitation."

And they still weren't out of trouble. They had no idea of the wind direction or speed. McVicar brought the flying boat down to 100 feet just below the clouds and took a reading by dropping a flame float. Despite poor visibility and a high-running sea, they were able to estimate the wind at 65 knots from 300 degrees. McVicar set course by keeping the front on his left. They were out of the worst of it, but because the direction-finding loop had been torn off during the storm, they were unable to hear the beacon from Ireland. They had to depend on their dead-reckoning ability—and luck.

At dawn the rain eased off and the ceiling lifted. Shortly afterwards they spotted land. Incredibly, they were off Galway Bay, precisely where they should be. It was uncanny luck, to say the least. Next they rounded the tip of Ireland and headed into Greenock on the firth of Clyde. Their flying time of 20.3 hours at a ground speed of 138 knots over 2700 miles came close to breaking an already established record of 19 hours and 50 minutes—commendable, even under normal circumstances. The miracle was that under the terrifying conditions they had encountered, they had achieved it at all.

Some months earlier, much farther south, close to the equator, one of the more memorable ferry flights took place; it was captained by one of Canada's most remarkable pilots, who merits a place in our aviation history.

Labour Day Weekend, 4 September 1971:
The Inn on the Park, Toronto, Ontario

I first met George "Pop" Phillips at Kapuskasing airport in northern Ontario during the summer of 1938 when I accompanied my father on a cross-country tour in which, as an Honorary Air Vice-Marshal of the RCAF, he was drumming up interest and support for the air force. He and Pop had been comrades-in-arms in the Royal Flying Corps during World War I. In peacetime, Pop became a bush pilot flying for the Ontario Provincial Air Services and was made eastern superintendent. In 1931 he was awarded the McKee Trophy for his work in forest fire air patrols. In 1940, at 47 years of age, he enlisted in the RCAF and was assigned instructional duties. By 1942 he was transferred to RAF Ferry Command where he was given the job of flying Hudsons across the southern Atlantic to Africa.

I next met Phillips in May 1946 when I was doing a series of feature articles on Ontario's northland for the Windsor Star. *Pop was piloting Norseman float planes for Ontario Lands and Forests, Division of Air*

*Service with headquarters at Sault Ste. Marie. He told me at the time,
"I'll go on flying as long as the world keeps turning."*

*When I met him again at the Canadian Fighter Pilots Association
(CFPA) reunion in Toronto in 1971, he had retired. But although he
was 84 years old, he'd lost none of his vitality—or capacity. After the
banquet on the Saturday night Pop and several others of us huddled
together in the hotel hospitality suite where, over more libations than we
needed, he related his story of his first flight to Africa in September 1942.
It was a corker that kept us up most of the night. To the best of my recol-
lection the conversation went something like this.*

BISHOP: George, what was this southern route you were all on
about?

PHILLIPS: We were supplying the British Eighth Army in Egypt with
bombers for an offensive against Rommel. The established route
was from Florida to the east coast of Brazil then across the Atlantic
to the south coast of West Africa and from there to Cairo. But on this
trip we never got that far. [Phillips' crew consisted of himself as
pilot, Flying Officer Bill Campbell, RCAF, as navigator, and
Sergeant George Seward of the Royal Australian Air Force as his
radio operator. After the war Seward was interviewed by Fred Hatch,
the RCAF historian, whose notes were filed with the Department of
National Defence Directorate of History.] For Bill and me it was our
first go at it. But George had done it once before so he knew the way
and he knew the ropes so far as radio was concerned.

BISHOP: This was when?

PHILLIPS: We picked up our Hudson at West Palm Beach on
September 26, 1942, and flew south to Natal on the east coast of
Brazil. It was a 4400-mile jaunt as the crow flies, so en route we
touched down at fields in Puerto Rico, Trinidad, and British
Guiana to stop over—drink—sleep—and refuel.

BISHOP: No problems?

PHILLIPS: Not yet. But on the next leg, across the southern Atlantic
to the USAAF base on Ascension Island, the fuel pump began to

act up so we had to lay over for repairs. This was unfortunate—
very unfortunate in fact—because I'd hoped to make Accra on the
coast of Ghana in Africa before it got dark since neither Bill nor I
had made this trip before and George wasn't all that familiar with
the territory either.

BISHOP: So you stayed over until the next day?

PHILLIPS: I wished to hell we had. But no. We decided to take our
chances and took off. On the way we ran into a storm that knocked
out the bloody radio. So we couldn't check our position. By the
time we could see the coast it was dusk. The sun was gone so we
couldn't take a sextant shot to get our bearings and it wasn't dark
enough to take a shot from the stars. We were too low and it was
too dusky to get a dead reckoning, so I decided to pancake the
aircraft on the beach wheels up. Then I spotted a landing strip
dead ahead and we breathed a collective sigh of relief that our troubles were over. Ha! Bloody ha!

As I lowered the undercarriage, I could see barriers across the
runway. What the shit was this? Then the air was suddenly filled
with flak. George fired off the colours of the day in the belief we
were over Ghana—British territory. It was too late to pull up and
I crashed into the barriers. The right tire blew and the Hudson
ground-looped.

We climbed out the windows to be greeted by these big coloured
soldiers—Senegal troops as it turned out—who arrested us as
prisoners of war. We had landed at Cotonou on the coast of
Dahomey to the east of Ghana—Vichy French territory.

BISHOP: They treated you as enemies?

PHILLIPS: Goddam right they did! They took us upriver, 1500 miles
by wood-burning paddlewheel boat in frightful jungle heat, to a
prison camp at Bamako, the capital of Mali. I held the rank of
flight lieutenant at the time, so I was the senior officer in the camp
and it was up to me to deal with our captors. It didn't do much
good. The men were suffering from malnutrition, mostly dysentery and malaria, but we did our best to keep up their spirits.

Fortunately, our imprisonment didn't last long. After the Allies landed in North Africa in early November, little more than a month since we were captured, French West Africa changed sides and we were released.

BISHOP: Quite an experience.

PHILLIPS: Not quite the end to the story, Bish. I made one more trip to North Africa, this one without incident. When I got back to West Palm Beach, lo and behold, there was the Hudson I had pranged [smashed up] at Cotonou fully repaired and ready to fly. Cheers! Let's have one for the road.

Pop ended the war as liaison officer with the RAF at Natal airfield in Brazil and was discharged with the rank of squadron leader.

During 1942, Ferry Command had delivered almost 800 aircraft across the Atlantic via the northern routes. In the closing months of the year, 127 deliveries were made to Africa through the southern route. The cost was heavy. Thirty-four planes had been lost, in which Canadian fatalities totalled 55.

But the deliveries achieved two significant results in the prosecution of the war at a stage in which air power was the critical factor. The aircraft supplied to RAF Coastal Command gave the Atlantic convoys complete air cover protection, and as a result the Battle of the Atlantic was beginning to turn against the dreaded U-boats.

In Africa, the success by the British Eighth Army at El Alamein in late October in defeating the German Afrika Korps, the first Allied ground victory of the war, was directly attributable to air supremacy made possible in great measure by Ferry Command.

Delivery of aircraft from the New World to the battle theatres of the Old was beginning to have a telling effect—and it was only just starting to get revved up.

Bending with the wind in light of British-American victories in North Africa and the capture of Sicily and invasion of Italy—not to mention the Russian successes in the east—in October 1943, Portugal granted the Allies landing rights in the Azores, a distance of 1500 miles from Gander. This considerably reduced the time, distance, and fuel costs of ferrying heavy aircraft to North Africa, the Middle East, India, and China. Like other transatlantic flights it had its share of perils. On Christmas Eve, 1943, Flying Officer Jack Uren and his crew experienced the eerie sensation of having their Liberator struck by lightning.

During that same year the ferry service underwent a major transformation. It was absorbed by the newly established RAF Transportation Command and reorganized into three wings, one of them, No. 45, stationed at Dorval under the command of Air Vice-Marshal Reggie Marix, a World War I RNAS pilot who had lost a leg in combat. "Ginger" Bowhill became AOC Transport Command with headquarters at Harrow, England.

It was through Reggie Marix, a close friend of my father's, that I was able to arrange passage in a Liberator to Nassau on my discharge leave in March of 1945. And it was there in the Bahamian capital that I learned about the chief nemesis of the Ferry Command pilots, the Canadian-built de Havilland Mosquito.

Until the advent of the jetfighter, as a combat aircraft the all-wood Mossie had no peers on either side. With a flat and level speed of well over 400 miles per hour, it was employed in multifarious roles: day and night fighter, bomber, torpedo plane, mine layer, photo-reconnaissance plane, and pathfinder. Installed with extra fuel tanks to increase its range to 2430 miles, it surpassed all records for speed in transatlantic delivery—the fastest known, from Gander to Prestwick, being just over five hours.

But the Mosquito was fraught with its own problems. Many planes disappeared on the transatlantic trip without a trace. Veteran ferry pilots reported possible reasons from their own experiences. There was a smell of gas in the cockpit emanating from the bomb bay fuel tank. The slightest spark could turn the plane into a blazing inferno. On more than one occasion, the air tank that fed the pneumatic brakes exploded due to temperature changes.

The pilots I talked to in Nassau were afraid of the Wooden Wonder, deathly afraid. I was told this was a general malaise throughout the ferry service. "That son of a bitch is nothing but a flying coffin," one of them said. Most aircrews in fact did their utmost to avoid being drawn for Mosquito flights. They blamed the accidents on oil dilution and sudden carburetor icing. When the starboard engine failed, it would knock the radio out of action. The Packard-built engines were unreliable. Dry rot could sabotage the plane—the wooden wings would simply disintegrate.

Ironically, a month later when I returned to Nassau after holidaying in Miami, I learned that 130 Mosquitos had been delivered via the southern route without a single loss. It is generally conceded that, overall, Mosquito losses were some 30 aircraft out of the 1000 produced in Canada. There is apparently no record of how many were safely delivered to Great Britain.

What the ferrying service and those who made it possible achieved went beyond the very important contribution made to the war effort, vital though that was throughout World War II. It established the ground and air work that could be successfully translated into peacetime air transport in which Canada has played, and hopefully will continue to play, a significant part.

Chapter 3

Ralph Manning and the Queen of the Underworld

The heaviest loss of all
was the sinking of oil tankers.
—Historian B. H. Liddell Hart

In the many years that I was associated with my friend Ralph Manning, first as RCAF Historian and later as Curator of the Canadian War Museum, I was only vaguely aware of his splendid war record. He was, in fact, an outstanding torpedo bomber pilot in Coastal Command, whose exemplary combat career ranged from operations off the coasts of the German-occupied countries to Africa and the Indian Ocean.

It was not until I had completed the research for Courage in the Air, *the first volume in my* Canada's Military Heritage *series, at the National Defense Directorate of History in Holly's Lane, Ottawa, that I felt adequately briefed to approach Ralph directly. Here is the long-overdue story of that remarkable career, which I gathered first-hand.*

In the fall of 1941, having completed his operational training as a torpedo-bomber pilot on twin-engine Bristol Beauforts, Ralph Manning and another graduate Canadian pilot on the same course were posted to 42 Squadron, RAF Coastal Command. On arrival they learned the unit had suffered heavy casualties in anti-shipping strikes off the coasts of France, Belgium, Holland, Denmark, and Norway. Morale was low, the mood in the mess sombre. When they reported to the squadron adjutant, they were greeted with the imperious pronouncement: "You probably won't make it. So far half the new types get the chop the first time out!"

"Typical know-it-all wingless wonder," Ralph said. "We didn't pay much attention to him." The adjutant was half right, though. On his first strike Manning survived, but the other Canadian newcomer went for a Burton. Manning continued to defy the odds, carrying out strike after shipping strike, seemingly undaunted by the risks such attacks entailed. He quickly became one of the best, most experienced practitioners of the trade.

No one ever suggested that shipping strikes were a piece of cake. In fact, they were the most precarious and exacting roles Coastal Command aircrews were called upon to undertake. But I did not fully appreciate the skill required and the risks involved until Ralph explained them to me.

"Torpedo bombing was the most lethal weapon against enemy shipping," he pointed out, "because the missile was designed to strike at a vessel's most vulnerable spot—below the waterline. Aerial bombing could inflict a lot of upper structural damage, but in the case of warships with their armoured decking, it would be negligible.

"A successful attack had to be carried out abeam of the target at low level and at reduced speed to assure accuracy. The correct distance and timing were essential when releasing the torpedo. Everything depended on getting that 'fish' right on target."

I interrupted to ask, "What about the flak?"

"The name of the game," Ralph replied. "Something you learned to live with. Actually you got used to it. In fact ignored it; your concentration was on hitting the target. Also by coming in low, you minimized the effectiveness of the enemy's guns. Half the time they couldn't lower their artillery sufficiently to fire down at you. Also it varied from time to time—whether it was merchant shipping, flak ships, E-boats, or warships—each case was a bit different."

On 17 May 1942, Manning was about to demonstrate his prowess against one of the most formidable German battleships. "At the briefing that morning," Ralph remembered, "we were told that *Prinz Eugen*, which had been undergoing repairs at Trondheim, Norway, was at sea under heavy naval escort on its way to Kiel, Germany. From there it could engage Allied convoys on the Murmansk run. It had to be taken out of action. Its demise was critical and our job was to sink it."

Such high stakes called for an all-out effort. At deck level, 12 Beauforts from Manning's squadron would form the attack force in three sections of four, while six Blenheims would create a diversion by faking a torpedo run to draw fire away from the attackers. To neutralize the escorts, four Beaufighters would riddle the destroyers with their cannon fire. And just to add a further distraction to the scenario, a dozen Hudsons would simulate a bomb run at altitude.

"We knew we could expect a lot of flak. From aerial reconnaissance, the flotilla was reported hugging the coastline well within range of the shore batteries," Ralph remembered. The moment it was sighted, *Prinz Eugen* began zigzagging to present as difficult a target as possible and the escorting destroyers laid down a heavy smoke screen.

Gunfire erupted everywhere from every direction, from the battleship, the destroyers, and the coastal batteries. The *Prinz Eugen* gunners had their work cut out for them, taking aim at the waves of attacking aircraft on the deck and the Hudson bombers above them. Manning's section was the last to go in; so far the battleship had escaped without damage, so it was up to them to inflict it. Suddenly, directly ahead of them, the sea erupted in giant spouts, high enough to block the pilots' view. The *Prinz Eugen* had trained her heavy guns to fire explosive shells into the sea, churning it up to form a wall of water. But this action didn't stop the four Beauforts, who flew right through it.

Now an additional menace presented itself—Messerschmitt

109s joined in the fray. "As I got ready to release the torpedo, I glanced out the window to see how my mates we making out," Ralph related, "just in time to see the 109s send the other three Beauforts crashing into the sea."

Manning was now very much on his own. From 800 yards he released his torpedo and at that very instant the Beaufort received a direct hit from one of *Prinz Eugen*'s flak guns that sent it into a half roll to one side. Struggling with the controls to straighten out the aircraft, he found himself in the perilous position of being caught in the crossfire between one of the destroyers on one side and the battleship on the other.

Having sustained even more damage to his mutilated torpedo bomber, Manning coaxed it back to base, but ground-looped on landing. The accident blocked the runway, which brought the squadron CO out in his car to tear a strip off Manning for obstructing traffic. Later on, learning of his stout effort in attacking the German battleship, he rescinded his admonition to congratulate Manning on what was indeed a "Good show!" However, that was but a dress rehearsal for the future challenge that lay in store.

Three months later, in August 1942, Manning was posted to 47 Squadron RAF, part of 328th Wing of the Northwestern African Coastal Air Force. That was a critical month in the struggle for North Africa. General Erwin Rommel's Afrika Korps was a scant 60 miles from Alexandria and the Nile Delta. A counteroffensive by General Sir Claude Auchinleck's Eighth Army had failed. On August 4, British prime minister Winston Churchill flew to Cairo to size up the situation, which resulted in General Bernard Montgomery taking over the Eighth Army from Auchinleck. But at Montgomery's insistence, to allow time for preparation and training the British offensive—the success of which was critical to the success of the Anglo-American landings—was delayed.

However, during the first four days of September, the tide had already begun to turn when Montgomery blunted an attack by Rommel at Alam-el-Halfa Ridge. In doing so, he had instilled a fresh spirit of confidence into an army hitherto plagued by defeat after defeat. By the time the British offensive was launched seven weeks later, on October 23, the troops felt assured of certain victory.

One of the most important factors in the preparation for the Battle of El Alamein was the strangling of the Panzerarmee's (the Afrika Korps' tank divisions) sea-arteries of supply. "That was my immediate assignment on arrival at Gianaclis airfield, southeast of Alexandria. We were at it day in, day out," Ralph told me. It paid off handsomely. During September, together with the British navy's submarines, the Coastal Air Force squadrons sank nearly a third of the tonnage shipped by the Axis via the Mediterranean and forced other vessels to turn back.

In October these attacks strangled the enemy's lifeline. The most serious losses of all were suffered by the oil tankers. On the eve of the battle the Panzerarmee had a mere tenth of the fuel supply it needed. Rommel had told Hitler, when he was invalided back to Germany in September with dysentery and jaundice, that the army could not advance or even hold its ground without sufficient fuel supplies. Hitler had assured him that Africa would get all the support needed. There was no way, of course, that he could possibly fulfill that promise.

On October 24, the day after the British offensive started, Hitler persuaded Rommel to leave his hospital bed at Semmering in Austria and take charge of the battle. Rommel first stopped in Rome, where he expressed to the German military attaché, General Enno von Rintelen, the need to dispatch oil supplies immediately. He then flew on to Crete and arrived at his North Africa headquarters that evening.

According to Ralph Manning, Rommel's conference in Rome must have reaped fast results; next day a 5000-ton oil tanker was diverted from Benghazi to Tobruk, 200 miles closer to the battle scene. The tanker, a Greek vessel christened *Proserpina* after the mythological queen of the underworld, was carrying 3500 tons of precious fuel.

"The first we heard about it," Ralph related, "was when we were called to a briefing that afternoon. Air Recce [air reconnaissance] had spotted this tanker and two freighters escorted by four destroyers off the Libyan coast. The gen [intelligence] was that sinking it was critical to the outcome of the battle. But then everything we were told to do was always *critical*."

A composite task force of five Bisley light bombers, four escorting Beaufighters, and eight torpedo-bomber Beauforts took off shortly after 1700 hours, headed out to sea, and set a course west. The drill was for the Bisleys to attack the freighters, the Beauforts to take out the tanker, and the Beaufighter crews to keep their eyes peeled for enemy fighters.

"When we made landfall two hours later, we were too far east of where we should have been. There was no sign of any convoy but below us a string of power barges opened fire with the shore batteries joining in." Charlie Bladen, Ralph's side-gunner, let fly a burst or two in retaliation, which drew a sharp rebuke from the Beaufort's other gunner, Nimmy Nimerovsky: "Save your ammunition, you stupid bastard. We still have to find that tanker!"

The formation flew on. Ralph continued his narrative to me. "Just past Tobruk I saw a couple of the Bisleys circling over some ships— three destroyers and two freighters, but no sign of a tanker. It must be further on, I thought. Then to my amazement—and fury—I saw our flight leader peel off towards the ships. Hell, he must know there was no goddam tanker there. Well to hell with him! In a rage I pulled up and headed further west—a bit chancy, two Eyties [Italian fighters] appeared above us. But there dead ahead was a column of smoke. Eureka! The tanker and a destroyer."

What the task force later realized was that when it was detected by German radar a trap had been set with all the ships, except one of the destroyers and the tanker, acting as bait to protect the *Proserpina*. It might have worked too, but for Manning's dogged determination.

"By this time," Ralph added, "two Bisleys had joined us, who thankfully chased away the Macchis [the Italian fighters], as well as one of our own Beauforts flown by Norm Hearn-Phillips who, unbeknownst to us, had elected to follow our aircraft instead of attacking the other ships."

That attack was not only a miscalculation but resulted in a disaster as well. Three of the Bisleys took on the smaller of the merchant ships, dropping their bombs on it. Concentrated antiaircraft fire brought down one of the fighter-bombers. Next, the Beauforts struck at the freighters. One of the torpedo bombers was hit by flak but managed to climb away even though half its rudder was shot off. Another Beaufort took a direct hit when it dropped its torpedo, flipped over onto its back, and crashed into the sea. What remained of the group formed up and, covered by the Beaufighters, headed west to try and find Manning and Hearn-Phillips.

Ralph added: "Norm made the first attack on the tanker, but as he swooped in, a shell struck the fuse box, shorting the electrical system, and his torpedo released itself, falling uselessly into the sea—a total write-off. I didn't know it then, but that left our Beaufort with the only torpedo left in the entire force.

"I turned the aircraft to aim at the tanker from right angles. But the *Proserpina*'s skipper took the correct evasive action by swinging toward us head on, reducing its silhouette as a target to a minimum. I was tempted to fire off the torpedo anyway, but decided instead to make an attack from the other—the landward—side. I turned around and approached the tanker at a 45-degree angle from abeam and, at 700 yards' range, I pressed the release button and saw the torpedo streak toward the target. At that moment, one of the Bisleys dropped a delayed-action bomb on the ship, then pulled up sharply—a second too late. Its port wing struck the vessel's foremast, which sheared the wing off just as the second Bisley came in to attack. Up in the nose of our aircraft my navigator, Norm Spark, captured the moment on his camera for posterity. But it looked like our attack had been a dud. The torpedo had failed to explode."

As the Beaufort flew on over the tanker, one of the bombs dropped by the Bisleys exploded, slamming the bomber upwards and momentarily stopping both engines. Manning pulled back on the control column and gave the engines full throttle.

"What with bombs exploding, flak all over the bloody place, and aircraft diving in all directions, I wanted to get the hell out of there," Ralph said. "Just then Nimerovsky yelled over the intercom: 'We did it! Wow! She's going up in flame and smoke!' Our attack had been a success after all."

When Manning took aim, the *Proserpina* was turning inward toward the Beaufort. By the time the torpedo reached the target, it struck it a glancing blow at an angle near the port bow that sent it rolling alongside the hull toward the stern before it finally exploded.

"We didn't stick around to watch the fireworks," Ralph stated, "but we weren't out of the woods yet. In the distance, one of the Beaufighters spotted a formation of ME-109s [German Messerschmitt fighters] to the north and well above. Fortunately, we were low enough so that they didn't see us, because we were certainly in no shape to take them on. But we had two more casualties before we reached base—a Bisley and one of our Beauforts collided and crashed into the sea. There were no survivors.

"I hadn't realized how lucky we had been until after we landed. We had taken several bullets in one of our fuel tanks as well as the main spar."

The sequel to the scenario was that, at dusk, a flight of Wellington reconnaissance bombers flew out to finish off the convoy. The smaller freighter had disappeared, sent to the bottom by the Bisley attack. The Wellingtons sank the larger merchant ship with torpedoes, but there was no sign of the destroyers. The *Proserpina* was still afloat, but the fire that raged in her was visible for miles.

A month later Manning was transferred again—this time to India to his old 42 Squadron RAF, carrying out army cooperation duties. In the spring of 1943 the unit moved to Burma in support of Major General Orde Wingate's Chindits guerrilla forces expedition against the Japanese. Later, Manning joined 217 Squadron RAF in Ceylon, where he was engaged in convoy patrols, converting pilots to Beauforts and instructing on air-sea rescue procedures. In the latter case, he was able to give his pupils a first-hand lesson when he was forced to ditch into the sea while on convoy patrol. The aircraft's dinghy wouldn't inflate and Manning and his two crew members—neither of whom could swim—had to rely on their Mae West life preservers to keep them afloat in shark-infested waters. Nevertheless, Manning kept their spirits up until all three were rescued by one of the ships they had been escorting.

Following World War II, Manning remained in the air force, serving at the RCAF Staff College in Toronto, Ontario, and at NORAD Headquarters in Colorado, before being appointed RCAF Historian in 1960. In that capacity he was instrumental in securing the hangars at Rockliffe Air Station in Ottawa, Ontario, to display the National Aviation Museum aircraft collection. In 1965, he retired from the air force and joined the Canadian War Museum in Ottawa as curator.

Chapter 4

One in a Million

The Royal Canadian Air Force Women's Division (WD) formed a memorable part of my own service life. My sister and one of my first cousins were WDs. At No. 2 Service Flying Training School at Uplands, Ottawa, WDs acted as timers, checking our flights in and out. In England I became closely acquainted with Flight Officer Nancy Smith, assistant to Air Marshal Harold (Gus) Edwards, Air Officer-in-Chief, RCAF Overseas, and many others. By that time women in uniform had become an accepted and very welcome fact.

During World War I the aerial bombing of civilians in England created the "home front," bringing women and men—as well as children—under fire. By war's end, more than 200 nurses had been decorated; 46 had given their lives. Canadian participation amounted to 3141 serving at home and overseas with the Canadian Medical Corps.

Although that contribution and its attendant achievement were still very much of a nonmilitary nature, it did bring about a change in thinking about women's involvement in the armed forces.

By 1937, as Nazi Germany prepared for war, the British began laying the groundwork for the formation of the Auxiliary Territorial Service (ATS), the Women's Royal Naval Service (WRNS), and the Women's Auxiliary Air Force (WAAF). In Canada, the Munich crisis of 1938 precipitated a revival of interest in women's direct participation in the military with the formation of dozens of auxiliary groups.

The outbreak of war in 1939 brought immediate pressure on the

Canadian government from several of these independent groups to create official auxiliary services to be part of each of the military services. A survey of commanding officers across the country drew mixed responses, but it was generally conceded that women were sorely needed to replace the manpower directed into combat and other field duties, and that this condition would prevail and increase as the war continued.

This awakened a clarion call that manifested itself in women from all walks of life volunteering to contribute to the war effort, not only with the military, but in nursing, as well as replacing men in factories, in offices, on farms, and in countless other occupations. Remarkably, for a nation of its size, out of a population of a mere 11 million at the time, during World War II a total of one million Canadian women served their country in one fashion or another.

On 27 June 1941, the Canadian Women's Army Corps (CWAC) was officially sanctioned. This was followed on 21 July 1941 by the formation of the Canadian Women's Auxiliary Air Force (CWAAF), later to become the Royal Canadian Air Force Women's Division (WD). On 31 July 1942, approval was given for the establishment of the Women's Royal Canadian Naval Service (the WRCNS or "Wrens"). By the end of hostilities, nearly 50,000 Canadian women had volunteered for military service, 22,000 with the CWAC, 17,000 with the RCAF WD, and 7000 with the WRCNS.

This story of those Canadian women in the military revolves around the record of one of them, who was, in effect—taking into account the overall contribution by Canadian women—one in a million.

On the wintry late evening of Friday, 19 February 1942, a former teacher at Berthelet School in Montreal, Air Woman Second Class (AW2) Mary Hawkins of the Women's Division of the Royal Canadian Air Force, along with eight other recruits from the same city, reported for duty at No. 7 Manning Depot (MD), Rockcliffe Air Station, Ottawa. This would be their home for the next two months as they began a period of initiation and integration into service life known as Basic Training.

Two days later, Mary Hawkins wrote to her mentor, Marion Strang, the Warden (Dean of Women) of her alma mater, Macdonald College, Ste. Anne de Bellevue in Quebec, who had encouraged her to enlist. While she enthused over service life in general, she lamented the lack of bathtubs. "You can't fall asleep in a shower no matter how hard you try."

Mary Hawkins' interest in joining the air force was first kindled in late 1941 when one of her closest friends left her position as dietitian at Macdonald College to enlist in the WDs as a Messing Officer. Mary longed to follow suit. The following summer, while attending a summer course at Queen's University in Kingston, Ontario, a female RCAF recruiting officer gave a spiel on the advantages and virtues of becoming a WD. Mary was hooked. But she still had to wrestle between the prospect of leaving her job when there was a severe shortage of teachers due to the number of men enlisting, and leaving her family responsibilities to her mother and younger brother, as her father and older brother were serving in the army. Marion Strang, to whom she turned for advice, soon solved her dilemma by encouraging Mary to enlist.

Mary's first letter as an Air Woman heralded the start of a correspondence with Mrs. Strang, involving some 150 letters from the time of her enlistment to her honourable discharge from the service two-and-a-half years later in September 1945. Her original intent had been to provide Mrs. Strang with some diversion from her concern over the fate of her own son Kenneth, a lieutenant with the Royal Rifles of Quebec who had been captured at Hong Kong in December 1942. At the time she had no idea that those WD letters were being kept in tidy sequence and would be given back to her by Mrs. Strang after the war.

Shortly after her arrival at Rockcliffe, Mary applied for an operational posting—her objective was finally to be sent overseas where the action was—and after an interview before a Selection Board she was rewarded with the post of Clerk Operational. In April she was posted to Halifax, Nova Scotia, along with 12 others as Clerk Op with duties in the Control Room of Eastern Air Command. They were stationed at the Y-Depot, an RCAF jumping-off point for transfers overseas, and billeted in Nissen huts (tunnel-shaped corrugated iron structures with cement floors), which Mary found lacking in the comparative comfort and privacy of their previous barracks. However, her posting was fortunate, because her fiancé, Lieutenant George Buch of the Black Watch Regiment of Canada from Montreal, was in the same outfit as her older brother Chris, and was also stationed in Halifax. (It was not until I was well into writing this chapter that it dawned on me that I had known George Buch at school—Bishop's College School in Lennoxville, Quebec. His choice of the Black Watch was a natural and logical one. Our cadet corps was affiliated with that regiment.)

On May 14, Mary was promoted to Air Woman First Class. Then a break in the normal routine took place on 23 May 1943, when the aircraft carrying Prime Minister Winston Churchill, code-named "Trident," was routed over eastern Canada. Churchill had been in Washington, D.C., attending the Washington Conference to discuss the disposition of the Allied forces after the Axis defeat in North Africa. Mary was on duty at the time in the Eastern Air Command Control Room. It was an unforgettable moment, but one that Clerk Op Mary Hawkins was compelled to couch in veiled terms in her letter to Marion Strang to avoid censorship, by referring to the Prime Minister simply and enigmatically as a "noted Briton."

After two months in the Eastern Air Command Control Room at Halifax, a contingent of the Y-Depot Clerk Ops was posted to the RCAF Sea Plane base at Dartmouth across the basin. After a somewhat routine existence, their new duties offered the excitement of "scrambling" flights of Canso coastal seaplanes to take off against potential "bandits"—enemy aircraft. But this still did not satisfy Mary Hawkins, who hankered for an overseas posting.

Added to this frustration was the departure of her fiancé, George Buch, for an undisclosed embarkation point awaiting orders to sail overseas. There would be no further contact between them except through the mails.

The Operations duties at Dartmouth gave Mary and her fellow Clerk Ops a firsthand insight into the danger presented by German submarines operating in the Gulf of St. Lawrence, whose positions were pinpointed by Eastern Air Command. By the autumn of 1943 the Allies had the upper hand over the U-boats in the Atlantic, but the risk of torpedoing had not altogether diminished. Mary was much relieved when she received a letter in October from George, postmarked Great Britain, that he had arrived safely on the other side of the Atlantic.

A few days later Mary received the orders she had been waiting for: to report to the Y-Depot in Halifax two weeks after November 3. In the meantime she was given Embarkation Leave. Mary was on cloud nine; it signified the overseas posting she had been long-ing for. With the posting went a promotion, to Leading Airwoman. Mary found it so difficult to contain her excitement that when she began sewing the propeller badges onto her uniform, she sewed right through both sleeves, and couldn't get her arms into her tunic.

Mary Hawkins' draft of 50 Clerk Ops was part of the 1300 RCAF WDs, the "lucky few" as they were known, to secure an overseas posting during the entire war. On 21 November 1943, Mary and her group boarded the Cunard liner *Mauretania* at Halifax. Her group of seven was quartered in staterooms normally reserved for officers. Meals were well above par; they also had the use of the officers' sun deck and there was lots of time for recreation and entertainment.

When the Y-Depot Women's Division contingent docked at Plymouth on the south coast of England 10 days later, having crossed the Atlantic in comfort compared to some of their fellow uniformed females in other overseas drafts (on some ships they had to sleep in their clothes for fear of being torpedoed), they were serenaded by the RCAF band, then whisked off to a waiting train for an overnight journey to Bournemouth on the south coast. There they were comfortably lodged in a resort hotel while awaiting postings to various air stations.

The next day Mary was reunited with her fiancé, who had three days' leave after completing a course in London. They enjoyed being together after their three-month separation. While they took in the sights Mary experienced her first air-raid alert; it came to naught, but she found the blackout somewhat eerie.

By the end of the weekend she and George had decided to get married in January, by which time Mary hoped to be settled in a new posting. Alas, that prospect ran into headwinds.

Shortly after the Clerk Ops draft got settled, they received a visit from the Officer Commanding, RCAF WDs Overseas, Wing Officer Kathleen Walker, who made a special trip to Bournemouth to advise them that for all intents and purposes they had been posted overseas under "false pretenses." A communications request for Clerks General from RCAF Headquarters in Ottawa had been bureaucratically misinterpreted as Clerks Operational. (This was not all that surprising; a similar request for a specified number of air *screws*—propellers—resulted in the sudden appearance of an unwanted number of air*crews*.) The problem was that the Clerk Ops were not really needed for jobs they had been trained for. There were more than enough experienced British WAAFs with Ops experience, many going back to Battle of Britain days.

W/O Walker assured the draft, however, that despite the circumstances of their arrival, they were most welcome in England; it had been like pulling hen's teeth to get Ottawa to release *any* WDs for overseas duty. So to protect the status quo, the less said the better. There were other jobs that needed filling. The matter was temporarily left up in the air, although the W/O suggested that most of them might want to come to London to retrain and muster to new trades.

Meanwhile, Mary busied herself adjusting to the ways of wartime Britain. "It's interesting to see the war effort close up," she wrote. She noted particularly that every square foot of land was put to arable use and every home had a vegetable "Victory Garden" as well as flowers growing in profusion. She also found that the British pound was worth far less than she had been led to believe— about two dollars.

She was surprised how well-fed they were—better than the civilians—which was contrary to what they had heard. It made her acutely aware of what sacrifices the British had made, imagining what it must have been like to leave home in the morning, not knowing whether by the time they returned that evening they still had a roof over their heads. "I ... am filled with admiration and wonder at the ability of the British people to withstand and carry on," Mary wrote to Marion Strang.

Half the draft had taken the WD Commanding Officer's advice to remuster to another trade. But Mary and the rest of the Ops filled in the time when and where they could, awaiting assignment to an Ops job or anything else available. One by one, the transfers came through, sometimes weeks apart and always on short notice; Mary attached herself to the permanent WAAFs stationed in Bournemouth, taking her turns in the RAF/RCAF post office awaiting a posting momentarily, virtually living from day to day.

Then suddenly her fortunes changed. In mid-December, word came through that Mary was posted to Digby Fighter Station in Lincolnshire, commanded by Canadian Battle of Britain ace Group Captain Ernie McNab and home to two RCAF Spitfire Squadrons: 402 and 416. Because the transfer did not become effective until early in February, Mary and George set their wedding date for Saturday, 22 January 1943, at 11 o'clock in St.-Martin's-in-the-Field Church in London. To overcome the proviso that either the husband or wife had to be a resident of the parish for two weeks prior to the marriage, George had left a suitcase in the Charing Cross Hotel a fortnight ahead of time.

His attention to the wedding arrangements was tinged with irony and humour. George asked some of his fellow officers whether they could recommend a suitable place for the reception. He was unimpressed with the places he'd been referred to. However, as he wandered through London's West End, he came upon the name "Claridge's" engraved on the sidewalk. On closer inspection he concluded that this place looked a cut above the others and went into the hotel to make further inquiries. The staff were more than helpful and quoted him a modest price for the reception—one pound per head.

Since the bride and groom planned to leave for Cornwall on their honeymoon early the following day, the concierge told George that the hotel's bridal suite would be available for their wedding night. What could be nicer? When George returned to his battalion, his friends were flabbergasted to learn that this naive young Canadian officer had been able to arrange a wedding reception at one of London's foremost hostelries, whose guest list included the names of many of Europe's crowned heads.

On Friday, the eve of the marriage, Mary and her brother Chris, her maid of honour and fellow WD, Mona Langley, Mona's brother Ellis, and George and his best man Tommy Havill gathered in the latter's room in the Dorchester Hotel. Scotch flowed liberally before they repaired to the dining room for some champagne and liqueurs with the evening meal and then set off to visit George's aunt, Olga Buch, who lived in the suburb of Streatham. But it was a visit they wouldn't make.

That night marked the beginning of the Luftwaffe's "Little Blitz" on London, in which 268 bombs fell on the city and surrounding area, the worst bombing the metropolis had absorbed since the blitz of 1940. While it didn't bother the wedding party one iota, it "put the wind up the taxi driver" (frightened him), who promptly turned back halfway to the destination, unnerved more by the thunder of the ack-ack guns than the bomb explosions.

Though the party returned to the hotel unscathed and still in the merriest of moods, the incident was not without fallout. Aunt Olga did not have a telephone, so the couple could not call and explain why they weren't able to come; they assumed she would have heard about the raid and understood their predicament anyway. But Aunt Olga understood no such thing. She was quite miffed that they had probably decided they had much better things to do and, as Queen Victoria might have said, was not amused.

In any event, on Saturday morning, George and Mary's wedding came off without a hitch and the bride and groom journeyed by rail to Cornwall for their honeymoon, where they stayed at the luxurious Tregenna Castle Hotel in St. Ives, situated on a cliff with a breathtaking view overlooking the ocean. The war seemed far away and almost forgotten for that brief period before Mary had to report for her new duties and George returned to his regiment.

At Digby Mary Hawkins, her buddy Helen Woodcroft, and two other WDs from Bournemouth spent the first month learning the ropes and getting acquainted with being part of an operational front-line station. It was a thrill to watch the Spitfires taking off and returning from their missions over German-occupied territory on the continent.

The WDs were billeted reasonably comfortably, but inevitably had to fight the cold, in a house originally designated Married Quarters for Warrant Officers on the grounds of Blankney Hall, a manor located a couple of miles from the fighter field itself that served as the station Operations Room. The accommodation was temporary until the erection of Nissen huts was completed. It took some time to settle in, and for their WAAF counterparts to understand that they felt like strangers and were suffering from homesickness. Quite naturally there was some resentment; after all, the WAAFs had been at it since the start of the war, while the Canadians were newcomers and with a higher rate of pay to boot. And unlike the Britishers, they were free of any domestic ties and responsibilities. On leave they could roam at will, like tourists.

Mary found it hard to understand the British attitude. "Their ideas [are] prehistoric," she wrote. They believed there was no place for women at the top in either a trade or a profession, and that the air force should have male officers; they were quite huffy, not to say stuffy, about it.

In fact there was a marked difference in the attitude of the WAAF (British) officers and that of Women's Division Canadian officers toward the other ranks. After inspecting Mary and her fellow WDs' quarters, their Canadian officer would remove her cap, sit on the bed, have a cup of coffee, smoke a cigarette, and have an informal chat. The Britons considered this informal behaviour inexcusable.

When Mary's "48s" (weekend hours' leave) coincided with George's time off from his duties, they joined each other in London, but on one occasion Mary went to Brighton on the south coast, close to where George was stationed. Toward the end of March, the south of England became a restricted area in preparation for the Second Front, the long-awaited invasion of Europe. All leaves were cancelled and all "48s" limited to an area 12 miles from camp. However, by applying for Compassionate Leave, which required the signature of an Air Marshal no less, she and George were united briefly when George's irregular hours of duty would permit.

As April drifted into May and the tempo of softening up *Festung Europa* increased, through daily Allied bombing, it became obvious that D-Day was imminent. In the Ops Room at Blankney Hall, the routine for Mary Hawkins and her WD and WAAF companions accelerated and they were called upon to put in longer and longer hours. Far from feeling overburdened, they looked upon their role with a sense of excitement. Then the big moment arrived.

Mary's shift went on duty at midnight on that historic date, 6 June 1944. As they walked to the mess for a pre-shift meal, they could hear the roar of planes overhead and see the navigation lights. They later learned that there were some 12,000 aircraft aloft that night, all heading toward France. The girls were in for a busy time in the Ops room, but they were allowed to relieve each other at 10-minute intervals. No one even dozed during those periods of respite; however, they couldn't risk going back to work half-awake.

When they went off-duty at 5 a.m., by which time most of the aircraft had returned, they trudged over to the Nissen huts, so exhausted they fell asleep the moment they lay down on their cots.

About nine o'clock, an excited WAAF arrived at their door announcing that D-Day had begun, which hardly came as a surprise and made the occupants so mad at having been awoken from a sound sleep that they greeted the intruder in decidedly unladylike terms, telling her in equally unladylike words to beat it.

Two days later Mary found herself preparing reports for her commanding officer, Grace Findlay, on the status of the women's baseball league, details of a birthday celebration, and the outcome of a recently held Canada Night lecture. It struck her as somewhat ironic to be writing about such relatively trivial matters, what with the up-to-the-minute reports from Normandy and the newspapers publishing extra editions reporting on the invasion.

At the end of July, Mary was transferred to the Intelligence Branch at Digby Headquarters. Her job entailed processing documents and mounting, filing, and keeping wall maps of the continent up to date, a task made difficult—but no less rewarding—with the situation changing so rapidly from day to day. Her duties also included issuing messages on the up-to-the-hour status of enemy coastal defences for the pilots' edification.

At the beginning of September, along with her pal Helen Woodcroft, Mary was transferred to 62 Base RCAF at Linton-on-Ouse in Yorkshire, one of the 6th Group Bomber stations. She never lost her fascination for watching the Lancaster bombers taking off for a bombing raid and rendezvousing over the field then flying into the distance. "They look like dogs with their ears back, in pursuit of a rabbit," she wrote.

She quickly learned all about bomber aircrews' superstitions. It was considered bad luck for girls to follow the crews out to the bombers before a raid. They even took a dim view of them hanging around their kites. Mary also discovered a piece of equipment issued on occasion before a mission that made aircrews cringe and shudder: an arm band, packed into a small plastic case, bearing a Union Jack and a message in Russian identifying the bearer as an Allied airman should the aircraft come down in Soviet territory. It meant the target was so deep inside Germany there would be no point of return if trouble occurred.

In her job, Mary was able to follow the course of events developing in France closely and, with her husband's regiment on the firing line, not without some concern. For instance she pondered whether the fearful battle south of Caen had really been necessary. On July 21, in an attack on Fontesay-le-Marmian, south of the Normandy capital, which the British and Canadians had captured 12 days earlier, the Black Watch lost 123 killed, 100 wounded, and 83 taken prisoner, the worst one-day loss in its history. Major Phil Griffin, whom both Mary and Marion Strang had known at Macdonald College, was one of those listed as killed. Not many of the original battalion were left. Thankfully, George Buch was not among the casualties, and his letters, though inevitably delayed, were cheerful and optimistic and reached his wife regularly.

On October 22, at the time of the Battle of the Scheldt Estuary to free the approaches to the Dutch port of Antwerp, Mary received a letter dated the 9th of that month in which George announced that he was taking over command of his company and for the next little while would be too busy to write. It was small wonder. On October 13, the Black Watch, which had been guarding the approaches to the Albert Canal, was called upon to capture Woensdrecht and seal off the South Beveland Isthmus linked to Walcheren Island, the westernmost German-occupied territory north of the estuary. Thanks to poor intelligence and planning, and lack of reconnaissance, it resulted in a massacre. "Black Friday" cost the Black Watch 183 casualties, 56 of them fatal— nearly half its regimental strength.

Ten days later, on November 3, Mary had made a date to meet Derrick Farmiloe, an RAF pilot friend from Digby, for dinner and an evening of dancing in York. Half an hour before she left to go into town she went to collect her mail. There was only a yellow envelope and her immediate reaction was one of disappointment; that Derrick couldn't keep the date. Instead, when she opened it the message read, "Regret to Inform You ... Missing in Action, October 13th."

"I had long thought that the word that someone was 'missing' was extremely bad news," Mary recorded later, but on the contrary, she actually found it reassuring; at least she knew he was alive.

Firsthand reports—one from the colonel of the regiment—quickly established that George had been wounded at Woensdrecht. As he was being carried off the field by German stretcher-bearers, he had called out for them to leave his hat behind; he'd be back for it. Sometime later, the Hackle—a red feather and a battle honour worn in George's balmoral—turned up at the No. 1 Canadian Neurological Hospital at Basingstoke in the south of England worn by a wounded Black Watch patient who had retrieved it from the battlefield. Mary believed that George had left the cap behind as a signal that he was alive.

Mary decided that she should cable both his family and her own to say that it appeared George was all right and that they hoped to be celebrating March 8 together (Mary's 22nd birthday). These well-meaning, obviously innocent messages set off a barrage of heavy red-tape flak from the censors. Who was "George"? Why was he "all right"? What was the significance of March 8? All this rigmarole delayed delivery of the cables for over a week. And it left those on the receiving end somewhat in the dark.

Meanwhile, George's Aunt Olga, who worked at the *Evening Express*, added to the imbroglio by availing herself of the newspaper's wire service to cable both families: "Deepest Sympathy." Unfortunately, her gesture did nothing to clarify the situation. Back came the queries. Who did she mean? George or Mary's brother, Chris?

Mary's father to the rescue. Using his army connections, Major Stuart Hawkins gained access to the casualty list that confirmed that George was among the 24 men from the Black Watch Regiment listed as missing on October 13. Later, official word came through that he was a prisoner of war in Northern Germany and it was eventually established that he was being held at *Oflag 79*.

Mary celebrated 31 December 1944 as she had never celebrated a New Year's Eve before: She had finally received her first letter from George since his capture. After being hit by shrapnel, he told her, he had taken cover and was spotted by German Red Cross paratroopers who he said treated him very decently. Though he had a shrapnel hole in his right leg and a slashed wrist, no bones had been broken and he was confident that, given time, his leg would heal properly. He also commended the first-class medical treatment he had received at the hands of the enemy doctors.

At the beginning of 1945, although hostilities in Europe still had nearly four months to run, victory was clearly in sight and the war effort focused in that direction had already started to wind down. One by one, the RCAF Women's Divisions in Europe were being sent home. Mary Hawkins had on several occasions been given her "ticket" to Canada only to have it cancelled at the last minute. Then, in mid-March, all home postings were temporarily frozen. In an about-face policy, HQ decreed that wives of POWs were to be treated as singles. Presumably the order had been made to facilitate sending both wife and husband back to Canada in the same draft, once the latter had been released from imprisonment. Yet for some inexplicable reason, it didn't work out that way for George and Mary.

Although the war was drawing to a close, at Linton-on-Ouse (and at the other RCAF 6th Group Bomber Command Yorkshire airfields), it was business as usual, with the Lancaster bombers almost daily, weather permitting, carrying out their final sorties of the war—not without casualties. On 25 April 1945, two squadrons from Linton—426 (Thunderbird) and 408 (Goose)—went out on what was to be their final bombing operation over Wangerooge Island, east of the Frisian Chain. One crew was lost and because the end of the war in Europe was imminent, the loss of these young lives seemed to Mary all the more tragic even though life went on as usual—parades, etc.—at the base.

Two weeks before the official German surrender at Reims on 7 May 1945, *Oflag 79* was one of the prisoner-of-war camps liberated from the enemy in the rapid Allied advance eastward. George Buch, thin and weak, but thoroughly recovered from his wounds, was repatriated to England and put on double rations, an extra quart of milk a day, and as much stout ale as he could drink. He and Mary spent 10 days at Shanklin on the Isle of Wight while he recuperated, then they returned to London in time to take part in the VE-Day celebrations.

George sailed for Canada in mid-June, not with Mary as the "WD singles" directive had led them to believe. His wife had to wait until November to leave England, but at least her time was spent at the "R" Depot (Repatriation) in the comfort of Torquay in Devon, a very scenic part of Great Britain.

While a few women had trouble adjusting to civilian life following their discharge from the service, Mary Hawkins Buch was among the majority who easily and comfortably fitted into the peacetime environment. Mary returned to the vocation she had left behind, serving on the local school board of Montreal's Lakeshore community and also becoming active in education at the provincial level working in Youth Protection. Since retiring in 1983 she has lived in Brockville, where she is past president of the District Historical Society.

Looking back on her days as an airwoman, she writes: "Many of [our] recollections are happy ones—of warm friendship, mirth and mischief in the midst of loss and grief. ..."

Slightly more than 5000 Canadian servicewomen served overseas— considered to be the "chosen few" by those left behind, but whose contribution to the war effort, though lacking some of the dangers and excitement, was no less of vital importance. From the time of the first female enlistment in 1941 to the end of World War II, 244 Canadian Servicewomen had been decorated with honours ranging from Mention in Dispatches to Member of the British Empire.

Chapter 5

Joy Cometh
in the Morning

In an address to the Toronto Branch of the Naval Officers Association of Canada on 17 February 1999, I said:

"In the early summer of 1943, when our squadron was stationed at Redhill south of London, we flew clipped-wing Spitfires on medium-bomber escort work. These planes were highly maneuverable at lower altitude, but the wing loading made them stall at higher speeds than normal. They certainly weren't designed for deck landings.

"And—neither was I.

"Ironically, one day a Royal Navy Fleet Air Arm officer arrived in our midst to teach us how to fly off and on a simulated carrier deck.

"Next morning we found one end of the grass field marked off with white tape, an area equivalent to a carrier on which we were expected to take off and land.

"On my first attempt, I pulled the control column right back. Air brakes tight on. Throttle fully forward. A crewman waves his flag. I let go the brakes and I'm on my way—splash! Right off the edge of the carrier—and into the English Channel. In this case—luckily—onto that lovely green grass.

"Climbing into a circuit, I looked down on that goddamn postage stamp I'm supposed to land on. Mission Impossible.

"I curved in, then when I got my correct glide angle, straightened out—flaps down, wheels down. Throttle back. The bloody bat boy waving those friggin' things like there's no tomorrow. And if this had been for real instead of just practice, there would have indeed been no tomorrow. I overshot by at least three carrier lengths. Into the good old Channel again. Thankfully, in this case the good old grass again.

"Over the next two weeks I managed to screw up six takeoffs and a like number of landings and yet I was one of the more successful ones. A star in fact.

"Our Fleet Air Arm friend took it all in stride. But after two weeks he'd had enough. He packed up and left—probably in disgust. I guess the Admiralty felt the same way because we never heard any more about deck landings."

After the speech it was pointed out to me that actual takeoffs from a carrier were immeasurably assisted by the headwind into which it sailed, markedly reducing liftoff length needed. Further, arresting gear aboard the carrier brought landings to an abrupt stop. Those amenities aside, there were still perils in abundance for those of our confreres in the Fleet Air Arm (FAA) on the sea.

By mid-May 1941, the battle at sea had become critical for the British and Canadian navies and the merchant marine. In their efforts to strangle the supply lifeline of men and material being convoyed from North America to the British Isles, German surface raiders had already cost the Allies three-quarters of a million tons of shipping. On the 21st of the month, the battle-cruisers *Gneisenau* and *Scharnhorst*, and the cruiser *Hipper*, were docked at Brest, France. That morning, the newly launched *Bismarck*, its 15-inch guns making it the heaviest armoured ship afloat—exceeding the latest Royal Navy battleships by nearly 10 tons—together with the battleship *Prinz Eugen*, was spotted by reconnaissance planes heading north in the Kattegat Channel between Denmark and Sweden. Later that day they were reported berthed at Bergen Fjord in Norway. Clearly, the German navy was preparing for a major assault on Allied convoys.

At Scapa Flow, shortly after midnight next morning, the Royal Navy commander-in-chief, Sir John Tovey, dispatched the battleships *Hood* and the *Prince of Wales*, along with six destroyers, to provide cover and support for the cruisers *Norfolk* and *Suffolk*, already on patrol in the Denmark Strait between Greenland and Iceland.

Next day, naval reconnaissance aircraft reported that the two German battleships had left Bergen—under cover of broken cloud and rain—heading for the Denmark Strait, by this time narrowed by pack ice to a width of a mere 80 miles and often shrouded in dense mist. Tovey immediately sent out the *King George V* and the aircraft carrier *Victorious*, with seven destroyers as added support for the cruiser patrols in the strait.

The *Victorious* had originally been scheduled to sail with a convoy of 20,000 men for the Middle East. She had only joined the Home fleet at Scapa four days earlier. She was carrying a cargo of crated RAF fighter aircraft that were destined for Takoradi on the Gold Coast, to be reassembled and flown to Egypt to support the Western Desert campaign. Escort was to be provided by Fulmar two-seater planes of 800Z Squadron of the Royal Navy Fleet Air Arm. But those plans were countermanded to meet the breakout of the German battleships.

Also aboard the *Victorious* were nine Swordfish torpedo planes of the FAA. Once the carrier got under way, they were loaded with bombs, while the 800Z aircrews were ordered to stand on readiness as fighter protection for the fleet. Montreal-born navigator John Hoare had second thoughts about the role. He, along with his squadron mates, had been trained for reconnaissance duties. Furthermore, the Fulmar was hardly in a class with the modern fighters of its day. With a maximum speed of 250 miles an hour at 10,000 feet (in contrast to the Spitfire's speed of 362 miles an hour at 19,000 feet), it was heavy, cumbersome, and difficult to maneuver, with a slow rate of climb—fifteen minutes to 12,000 feet (in contrast to five minutes to 10,000 feet in a Hurricane). Additionally, it had no armament in the rear cockpit (the observer's seat), putting the observer/navigator at severe risk. Yet, incredibly, over a two-year period during the war Fulmars actually scored 112 kills against the enemy.

Despite the fact that he had spent six months in training before actually taking to the air and another year of aerial navigation instruction and practice prior to going to sea, Hoare had strong misgivings about how he would react under fire. "The great fear of course was fear," he wrote later. "I was sure I would be scared stiff."

As early as 1933, 19-year-old John Hoare knew precisely what and whom he would one day be fighting against. He had spent some months learning to speak German in Freiburg-im-Breisgau, where he had been witness to a pogrom in which Jewish shops were smashed by the Brownshirts.

In 1938, working as an apprentice with the British publishing firm Constable in London, he was turned down by the Royal Navy Volunteer Reserve; there were no vacancies in the Rosyth division. A year later, when war broke out on 3 September 1939, he was luckier; he was accepted for service with the Fleet Air Arm. But his chums in Bayswater, London, where he lived, looked upon his future with some skepticism. This was not without some justification: only two weeks after the declaration of war on September 17, the aircraft carrier *Courageous* had been sunk off the Western Approaches by a U-boat. Three days later, the carrier *Ark Royal* narrowly escaped a similar fate. These incidents led to aircraft carriers being withdrawn from submarine hunting.

When on a Sunday in October Hoare reported to H.M.S. *Vincent,* he was posted to a land-based training establishment at Gosport across the harbour from Plymouth. In joining No. 38 Observers'

Course, he was about to be inducted into the branch of the navy that the Admiralty regarded as an extension of the Royal Air Force and viewed with both misgiving and mistrust. After four months of basic training in wireless telegraphy, navigation, and seamanship, the fledglings were promoted from naval airmen second class to leading naval airmen, and were posted to Whale Island for gunnery instruction. This was ironic for John Hoare, whose first operational assignment was in a Fulmar—whose rear cockpit, as has been mentioned, had no armament. That course completed, the next step was Signals School at Portsmouth. Finally, in early June the group was transferred to Ford aerodrome on the Sussex coast for flight training in antiquated Shark biplanes and Proctor monoplane trainers, both open-cockpit aircraft.

At first, that early summer of 1940 seemed a bit unreal to Hoare and his fellow students. Around Ford, the English countryside remained unchanged. Beer was in ample supply. Coates' distillery in Plymouth continued to produce copious quantities of gin. "Food rationing" was a phrase more than a practice. Although the Battle of Britain was at its height, and evidence of war was all around— there were sandbagged antiaircraft placements on the perimeter of the field, and smoke trails high in the sky were almost daily reminders of fierce aerial combat—the war seemed remote.

Then one weekend the peacefulness came to an abrupt end. German bombers struck Ford, inflicting severe damage and several casualties, making it impossible to continue flying training or even ground school.

The trainees were transferred to Arbroath, on the east coast of Scotland, where their training continued until mid-September. They were given their observer's wings and graduated as sub-lieutenants. After a weekend's leave, they reported to the Royal Naval College at Greenwich, London, for officers' training. Then, in October—a year after he had been enrolled in the FAA—John Hoare and fellow officer Pat Goodger were posted to 828 Torpedo-Spotter-Reconnaissance Squadron, which was being

formed at St. Merryn in Cornwall, and was eventually destined for
H.M.S. *Victorious*.

The 828 Squadron was equipped with Albacore biplanes, the
latest in torpedo bombers complete with covered cockpit. Hoare
was assigned as observer to Lieutenant "Skid" Bellairs, an experienced pilot who had held a private licence in peacetime but whose
lack of appreciation of aerial navigation appalled his observer. He
refused to allow him to set the course, relying instead on his own
instincts, which consisted of following railway lines. To his horror,
Hoare soon learned that his pilot was also blind as a bat. On one of
their first air-to-sea firing exercises, they ended up in the middle of
the Plymouth balloon barrage, the ack-ack gunners below scaring
them off. But as a flyer, Skid had few peers.

In Hoare's own words, Bellairs could "land on the head of a railway engine. His deck landings, not the easiest of arts, were impec-
cable." The pair learned to team up happily and were later joined
by a third crewman, a telegraphist air gunner.

However, the amount of flying was limited by the highly restricted
area in Cornwall, particularly at St. Merryn, which was adjacent to a
fighter field at St. Eval. In November, the squadron moved north to
Campbelltown in the Mull of Kintyre, on the west coast of Scotland.

There the practice flights continued. The *Victorious*, berthed at
Rosyth, on the west coast east of Edinburgh, was still undergoing
modifications and not ready to accept the squadron. Then in March
1941, 828 Squadron was posted to Hatston in the Orkneys to the
north. There at last, though it was not yet aboard a carrier, the
squadron became truly operational, flying antisubmarine patrols.

Early in May, the *Victorious* was finally deemed ready for sea
duty, but 828 was not transferred to her as expected. Instead, John
Hoare and Pat Goodger were posted to 800Z Squadron aboard the
carrier, effective on the 13th of the month. Hoare found himself
assigned to duty watch with a fellow Montrealer, Fred Flynn.

For five days the crews familiarized themselves with the Fairey
Fulmar bombers, then on May 18 the *Victorious* set sail from Rosyth

to join the Home Fleet at Scapa flow. An unforgettable sight greeted them, Hoare remembered. Astern lay the new-class battleship the *King George V (KGV)*. On the beam was the *Hood*, "perhaps the most beautiful ship of war I ever saw"—and the largest warship in both the British and German navies. In addition there was the *Prince of Wales*, sister ship of the *KGV*, and several cruisers.

On May 21, the Fulmars were out on gunnery exercises. On their return there was a flap on, though the aircrews were unenlightened as to what it was all about. It was no false alarm; through aerial reconnaissance and intelligence the Admiralty had learned that the *Bismarck* and *Prinz Eugen* were steaming toward the Denmark Strait, south of which they would intercept a Canadian troop convoy. That night, on first watch, Hoare and Flynn noticed the *Hood* and the *Prince of Wales* slipping out of the harbour.

The next morning, the 22nd, the *Victorious*, in company with the *KGV* and four cruisers with a seven-destroyer escort, set sail from Scapa Flow on a course steering northwest. All day the weather—broken cloud and rain—steadily deteriorated, and by the following morning, at which time the flotilla was joined by the battleship *Repulse* from the Clyde, it was even worse.

Despite these atrocious conditions, at 1700 hours the two cruisers patrolling the Denmark Strait spotted the two German battleships approaching from the north, skirting the edge of the ice east of Greenland. First *Suffolk* sighted the enemy, then the *Norfolk* reported "one battleship, one cruiser, bearing 330, distance six miles, course 240."

Aboard the *Victorious*, the aircrews were told that the *Hood* and *Prince of Wales* were hurrying to the scene, expecting to intercept the *Bismarck* and *Prinz Eugen* at daylight next morning. Frank Furlong, the pilot to whom Hoare had been assigned, told him they had been put on starter's orders. Furlong, a small but rugged Irish prewar pilot, held the rare distinction of having, as an amateur, won the Grand National on his father's horse, Reynoldstown. He and Hoare hit it off at once.

Toward midnight the Swordfish were "bombed up" and the crews given orders to stand by at first light around 0300 to 0400 hours. In the Denmark Strait, the British battleships sighted the German warships at sunrise, 0535 hours, the following morning. At a range of 14 miles, or 25,000 yards, all four vessels opened fire. The British attacked head on while the Germans joined battle broadside, giving them the distinct advantage of bringing more and greater firepower to bear.

Almost immediately the *Bismarck* scored a direct hit on the *Hood*, starting a fire that quickly spread throughout the ship. Four more salvos from the *Bismarck* finished her off and she vanished beneath the waves, taking all but three of her 1500 crew to the bottom.

Both German ships now concentrated their fire on the *Prince of Wales*, which put up a gallant, uneven fight, receiving four hits from 15-inch shells. One of the shells demolished the bridge and another put a hole in her hull below the water line. Her captain decided to break off the action under a smokescreen. However, she had managed to damage the *Bismarck*. One shell had penetrated its hull underwater and another had pierced the oil tank, reducing its fuel endurance. Admiral Gunther Lutjens decided to head south and make for a western French port, but at a reduced speed. The *Bismarck* left a telltale trail of oil in its wake.

When news of the *Hood's* demise reached the *Victorious*, it was greeted with dismay and a sense of impotent fury. The carrier was speeding to the scene as fast as she could—ahead of her flotilla— with the objective of making an air attack against the *Bismarck* as soon as she came within aerial range.

For the aircrews, as they awaited orders to take off, that afternoon of 24 May 1941 was a long one indeed. It was hardly a day for flying either, what with a rough running sea and ever-increasing winds. The men busied themselves as best they could. Furlong borrowed a parachute dinghy from one of the contingent of RAF pilots aboard, destined to fly Hurricanes from the Gold Coast to Egypt—

if that project was ever to be reinstated. Unlike the RNFAA model, it was bright yellow for easy spotting instead of the dull, drab green navy issue. Hoare filled his flask with brandy and stuffed two paperbacks into the pockets of his flying jacket: Evelyn Waugh's *Decline and Fall* and *Vile Bodies*—just in case!

Toward the end of the day, orders came that, despite the weather, the Swordfish were to take off at 2200 hours and the Fulmars, being the faster aircraft, an hour later to fan out and search. Furlong and Hoare downed a couple of gins, ate a hearty dinner, then proceeded to the hangar to make a final check of their equipment. The Swordfish were wheeled to the lift and brought up to the flight deck. The carrier faced straight into the wind, which at this point was of gale proportions, so that the bow fell and rose with the waves. The signals officer flagged each aircraft off at the beginning of the rise. Even so, burdened with 1500-pound torpedoes, they dipped ominously below the bow before reappearing, then climbing away under the grey overcast and in the face of snow flurries.

The Fulmars' turn came next. Furlong and Hoare, clothed in sheepskin-lined Irvine jackets—but forgoing the accompanying cumbersome pants—Mae West life preservers, leather flying helmets, and leather gloves, silk-lined for warmth, climbed into their cockpits and tested the intercom. Hoare made a last-minute check of his navigating equipment, chart board, compass, protractor, and pencil and erasers. The signals officer wished them luck, then promised them a sandwich and a beer in the ward room when they returned. And off they went—into the dreary, sombre, forbidding skies.

The ceiling was about 200 feet with visibility, between snowstorms, close to two miles. Furlong kept the Fulmar at an altitude of between 100 feet and the bottom of the cloud layer on the outward leg of their search, which lasted some two hours. At the stage when they were about to turn about and return to the carrier—the Fulmar had an endurance of four-and-a-half hours—through a snowstorm they thought they saw a ship below—the

Bismarck! But when the snow cleared, there was nothing to be seen. A mirage! In any case, they decided not to radio their "sighting" for fear of leading the fleet on a wild goose chase. They made a small square search, but finding nothing and with the light fading, they set course for home.

Two hours later, when they failed to find the carrier, they knew they were in trouble. They learned afterwards that the fleet had changed course and that the *Victorious'* homing beacon had failed. In fact, their aircraft had been heard below and a searchlight had been aimed in their direction; but the darkness and the snow squalls had prevented them from seeing the signal.

After nearly five hours in the air, Furlong said, "We'd better get down while we still have an engine." They ran through their ditching drill and then Furlong began a long, slow descent into the wind. Hoare fired off several Very lights to allow the pilot to judge his height off the water.

Considering the circumstances and the rough, high waves, the ditching was remarkably smooth, quick, and efficient. The aircraft hit the surface once, bounced, thumped down again, and came to a stop. The Fulmar's large, round dinghy inflated immediately from the shock and floated alongside Furlong's cockpit, allowing him to calmly step into it without even getting wet, and he was able to empty his emergency rations box into it. Hoare had to swim a few strokes to get to the dinghy, but managed to get into it wet but none the worse for wear.

Furlong's prescience in borrowing the RAF dinghy proved a godsend. They inflated it, then stood it at a 45-degree angle, taking turns holding it against the waves to act as a sort of protective shield. Otherwise, the larger dinghy would have been swamped and likely sunk. After getting organized they now had to settle down to wait in hopes of being rescued. It was a bleak prospect and they cursed their luck. It was rough, intensely cold, and wet—they were sitting in water—and they were utterly miserable.

At dawn, Hoare's foresight in filling his flask proved to be a second salvation. They each took a swig of brandy that burned its way down their gullets. It had a calming and soothing effect—momentarily. Suddenly in unison they leaned over the side and spewed their guts out. As the sea began to abate and the snow stopped, they began to feel warm. Hoare realized that vomiting increases the heartbeat, creating body warmth. He hit on the idea that if they regularly took a mouthful, ran it around inside the mouth, then spat it back into the flask, the exercise would be enough to induce vomiting and that would keep them warm. At the same time the brandy supply would last.

As time went on they were plagued by two things. They were suffering from delayed shock and frostbite. Sitting in the icy water was the cause of the latter. They slapped each other's legs to keep warm and then urinated down the side of their legs. What kept them on an even keel and probably from becoming delirious was their ability to entertain each other and keep their spirits up and their minds off their predicament.

Furlong recounted his Grand National win so many times that Hoare said after they were rescued he could have ridden that race blindfolded. In retaliation Hoare amused his pilot by reading excerpts from his thoroughly soaked *Decline and Fall* and *Vile Bodies* paperbacks. Waugh's dark satire and sardonic sense of humour produced laughs between the pair when laughter was sorely needed.

By the late night of May 25, by which time they had been in the dinghy for some 20 hours, they broke out the emergency rations—chocolate squares and Horlick's malted milk tablets. Hardly a feast nor nutritious enough given the conditions under which they laboured—but this was typical of the offhand approach to such matters by those responsible, who compiled these rations without the slightest regard to or study of what was properly required to meet emergency situations.

By the next afternoon they were still cold and uncomfortable, with no sign of rescue in sight, but at least the sea had calmed down almost completely, with only a slight wind blowing. Furlong, who had become somewhat morose with frostbite, suggested that they use the yellow dinghy as a sail and make for Iceland. But Hoare estimated that they were being blown away from land by a northeaster and that their only hope lay in the search by the *Victorious*, which he was confident she would have mounted. He advised Furlong to be patient and wait it out with the consoling verse "Heaviness may endure for a night, but joy cometh in the morning," from the Book of Common Prayer. They did not have that long to wait.

On the afternoon of May 26, the weather began clearing rapidly, the sea was calm, and it was getting warm. The sun was high in the sky and visibility was unlimited. To the west Hoare could make out a wisp of smoke that steadily got larger. In his excitement, he awakened Furlong. By that time they could make out a mast and funnel of a merchantman coming over the horizon. There was no mistaking that it was headed in their direction.

In his thankful Irish exuberance, Furlong shouted, "Christ, now I suppose I'll have to be faithful to my wife for the rest of my days." The pair hoisted the yellow dinghy to identify themselves and make it easy for the ship's crew to see them. Initially, however, it had the reverse effect; the skipper of the Canadian Pacific freighter *Beaverhill* had mistaken the yellow dinghy for the camouflaged conning tower of a German U-boat and was reluctant to proceed any nearer. Luckily, his first officer had spotted the two airmen sitting in the navy dinghy and the freighter quickly pulled alongside and lowered a ladder.

With the help of the crew, Furlong and Hoare slowly and painfully hauled themselves aboard and tumbled onto the deck. Each was given a large shot of rum, knocking them both out. When they came to, members of the crew gave them a hot bath, provided them with a pair of pajamas each, and put them to bed. They slept the rest of the day and through the night to awaken next morning to the smell of a sumptuous breakfast of bacon and eggs, "the great meal of my life," Hoare remembered.

When asked if they would like a second helping they were astounded, certain that they'd had more than their fair ration. The steward assured them that the freighter was carrying a cargo of two million eggs, 500 tons of the best Canadian bacon, and a huge load of TNT. "Think what an omelet we'll make if we go up," he laughed sardonically.

Following the meal, they were given an electric vibro-massage by the ship's doctor in the sick bay, then sent back to bed where they slept until evening. On awakening they were invited to join the skipper and First Officer in the captain's cabin where they were offered glasses of rum and their speedy recovery, toasted by the captain.

The captain also gave them the welcome news that the *Bismarck* had been sunk at 11 o'clock that morning. Some time later, when they reached shore, they learned the details. Around midnight of May 24 the Swordfish from the *Victorious,* guided by radio from the cruiser *Suffolk,* which still had contact with the *Bismarck,* after two hours finally found the German battleship and attacked in the face of fierce fire. One torpedo found the target, striking it just under the bridge. Despite the darkness, blinding rain, high winds, and failure of the carrier's beacon, all aircraft returned to the *Victorious* safely. The Fulmar squadron was not so lucky. In addition to Furlong and Hoare's apparent demise, the latter's buddy Pat Goodger and his pilot were never seen again.

At 0300 hours on the morning of the 25th, the *Suffolk* lost contact with the *Bismarck.* The rest of the day was spent in a fruitless search for the enemy warship by the rest of the fleet. However, at 1030 hours the next day, Catalina aircraft from RAF Coastal Command flying out of Lough Erne in Ireland spotted it en route to Brest, but still 700 miles from its intended destination. Fire from the battleship damaged one of the flying boats and again contact was lost.

But within the hour two Swordfish from the carrier *Ark Royal,* part of Admiral Sir James Somerville's Force H that had sailed north from Gibraltar, spotted the *Bismarck* once more. At 2100 hours that evening a force of 15 of the torpedo bombers attacked the battleship, registering hits that damaged the propeller, wrecked the steering wheel, and jammed the rudder. That night they attacked again, inflicting further damage. Shortly after midnight on May 27, with his ship still 400 miles from Brest, the commander, Admiral Lutjens, reported: "Ship unmanoeuvrable. We shall fight to the last shell. Long live the Fuehrer!"

At 0847 hours, the battleships *Rodney* and *King George V* began relentlessly pounding the crippled *Bismarck* with armour-piercing shells, a barrage that lasted one-and-a-half hours, leaving the warship a blazing wreck. The British battleships then withdrew before U-boats and long-range Luftwaffe bombers, which were reported on their way, arrived, and left the cruiser *Dorsetshire* to deliver the *coup de grâce*.

By 1040 hours it was all over. The mighty *Bismarck*, which had absorbed as many as 12 torpedo hits and countless shell strikes and was still afloat—a tribute to its designers—finally turned turtle and sank, taking 2000 of the crew including its commander, Admiral Lutjens, to the bottom. One hundred ten survivors were rescued by the British and five others by a U-boat. The *Bismarck*'s consort, the *Prinz Eugen*, which had been forced to disengage on May 24 in the Denmark Strait, safely reached Brest a week later.

So ended what Winston Churchill described as "a naval episode of the highest consequences." It marked the climax and final defeat of German plans and efforts to win the Battle of the Atlantic with surface ships.

The freighter *Beaverhill*, which rescued Furlong and Hoare, was part of a convoy en route from Saint John, New Brunswick, to Liverpool. When news of the breakout by the German raiders was received, *Beaverhill*, being a fast ship, was detached from the convoy to make it to Liverpool on her own. When she picked up the two drifting airmen, she was 100 miles off her normal course. A rescue against all odds!

Both men recuperated satisfactorily from their ordeal and

returned to active service. Furlong was killed flying fighters. Hoare survived and eventually became an instructor. After the war, he returned to publishing and also served as Secretary of the International Wine and Food Society. He eventually turned to full-time writing, making his home in France.

Chapter 6

Tail-End Charlie

Charlie Hobbs and I shared a common experience. We both sailed to war in style, crossing the Atlantic in comfort and ease aboard the Akaroa, a New Zealand refrigeration ship. Charlie, who was from Toronto, embarked at Halifax, Nova Scotia, in the fall of 1941. I followed in another convoy on the same vessel almost a year later.

It was a luxurious way to go—the 16,000-ton cargo ship had a single passenger deck accommodating 200, a wood-panelled lounge and dining room, separate bar, individual and double staterooms complete with cabin steward, and gourmet meals served on linen tablecloths.

Rank notwithstanding, there was no distinction made between RCAF aircrews aboard: pilots, observers, wireless operators, and air gunners were all lumped together. Charlie had become one of the latter, both by accident and by choice.

Two weeks before he was scheduled to graduate as a twin-engine pilot from the Service Flying Training School at Brantford, Ontario, he pranged his Anson into another trainer in full view of all those in the control tower and was promptly washed out.

He was given a choice of remustering as an observer, wireless operator, or air gunner, which meant another six months of training. However, the replacement of twin-engine bombers by four-engine types in RAF Bomber Command—not to mention aircrew casualties— created a heavy demand for air gunners. The RCAF introduced a crash

training course on a volunteer basis and Hobbs wasted no time apply-
ing. In less than six weeks, he was on his way overseas.

Charlie Hobbs received his baptism of fire on the night of 30/31
May 1942, while he was still in training. This was the night of the
first 1000-bomber raid, conceived by Bomber Command's Air
Chief Marshal Sir Arthur Harris. Charlie was the rear gunner in a
Wellington bomber on this fateful night, described by Winston
Churchill as "the introduction of a new phase in the British air
offensive."

One of the main objectives was to deliver such destruction in a
single blow that it would allay all opposition to creating a large
bomber force. The target was Cologne in the Rhine valley south of
the Ruhr, the crossroads of trade since Roman times, and in World
War II one of the most heavily defended cities in all Germany
against air attacks.

Up until that time the largest bomber force sent out against a
single target had been 235 aircraft. To marshal a force nearly five
times that number for "Operation Millennium," Bomber
Command had to draw upon bombers from the Operational
Training Units as well as from all of its other groups.

Early in May, having graduated from two gunnery school courses
since arriving in Great Britain in November of the previous year,
Sergeant Charlie Hobbs and his classmates were posted to No. 16
Operational Training Unit (OTU) at Upper Heyford in Oxford-
shire. There they were divided into bomber crews. Hobbs was
assigned to a crew made up of Glen "Nic" McNichol, from Ricklea,
Saskatchewan; George Bishop (no kin), bomb-aimer from Owen
Sound, Ontario; Harold Jean de Beaupré ("Bo") of Waterloo,
Ontario; and Stan MacFarlane, an Englishman and the only
married man in the group.

They spent the next few weeks familiarizing themselves with the
bomber, which was new to all of them, and learning to work
together. But for the Millennium raid, because their experience was

still limited, McNichol was replaced as pilot by Squadron Leader Couch, who had several hundreds of hours flying Wimpeys (as the Wellingtons were known), but who like the others had no operational experience. McNichol would act as second "Dickie" (pilot).

The raid had been planned to last 90 minutes over the target, the bombers making up the stream flying out of 52 different airfields. The bulk of the force consisted of twin-engine Hampdens, Wellingtons, and Whitleys, bombers past their prime, numbering 708 in all, and 388 of the new Manchesters and four-engine Halifaxes, Lancasters, and Sterlings, a total of 1046 aircraft. Of these, 367 came from the training units.

Around 2200 hours that evening the crews of 11 Wellingtons at Upper Heyford climbed aboard their aircraft and went through the pre-startup drill before starting the engines and taking off. When Couch reached a cruising altitude of between 10,000 and 11,000 feet over the North Sea, Charlie Hobbs tested his Browning machine guns. As the coast of Holland came into view, the crew could see tracer flashes in the clear, moonlit sky. Nearer to the target, their bomber was caught by a searchlight. Intense bursts of flak, which sounded to Hobbs "like someone eating apples in church," quickly followed. The Germans then swung the main searchlight onto the bomber, then more lights concentrated their beams on the Wellington, blinding the crew. Couch coolly told them to hang on and began evasive action by diving at the main searchlight. By doing this, however, he temporarily lost control of the plane. The Wellington spun. Overcorrecting, Couch sent it spinning in another direction. At 4000 feet, having shaken off the searchlights, he managed to pull out of the dive, quite a feat with a full bomb load, and gradually began regaining altitude.

In the process, Hobbs suffered severe whiplash in the tail turret and completely lost his vision. He was vaguely aware of the bombs being dropped. By the time they returned to Upper Heyford, he had recovered his vision.

The raid had been a huge success. Eight hundred ninety-eight crews claimed to have reached and attacked the target, dropping 455 tons of bombs, nearly two-thirds of which were incendiaries. More than 600 acres in the built-up area of the city were destroyed, 250 factories obliterated, 486 people killed, 5027 injured, 59,100 rendered homeless. Eighteen thousand four hundred thirty-two houses, apartments, workhouses, and public buildings were destroyed. By what must be construed as an act of divinity, the Cologne Cathedral, one of the most important Gothic structures in the world, escaped unscathed not only by this raid but also by the host of others that succeeded it during World War II.

The cost to Bomber Command was light considering the magnitude of the operation and the inexperience of a large number of the crews—40 aircraft lost, one of them from Upper Heyford, with 112 suffering damage, 12 of which had to be written off.

On June 1, 48 hours after the raid on Cologne, the second of the 1000-bomber raids took place. This time the target was Essen, a Ruhr city to the north which was even more heavily defended than the previous target. The Upper Heyford Wellingtons were again in evidence. But this time the target was shrouded in mist and results were spotty. Most of the bombs fell on neighbouring towns, and Essen itself got off lightly. On the return flight, Hobbs had his first encounter with an enemy fighter. He managed to get off 50 rounds but without solid result, although he did scare away the Messerschmitt 110.

Before embarking on a week's rotation leave, Hobbs and his crew were asked if they would like to volunteer as part of a Pathfinder Force, an elite group of crews being trained for target marking. They eagerly agreed. First they would be transferred to 83 Squadron RAF at Scampton in Lincolnshire for conversion to the four-engine Lancaster bombers. Meanwhile, following their furlough, they had another operational training flight to make.

On the night of 25/26 June 1942, their final raid in the Wimpy took them to the heavily industrialized—and defended—port of Bremen in the north, 200 miles farther than either Cologne or

Essen—a seven-hour round trip. As in the case of Essen the target was obscured—this time by cloud. The four-engine bombers in the top layer of the stream had to descend below the cloud layer to drop their loads, or their bombs would have fallen among, or even on, their twin-engine counterparts at 10,000 feet below them.

As the aircraft left the target, German fighters plunged through the cloud cover to pounce on them. Though Hobbs' Wellington escaped attack, there was plenty of evidence around them of the carnage done by the night fighters. One Lancaster nearby exploded and only one parachute appeared. Below, they could see the wreckage on the ground of other aircraft, most of which were burning grotesquely.

Forty-nine aircraft went missing that night, 5 percent of the total bomber force, the highest percentage casualty of all three of the first 1000-bomber raids. Results were rewarding, however. Some 27 percent of the business and residential area was destroyed and heavy damage was inflicted on the Focke-Wulf fighter aircraft plant, the principal objective.

When the Wellingtons landed at Upper Heyford around 0300 hours, four of the 11 were posted as missing. However, later one of them was reported as having landed safely at a nearby aerodrome. That marked the end of the 1000-bomber raids until the next full-moon period.

Before Hobbs and his crew reported to their new posting at Scampton after a week's leave, they continued to make practice flights, one of which was even scarier than any of the three air raids. Unwittingly, "Bo," the navigator, led them smack-bang into a balloon barrage. Fortunately, the leading edges of the wings were equipped with cable cutters. Hobbs was well satisfied with his end of the training course. He left Upper Heyford with an above-average air-firing rating.

On July 21, the new arrivals at Scampton flew a Lancaster for the first time as a crew. The only difference for Hobbs as rear gunner was that four machine guns were mounted on the turret, as opposed to two in the Wellington. Hobbs made three operational sorties as an upper gunner with other crews, one to Osnabrück, another to Nuremberg, and one more dropping mines off the coast of Denmark, while the rest of the crew continued their familiarization flights.

Early in September they were transferred to 207 Squadron RAF at Bottesford in Nottinghamshire, where they made their first operational flight as a crew on 12 September 1942, with Bremen once again their target. Two more raids followed that month, one to Essen and another to Wisher. By this time Hobbs had nine ops to his credit and was promoted to flight sergeant. Nic McNichol earned a similar promotion in rank.

At a squadron briefing on October 2, the crews were told they would immediately begin intense low-level practice flying in preparation for a 100-Lancaster-bomber raid, flying at rooftop level in daylight without fighter protection, relying on the element of surprise. No further information was offered and the strictest security was observed. At this time, Hobbs' crew was joined by two new members, both Scotsmen: Bill Willis as mid-upper gunner and Alex Willis to man the mid-lower guns.

The squadron moved to another aerodrome at Langar, a dispersal field near Nottingham, where after the evening meal at 1900 hours on October 16, the aircrews learned that the raid would take place next morning. The target was the ballbearing factory at Le Creusot in Vichy. The formation would be boxed, 10 aircraft across by 10 deep. As a precaution, special armour had been fitted in front of 207's rear gunners since their bombers would form the rear row of the formation and would be preyed upon by German fighters.

It took two hours to form up over Cornwall—groups were arriving to rendezvous from all over the Midlands. This in itself was an accomplishment. Once in the box the Lancasters proceeded south over the English Channel west of France, down the Bay of Biscay turning east, still well under 200 feet to avoid radar detection, to cross the coast at Les Sables d'Olonne, a safe distance south of the well-defended port of St. Nazaire.

They had reached a point some 100 miles inland when the 217 Squadron Lancaster on Hobbs' right was forced to turn back as one of its engines had failed. The remainder of the formation continued on at low level over the rolling French countryside until 25 miles from the target, at which point they climbed to a safe bombing height of 2000 feet. Through the Underground, the French workers had been told to leave work five minutes early that afternoon, so that not a single Frenchman was killed.

By the time Hobbs' aircraft had its turn to bomb—one of the last—a heavy cloud of dust and smoke was rising from the target, obscuring it, though flames could be seen through the haze, and the Lancaster was buffeted by the bomb explosions below.

The raid over, the formation broke up, the aircraft returning to the deck to make their way home individually—warily scanning the sky for enemy fighters. The danger was minimized as dusk fell and darkness closed in, allowing the Lancasters to climb to height for the remainder of the journey home.

The sortie had been an enormous success, the surprise complete. The bombers had not encountered a single enemy fighter and the ground defences around the target had been taken unawares. Results were very gratifying. Photographs taken by Mosquito reconnaissance planes showed that the factory had been flattened. Only one Lancaster had been lost—the bomber that was forced to turn back with a dud engine; it had ditched in the Bay of Biscay where it was attacked by three Arado fighters, one of which the rear gunner shot down, with a second crippled by the mid-upper gunner who also warded off another that flew away in flames. The crew, one of whom became a casualty, were picked up by the British Air Sea Rescue Service. Hobbs summed it up quickly: "Debriefing was a champagne party that night."

The Le Creusot raid marked Hobbs' 11th operation, and once again he had leave coming to him. On his return to Langar, the squadron was assigned to targets in Italy, where bombing would be concentrated now that the British were victorious at El Alamein and the Allies had landed in Morocco and Algeria. Another consideration was the worsening winter weather across Germany. As Churchill put it: "The heat should be turned on Italy ... but Germany should not be entirely neglected."

There had been changes in the composition of the bomber crews at this stage. The second pilot was replaced with a flight engineer; in the case of Hobbs' crew, this role was filled by a Cockney, George Mott. George Bishop opted for a transfer to another squadron where his talents as a navigator could be put to more productive use. His place as bomb-aimer was eventually taken by an American named Bill Lewis.

On November 7, the squadron made its first trip over the Alps, as part of a force of 175 bombers to bomb the industrial centre of Genoa on the coast of the Ligurian Sea—a nine-and-a-half-hour sortie. Swiss antiaircraft gunners thoughtfully fired straight up in the air, providing the navigators with a positive fix. It was Switzerland's contribution to the Allied cause while still preserving its neutrality. Bombing from 8500 feet was accurate; not only was the raid successful but losses were light. However, two nights later while bombing Hamburg, Germany (fulfilling Churchill's intentions), cloud over the target forced the bombers to make a second run during which they were attacked by fighters. Losses that night amounted to a severe 7 percent.

Two nights later, Hobbs and his crew were forced to abort a raid on Genoa when the turret pressure failed. Next morning he received news that one of his former classmates and a close buddy, Jack Cameron (with another squadron), was reported a prisoner of war, hospitalized in Germany. Hobbs had been on Ops for just under six months at this point and he reflected on the fact that half the gunners in his training course had already gone missing.

On November 15, the target was again Genoa. On this occasion the squadron demonstrated its mettle as a bona fide Pathfinder (PF) unit, setting the pattern for marker operations to follow. Once over the target, the bombers dropped chandelier flares to light it up, then unloaded their bombs through the sky markers. A minute later the main force followed using the same markers. This was the earliest form of target marking. The results were excellent and, incredibly, all 78 bombers on the raid returned home.

Before going on Christmas leave, Hobbs' crew made two more sorties to Italy, this time the target being Turin, near the Franco-Italian border. Both were uneventful—clear visibility over the target, no enemy fighters, and little flak. They began the new year, 1943, with a planned raid to Essen, but due to a navigational difficulty, they were forced to turn back. Three Lancasters were lost.

In January they retransferred to 83 Squadron at Wyton, Huntingdonshire (Wyton Hunts), the Pathfinder Headquarters, at which time the unit was officially designated a PFF squadron. All aircrew were given a golden eagle emblem to wear on their breast pocket under their pilot's wings.

The role of the Pathfinder had by now been both defined and refined. Their job was to pinpoint the target by flying in ahead of the main bomber stream and putting down incendiary markers as bomb targets. In time, this pinpointing resulted in highly accurate bombing, and raids began inflicting greater and greater damage.

Then 83 Squadron made its first sortie employing the new technique over Düsseldorf and this proved quite successful. The process was repeated on February 2 and 3 at Cologne and Hamburg. These were followed by Pathfinder operations against the enemy seaports and submarine bases—Lorient, Willemshaven, and Bremen. By the end of February, Hobbs had completed—and survived—30 ops over a period of nine months, defying all the statistics for the longevity of a rear air gunner. This data varied. According to one source, the average life was only six trips. By any measurement, however, Hobbs' time was running out. Providentially—or otherwise—he still had a few more ops to go.

He spent his 34th and 35th operations over Berlin. On 3 April 1943, he and his crew were part of a 348-bomber armada for a raid on Essen in which 252 were Lancasters, the largest number of the breed to be sent out all at once up to that time. Twenty-one bombers failed to return. Next night the bombers were out in even heavier strength over Kiel. For Hobbs and his crew this was their third night of operations in a row.

Two days later, 5 April 1943, marked a milestone date for the crew. That night they flew a plane nicknamed "Q" for Queenie on a raid against the St. Nazaire submarine pens. Lancaster R5868, which had just returned from inspection, was to become a legend—the longest-surviving bomber of that make of the war—recording 137 operations from 1942 until the end of hostilities. (Today it is on display at the RAF Hendon Museum north of London, England.)

By mid-April, Hobbs had an operational total of 43 raids to his credit, two short of the 45 he had contracted to fly with 83 Squadron, lumping together his first and second tours. On the night of 16 April 1943, he was destined to fall one short of securing that covenant.

The target was an important one—the Skoda Gun Works at Pilsen in Czechoslovakia. The trip en route to the target under a moonlit sky was uneventful. The bomb run went like clockwork. As soon as Bill Lewis signalled "bombs away," Nic McNichol dove the Lancaster to rooftop level to avoid the heavy flak and the searchlights. The strategy failed; almost immediately one of the starboard engines was knocked out. Then several searchlights lit up the bomber, giving the enemy ack-ack gunners clear aim. Hobbs fired his four Browning machine guns to try and douse the lights, while McNichol climbed the aircraft to regain altitude for the flight home. Ten minutes later, the other starboard engine began to run rough and then caught fire. George Mott, the flight engineer, feathered the propeller and flooded the engine, successfully putting out the fire. Now McNichol and Mott wrestled with the two port engines still functioning to maintain level flight, but the process of gaining altitude was slow.

They made steady progress across Germany and were well into France when a third engine conked out—the one that supplied the pressure to Hobbs' gun turret. The intercom went haywire also. The navigator, "Bo," came back to the rear turret to tell Hobbs that McNichol had ordered the crew to bail out and that he was to go forward. As he made his way he saw that the Lancaster had been badly damaged and that Alex Willis, the mid-upper gunner, had been so badly wounded he was unable to bail out.

Hobbs was halfway forward when a night fighter raked the aircraft with cannon shells. No one was hurt but it set parts of the bomber on fire. Mott, Beaupré, Bill Lewis, and Stan MacFarlane, the wireless operator, had already bailed out. McNichol was still in the driver's seat holding the plane steady, but it was rapidly losing height. Hobbs volunteered to go back and see if he could put out the fires, but found they were out of control. McNichol asked him to unbuckle his parachute. They were now too low to bail out.

Hobbs was standing behind the pilot's seat, bracing himself for the impact of hitting the deck, when the night fighter struck again, the cannon shells shooting the control out of McNichol's hands. The nose of the Lancaster rose up, then the aircraft plunged down and struck the ground.

The crash killed the pilot and knocked Hobbs out cold. When he came to, he saw that Alex Willis had also survived and was struggling to work his feet out of the wreckage. Hobbs was badly cut and his hip pierced by pieces of shrapnel. Willis managed to extricate himself and the pair made their way to a nearby house, where they found the rest of their crew had also taken shelter, all except for Lewis, who as bomb-aimer, being in the most forward position of the aircraft, had bailed out first and was probably some miles away. The rest of them made a sorry lot, badly banged up, some with broken bones.

German soldiers soon arrived, herded the airmen into a truck and drove them to a nearby Luftwaffe night-fighter airfield. There the pilot who had shot them down had the temerity to ask Hobbs why he hadn't fired his guns. Holding his tongue, the dejected, downed, and irate rear gunner refused to answer.

That morning they were driven to Reims, northeast of Paris, where their wounds were attended to at the American Memorial Hospital. Next day they were driven to Paris where they boarded a train for a *Dulag Luft*, an interrogation centre at Frankfurt-am-Main under the jurisdiction of the Luftwaffe. Each prisoner was shoved into an 8-by-12-foot cell.

For the first two days, the POWs were left alone, a move designed to prey on their nerves. On the third day, a German identifying himself as a Red Cross representative visited Hobbs and handed him a form to fill out so that his family could be notified that he was alive. All aircrew had been instructed that if taken prisoner they were to provide nothing more than name, rank, and serial number. The form asked for information about Hobbs' squadron, aircraft flown, and other details. Hobbs handed it back and identified himself simply as Charles Hobbs, Flight Sergeant, R85583. The German flew into a rage and told him that if he refused to cooperate his family would never learn of his fate. Hobbs calmly replied that he was sorry he could give him no further information. But inwardly he was thoroughly unnerved.

Next morning Hobbs had another visitor, a civilian who offered him a cigarette—a Chesterfield! Then he got down to business badgering his prisoner with questions for an hour or so, but which Hobbs steadfastly refused to answer. The interrogator departed leaving Hobbs with two more Chesterfields and the threat that the Gestapo would now take over.

Two days later an angry Nazi Luftwaffe officer came to see him, ranting at Hobbs, who did his best to keep his nerves under control. He kept a safe distance between himself and his interrogator, who finally left in a huff promising that things would now get tougher. The implication was clear: torture or execution—or both. A week went by, leaving Hobbs in terror as to when the axe would fall. The next visit would come from the Gestapo.

To Hobbs the burly individual who came to interrogate him could have stepped right out of a Hollywood war movie of the day—knee-length black leather coat, dark fedora with the brim pulled down on all sides, a holstered oversize revolver strapped to his waist. Now the grilling, bullying, and threats began. Who was the pilot? What kind of aircraft? Where was he stationed? Hobbs kept to the standard reply—name, rank, and serial number. Suddenly a shot rang out from down the hall. That, the Gestapo officer advised him, was the result of one of his comrades refusing to cooperate. He might well share a similar fate. Stoically, but with his nerves at the breaking point, Hobbs stood his ground: name, rank, and serial number. The man rose to his feet, snarled at Hobbs, and stomped out of the cell.

After Hobbs had 16 days in solitary, during which he was hungry the entire time, a guard asked him if he would like to shave, but the blunt blade he was given made that luxury impossible—more deliberate discomfort—and he gave up. Later in the morning, the civilian who had visited him earlier returned and told him that because they now had all the information they needed to know about him, he would be released into the prisoner compound. He then recited some of that intelligence from a file. He named his pilot: "*Bren* McNichol" instead of "Glen." Aircraft in which he was shot down, a *Halifax*, not a Lancaster. Hobbs realized he was being led into a trap to correct his interrogator. Refusing to rise to the bait, he simply thanked his intimidator who promptly left. Mercifully, the carefully orchestrated and rehearsed mental torture regimen—a deliberately cruel charade designed to break down a prisoner's will to resist—from which he had emerged often frightened to death and half-starved, had come to an end.

That afternoon he entered the camp compound, a bleak, barren, and depressing enclosure surrounded by double rolls of barbed wire inside of which was a warning wire supported by posts. Six sentry boxes sat high above the fences, each with two machine guns. Hobbs was greeted by a sergeant who advised him to keep his mouth shut; there were listening devices in all the huts and German "plants" among the *Kriegies* (POWs). It might not be solitary confinement, but it was still an interrogation camp.

Along with others released from solitary, Hobbs received a Red Cross parcel—hardtack biscuit, a tin of jam, three cans of meat, a pound tin of Maple Leaf butter, a tin of Klim milk powder, a compressed tin of rolled oats for cooking, a tin of cheese, two chocolate bars, and two packs of cigarettes. All these were welcome additions to the meagre rations of a slice of bread, margarine, and a potato the Germans were still dishing out as a meal. Had it not been for those Red Cross parcels a great many prisoners would have starved to death.

Hobbs found two of his crew in the compound who had survived the interrogations: George Mott, the flight engineer, and Stan MacFarlane, the wireless operator. The fate of the others remained a mystery and cause for concern.

Some days later, the 40 prisoners in the compound were driven by truck to the Frankfurt railway station and herded into a cattle car where they spent the next five days en route to Stalag I at Barth in northwest Germany, close to the Kadat Channel. On arrival they were made to shower and dusted for lice before being allowed in the compound where, ironically, they were given back their dirty clothes.

Inside, Hobbs met his old buddy Jack Cameron, who asked what had kept him so long and proceeded to show him the ropes. He also acted as his sponsor, a security measure with new *Kriegie* arrivals who were suspected "plants" until someone vouched for their identity. Cameron introduced him to the Senior British Officer (SBO) in the camp, RAF Warrant Officer First Class Dixie Deans, who became famous for ensuring the well-being and proper treatment under the rules of war for the prisoners under his elective command.

Uppermost in the minds of prisoners of war (not only at Stalag I but in all camps) was escape. The camp was heavily enclosed with barbed-wire entanglements and inside trip wires. Raised sentry (*Posten*) boxes manned by machine guns were strategically spaced and at night searchlights flooded the compound. Occasionally some prisoners did manage to get over the wire, but their freedom was short-lived. After a few days they were captured and ended up in the "cooler"—the isolation cells—for two weeks. But the adventure was worth the candle—it boosted morale, not only for the "escapers" but for the entire camp. However, the best and only feasible means of escape was through underground tunnels from within the compound out under the fence and beyond it. Construction of two of them was under way at the time Hobbs arrived and he volunteered as digger in the main one.

It was well on the way to completion when one morning the "honey bucket express," the horse-drawn cart carrying a full load of human manure pails, made a detour that took it right over the roof of the tunnel. Under the weight of the wagon it collapsed, the cart sinking into the soft earth up to its axles. Dozens of *Kriegies* tried desperately to move it but the game was up. The "Goons"— German guards—soon caught on and traced the tunnel to its origin in the washroom of one of the huts. The tunnellers spent the next fortnight in the cooler. Undaunted, diggers quickly began work on another tunnel.

The second tunnel, which had been started earlier, was only 20 feet from being completed when it was announced that in three days the prisoners were being moved to a new camp, Stalag Luft 6 at Hyderkrug near Koenigsburg in northeast Germany.

It took four uncomfortable, unsanitary days confined to a cattle car to reach their destination, a much bigger camp that altogether accommodated more than 1000 noncommissioned officers. The Canadians were separated from the rest.

At the end of August 1944, Hobbs developed acute appendicitis. Because there were no medical facilities, the sole medical officer at the camp, a British army major, persuaded the German commandant to allow Hobbs to be taken to a hospital in Koenigsburg where he was handcuffed to his bed. Following the operation—which was successful—he was driven back to the prison camp where he spent some weeks in the recovery hut under the care of the British M/O.

A hidden radio, which the Germans were never able to find because the prisoners kept moving it and took pains to have look-outs stationed to warn of any searches being undertaken, kept the camp informed of the war's progress, and by this time— September 1944—it was good news indeed. The Allies had invaded Europe in June, and now all France, most of Belgium, and parts of Holland had been liberated. Morale among *Kriegies* soared.

Near the end of October the prisoners were moved to another camp at Thorn in Poland northwest of Warsaw in an effort to distance them from the advancing Allied armies. It was another uncomfortable rail journey by cattle car with the danger that they might be strafed by their own planes—the RAF and the USAF were shooting at anything and everything that moved.

The Stalag at Thorn held Canadian personnel captured during the Dieppe raid of August 1942. At night they were shackled in chains, a reprisal for orders captured by the Germans during the raid stating that any enemy taken prisoner during the raid were to be chained and/or tied up. What the Germans never did learn was that as soon as the doors were shut and locked up for the night, the soldiers unchained themselves with the help of a sardine can twister key.

The stay at Thorn did not last long. In November 1944, the thunder of Russian artillery could be heard coming from the east—the Red Army was advancing in great strides. The *Kriegies* were once again herded into boxcars and moved west to Fallingbostel, an air force POW camp near Hanover in the heart of the air war zone. The lack of sanitation, because the latrine pails could not be emptied due to German guards' refusing to open the doors even when the train was at a standstill, resulted in an outbreak of dysentery—*bleeding* dysentery.

Christmas 1944 came and went, but there were no presents or Christmas cards that year. The latter had to wait until 1 February 1945, Charlie Hobbs' 24th birthday, when a special embossed card arrived:

All Canada joins
in
Warmest Christmas Greetings
and good wishes to you
(signed) *W. L. Mackenzie King*
Prime Minister

By March the Allies were closing in on the west, the Russians in the east, having crossed the German border from both directions. The Canadian army was 200 miles away. Now the Germans issued orders that the camp at Fallingbostel, which by this time had swollen to over 1000 prisoners, was to be evacuated and the long march begun to the southwest. At night they slept wherever they could. On the first night, Hobbs remembered, he slept on the road. Mostly, the German officers in charge commandeered barns for sleeping quarters.

Food was scarce and the prisoners were desperately hungry. En route they foraged for poultry and eggs. On one occasion they butchered a young heifer. Adding to their discomfort, one day a flight of RAF Typhoon fighter-bombers mistook the prisoners for German soldiers and strafed the column with their cannons. Hobbs and his buddy, Cameron, took cover in a ditch. Others were not so lucky and many were killed.

The incident had an unnerving and unsettling effect on Hobbs. He decided that since the Germans were neither feeding them nor protecting them he would take off on his own—escape!

Apathy on the part of the German guards—and their dogs— made the venture surprisingly simple. When the column trudged through some woods, Hobbs took off, running for all he was worth for 10 minutes and then hiding out for two hours, lying on the ground under some leaves. In the distance he thought he could hear something that sounded like a tractor but realized it was more likely a tank. He had seen the marks of tank treads on the road he was following. He sat down to rest when two other prisoners that he knew appeared. But when he called out to them, they were so alarmed that they ran off.

By dusk the years of imprisonment, the lack of proper diet, and the experience of escaping all caught up with him. He was absolutely spent. He headed for an open field, lay down, and promptly fell asleep. At dawn he awoke—still thoroughly exhausted—wandered over to the shelter of some trees, lay down, and fell asleep again. This time he was awakened by a deer looking down at him. Even this mild creature scared him out of his wits.

Before moving on, he treated himself to all the water in his kit bottle and what food he had been able to scrounge. He knew he would soon have to find food and shelter to sustain himself. He kept walking and once again ran into two fellow air force prisoners on the lam, more *Kriegies* he knew by name. They were discussing which direction to take when, from 200 yards away, a German flame thrower opened up at them. Hobbs jumped into a stream and lay low while the others took off.

When the danger passed, Hobbs began walking down a road where, in the distance, there was a farmhouse set well back from the edge of the field. He was crossing the field toward it when some children spotted him and ran into the house. Five minutes later, the farmer appeared and asked if he was a prisoner. When Hobbs affirmed that he was, the farmer beckoned him to enter. Inside were the other two prisoners—the survivors of the flame-thrower incident.

The farmer told them that the British had already passed through and gave them directions to the army bivouac. Before dark, they left and had gone a mile down the road when Hobbs, who was well ahead of the other pair, was challenged by a sentry. When he identified himself and the other two as Canadian air force POWs, the sentry pointed toward the camp and told them to ask for the Officer of the Day.

When they reached the bivouac, their first sight—and it would be hard to picture a more welcome one, given the *Kriegies'* particular circumstances—was that of the cookhouse, where they were treated to bacon and eggs, something Hobbs had only been able to dream about for the past three years.

That night, they slept on straw in a barn, and early next morning were driven to the nearby town in a jeep with a German POW seated on the hood to watch for aircraft. It was a wise precaution. When a low-flying plane swooped toward them, the driver stopped the vehicle and everyone headed for the safety of the ditch. There they got their first look at the twin-nacelled aircraft with no propeller—the Messerschmitt 262, the first jet fighter in the history of aerial warfare.

From the town where the British 7th Armoured Division was positioned at mid-afternoon the trio piled into a truck full of other *Kriegies* to be taken to an evacuation centre. Ironically, it was their old alma mater, Fallingbostel, where they would await transport to Brussels, Belgium, 255 miles to the southwest, for a flight to England.

Hobbs was driven across Germany to Belgium during the third week of April 1945. From Brussels he was flown to England, where he spent a leave and waited to return by ship to Canada. During his stay he passed through London on a train on May 9, VE-Day, the date World War II in Europe officially ended. Before leaving England he was commissioned a flying officer, a promotion back-dated to the time the RCAF had been officially notified through the Red Cross of his capture by the Germans. He was told by inter-viewers at air force headquarters that he had three options: take an honourable discharge and receive full benefits, remain in the service, or volunteer for the Far East to fight in the war against Japan. He needed no persuasion to request a discharge. "Five years was enough!" he responded.

In civilian life Charlie Hobbs became a self-employed manufac-turer's agent.

Chapter 7

The Jet-Job Jackpot

I wasn't in when Smitty called. But I knew from the tone of his voice on my answering machine that he was upset. Upset? Incensed or irate would better describe it. The source of his displeasure, which had been boiling under the surface for some time, had come to a head when he read a newspaper report of the death of one of our fighter-pilot brethren. The article alleged that the individual concerned claimed to be the first Commonwealth pilot to shoot down a German jet fighter.

"Did you see that crap?" he shouted at me over the blower when I returned his call. "It's enough to make me want to throw up!"

While the news item was misleading, the cursory official 401 RCAF Squadron diary entry, though accurate, could *hardly be called enlightening:*

October 5 [1944]. Twelve a/c took off and while on patrol one ME-262 was spotted diving toward Nijmegen. The Squadron promptly dived after it and after a chase during which five members of the Squadron took a squirt at it, the e/a started to burn in the air and finally crashed. ... This ME-262 shot down today is the first one destroyed by anyone in the RCAF or RAF.

Because he was the key player in that drama, the right guy in the right place at the right time, the role of Squadron Leader Roderick Illingsworth

Alpine Smith, Distinguished Flying Cross and Bar, who flew 225 combat missions and destroyed 13-1/5 (the fraction denoting partial credit for a shared kill) enemy aircraft—and the subsequent controversy arising out of that role—warrant special attention, commendation, and consideration. To set the record straight, this is what actually happened.

Rod Smith's appointment as commanding officer of 401 Squadron in the fall of 1944 coincided with the end of Montgomery's ill-conceived airborne operation to seize the Rhine bridges and capture the Ruhr. To support the operation the squadron had been moved to Le Culot airfield in Belgium from Brussels. Though "Market Garden" had failed, the German Luftwaffe was determined to destroy the Rhine bridges, so there was still plenty of aerial activity about. The 401's new CO wasted no time demonstrating his ability and skill as a fighter-leader to take advantage of that situation. Not with a lot of ballyhoo, bullshit briefings—but up there, airborne in the middle of it, where it counted. He didn't take long to prove his point.

Two days after taking over as "boss" on September 29, having completed a routine patrol over Nijmegen bridge, Smith was leading the squadron back to base when they spotted a gaggle of more than 30 Messerschmitt 109s and Focke-Wulf 190 fighters hassling a Typhoon squadron. Spread out in battle formation with the height advantage, the 12 Spitfires waded in. Tex Davenport, flying wingman to the leader, was impressed. "Smith maneuvered us quickly and easily into perfect attacking position," he commented. "No trouble at all."

In the ensuing melee, the Spitfires shot down nine of the enemy fighters and damaged five others, Smith accounting for two destroyed himself. "It was like swatting them with a tennis racquet," he recalled. "I'd never seen so many aircraft hit the ground in so short a time. It made me realize what a great squadron I'd inherited." By the same token, 401 Squadron had just acquired one of the best, most experienced tactical air fighter-leaders in the business.

Smith had gotten into the game early on. A native of Regina, Saskatchewan, he joined the RCAF in 1940 and, after graduating as a pilot, went overseas to England in March 1941 where he joined the newly formed 412 Squadron, flying Spitfires on fighter sweeps and close-escort medium-bomber missions over France from the Digby airfield in Lincolnshire.

"These sweeps and circuses were highly unprofitable," Smith said. "The Spitfire V models we flew at the time were badly outclassed by the German ME-109s and later the FW-190s. Also, the bombing was ineffective, not just due to the meagre bomb loads the Blenheims and Bostons carried, but because of their pitifully small formations of six or twelve. They were simply there as bait."

It was perhaps fortunate and fateful that during his tenure with the Digby fighter wing he never encountered or even saw an enemy aircraft. But that was about to change—dramatically. In May 1942, Smith was posted to beleaguered Malta. The Mediterranean island between Sicily and Libya in North Africa represented a thorn in the side of the Axis. Though the incessant German and Italian bombing forced the Royal Navy's Mediterranean fleet to abandon it in favour of the safety of Gibraltar, from Malta airfields the Royal Air Force bombers and torpedo planes struck at ships carrying fuel and supplies to Erwin Rommel's Afrika Korps, threatening its success against the British Eighth Army. Hitler wanted Malta crushed. Churchill was prepared to defend it to the death. To the Spitfire pilots stationed there, it became a shooting gallery.

On arrival, Smith reported to 126 Squadron RAF in which he was shortly joined by his brother, Jerry. On July 18 the brothers teamed up to share in the destruction of a German Junkers 88 twin-engine bomber, a first kill for both of them. On the 23rd they made it a family affair once again by each bringing down a JU-88 in the same combat. Four days later Rod shot down another Junkers. Then tragedy struck. On August 10, Jerry was posted as missing, presumed killed in action.

Three days later Rod brought down an Italian Savoia Machetti tri-motor bomber. Then for the next month he was laid low with sinusitis, which took him out of the fighting. But in October, when the Germans launched a fresh blitzkrieg against the island, Smith was right back in the thick of it. On the 11th of the month he became the first to bring down an enemy aircraft during the new assault when he shot down a JU-88 in flames. Five days later he destroyed an ME-109, the first enemy fighter he had brought down and his fifth victory, establishing himself as an ace. On October 15 he found himself on the receiving end of a Messerschmitt's guns, forcing him to bail out of his badly-shot-up Spitfire.

Smith scored his sixth and final victory over Malta on October 28 when he shot down an ME-109. Then a severe case of jaundice took him out of action as he was sent to England to recover. After recovering from his illness, and following a stint as an Operational Training Unit instructor, he returned to Canada on leave. In December of 1943 he joined 401 Squadron at Biggin Hill, Kent, as part of the 83 Group Tactical Air Force—which is when I first met him. To his delight, we had just been re-equipped with the powerful Spitfire IX-Bs. The two-speed, two-stage after-cooled supercharger gave us a decided edge over the Luftwaffe fighters at any altitude.

In March 1944, Smith was appointed a flight commander with his old unit, 412 Squadron, which was part of our wing. One of the first victories he scored in his new role occurred on July 7, by which time we were stationed at Beny-sur-Mer in Normandy following the Allied invasion. It was an experience he would never forget. He had tangled with an FW-190 somewhere south of the bridgehead at around 1000 feet. The fight didn't last long, it was so one-sided. Smith got on the tail of the Focke-Wulf and gave it a short burst from his cannon and machine guns. His tracers set the cockpit on fire. As he pulled up alongside, the pilot jettisoned the hood in an effort to bail out. He was half-in, half-out of the cockpit when flames engulfed him. Finally he fell from the inner wing root, burned beyond recognition. "It shook me rigid," Smith admitted.

During August, September, and early October, in the wake of the

British-Canadian armies' advance across France and into Belgium and Holland, 126 RCAF Wing, of which 401 and 421 Squadrons were a part, made a series of successive moves east from Beny-sur-Mer to airfields at Brussels and Le Culot and finally on October 3 to a grass field near the village of Rips in the Netherlands. By this time the 83 Group control station—"Kenway"—had moved forward to the village of Nijmegen, near the bridge which had been captured during the Arnhem operation.

Two days later, after 48 hours of relative inactivity due to a low ceiling, on the afternoon of October 5, 401 Squadron was vectored to patrol the Nijmegen bridge, by this time a routine chore. Rod Smith, the new CO, remembered the altitude—"angels"—of 13,000 being unusual for the tactical air force and, after weeks of low cloud, the sky was almost completely clear. The patrol was quiet, with nothing to report, when Kenway called to announce to Smith that a "bogie"—enemy aircraft—was heading toward the squadron at the same altitude. Smith climbed the 12 Spitfires another 500 feet and levelled off three or four miles northeast of the town.

Almost immediately, he spotted the aircraft dead ahead about 500 feet below, travelling southwest towards Nijmegen, head on at the squadron "very fast." Smith alerted the others, then swung out some distance to the right to give himself enough room to swing sharply back to the left all the way around to the southeast "so that I would be able to pull in close behind the aircraft at a small enough angle to its path to be able to aim ahead of it, if it should be obliging enough to keep on coming." Several of the other pilots duplicated the maneuver.

Smith quickly recognized its futuristic lines, with the leading edge of the fin swept well back and the tail plane set high on the fin. It was a Messerschmitt 262. The German pilot continued to fly straight and level, seemingly oblivious to the presence of the Spitfires, probably because Smith had positioned the squadron between the jet aircraft and the sun.

"I felt a peculiar thrill," he said later. "At long last here was a jet plane that had made a mistake and was going to leave itself open to a burst of fire, if only to a short one because of the speed with which it would be able to draw away."

Smith began a final swing back to the left, and around to the southwest when the ME-262 climbed slightly up and to the left improving his angle of deflection, in fact presenting his would-be antagonist with a perfect shot. He was aiming along a path ahead of the jet and about to open fire when another Spitfire, in a tight left turn like his own, cut in front of him. However, the pilot had not pulled out far enough to the right to position himself for a shot with any hope of hitting the enemy plane. Smith was stymied; he still had the 262 partly in his sights, but if he opened fire he risked hitting the other Spitfire. He was tempted to chance it anyway, when fate intervened.

The enemy pilot must have finally realized he had flown into a hornet's nest because he suddenly half-rolled his aircraft to starboard in a fairly steep dive, then half-rolled the other way and began banking and swerving from side to side, all the while in a dive crossing over Nijmegen in a southwesterly direction with 12 Spitfires in hot pursuit. It was a strange evasive action for a pilot with an aircraft whose speed outpaced his pursuers in a normal straightforward dive by over 100 miles an hour.

It was not until 45 years later that Smith learned that the culprit who cut him off was Hedley Everard, the same pilot who had been reported in the media as the first one to spot the jet (when it had been Rod Smith) and also the first to hit the 262. This last was another fallacy; that particular honour went to Everard's wingman, John McKay. When the squadron had been diving after the enemy plane and he had seen Everard was in no position to hit it, he had opened fire himself.

Smith reported that two or three cannon shell strikes had appeared on the trailing edge of the ME-262's starboard wing root alongside the engine nacelle, from which issued a thin stream of

grey smoke. For a moment it had looked as if the engine might catch fire, but it hadn't. Several Spitfires had still been firing at the enemy plane, but without result. Smith and his wingman, Tex Davenport, had been forced to pull out of the dive at 7000 feet to avoid colliding with each other. Meanwhile, the ME-262 had pulled out of its dive at 3000 feet over the southern edge of Nijmegen, still heading southwest but no longer trailing smoke and by this time increasing its lead on the pursuing Spitfires.

That had seemed to end the action then and there. But once again the action of the German pilot had proved unpredictable. Suddenly the ME-262 had zoomed up "into the most sustained vertical climb I had ever seen," Smith would later comment, "leaving far behind the Spitfires which had followed it all the way down." To their great surprise, its climb brought it up to the point where Smith and Tex Davenport had levelled off. Smith described the action that followed:

As it soared up to us, still climbing almost vertically, the sweepback of its wings became very noticeable. Its speed, though still considerable, was beginning to fall off, and with full power on I was able to pull up in an almost vertical position to within about 350 yards behind it, the maximum range. I aimed at one of its engine nacelles and began to fire a burst which lasted about eight seconds, shifting my aim to the other nacelle partway through. I saw strikes around both nacelles and within two or three seconds a plume of fire began to stream from alongside one of them. The 262 was then slowing down more than I was and I was able to close the range to about 200 yards.

Eventually, because the 262 and my Spitfire were pointing almost vertically upwards and were quickly losing momentum, we both began to fall off slowly and in unison into stall turns to the right, thereby losing all control for the time being. Halfway through our stall turns, when our noses had come down level with the horizon but our wings were almost vertical, I felt as if I were in slow motion, line-abreast of the 262 to its right, and directly below it. As the 262 was only 100 yards above me at this point, I had a remarkable and unhurried look at it, side on. I particularly noticed its shark-like nose, the triangular cross-section of its fuselage, and its superb cockpit canopy, which gave its pilot an all-round view. To my surprise I couldn't see the pilot's head, although the canopy was fully closed. He must have had his head down for some reason.

At this point it dawned on Smith that when they came out of their stall turns, they would both be facing downward but their positions would be reversed; that is, the jet would now be on his tail instead of vice versa. And that's exactly what happened. When the Spitfire's nose went down, for a few critical seconds Smith had absolutely no control. Because the aircraft had no rear vision, he lost sight of the ME-262 completely. Tex Davenport, who had stuck with his leader all through the exercise and managed to get in a few squirts himself, reported that at that very moment the jet had fired at Smith. But when he recovered control, the ME-262, only a few yards to his right, was diving vertically, leaving a plume of flame behind it. Seconds later it crashed into a cornfield just southwest of Nijmegen.

Smith called Kenway Control to report: "We've just shot down a jet-job southwest of Nijmegen."

"I know, we've seen it," shot back the reply. "Good show!"

Good show! An understated accolade for a historic moment—the first German jet to fall to Commonwealth pilots.

When the squadron landed back at the airfield at Rips, the pilots were understandably jubilant. Though there is no question in my mind today that Rod Smith was responsible for the destruction of the ME-262, back then, because five pilots had fired at it and in the interest of squadron morale, it was decided to share it. (I am sure that decision was Smitty's.)

The 83 Group had confirmed that this was the first jet ever

destroyed in the air, but it was learned later that American pilots had beaten the Canadians to the punch, having already brought down two German jets themselves. But that in no way diminished the epic deeds on the part of Smith and his comrades.

The body of the pilot of the ME-262, his chute unopened, was found a few days later a short distance from where his aircraft had crashed. He was identified as Hauptmann Hans Chr. Buttman, a bomber pilot, which may account for the tactics that no fighter pilot would ever have employed in a scrap.

Post-Mortem

In 1988 Hedley Everard published his autobiography entitled *A Mouse in My Pocket*, about which Rod Smith wrote, "The less said the better." In the book, the author took credit for the 5 October 1944 action. John McKay was furious, as was Smith. When Everard's obituary appeared in the 6 March 1999 edition of the *National Post*, crediting him with drawing first blood in the incident, Smith wrote to the editor that the obituary "was demeaning of the parts played by some of his fellow squadron pilots."

This chapter is my personal contribution to giving credit where credit is due.

Chapter 8

Liberator Skipper

Most of us flying on operations over Europe in World War II were well aware that we could end up in enemy territory if shot down or if our aircraft packed up. With luck you might evade capture, as many did. Pilots were well briefed on what to expect and how to respond if taken prisoner. Initially you would be imprisoned in isolation and interrogated. You would be alternately cajoled and threatened. You were under strict orders (in accordance with the articles of war) to divulge nothing more than your name, rank, and serial number. After a short period— usually a matter of weeks—of failing to cooperate with the enemy, you would finally be determined a lost cause for any intelligence and sent to a prisoner-of-war camp. There, as all of us were told, the worst privations were hunger and, in winter, the cold. And sheer boredom.

During the winter of 1943–44, when I was stationed at Biggin Hill fighter field south of London, we were given a first-hand report on just how the Germans treated prisoners, as well as POW camp conditions. Don Morrison, one of a group of POWs repatriated by the Germans on an exchange basis, visited our station. Flying with our squadron (401 RCAF), he had lost a leg when he was shot down over France on 8 November 1942, and ended up in a Luftwaffe hospital before being sent to prison camp. He described life as a prisoner as "colorless and dreadfully monotonous." Otherwise, he had no complaints about the treatment at the hands of his captors. In fact, of the medical care he received while in hospital, he was most laudatory. Somehow, although I dreaded the thought of ever becoming a POW, God forbid, I found Don's remarks somewhat reassuring.

However, Don's experience and that of his fellow POWs in Europe contrasted sharply with the deplorable treatment Allied prisoners of war were suffering at the hands of the Japanese, who refused to respect the terms laid down by the Geneva Convention for the treatment of prisoners. Allied POWs faced beatings, torture, starvation, and even execution. Many POWs died from overwork, disease, malnutrition, and beatings, particularly in Siam where the Japanese were building a cross-country railway to Burma, since the defeat of their navy at the Battle of Midway had put an end to their sea supply routes. As a Liberator bomber pilot captain flying out of India over the jungles, swamps, mountains, and plains of Burma, Thailand (Siam), and Indo-China, Wally Frazer of Ottawa, Ontario, lived with that horrifying prospect on 35 individual bombing missions during 340 hours of operational flying time.

At the briefing before he and his crew made their first bombing sortie flying from Digri, a two-hour train ride from Calcutta, on 4 November 1944, the Intelligence Officer outlined ways and means of escape should they be forced to parachute or crash-land in enemy territory. The mission was a 1400-mile round-trip daylight raid on rail targets at Rangoon, the most heavily defended target in all of Burma, protected by a large fighter base at nearby Mingaladon.

It would be hard to differentiate whether the IO was warning the pilots or trying to scare the hell out of them. He seemed to take a macabre delight in painting a picture of a 500-mile trek through snake-infested jungles, leech-ridden swamps, and bypassing Japanese-occupied villages to get back to India. Hardly a likeable proposition.

Every airman was given an English-Burmese dictionary and a supply of Burmese currency to reward the Burmese natives helping him reach safety. But by the same token, the IO pointed out that the possibility of the Burmese turning them over to the Japanese to collect a further reward could not be ruled out.

The crews were also advised to give the Arakan mountains on the east side of the country a wide berth, because the natives there were thought *to be cannibals. That night when Frazer bedded down, he couldn't sleep. The IO's comments nagged at him: "Stay away from the headhunters." Frazer mused "Maybe I could make it to the coast, find an uninhabited island, do a Robinson Crusoe bit until the war's over. Damn that intelligence guy and his escape routes."*

That First Op

The morning dawns clear and bright. At sunrise, the plane nicknamed "P" for Peter—Wally Frazer and his copilot, Jock Govan, at the controls—loaded with two tons of bombs and 2334 gallons of high-octane fuel, eats up every inch of the 2500-yard-long runway, the four 2400-horsepower Pratt and Whitney engines groaning in protest as the full weight of the 31-ton Liberator struggles into the air.

Inch by inch Frazer climbs his bomber to 4000 feet under a blue sky over the Bay of Bengal. Over Saga Island, the rendezvous point, he begins circling, waiting for the other aircraft from 215 RAF Squadron to catch up. There are only five in all; mechanical failure has grounded a sixth. They are joined by 22 other Liberators from 355 and 356 Squadrons, and the three units split into sections of three in "V" formation 100 yards apart. In the lead is 355 Squadron. The other squadrons are on the flanks, 215 on the left. "P" for Peter and "D" for Dog make up Frazer's two-plane Vic, with "D" the leader.

Burma is three hours away, and the bombers begin a steady climb to bombing height, 12,000 feet. Frazer turns the controls over to Govan, relaxes, and reflects on what they had been told to expect over the target, Rangoon: heavy flak and a certainty of enemy fighters from the nearby Japanese Mingaladon fighter base—a great initiation for a "First Op" (operation).

At 10,000 feet the crew members of "P" for Peter hook up to the oxygen supply. Suddenly Bob Done, the navigator, barks over the intercom that they are passing over Cheduba Island; the coast is drawing near. A second message follows a moment later. It's the upper gunner, Eddie Hill, to report they have been joined by

American fighters—Thunderbolts and Lightnings. A comforting thought, but Frazer is reminded that the limited-range fighters could only escort them to within 100 miles of the target. From then on the bombers would be on their own.

The formation crosses the coastline, below them rugged green country without a sign of life. At 1155 hours, the bombers level off at 11,600 feet with the target only 45 minutes away. The fighters have already turned back.

Then comes the moment of truth. As they near the IP (Initial Point) where they begin the target run by turning south to starboard, P–Peter and D–Dog are ass-end Charlies in the overall formation—out in left field. Frazer decides they will be less vulnerable to enemy fighters if they move out of the echelon position into line-astern behind D–Dog, forming a double-plane box with all guns above them. As the copilot slips the bomber into the slot, Bob Done reports that by following the Rangoon River their estimated time of arrival to the target is now 12 minutes. Two minutes elapse before Frazer takes over the controls from Jock Govan. He pulls to within 15 yards of D–Dog, which is only 10 feet above them.

It's tough trying to stay in position, constantly adjusting the throttles as the planes ahead keep jockeying about and changing speed. It's not made any easier by the rough air and changing winds. Bob Done reports three minutes to the IP, seven to the target. Then Phil Jones, one of the gunners, reports a heavy concentration of flak ahead, the first this crew has ever seen. Ugly grey puffs of smoke are everywhere—above, alongside, underneath—they fly right through it as Frazer does his damnedest to maintain a steady course.

The bombardier Alan Smith butts in excitedly: "I see the target, Wally. Straight ahead. Railway yards ... just like the pictures. We're right on line!"

Frazer can see the bomb bays opening ahead on D–Dog, the bombs ready to drop. But P–Peter's doors are still closed. Frazer shouts over the intercom to Smith, "Open the damn doors!" The bomb-aimer meekly admits that he forgot. Now the doors are open. Only seconds to the drop point. But Frazer is having trouble holding the aircraft steady. Then, suddenly, the bomber sustains a sharp jolt like a kick from a mule. Then another one. The aircraft shudders under the double impact, but Frazer is too busy maintaining his speed at 170 miles an hour for Smith to release his load to give it much thought.

Smith presses the release button, and to the relief of the entire crew signals "Bombs away!" Now two tons lighter, the aircraft leaps forward. Frazer yanks back the throttles to slow the plane down and avoid smashing into "D" for Dog directly ahead. But—there is no "D" for Dog. In fact, there are no aircraft anywhere to be seen. They're all alone. Well—not quite alone.

From the upper gun turret Phil Howse blurts: "Bandit! Twelve o'clock ... attacking." From the pilot seats Frazer and Govan stare ahead at a sight neither will ever forget—a Japanese Oscar fighter coming straight at them head on with guns blazing. They can hear Howse's five machine guns rattling in return and the repugnant stink of cordite. Then, in a flash it's all over—the enemy fighter is gone.

Govan is pounding Frazer's arm and shouting at him. Frazer ignores him. He has more important things to cope with as Hill, the top gunner, yells into the intercom that there are more "bandits" diving down from out of the sun. All of "Peter's" guns open up again, the gunners shouting at each other. Frazer is in a quandary as to just what action to take. Dive, twist, and turn? Nope. The risk of collision with the other bombers—wherever the hell they are—is too great. Better to steer straight and level and let the gunners battle it out.

Meanwhile, his copilot is still pounding his arm—harder—and still shouting. Frazer dips the starboard wing to see what Govan is pointing at. There, below them, are the other bombers—the entire formation heading for home, but in the opposite direction!

P–Peter is at least a quarter of a mile from the nearest plane. The guns are still warding off the Japanese fighters as Frazer jams the throttles forward and dives the bomber straight at the ground to pick up speed while making a turn to starboard. The Liberator tops 300 miles an hour as it comes nearer and nearer to the formation and catches up to D–Dog. It feels good to be back in the safety of the fold. The enemy fighters have broken off.

As Rangoon fades in the distance the crew relaxes, enjoying a sense of relief that on their first operational sortie they have actually made it to target and are alive to talk about it. Smith reports that the bombing was fairly accurate with several strikes on buildings and the marshalling yards, which were heavily damaged.

Arthur Cooper, the flight engineer, and the gunners check for damage. P–Peter has taken quite a few hits. There are holes in the tail assembly and a large gash in the port aileron. But after putting it through a series of tests, Frazer is convinced the bomber will make it back. Eddie Hill reports that a large piece of jagged metal is sticking straight up from the cowling of number-two engine. It is difficult to determine whether it was from flak or is a piece of an enemy fighter. In either case, it was a close call. Only six feet from the cockpit, it bloody nearly knocked out the inner power plant on the starboard side.

The gunners are claiming they shot down one of the Japanese Oscars, though their versions conflict with one another. It is generally agreed, however, that the fighter rolled over on its back, vomiting black smoke, that it was probably on fire, and that a piece of the wing fell off as it dived.

Once over the water, the formation breaks up—everyone on their own. Frazer puts the controls on "George"—the automatic pilot. The crew busy themselves with routine tasks—checking the fuel gauges, adjusting the trimming tabs, munching into bully beef sandwiches, and taking a leak—into a bucket. Though there is a tube for the purpose, when it is used it sprays the rear gun turret. That pisses off Jim Slight, the rear gunner—literally—to the extent that he delivers an ultimatum that if they use it again he'll quit the crew.

With half an hour to go to reach base, the coast of Bengal looms ahead shrouded in thick ground mist. Govan goes back to use the pail and Cooper, the flight engineer, takes his place in the right-hand second dickie seat. As they near the airfield, Frazer tells him to buckle up; it'll be good experience to practise the landing procedure in case in the future something happens to both pilot and copilot.

On the approach, Frazer calls for the undercarriage down, and partial flaps. Cooper responds accordingly. Lining up the runway, Frazer reduces speed and asks for more flap, checks the fuel mixture and propeller pitch as Cooper steadily reports the descending height and airspeed. "P" for Peter touches down as smooth as can be—like landing on a featherbed mattress. But something is wrong. The aircraft begins to veer to the left and skids off the runway, bouncing in and out of ditches and smashing through brush and saplings at 90 miles an hour.

Frantically Frazer screams at Cooper: "Arthur, get off the goddamn [rudder] pedals!"

"I'm not touching the pedals" is the frenzied reply.

"You must be!"

"I'm not!"

The plane continues to veer to port. Frazer has his right foot down to the floor on the right brake pedal but it fails to correct the swerve. "Peter" is now completely out of control, bouncing over the rough ground. The aircraft avoids a grove of palm trees and begins to slow down. It hits a ditch, bounces and hits another, and comes to an abrupt stop. Frazer orders the bomb bays opened and tells everybody to jump out—quick.

Once on the ground, the crew scampers away from the ship as fast and as far as possible in case of a fire and explosion. But "P" for Peter sits, forlornly immobilized, canted to the left, the port wing tip touching the ground. One of the oleo legs is bent, and there are holes all over the aircraft the crew couldn't see from inside. It's a mess.

Sirens wail as the fire-truck drives up followed by the commanding officer in his jeep. The CO asks if anyone is hurt. Frazer shakes his head, then is asked what happened. The truth is Frazer doesn't really know, though he senses he is under the gun. Perhaps he shouldn't have let Cooper take the copilot's seat, but he keeps that potentially damning admission to himself. He stammers out an explanation that possibly the brake seized. It's all he can think of to say.

But an examination by the engineering officer reveals that the left tire was flat. That accounts for the swerving. Furthermore, there was a cannon hole in the front of the number-two wheel nacelle and another one behind. Overall the aircraft took quite a clobbering. Frazer, who just a moment ago was sure his ass was in a sling, finds himself being congratulated by the CO now, shaking his hand for a job well done in getting the aircraft down in one piece. The downside is that the EO declares "P" for Peter will never fly again. When she was towed away to the Maintenance Section where she would be put to good use to serve less damaged Liberators than herself with spare parts, her crew went with her to wish her a reverential farewell.

With the fall of Singapore, which lay at the southern tip of the Malay Peninsula, on 15 January 1942, the stage was set for the occupation of Malaysia and Burma. On March 8, the key port of Rangoon had been captured, and Mandalay surrendered on May 1. By the end of the month the British forces, which numbered some 35,000 men supported by only 37 outdated fighter aircraft, had been forced to retreat back over the mountains into India.

That was the extent of Japanese expansion in Southeast Asia for the time being. The British, meanwhile, began planning to drive the enemy out. To build up a viable fighting force wasn't easy. The Assam/Bengal area bordering Burma lacked facilities such as airfields, depots, roads, railways, and pipelines.

The Indian-Burma theatre of war was low on British priorities, particularly where RAF expansion, a prerequisite to the success of any attempted ground or amphibious operations, was concerned. Due to Rommel's victories in the Western Desert in June 1942, supplies and equipment earmarked for India were diverted to the Middle East.

As a result, the limited offensive to recover the Arakan coastal region, with a 100-mile march down the Malay Peninsula from December 1942 to May 1943, was an unmitigated failure.

The good news was that in November, the Southeast Asia Command (SEAC), which had been officially created at the Quebec Conference in August, ordered that all RAF operational units were to be combined with units of the United States 10th Air Force. By year's end this combined aerial strength, which numbered 48 British and 17 American squadrons, had as its primary strategic purpose the destruction of the Japanese air force which in Burma alone totalled 740 aircraft spread over four airfields.

Tactically it was called upon to support the SEAC objective of reoccupying northern Burma with the aim of reopening the road to China. In anticipation of this offensive, the Japanese planned a "preventative" attack of their own into Assam, which they opened in March 1944, to capture Kohima and Imphal (the latter reputedly the home of the sport of polo).

It was perhaps propitious that Flying Officer William Wallace Frazer, RCAF, aboard the P&O (Peninsular and Oriental) luxury liner on the Indian Ocean while en route from England to Bombay, heard over BBC Radio news that a battle was raging at Imphal where the Japanese were trying to cut the British supply lines. He also learned that Tokyo Rose was predicting that the glorious army of the Rising Sun was about to break out and march all the way to Delhi, the capital of India.

Speculation between two British army intelligence officers aboard the liner was that if Imphal fell, anything could happen. When the Japanese arrived in Burma, many of the Burmese threw in their lot with the invaders. Apparently the same thing could happen in India where the British weren't any better liked. One of the IOs told Frazer that in April 1942, negotiations between Sir Stafford Cripps—the former British ambassador to Moscow who had been appointed special emissary to India—and the Indian Congress broke down, which led to a half-baked rebellion against the British Raj, impeding the development of airfields and supply lines. Apparently the prevailing native mood hadn't changed much since then.

The insight made Frazer wonder what he was getting into. Being on this ship, bound for India. Told that he would be flying Liberators, the four-engine B24 American bomber. None of it seemed to make much sense.

Back home in Canada where he had joined up at the end of 1941, he took his elementary training on Tiger Moths, then service training on Harvards. After graduating as a fully fledged single-engine pilot, he found himself overseas at an Operational Training Unit at Harwell near Oxford, England, learning to fly twin-engine Wellington bombers. On completing the course, he awaited the usual posting to RAF Bomber Command. Meanwhile, three South African air force crews in the same course were selected for India, but refused to go on racial grounds, threatening the RAF that their government would back them up. Incredibly the RAF yielded to the threat, leaving an opening for three volunteers for India.

Frazer indicated—merely indicated—he just might be interested. On balance the odds of survival there might just be a whole bunch better than on the almost nightly air raids over Germany in which losses averaged as high as 10 percent. But he still did not commit himself. That didn't make any difference; next thing he knew he found himself on a list of "volunteers" to be sent abroad as did, unbeknownst to him, two of his OTU crewmates. Just like that. All three accepted the posting, not quite sure whether they were sorry or glad.

They reached Bombay on 21 March 1944. The gateway to India. No turning back now, even if they'd wanted to.

Frazer and his fellow officers spent the next eight weeks at the RAF Reception Depot at Worli, a suburb of Bombay, awaiting a posting to a conversion unit before joining a squadron. It took a while for them to become accustomed to the heat, insects—malaria-carrying Anopheles mosquitos requiring netting over the camp cots for protection, cockroaches, flies that went with every meal, and spiders—and lizards. They soon learned that while khaki shorts were comfortable, slacks were more practical unless you wanted to be bitten by insects behind the knees, causing sore red welts to rise. And then there was Delhi Belly or Bombay Bum, a local form of diarrhea that left you feeling weak and tired.

They took in the sights, the splendour and the filth, the incredible contrast between wealth and poverty, the ritzy hotels and the beggars, camel and elephant rides and bartering with the street vendors. To pass the time they played golf and swam at the exclusive Willington Sports Club, where as officers they were allowed temporary guest memberships. They settled into a routine—card games in the morning, a siesta after lunch, and a late afternoon swim at the Beach Candy Baths where there were no rank barriers and where Frazer could join up with his two OTU bomber crew, noncommissioned officers Sergeants Bernie "Mac" McIlwaine, a wireless operator, and Stan Jones, an air gunner.

But eight weeks was a long time with nothing to do but amuse themselves. When orders came on 8 May 1944 to move to Poona south of Bombay to make way for an incoming draft arriving by ship from England, although it was only a holding station until they could be accommodated at the Heavy Conversion Unit to train on Liberators based at Kalor near Bangalore on the south tip of India, the posting was welcome.

Frazer did not get to look at a Liberator until late May, but then it was love at first sight. He was absolutely captivated by the huge mottled-grey bomber with a giant wingspan which, he was told, was the largest of any aircraft in the world—a whopping 110 feet. And by the four powerful radial engines, capable of generating a total of 4800 horsepower. But what awed him most was the size of the twin tails—four feet wide and six feet high. From the ground they were higher than a house.

The fuselage looked stubby compared to the British Lancaster, for example, and, at 66 feet, seemed out of proportion to the wingspan and tails. But what it lacked in length it made up for in width and inside roominess, which he now saw for himself.

Climbing in through the bomb bay, Frazer made his way up to the pilots' cabin—two big seats side by side felt like easy chairs. This was pilot comfort—so unlike RAF aircraft. After touring the rest of the interior—the navigator's work station under the flight deck, the bomb sight in the nose, the ball turret lowered by hydraulics to be underslung outside the fuselage, on either side two other gun turrets and another in the rear—Frazer lowered himself to the ground through the escape hatch. "Yeah, I'm going to like this aircraft," was his assessment.

His introduction to the Liberator reinforced Frazer's determination to become a bomber captain—not a second pilot. He wanted to give orders, not take them. At OTU the Wellingtons did not need a copilot, so he automatically became the skipper. But at Harwell, he had made a bollix of picking a crew. He left it until too late so that the only people left were those no one else wanted. Only two measured up—Bernie McIlwaine and Stan Jones. He wasn't going to make that mistake again. Oh no?

Over the next few days his time was so taken up with ground classes, studying the B24 and related pilot procedures, and brushing up on navigation, radio, and armament—that in off-hours he just didn't seem able to concentrate on the task of rounding up a crew. Procrastination, one of his messmates chided him; if he didn't get going, it would be like the OTU balls-up all over again—he'd be left with a bunch of characters nobody else wanted. Others bragged to him about the crews they had already enlisted. He felt like a jerk. But that was the very catalyst he needed to make his move.

A day later, during a recess between classes with the students pouring out of the buildings for a tea break, Frazer made his move. His first step was to find a pilot and go on from there. He approached Sergeant Stan "Jock" Govan, with whom he had shared a desk and talked on several occasions, chatting with a pair of NCOs wearing air gunner's wings. Frazer waded right in, told them he was trying to form a crew and would they be interested. Govan readily agreed (to act as second dickie—no problem there), provided his two gunner mates, Jim Slight and Phil Howse, came with him. No problem there either. Along with McIlwaine and Jones, that made up a crew of six. Frazer still needed a navigator, a bomb-aimer, a flight engineer, another gunner, and a wireless operator.

That problem quickly resolved itself. Jock Govan enlisted Bob Done, a navigator looking for a crew. "Mac" McIlwaine recommended a former classmate, Joe Barlow, as the extra radio man and another friend, Eddie Hill, as top gunner. A deal. Govan brought aboard Arthur Cooper for the job of flight engineer. This left the crew short only a bomb-aimer. That slot had to wait to be filled until late September when four graduated bomb-aimer pilot officers arrived from England, and this time Frazer made sure he had the first pick—a fellow officer, Alan Smith. That not only brought the crew up to the full complement of 11 but, with the rest of the crew being NCOs, it provided Frazer with a roommate.

After finishing the ground school course on 16 June 1944, the crew was pronounced ready for the supreme test—their first flight working together in a Liberator. An instructor occupied the right-hand seat while Govan, the copilot, looked on. Frazer went through the cockpit drill he'd rehearsed so often. It drew a sharp rebuke from the instructor who ordered him to run through it again. He'd forgotten to lock the brakes before ordering the engine startup. Second time around he got it right. He flicked on the intercom switch and gave the order to start engines, hoping he didn't sound half as nervous as he felt.

As the instructor flipped on the fuel booster pump, Frazer

pushed the mixture control to "auto lean," checked the oil pressure which registered normal, then throttled back from full power. An angry voice from the right seat barked in his ear: "Aren't you going to tell me to turn off the booster pump?" Yes. He'd forgotten. "Pilot to second pilot. Turn off the fuel pump."

With all four engines synchronized and the hydraulic, fuel, and oil gauges reading normal, the instructor gave Frazer the okay to taxi out to the runway. He did a lousy job. He picked up too much speed and as the aircraft headed off the runway toward the sand he was unable to control the swerve. Desperately he throttled back and tried to slam the brakes down, but the instructor got to them first and saved the situation by making a sharp 90-degree turn that put the bomber back on the straight and narrow. His only admonition was to tell Frazer to take it easy until he got the hang of it.

Now they were ready for takeoff. Frazer went through a final cockpit check, called the control tower for permission to take off, received it, and proceeded to taxi onto the runway. Lining up the nose dead centre, he began his takeoff run with full throttle and extended flap for extra lift. Holding the Liberator steady with gentle use of the rudders, he gradually increased his speed until, at 120 miles an hour, the instructor calmly told him to pull back on the stick and take her up.

Gingerly Frazer pulled the control wheel toward him, but not hard or far enough. Nothing happened. The plane was still on the runway and fast running out of it. He eased back on the wheel some more. Still nothing. Then, suddenly, he felt the wheel slam hard against his chest. The instructor had taken over and up she went. A soothing voice crackled over the intercom: "All right, Frazer, you take it."

As the big bird began to climb, slowly, reassuringly, the instructor politely asked Frazer to pull up the undercarriage. Tit for tat. At 600 feet altitude Frazer eased back on the throttles and courteously requested his mentor to raise the flaps.

When he reached 1000 feet, Frazer was instructed to level off and make a full circuit to familiarize himself with the feel of the aircraft while airborne. The instructor warned him to watch for the hill beside the runway (scoffing that whoever chose this site for an airfield must have bought it from his brother). Frazer levelled out, carefully adjusted the engine settings, made a gentle turn to port, then another, and they were on the downwind leg, straight and level.

For the moment they could relax, and the instructor took the hiatus to tell Frazer that his takeoff was pretty good for a first effort but that he should have taken matters into his hands when he saw he wasn't going to lift off soon enough instead of waiting for the instructor to take over the controls. It was a far fairer appraisal than he had expected. After making a second circuit, Frazer was now told to try a landing. The moment of truth!

Frazer started the procedure as he turned the aircraft cross-wind—flaps down, wheels down and locked, brake pressure fine, fuel booster pumps on, fuel mixture and propeller pitch set, reduce speed. Now he turned in to line up on the runway. But he left it too late. As he straightened out he was 200 yards to the right. He maneuvered the ship to the left and finally straightened out with the runway now dead ahead. But he had much too much height—900 feet and he was almost on top of the beginning end of the concrete strip. Frantically he called for more flaps—40 degrees—then yanked back on the throttles and shoved the nose down.

At this point the instructor intervened—all business—calling off the descent—800 feet, 700 feet, 600—and ordered Frazer to further reduce throttle and gave him full flap. Frazer dived the aircraft to lose height, but he was still too high and coming in too fast. At 150 feet with a speed of 130 miles an hour he was right over the beginning of the runway. The instructor sounded worried. "Height 50 feet, speed 115. Start to level off and hit the deck. We're running out of runway!" Then: "Speed 110. Cut the engines!"

Fifty feet from the ground Frazer pulled back the throttles, but then he felt the instructor's hand over his own slamming them right back to the "off" position. With a loud thump, first one wheel, then the other, struck the concrete. At 100 miles an hour the Liberator raced down the runway, but as the speed dropped the nose wheel hit the runway and the instructor's experience took over. He shouted for brakes, but before Frazer could hit the brake pedals the instructor beat him to it. The aircraft was standing on its nose before it finally screeched to a stop with only 50 yards of runway to spare. At 100 miles an hour that could be measured in terms of time of only a single second.

The instructor looked drained, as if he would rather take his chances back on Ops than training these bloody novices. But he soon simmered down enough to order Frazer to taxi back to the dispersal, then relaxed sufficiently to issue orders that the aircraft was not to be flown again until the undercart, the brakes, and the nose wheel had been checked.

Frazer had made a ropey landing and fully expected, with some justification, that his instructor would tear a wide strip off him. But to his astonishment, instead of chewing him out he told him that for a first try his performance overall had been passable. But he should have gone around again when he misjudged his landing approach. And, as a word of advice, generally he should be more decisive.

Another month followed taken up with practice flights—circuits and bumps, cross-country, bad weather, over-the-ocean, and night flying, as well as fighter affiliation with Spitfires—before they were finally posted to an operational Liberator bomber squadron, No. 215, at Jessore, 80 miles northeast of Calcutta.

300 Hours to Go

By the end of July 1944, the situation on the northeast Indian front had changed dramatically. With the collapse of the Japanese offensive around Imphal and Kohima, in which they lost an estimated 65,000 men, Operation Capital, an overland thrust to recapture north-central Burma spearheaded by Lieutenant-General Sir William Slim's British Fourteenth Army, was well under way.

On August 15, Frazer and his crew picked up a spanking new $200,000 B24 Liberator, fresh from the Ford plant in Dearborn, Michigan, at Alahabad, halfway between Calcutta and Delhi, and flew it back to their new home at Jessore where they christened it with a big black "P" painted on both sides, denoting "P" for Peter.

Though they were eager to get on with the war—flying operational missions—that wasn't in the cards just yet. First off, 215 Squadron was moved to another field at Digri north of Sabloni which, as part of 185 Wing, it shared with 159 Squadron. Conditions were much improved over Jessore; it was more rural-like, less jungle. Frazer and his roommate, bombardier Alan Smith, were faced with having to hire a new bearer—a native manservant. But Abdul, who had a sheaf of letters of recommendation including one from the local police chief, seemed to meet their needs nicely. And at 10 rupees a month (four dollars) plus another 15 rupees for a uniform ("To serve sahibs in dine room ver' important for uniform, sahibs"), it seemed a fair enough deal even though there was a caveat. He refused to sweep the room ("I personal servant, not sweeper").

Most of their flying schedule was taken up with practice flights—formation flying, air-to-ground firing, and bombing over a practice range. But on October 7 they were called upon to fly an air sea rescue (A/S/R) mission after two Liberators from 159 Squadron were badly shot up while attacking a bridge at low level north of Bangkok in Siam. One was last seen trailing smoke and was not heard from again. The other made it halfway home and signalled that it could not maintain altitude and would have to ditch. Liberators were dispatched to search, but the crews were none too hopeful that they would find what they were looking for. The Liberator was known as a "poor swimmer"—it could sink in minutes. But there was always the chance that the crew might be able to escape and take to their *dinghy* (from the Hindu word meaning "small boat"). "P" for Peter was one crew sent out the following

night. But after 12 hours of square searching and a repeat performance the following day, the search was called off.

Nevertheless, the A/S/R exercise was good practice for the "P"
for Peter crew from a navigational standpoint, particularly over
water and at night. In addition, the 24 hours in the air stood them
in good stead from another aspect; they counted against the total
number of hours—on a 6-for-10 basis—that their operational tour
with Southeast Asia Command called on them to complete. In
Europe a bombing tour was calculated at 30 trips. But because in
India the length of the missions varied so much, a bombing tour
was measured in terms of hours instead of trips—for "P" for Peter,
286 to go. Then their maiden combat mission to Rangoon on
November 3 cut into that total.

Their second Op, on November 28, was a piece of cake. Target:
the railway cars and locomotives in the Mandalay marshalling
yards—the third attack in a row against the Burmese railway
system. This was vital to the success of the British army's drive
southward—Myikmyan, the Japanese stronghold 175 miles to the
north, had already fallen and Bhamo was under siege. Next stop
Mandalay. Route to the target: east past Chittagong on the India
coast and over the Chin Hills. No fighters over the target but plenty
of flak. "Peter's" replacement bomb-aimer puts her bombs right on
the marshalling yards and the Liberator gets away without a
scratch. A seven-hour round trip and the crew is back at Digri. No
trouble at all.

This raid and its afterglow were characteristic of the life of
bomber crews in India. On landing Frazer attends the debriefing,
the intelligence officer wearing a skeptical scowl as crews report
their "successes." He'll accept them only after analyzing the reconnaissance target photos. On his way to shower and shave, Frazer
stops at the bar for a gin and lime. Then, after donning his finest
khaki, slacks, and bush jacket, all spick and span, he takes his place
at the white-linen-covered dining table where Abdul serves him a

plate of curried chicken. The officers' mess code of dressing for dinner preserved an aura of civilization in a somewhat uncivilized—snakes and tigers about—atmosphere and surroundings.

On December 2, Frazer's crew was off early on another, their second, air sea rescue search mission. An American B29 Superfortress had ditched in the Bay. As it turned out, "Q" for Queenie ("P" for Peter was undergoing a maintenance overhaul), but for a stroke of good fortune, might have needed rescuing itself. Fortunately, it had been prepared for a long haul. Instead of bombs the bays had been fitted with four auxiliary fuel tanks, bringing total fuel capacity up to 3000 gallons.

At approximately 0700 hours they were off the deck, and three hours later, at 800 feet with two miles' visibility, they began their patrol, a square search. Starting at a centre point they flew a square pattern around it. At 1600 hours the sun began to set and darkness closed in. By 2030 hours, they completed their search. They had seen absolutely nothing of the Superfortress.

Frazer checked the fuel gauges—the auxiliary tanks had been drained dry and the engines were feeding off the main tanks in the wings. Arthur Cooper, the flight engineer, calculated they had enough fuel for another four hours. Frazer decided on another half an hour search—it would count for 18 minutes more against the 300-Op-hour total.

At 2100 hours he headed for home. Two-and-a-half hours later the lights below told Frazer they were over land—but where? The navigator, Bob Done, took a star fix—only 20 minutes off course. Not to worry—plenty of fuel to spare. Exactly half an hour later they could see the lights of Digri dead ahead. Frazer brought the aircraft in for a landing, a bit bumpy, but down safe and sound all the same after nearly 17-1/2 hours in the air.

When Frazer climbed from the plane he was greeted by the ground crew chief, whose first question was how the fuel had held out. No problem, Frazer assured him; at least 100 gallons left. But when a crewman checked the wing tanks with a dip stick it registered nearly dry—almost empty—five minutes to spare. At the most! A close call!

The matter did not quite end there. Although Frazer and Arthur Cooper, the flight engineer, were adamant that the fuel gauges showed 100 gallons on landing, the CO did not believe them. They couldn't have read them properly. It was the engineering officer who came up with the solution to the puzzle. After satisfying himself that the ground crew had topped the tanks before the plane took off, he asked Frazer how long the ball turret, the one slung under the belly, had been extended. Frazer guessed perhaps 10 hours; the lower air gunner preferred it that way. That, the EO explained, would create extra drag and would account for the increase in fuel consumption they would not have calculated on. Plus, he said, the fuel gauges weren't all that accurate anyway. He promised to issue a bulletin to that effect.

The next mission took Frazer's crew to Siam, ironically at the time renamed Thailand—"The Land of the Free." The target was the far end of the rail line that the Japanese built, using slave labour—British POWs captured at Singapore as well as Burmese, Siamese, and Malays—running from Bangkok on the Gulf of Siam to Moulmein on the Bay of Bengal southeast of Rangoon, to supply their troops in Burma.

At 0830 hours on December 10, the day before the British 15th Corps under General Sir Philip Christinson launched an offensive to clear the Arakan coast of Burma, nine 251 Squadron Liberators took off from Digri, joined by another 12 from 99 Squadron at Jessore, to bomb targets of opportunity at low level in the Kanchanaburi district 70 miles east of Bangkok. It was an assignment usually entrusted to single-engine fighters. For four-engine bombers it was a new experience; so was getting to the target zone—individually instead of in formation.

They followed a course south down the Bay of Bengal with the intention of skirting Burma proper and turning east to cross the coast over the narrow Burma-Siam peninsula at Tenasserim, then over the Bilauktaung Range of hills before dropping down over Siam and the target area.

But after flying for 600 miles over water and with no sight of the Andaman Islands as a checkpoint, nor any sign of the 21 other bombers taking part, Frazer realized they were lost. Bob Done, the navigator, dropped a smoke pot on the water to take a drift reading which indicated the wind had increased from 10 to 20 miles an hour, so "Peter" had been blown 50 miles off course. He gave Frazer a course correction, advising him that they were two hours from the Tenasserim coast.

Sometime later, Jim Slight, the nose gunner, reported land ahead—the Heinz Islands. Then several other Liberators came into view. They were back on track and back in business.

With the Bilauktaung Range behind them as they descended to 2000 feet, the sky became crowded. Frazer was acutely aware of the danger of collision. Two Liberators from 99 Squadron had banged into each other a week earlier under similar conditions. They now had to keep a sharp lookout for the other aircraft around them as well as locating the railway. One of the gunners had only just reported having spotted it when he also advised that Alan Smith had been taken ill. Frazer called his bomb-aimer on the intercom, but Smith assured him it was nothing more than a touch of flu and he continued to try and track a target.

As Smith began map-reading aloud—a hamlet, streams, a river—Bob Done suddenly broke in to announce excitedly that they'd reached the stretch of railway they'd been assigned to. Then gunner Phil Howse spotted a locomotive pulling 10 cars behind it and asked for permission to fire. Frazer gave the OK and all the gunners opened up—except Eddie Hill in the upper turret, who was told to keep a lookout for Japanese fighters and gun posts on the hills they were flying through. P–Peter's gunfire stopped the train in its tracks and pierced the locomotive's boiler, which started belching steam.

Frazer now faced the choice of circling around and making a bomb run on the same target or seeking out a fresh one. He opted for the latter and proceeded on. Then, just as they had feared, another Liberator at the same level was heading toward them on their left. It swished by with several feet to spare, but too close for comfort.

At almost the same instant, Smith reported sighting two locomotives at a siding hidden under some camouflage netting—a worthwhile target indeed—but too late. They'd passed over it. Frazer wheeled the bomber around to take another run. As Smith released a bomb, machine-gun fire erupted from a gun nest below. P–Peter's gunners quickly took it out. However, Smith reported they'd overshot the target. Frazer circled round once again for another go.

This time there was no machine-gun fire from the ground. On this run Smith dropped two bombs, and although they missed the target again they created havoc, debris scattering in all directions. Frazer turned the aircraft around again for a second run. Now the problem was sighting on the target; there was too much smoke and dust to take proper aim. Nevertheless Smith dropped three bombs and the gunners reported the missiles landed right in the middle of the miasma, causing plenty of damage. They still had three bombs left. What now?

Frazer decided on the secondary target, the Kanchanaburi railway station, right in the path of their homeward route. This was tricky. The area was well defended by flak guns and accuracy was paramount. A POW camp was situated alongside the storage sheds. Smith suggested a dummy run. Negative.

"Just one run, then we get the hell out of there," was the skipper's curt directive.

At 2000 feet the flak was fierce. Not thick like the Rangoon and Mandalay raids, but bloody accurate. However, the bomb run scored a perfect hit. All three missiles landed right in the midst of the storage buildings, one structure exploded, another caught fire. Then it was to hell and gone away for P–Peter. Over the jungle again and out over the Bay. Seven hours to base.

All Liberators on the attack landed safely with only two casualties. In the CO's bomber, which had gone in almost on the deck, the rear gunner died from wounds on the way home. The other casualty was Alan Smith, who despite feeling under the weather, had done an outstanding job of getting his explosives on the target. But it wasn't flu that was ailing him. The Medical Officer immediately diagnosed it for what it really was—malaria—and it was off to the sick bay for P–Peter's bomb-aimer.

A week later the Digri Liberators were out in force over Siam again—this time in a formation attack on a railway bridge 20 miles out of Bangkok, Ken Silcocks filling in as bombardier in P–Peter for Alan Smith who was still unserviceable with the Anopheles Ague.

It was a botched effort. Bombing in formation, the lead plane's missiles fell well short of the target and the others followed suit. Only the fishes were disturbed by the 10 tons of bombs that exploded in the water—a costly failure not only in terms of bombs wasted but also in fuel, oil, and Ops time. At least the bombers and crews suffered no damage, though they well might have if a Japanese fighter pilot who was practising aerobatics below them on the way home had bothered to look up—all those nice, juicy, fat targets. Perhaps not; Japanese fighter pilots never did like bomber formations—too much firepower even for the Sons of the Rising Sun.

Before the year ended, 215 Squadron made one more sortie, at which time the unit moved to Dhubalia to join 99 Squadron as part of 175 Wing. The objective was to bomb the supply pump at Taungup near Cheduba Island off the Arakan Coast. It turned out to be a milk run, no flak—the Japanese had already begun withdrawing from Arakan in the face of General Christinson's advancing 15 Corps inland.

1945—On to the End

The lack of Japanese opposition prompted Christinson to accelerate plans to occupy Akyab and Ramree Island for use as air bases. On

January 4 the British found Akyab abandoned. Meanwhile 175 Wing concentrated on disrupting the BSR, the nickname the aircrews had given the Burma-Siam Railway.

On January 11, P–Peter and five others set out to plaster bridges at low level along the BSR north of Bangkok, each one armed with ten 500-pound bombs. Over the target, a single-span bridge spanning 60 yards across the river, it was clear and free from ground fire. At a 300-foot altitude, flying 165 miles an hour, it was just as well—the Liberator would have been a sitting duck. In this case the positions were reversed. It was the target that was mincemeat—or should have been.

However, the new bomb-aimer, Alf Reed, replacing Smith, who was on Recuperation Leave, wasn't quick enough on the trigger. The five-bomb stick overshot the bridge by 50 yards. Round again. Another miss, and Stan Jones in the lower gun turret reported only four explosions. A bomb hang-up. They tried once more, dropped the recalcitrant missile, but again Jones signalled a miss, a near one this time. Disgustedly Frazer turned the "Lib" for home.

They reached the coast north of Ramree Island. Then navigator Bob Done gave Frazer the news that they were heading into a 20-mile-an-hour headwind, an ugly realization for the ship's captain who had to decide which route to take. By detouring around Akyab (through faulty intelligence on the part of the RAF they didn't know that it was now in British hands) Frazer and Done reckoned they could just make it as far as their old alma mater, Digri, in three-and-a-half hours with about a half-hour's fuel to spare.

A while later Done advised that the headwind had increased to 27 miles an hour and by that time it was getting dark. Frazer decided to play it safe. He asked Done for a new heading to Cox's Bazaar, a USAF base on the Burmese coast, where they spent the night.

Between January 16 and 21, P-Peter made three more Ops. The first of these was a mass Liberator attack—made up of 215, 99, 355, 365 Squadrons and a USAF unit escorted by 88 Lightning and

Thunderbolt fighters—on the Japanese fighter field at Zayatkwin near Rangoon. Enemy fighters were no problem but clouds were; the bomb-aimers had to drop their loads by guesswork.

The next trip, three days later, was aimed at knocking out the runways on Meiktila airfield in the same vicinity. This was part of the strategy of preventing Japanese fighters from harassing the British troops now only 70 miles from Mandalay. On this occasion Alan Smith, P–Peter's bombardier, was back in the saddle. But it was touch and go whether he would have a chance to hit the target.

As the formation neared the Initial Point, the cumulus clouds got bigger and the gaps between them smaller. Leading one of the Vic formations of three, Frazer decided that instead of following the leading Vee, it would be easier to fly around the cloud, thereby reducing the risk of collision. But the cloud was bigger than he counted on and, while the rest of the formation squeezed through without any trouble, by the time his Vic made it around the cumulus he couldn't see them. That left his formation out on a limb, the only choice being to head back toward Burma. Finally, however, he spotted the rest in the distance and by putting on extra throttle soon caught up with them.

On January 21, 215 Squadron took part in the invasion of Ramree (code: Sandwip) Island. During this amphibious assault, while the Royal Navy shelled the coastal batteries, strafing Lightnings, Thunderbolts, and Spitfires covered the assault troops, American B24s raided the Japanese Headquarters, and four RAF squadrons bombed the fortifications; 215 Squadron's target was Mount Peter, a wooded ridge believed to be harbouring ground defences.

Flying toward the target, two of 99 Squadron's 16 Liberators following them collided. It was an eerie, frightening sight. One minute there were aircraft, then one of them turned into the sun and crashed into another. Both simply disintegrated into bits and pieces and in that split second 22 men perished.

Ramree, garrisoned by 1000 fanatical Japanese, fell later in the day. All but 20 of the defenders chose to die rather than surrender. The capture of this island was of particular importance. Being flat it provided an excellent site for airfields from which to supply the army in the field. But it was not operational until two months later. Meanwhile, to support the advance inland, the Liberators were assigned tactical low-level raids.

By mid-February P–Peter's crew had logged 143 Op hours—almost halfway home—and were given 10 days' leave, at the end of which they all received promotions in rank, Frazer to Flight Lieutenant, Smith to Flying Officer, and all the NCOs to Flight Sergeant.

On the second mission since returning to "Dusty Dhubalia," on the run-in to bomb Japanese fortifications at Paganyat just outside Mandalay at low level, the small propeller jettisoned from a bomb dropped by an aircraft above them smashed through P–Peter's windscreen and slashed Frazer in the face.

With the wind blowing through the hole in the Perspex at 160 miles an hour, the skipper turned the controls over to copilot Jock Govan, while self-appointed medic Joe Barlow, one of the wireless operators, applied first aid to patch up Frazer's face.

On 25 February 1945, they returned to Siam, this time to plaster the BSR at Kohrat near Bangkok. Bombing at dusk meant a long trip home in the dark, but their worst vexation was that not one member of the crew had a single cigarette among them with which to relax and pass the time. One consolation: by the time they landed their Ops hours had climbed to 177. Getting there!

On March 2, another first—bombing at night. Target: the Makasan railway workshops in Bangkok. A big operation this one—a total of five RAF Squadrons—50 Liberators in all. Using the pathfinder technique employed by Bomber Command over Europe, each squadron sent two aircraft down to 300 feet to drop marker flares.

Because the bombers were carrying three tons of bombs, crews were reduced by two to conserve weight and extend fuel range over so vast a distance. Left behind were the nose gunner (on the assumption that night fighters would not attack head on) and one of the wireless operators.

By the time P–Peter reached the target area, Bangkok was ablaze. There were fire and explosions everywhere, on the ground from bombs bursting, in the air from the flak, added to which was the disquieting spectre of searchlights probing the sky.

Over the target Frazer and crew saw a Liberator going down in flames, coned by three lights, twisting and turning to try and escape. It was alarming but they had little time to ponder its fate; their job was to concentrate on hitting the target. Finally after what seemed like an eternity those two magic words: Bombs Gone. All 54 bombers from Dhubalia got home, some damaged by flak, but not a single man was lost or even injured.

On March 17, 215 Squadron bombed supply dumps at Rangoon, each aircraft dropping 8000-pound loads on the target, the largest loads so far. The increased weight didn't make it any easier executing the takeoff, and Group operations promised the loads would gradually increase and not stop until a safe maximum was reached. It seemed the RAF was in a hurry to get the war over with.

In fact it was going in the right direction. Three days later Mandalay fell to the 19th Indian Division. Fighters and medium bombers had blown gaping holes in the thick walls behind a moat, backed by 45 feet of dirt surrounding the great red castle, Fort Dufferin. The defenders did not wait to engage the assaulting ground forces but fled through a sewer. By day's end the flag of the British 14th Army was flying over the ancient home of the Burmese Kings. The Road to Rangoon was now open.

Frazer spent the last week of March in Calcutta taking a Radio Range Beacons course, living the life of luxury in the Grand Hotel, enjoying such niceties as running water, a toilet, and a cooling fan that did away with the need for mosquito netting, and gorging himself on first-class meals—a welcome change from curries and bully beef. Quite a difference from camp life. His crew had the week off but they soon became bored with nothing to do and were glad when the skipper returned, mostly to take them on missions to Rangoon as the army continued its advance south toward the Burma port. In fact, attention to that particular area of operations had become a priority for the air forces—to the chagrin and dismay of 215 Squadron.

On April 17, without any prior notice, like a bolt out of the wild blue yonder, they received the stunning news that they would no longer fly bombing missions, in fact would not even be manning Liberators. Instead they would convert to transport duties flying DC3 Dakotas. Supplying the army by air had by now become an essential adjunct to ground operations. Next day the Daks arrived. Conversion to the lighter twin-engine transports was a cinch. But it was the disruption of the aircrews that stung. They regarded it as degrading, as if they had suddenly been demoted.

The Dakota needed only a crew of four: pilot and copilot, a radio man, and a navigator. So the rest of the crew were assigned to other captains. P–Peter's crew were understandably upset. With 238 hours Ops time under their flying helmets, they needed only five more trips to complete their 300-hour tour. Nor did they relish the move to Tulihal in the vicinity of Imphal. It offered scant amenities and they would be living under canvas.

They were equally disenchanted over their new duties: several trips a day delivering supplies over a drop zone or flying into short-takeoff-and-landing strips to bring in cargo and take out the wounded and those going on leave. These flights, though short, were over disputed territory at low level with the risk of being hit by flak or machine guns—or running into the Burmese hills in poor weather, of which there was always a plethora.

Frazer was not one to take such a situation lying down and spouted his objections and his views in no uncertain terms to anyone and everyone who cared to listen—even to some who didn't. It was ridiculous and inane, he argued vociferously, to waste all that four-engine bombing experience and talent learning to fly different aircraft for an entirely new job. It just didn't make sense.

For Frazer and his crew, and one other, that dogged persistence paid off. Both were posted to Sabloni to join 356 Squadron as replacements bringing their Liberators with them. The rest of 215 Squadron was not so lucky; they remained at Dhubalia with the Dakotas.

The two Lib crews wasted no time leaving Dhubalia, afraid that there might be a change of heart at the last minute. On April 20 they arrived at Sabloni, where, as experienced operational types—and with their own bombers yet—they were welcomed with open arms. They also learned that three-quarters of the aircrews with their new squadron were Canadians. Frazer's Liberator was compelled to undergo a slight transformation—to "D" for Dog. "P" for Peter had long been spoken for in 356. Before they left there had also been a crew change in the lineup. Alan Smith had asked to be posted to England—on compassionate grounds, his mother being seriously ill. His role as bomb-aimer had been filled by Joe Reid, a fellow officer, with whom Frazer shared a room.

By this time the British 14th Army was advancing so rapidly that further attacks on bridges were prohibited lest it should hold up forward progress. One mission, in which 356 Squadron was assigned to bomb the defences at Toungoo, 15 miles north of Rangoon, had to be rerouted at the last minute; a tank column had already captured the town. The Liberators were diverted further south to drop their loads on the Rangoon defences.

That was timely. On May 1, the British launched Operation Dracula, the invasion of Rangoon. It began with Gurkha parachute troops being dropped to the south, followed by fighting units of the Royal Navy sailing up the Sittang River preceding the 26th Indian Division invasion force, which landed the next day and took the city. There was no resistance. To avoid being cut off from Siam as the British 14th Army swept south to the east, the Japanese had fled after setting fire to the docks and other installations.

In Europe on 7 May 1945, Germany officially and unconditionally surrendered to the Allies. Next day the victors celebrated VE-Day. In Southeast Asia, meanwhile, World War II continued with a vengeance.

On May 14, 356 and her sister Squadron 355 in 184 Wing at Sabloni were given a "suicide job": attacking the Japanese Navy—well, part of it anyway. Reconnaissance aircraft had spotted a flotilla of naval vessels, the cruiser *Nachi*, four destroyers, and a supply ship headed for Port Blair in the Andaman Islands off the southeast coast of Burma, which were still in Japanese hands. The assignment was dicey: bombing at 5000 feet—against a floating gun platform, far too low. But they had no choice but to press on regardless—or, in the air force vernacular, "rewardless." So into the Valley of Flak flew the 24 Liberators.

They were lucky. At a point where they should have intercepted the warships, orders were received to return to base. Whew! The *Nachi* had disappeared. However, four days later several warships of the Royal Navy registered several hits on the cruiser, which was last seen limping for Singapore. The Indian Ocean was once again in RN hands. But the Japanese still occupied Port Blair and next day 184 Wing was dispatched to bomb it. This time, they were not so lucky. One of the 355 Squadron bombers was hit and crashed into the harbour.

At this juncture Frazer and most of his crew had almost completed the 300 hours needed to complete their tour. The exception was Joe Reid, the new bomb-aimer, but he had nearly enough hours from previous service with another squadron before joining D–Dog. However, now the requirements changed: the length of a tour was extended to a total of 400 hours. The crews accepted it philosophically; they had to. What the hell else *could* they do?

The Liberators at Sabloni were now introduced to an innovation for four-engine heavy bombers: dive-bombing. Anything for a laugh. But the USAF had reported great success with the technique. On May 25, D-Dog was part of a formation of four charged with dive-bombing a tiny railway bridge over the Ta-ko River on the Malay Peninsula, a 15-hour round trip in stinking weather. The Meteorological Officer had warned them of low stratus cloud over the Bay but clear skies over the Isthmus of Kra. In fact conditions were so bad across the water to Mandalay that the crews were forced down to 200 feet.

When navigator Bob Done reported that they had reached a point somewhere north of their intended course, there was still heavy overcast but, thankfully, at 1200 feet it was higher. Suddenly off the starboard beam another Liberator flashed by going in the opposite direction, its captain having either completed his mission or decided to abort. In any case Frazer cursed the stupid clot for flying right into the incoming traffic.

The question now was what route to take across the Isthmus. The map showed the hills to be as high as 2500 feet. Climbing into the cloud and flying over the top of them, then descending into who knew what, was far too chancy. Frazer decided to follow the river valley running between the hills, and pick up a road to Chumon on the far coast, a flight no longer than 20 minutes. They made it with no trouble. Skirting the town, they headed north to find the target.

In practice bombing with smoke bombs, they had dived from a height of 3000 feet, which gave them lots of room to spare. This was different. Due to the overcast they had to start from 1200 feet and it was raining. When they sighted the bridge, they saw that it had already been damaged; but it was still standing, so they agreed they should take it out altogether. They knew from Intelligence that there was no flak, so they made a dummy run. Joe Reid, the bomb-aimer, suggested two bombing runs but Frazer nixed the suggestion. It was a long way home in crappy weather and fuel would be at a premium.

Directed by Reid, Frazer shoved the nose down to begin the dive. His angle, though not quite vertical, was steep enough for the speed to build up fast. To check it, he asked the copilot for 20 degrees of flap. Though he did not have the nose aimed quite on the target, at 600 feet diving at 220 miles an hour, Frazer gave the order to drop the bombs anyway, then pulled the control wheel back into his gut and advanced the throttles. As the aircraft levelled out at 180 miles an hour 150 feet off the deck, Jock Govan suggested he begin climbing. Joe Barlow, the wireless operator, signalled a near miss, 10 yards to the right of the bridge and it was still standing. Damn! At least they had the consolation, on landing back at base, of knowing that they had accumulated another 15-1/2 hours Ops time toward their extended 400-hour tour.

Though they had no indication of it at the time, the D–Dog crew flew their last mission on 30 May 1945, two and a half months before the Japanese surrender, marking the end of the deadliest conflict in history, in which an estimated 53,447,000 human souls met their deaths.

The foray was a long one—14 hours—to bomb a merchant ship at Sattahip across the Bight of Bangkok. The Met Officer advised that there would be cloud over the Isthmus of Kra and this would prevent them flying through the valleys this time—as they had done when dive-bombing the bridge over the Ta-ko River—but from then on it would be clear all the way to the target.

Only five aircraft were available for the sortie and D–Dog, to conserve fuel and allow for an increased bomb load, would fly short three crewmen, one of the wireless operators and the upper and lower gunners. Not to worry. Although Sattahip was a naval base, the Intelligence Officer assured the crews there would be no fighters in the vicinity. Frazer's crew would also fly with a relief bomb-aimer, Jim Hamilton, replacing Joe Reid, who had been killed flying with another crew while trying to make up extra Ops time, and D–Dog would be last aircraft off the ground for the mission.

Shortly after takeoff, Stan Jones in the nose turret reported a solid bank of cloud ahead. Frazer ordered the crew to put on oxygen and began climbing to 11,000 feet to fly over it. Halfway across the

Isthmus, through a break in the overcast, they could see the water of the Gulf of Siam, and Frazer began to let down. They then noticed two Liberators some distance away flying in the opposite direction, presumably returning from having completed their bombing.

Twenty minutes to the target Hamilton advised that he was on sight tracking. They then saw two other Liberators returning; that meant D–Dog was on its own. Shortly afterwards Hamilton reported that the harbour lay straight ahead. It was turning dusk by the time D–Dog crossed over the coast. The flak gunners opened up, then just as quickly the bomber was past the batteries and over the harbour. Hamilton reported that there was no sign of the merchantman—only several small ships and two destroyers. Could the other bombers have sunk it? No. They must have missed it. There it was, clear as could be, outside the harbour, a perfect target well out of range of the shore batteries, protected only by its limited armament, with which it began firing at the bomber. But its shells never even came close.

The ship began zigzagging furiously as the Liberator started circling to get into position to bomb but its wake in the calm water made it easy to follow. Hamilton called for one bomb, out of the nine the Liberator carried to drop as a sighter. The air was smooth so that there was no trouble maintaining a course. Bomb gone—50 yards short but right on line.

With the sun beginning to set they would soon be running out of daylight. Only time for one more run. The aim was perfect but at the moment Hamilton pressed the bomb release button, the ship veered sharply to the right and all eight missiles splashed into the sea 20 yards to the left.

Disappointing as it was, there was no time for remorse or regret. Without waiting for Done to give him a course, Frazer swung the aircraft to the west in the direction of the sun as it began to slide below the heavy cloud bank in the direction of the Isthmus ahead. It was turning dark fast and they knew there would no moon that night. It would be fatal to try and get across the peninsula in the darkness of the clouds and impossible to get over the bank rising to over 20,000 feet; they didn't have enough fuel. Frazer pushed the throttles fully forward to coax as much power as possible out of the Pratt and Whitneys to give him the speed he needed to get across the peninsula before the light gave way. But when they reached the cloud bank at an altitude of 10,500 feet, the sun had completely disappeared and it was solid black. What now? Turn back and try and fly around it? Not a likely prospect with limited fuel reserves.

Providentially however, the nose gunner reported a spot of red— the setting sun burning through a break in the cloud, a beacon to follow even though it gradually began to turn to pink, then halfway across the Isthmus of Kra disappeared altogether. Now there was nothing but black darkness. Frantically, Frazer yanked the machine to starboard and began to climb, blind as a bat but hoping for the best. Luckily his instincts had urged him in the right direction. A little farther to the starboard Stan Jones in the nose picked up a faint trace of colour—not much, a bland grey—but colour all the same, a gap in the cloud revealing the open water below. Frazer turned toward it. The air suddenly got rough, then became smooth as thankfully they emerged from the far edge of the accursed cloud bank and out over the Andaman Sea.

Ten days later Frazer went on leave by himself, determined to take in the sights before his time was up, though how much longer the war would last was anybody's guess. First stop, the Taj Mahal, where Frazer teamed up with a British Army medical officer. Having explored that phenomenon, the pair took a train north to Kathogodam at the foot of the Himalayas. There, they were denied accommodation because they had no reservations; however, a military policeman took pity on their plight and arranged for them to stay at a private residence in Ranikhet 20 miles farther on. In this exclusive and picturesque village, which reminded Frazer of a Laurentian resort, they enjoyed the facilities of the officers' club, golfing and tennis, and dances in a holiday that ended all too soon.

A week later Frazer was on a train back to Calcutta and thence to Sabloni.

10 July 1945—a historic day for Frazer and his crew! They were taken off Ops. Tour-expired at long last! No more flak, no more Jap fighters, no more slugging through clouds and rough air and rain and winds. No more wondering whether the fuel will give out before they can reach home. No more, period! It's over! Time for celebration, then the inevitable wait—*wait*, an air force prerequisite, a routine, a ritual—to be put on the Boat List.

Hallelujah! On 15 August 1945—a week or so after the atomic bombs dropped on Hiroshima and Nagasaki—peace at long last. By the end of the month Frazer and his buddies were on their way by train to Bombay to board a troopship "Bound for Old Blighty Shore," as the song goes, on their first leg home.

Postscript

Following the war Wally Frazer became a chartered accountant and opened his own firm in Ottawa. In 1982 he retired and he and his wife spent their summers at their cottage in Perth, Ontario, and their winters in Florida.

On the Battlefield

Chapter 9

Guest Appearance

I rate Wallace Reyburn as one of the best, bravest, and most introspective of Canadian war correspondents. I first met Wally Reyburn in May 1946 when, as a reporter with the Windsor Star, *I was applying for an assignment as a stringer for the* Montreal Standard, *where he was a senior editor. I knew that he had been a war correspondent of some note and that, among other World War II battles, he had covered the Dieppe raid. "You might say I was a 'guest,'" he pointed out modestly. I was particularly interested in his participation for two reasons. Windsor was the home of the Essex Scottish Regiment, which had taken such a beating during Operation Jubilee. I was one of the reporters on hand when those taken prisoner were welcomed home. And, although it was before my time, my own Spitfire squadron, 401 RCAF, had figured prominently in the operation. "We scored an outstanding victory in the air," Reyburn told me. "We gave the Luftwaffe a thorough licking that day."*

Some years later in my research for Our Bravest and Our Best, *my account of Canada's Victoria Cross winners, I came across Reyburn's description of Cec (pronounced sess) Merritt winning his VC at Dieppe. This led to my interest in Reyburn's own part in that raid. What follows is my interpretation of my interview with him after studying his thrilling book* Glorious Chapter.

By mid-August 1942, Canadian war correspondents in Great Britain were getting pretty fed up. For two-and-a-half years they'd been sitting on their duffs waiting for the big Canadian war story. True, they were filing accounts of Canadian air force fighter and bomber combat operations. But though heroic and exciting, these reports were isolated and for the most part second-hand. And what could you write about the army? Impatiently waiting, training, waiting, training, waiting, and more training, the poor bastards. Not exactly good copy.

That was about to change. On Friday, the 14th of the month, Wallace Reyburn, war correspondent with the *Montreal Standard*, got a phone call from Major Cliff Wallace, public relations officer of the Canadian Army, summoning him to his hotel. It sounded urgent; he wanted to talk to him confidentially. When Reyburn arrived at Wallace's room, the major checked up and down the hall and tapped the walls to make sure their conversation would not be overheard—maximum security, all very hush-hush. Even then he did not reveal the nature of the assignment except to say, "This is the real thing. The biggest Canadian Army story that has broken so far in this war." Period. Other than instructions to be at a certain railway station at 3:30 the following afternoon there was no further explanation.

On the journey to the south of England Reyburn joined some 20 other official war correspondents and photographers, not all Canadians—the noted American author Ernest Hemingway and Drew Middleton of the Associated Press from New York were among them—the largest assembly of pressmen assigned to any military operation up to that time. Something big was in the offing all right. But even though they were split into small groups of five and six and dispersed among the various army units—Reyburn was assigned to the South Saskatchewan Regiment (SSR), an infantry battalion—they were still left in the dark as to what lay in store.

Two days later, at a press briefing conducted by Major Wallace, they were told that the operation in which they would be partici- pating was an amphibious one—air, land, and sea—by a large force at a town on the coast of France. But Wallace did not identify the town; the destination was still kept under wraps as far as the press was concerned, though it in no way detracted from their sense of anticipation and excitement.

As war correspondents they were issued Canadian Army battle-dress uniforms and came under army discipline. They were given privileges equivalent to those of captains but wore no insignia except "Canadian War Correspondent" badges. Since they were noncombatants they were forbidden under the articles of war to carry arms of any kind. Reyburn balked at this. He wanted to be in on the action. He considered arming himself with a revolver. However, one of the "South Sask" officers talked him out of it; if he was captured, as an armed noncombatant he could be shot on the spot—or worse.

Late in the afternoon of August 18, the SSRs boarded a destroyer, part of a Royal Navy flotilla of 237 ships set to sail at 9:00 that evening from four ports along the southern coast of England to carry an invasion force of 6000 men across the English Channel, the destination of which Reyburn at last learned when he reported to the regimental intelligence officer who handed him an envelope marked "Secret." It contained maps of Dieppe and the surrounding area.

At supper that evening Reyburn was seated next to the SSRs' commanding officer, Colonel Cecil "Cec" Merritt, who filled him in on the details. The first troops to go ashore, the regiment would land at 0505 hours next morning on "Green Beach" near the town of Pourville, a continuation of the main beach a mile or so west of Dieppe itself. There a bridgehead was to be established that included seizing the town as well as the Quatre Vents Farm to make way for an advance by the Queen's Own Cameron Highlanders of Winnipeg who would hit the beach half an hour later.

After supper Reyburn went below decks to snatch some sleep. He had just dozed off when a steward awakened him ordering everyone on deck. The troopship was passing through a minefield. The night was clear, cool, and starry with almost a full moon and the sea was calm. Shortly afterwards the order came to embark into the motor landing craft (MLC) slung from davits on deck. As he gripped his pencil and pad and stared down at the men armed with Bren and Sten guns, rifles with gleaming bayonets, revolvers, mortar shells, and grenades, he thought to himself that this was one time it seemed that the man who said the pen is mightier than the sword didn't know what the hell he was talking about.

Reyburn had been assigned to go ashore with the Battalion Headquarters (BHQ) under the command of Major Jim McRae, Cec Merritt's second-in-command. As the barge was lowered into the water from the mother ship the men were grateful they were in an MLC, which was larger than a ALC (assault landing craft), had higher sides, and was covered by a steel deck for greater protection.

As the destroyer—the mother ship—pulled away, the MLC was left on its own, but only figuratively. In the darkness the men could make out the shapes of other landing craft around them and ships of the Royal Navy shepherding them forward like a flock, leading them to their destination. Then suddenly the sky was lit up from behind and to the northeast by a flare that seemed to illuminate the whole English Channel. Tracer bullets etched themselves in brilliant pencil lines across the darkened sky like a fireworks display interspersed with balls of fire and rocket explosions. They had no idea what they were witnessing, but to the men on the sea that early morning it was a scene at once awesome, eerie, frightening, and thrilling. Only later would they learn that it was a chance encounter between British landing craft carrying an advanced force of commandos and a German tanker escorted by motor torpedo boats that was over as quickly as it had begun—the enemy completely unaware that they had intercepted the vanguard of an invasion force.

As the boats neared the beach the first rays of dawn broke through. When the cliffs came into view the men cocked their weapons and assumed a crouch position in the bottom of the barge, ready to spring forward at the double. They could hear the lapping of the water onto the beach and make out the shape of houses and hotels. Then with a crunch the landing craft hit the shore. The ramp came down and the men poured out of the barge and dashed forward 50 yards to the refuge of a 12-foot-high sea wall. By this time it was quite light. But in spite of it and the noise they made with their boots pounding over the pebbles on the beach, there was no sign that the Germans were aware the SSRs, spread out behind the parapet, were ashore.

There was a heavy smell of seaweed and salt in the air. So far, so good. Then, inevitably, the South Sasks were suddenly spotted by the enemy. A spattering of spasmodic machine-gun fire broke out aimed in their direction. Huddled behind the sea wall they felt safe and sound—at least for the moment. They knew they still had to scale the barrier to reach their objectives, Pourville and the Quatre Vents Farm. To clear the way wire-cutters climbed to the top of the wall to cut through the barbed wire protecting it. Reyburn marvelled at their courage: working away, ignoring the danger of German gunfire. But their gallant efforts proved futile, a lost cause. Bunched up and tangled, the barbed wire was impossible to cut through. They had to find another way to get over the parapet.

Fortuitously, at that very moment, someone noticed a section of the sea wall that had no barbed wire. Instead there was a heavily sandbagged blockhouse with thick walls. Unhesitating, Reyburn and 40 others climbed up and into it. But they quickly had second thoughts. Getting up the wall had been just too easy. Reyburn pondered—had they walked into a trap? The blockhouse could be mined and might go off at any moment. They cleared it as fast as they could, finding themselves safely on the inner side of the sea wall. Reyburn's instincts were soon to prove only too fatally prophetic. Half an hour later, when members of the Cameron Highlanders reached the blockhouse, someone somewhere pressed a button that set off an explosion and blew them to pieces.

Meanwhile, along with Jim McRae and other members of the Battalion Headquarters, Reyburn made his way across the promenade to an empty house behind which lay a grass square fringed with trees—a community park. In the house's two-car garage the wireless operators set up shop and went to work communicating with the forward units.

From the doorway Reyburn and others watched as infantrymen went about the task of housecleaning, flushing out Germans hiding inside. This battle-drill exercise by the Canadian Army had been brought to a state of the art by practice, practice, and still more practice. Now all that drilling was paying off under actual battle conditions. While a pair of infantrymen covered the house with their Bren guns, two others battered their way into the building through the door and windows with their rifle butts, then ran inside. Their purpose was to flush out Germans and take them prisoner for questioning—one of the main objectives of the Dieppe raid itself. Through this device Reyburn came face to face with an enemy soldier for the first time, though it was hardly what he expected.

This German was in no condition to be interrogated, at least not until he received some medical attention. He had dislodged from his hiding place by hand grenades, and shrapnel had torn the flesh from his right shoulder and forearm. His right hand, which he was holding in his left, was hanging by mere shreds of tissue. His wounds aside, he was the antithesis of the superman painted by the Nazi propaganda machine: He wasn't youthful, he was bespectacled, and he was pudgy. More like Sad Sack.

Other prisoners that followed, brought in at bayonet point with their hands raised, were not exactly advertisements for the mighty Wermacht either. Sullen-looking, in poor shape, they were either quite old or very young. By comparison the Canadians, all of them in their early twenties, virile and powerfully built, looked strong and sturdy.

By this time the garage serving as the BHQ came under enemy mortar fire that appeared to be emanating from a hilly golf course situated between the Pourville suburb and Dieppe itself. This was followed by the boom of heavy artillery, the rattle of machine guns, and the ping-ping of sniper bullets. Aircraft roaring overhead, both Allied and German, added to the crescendo. Reyburn felt a sense of excitement; this was the real thing.

In the midst of all that bombardment, he was also filled with admiration, amazement, and awe at the conduct of the French people. As soon as the landings took place, the British Broadcasting System (BBC) had warned that this was only a raid rather than an invasion, and that the French should take no part in it for fear of later enemy reprisals. Incredibly, with all hell breaking loose right in the middle of their home town, these unarmed civilians stayed cool and unflustered. There was no stampede to the fields. The morale of those Frenchmen left a lasting impression on Reyburn. "They remained perfectly calm," he wrote, "and showed not the slightest sign of panic."

Thus far Reyburn had been nothing more than a spectator to what had been happening around and about him. Now that communications had been established Jim McRae was able to brief him on the overall picture of what the regiment as a unit was actually engaging in. "A" Company of the SSRs, he was told, was advancing through the Scie valley, in which the Pourville suburb lay, with the objective of taking a German radio-locating centre and an antiaircraft battery out of action. Meanwhile "B" Company was working the streets of the town to clear the houses, take prisoners, and pave the way for the Queen's Own Cameron Highlanders to advance on through. On the right flank "C" Company was up on the terraces silencing machine-gun nests for the advance, while similarly on the left flank "D" Company was carrying out the same exercise.

BHQ now moved out of the two-car garage, which had become too much of a hot spot from German mortar fire, onto the grassy square behind the house where other SSR personnel had stationed themselves guarding their enemy prisoners. Jim McRae, his adjutant, and the two wireless operators had just got themselves reorganized to begin signalling and receiving again when a shell landed in the middle of the square and exploded.

The blast killed a BHQ staff officer and four of the German prisoners.

Reyburn was lying on the ground at the time when the explosion sent him flying. His ears started ringing and he felt dizzy and it seemed as if a handful of sharp pebbles had struck him in the back. But he gave it no more thought until later when his shirt and pants started to feel damp. He soon found that what he had taken to be sweat was actually blood—the pebbles had been pieces of shrapnel.

Undeterred and anxious to get a first-hand glimpse of the front-line action, Reyburn joined a group of SSR infantrymen advancing at a crouched trotting gait along the main street of Pourville toward the bridge across the River Scie that led to the centre of Dieppe. He had no inkling that he was about to become a first-hand witness to one of the most gallant and stirring moments in Canadian military history.

The wide avenue, flanked by shops, hotels, and picket-fenced lawns on either side, was being systematically peppered with sniper fire. Reyburn wasn't scared, although he had certainly expected to be. The concern uppermost in his mind was reaching the relative security of an alleyway between two buildings some 20 yards short of the 200-yard-long bridge, totally exposed from one end to the other and without railings or balustrades of any sort, at the end of it a towering concrete fort that looked menacingly down on any force challenging the crossing.

The infantrymen now formed up into sections. Reyburn watched as they surged forward one section after another. From the concrete fort the Germans let fly a merciless hail of machine-gun-bullet and mortar-shell fire. Men fell in their tracks, some dead, some wounded. Others retreated to the safety of the alleyway. Reyburn dashed out with the stretcher-bearers to drag in the wounded, whom they laid out in the alleyway or on the gravel road itself.

As the men got ready to tackle the bridge again, their CO, Colonel

Cec Merritt, came ambling up the street. Taking off his tin helmet and wiping the sweat from his brow, he asked, "What's the trouble?"

"This bridge is a hot spot sir," came the reply. "We're trying to get across it."

Merritt walked up to the start of the bridge and announced matter-of-factly: "Now, men, we're going to get across this bridge. Follow me. Don't bunch up. Spread out. Here we go."

Twirling the helmet that dangled from his wrist, Merritt strode across the bridge showing no reaction to the enemy fire erupting all around him. His men followed as he advanced.

"Watching this display of bravery and inspired leadership," Reyburn would later write, "I felt a thrill run through me ... I'd never seen anything like it before in my life ... What makes bravery like that? ... A stretcher-bearer standing beside me shook his head incredulously and said, 'My God!'"

Most of the men got across that first time, but Merritt was to cross that bridge no fewer than four times. Leading other men across he would set off saying, "Come on over—there's nothing to it." *(In 1995 when Cec and I were being interviewed by the Vancouver television stations to promote my book* Our Bravest and Our Best, *of this action which earned him the Victoria Cross he said, "There was nothing heroic about that. That was my regiment—it was my job!")*

Later Reyburn seated himself against the side of a three-storey house safely away from where the Germans were lobbing mortar shells toward the BHQ. His job as a reporter was to observe the operation from as many views as he could find. In this case he had an unrestricted and uninterrupted ringside seat to the air battle raging overhead. Though the outcome of an air battle seen from the ground was impossible to ascertain, Reyburn was nonetheless fascinated with the dogfights twirling and whirling above, the whine and snorting of aircraft engines, and the *pop pop pop* of sporadic machine-gun and cannon fire, in what actually turned out to be the worst drubbing the Commonwealth air forces had given the Luftwaffe since the Battle of Britain. Reyburn was also at times distracted from the fighting taking place above and around him by the sometimes lackadaisical and occasionally comical way in which the French went about their lives, taking it all in stride:

A farmer going about his chores—herding his cows into the shelter of the barn then bringing in a pile of hay to feed them—seemingly oblivious that the concrete fort on the golf course was firing mortar shells right over his head.

An elderly gent having just left the bakery, pedalling along on his bicycle, ... quite unconcerned with all the military activity around him—None of this commando-style raid nonsense was going to prevent him from enjoying his daily fresh bread.

A lad of nine appeared to be having a field day watching the Canadians firing off mortars and marvelling at the signallers working their wireless sets. Before crossing the street, taking off his beret, projecting it around the corner on the end of a stick—Cowboys and Indians style—and when no sniper took a shot at it, scampering across.

When a SSR officer, having dodged sniper bullets down the road plunked down beside him, Reyburn pointed to the verandah of the Albion Hotel across the street where a figure seemed to be moving. The officer peered through his binoculars then handed them to Reyburn. It was no sniper but a fattish Frenchman pacing up and down the verandah who appeared to be enjoying the sight of a building on fire down the street, even though part of the roof of his own hotel had been blown off.

After Reyburn's companion left, when a bullet glanced off the brickwork above his head he also decided it was time to move on. Obviously a sniper had him pegged. But where to go? In what direction? Lying face down on the grass he lodged himself as close to the wall of the house as he could, hoping the sniper's aim wouldn't improve. It was like waiting for the other shoe to drop. Then the sniper fired off another shot a good two feet off the target. Too close for comfort. Reyburn decided on the lesser of two evils: to make himself a moving target instead of a stationary one. He joined a pair of soldiers headed on the double toward the terraced hill on the side of the River Scie. Two hundred yards further on they came to a stable where several others had taken shelter inside. One of them was Sergeant Howard Graham with a Sten gun slung over his shoulder, whose battle-dress tunic was bulging with incendiary bombs. There was no denying he meant business. "See that street out there," he announced belligerently. "There's a goddam sniper out there picking our boys off. I'm going along the road setting each house on fire until I get him or he gets me. He'll come running out of doors, and I'll pick the bastard off with this Sten gun." With that he headed down the street.

Reyburn left the security of the stable for a closer look at where the action was taking place. Passing houses on the slopes west of Pourville, all the signs of war were there. Carnage. There wasn't a building still standing that hadn't had part of it blown away. Many houses were burning. Severed telephone lines were left dangling. Trees had been decapitated, leaving them looking forlorn and sad. Streets were littered with rubbish, wreckage, discarded helmets, and equipment. Reyburn talked to a corporal and a private escorting four Nazi prisoners and asked if any of them spoke English. "No," the corporal replied derisively. "All they can say is *Kamerad* [surrender]." This was symptomatic of the Canadian soldiers' poor opinion of the enemy as a fighting individual. Summed up: the German was fine sitting behind the safety of his machine gun in his pillbox firing at his attackers below and in the open, but when faced with close hand-to-hand combat he threw in the sponge.

Reyburn attributed the Canadians' tenacity throughout the raid to the fact that after a long period of inactivity they were spoiling for a fight, anxious to prove themselves the equal or better of the other Commonwealth troops that had already seen combat. They had certainly given a good account of themselves but the cards were stacked against them. In the first place the Germans knew they were coming; they were ready for them. The Germans controlled the battle from the heights of the cliffs overlooking Dieppe. They enjoyed a preponderance of firepower—heavy German artillery against mortar and small arms fire. Like popguns versus cannon. That the Canadians lasted on the beaches as long as they did would have been impossible without air supremacy. But by 1000 hours the order was given to withdraw from the beaches onto the landing boats.

The SSR BHQ had been moved to another house closer to shore, some 50 yards inland from the promenade where the dead and wounded had been taken into an empty building. Cec Merritt signalled by wireless to the headquarters ship that the regiment was ready to be taken off and requested landing craft be sent in. The ship replied that the boats would be into the beach by 1100 hours.

Several companies of South Sasks and Cameron Highlanders were jointly fighting a rearguard action to hold up German reinforcements determined to prevent the evacuation. Enemy rifle and machine-gun fire from the wooded slopes to the north had begun to penetrate as far as the BHQ. Bullets were striking the roof of the house.

The buildings were also being strafed by low-flying German Messerschmitt and Focke-Wulf fighters. Some of the troops left the houses and blocks of buildings in which they were sheltering to come out into the open onto the streets and squares and fire back at the enemy aircraft with their Bren and Sten guns—even their rifles.

All the while Merritt was busy directing operations from a gravel pathway that ran alongside the house in which the BHQ had been set up. Ignoring the German planes buzzing overhead and the bullets coming from the woods, he stood out there in the open without even his helmet on, so that he could get an unrestricted view of what was happening. The Germans were getting closer; bullets now splattered the upper storey of the house. Worse still, he saw no sign of the boats, looking out to sea.

From the doorway Reyburn watched the dead and wounded being brought out onto the promenade. It was obvious it was going to be difficult enough to load them into the boats along with those still alive let alone all the prisoners they'd taken. The problem was quickly solved; Merritt ordered the captives to be left behind.

The Germans were getting closer; they had reached the valley and there was still no sign of the landing craft. "I started to wonder what it would be like to be a prisoner of war," Reyburn wrote later. Then a shout went up, the boats had been sighted. At that moment Reyburn ran into Sergeant Howard Graham, whom he'd last seen trundling out of the stable, armed to the teeth, determined to hunt down a German sniper. He recognized Reyburn instantly. "I got that sniper alright, newspaperman," he told him.

Now the exodus to the beach began. The wounded were taken first, then Merritt signalled the next 100 men to go forward, Reyburn among them. As they set off the CO commanded: "Don't run, men, slope arms and march to the beach!" Reyburn had been dashing forward in a crouch to avoid being hit by a sniper, but when the order came he pulled himself erect and marched smartly with the others.

At the edge of the promenade there was a ladder propped up against the sea wall at the bottom of which was a pile of khaki-clad bodies. It occurred to Reyburn that as the troops descended it they were creating a bottleneck and a target for the German gunners. So he decided instead to jump the 12 feet, miraculously landing on the pebbly beach without even bruising himself let alone spraining an ankle or breaking a leg. "In my normal senses," he wrote of the incident, "I'd think twice about jumping that distance onto merely grass, but you do those things in the heat of battle without thinking about it."

From under the parapet, Reyburn gazed out onto a scene he would never forget. The tide was fully out and apart from the 50 yards of pebbles extending from the sea wall toward the shoreline the beach was sandy. From where Reyburn stood the distance to the water's edge was about 300 yards. Visibility out to sea was limited by smoke and haze from Dieppe's burning buildings. A dank, nauseous mixture of seaweed, salt water, and blood stung the nostrils. The beach was dotted with men on the sand running out to the boats whose bows had grounded into it every 100 yards or so. Other landing craft were coming and going behind them. Some were circling about, picking up survivors from those that had been sunk.

Now that the troops were on the beach the Germans concentrated all their firepower onto that limited, narrow stretch of pebble and sand. From either end they raked it with their machine guns while, from the cliffs above and from behind the town, heavy artillery shells rained down throwing up fountains of sea spray as they exploded among the boats. Mortar shells burst on the beach sending up showers of sand and pebbles. Snipers picked off men as they dashed for the boats. Focke-Wulf fighters roared down low, spitting machine-gun and cannon fire. A Junkers 88 twin-engine bomber that managed to slip through the Spitfire fighter screen dropped bombs on the boats from 100 feet.

Fire and brimstone! For Reyburn, the hazy smoke, the little boats, the men on the beach, conjured up a vision of newsreels and photographs of the evacuation at Dunkirk. A replay—only on a smaller scale. But no less terrifying. Hell on earth!

Someone shouted to Reyburn: "That's your boat there—along at the end." Dashing forward, he cursed his clumsy clodhopper army boots as he stumbled over the pebbles. Then suddenly he had the queer sensation of sailing through space as he raced across the sand. Bullets whistled all around him but he was barely aware of the danger, his mind so intent on reaching the boat. But when he got there, to his dismay, the ramp was up. As he prepared to clamber over the side, someone said, "She's stuck! We've got to push her off the sand!"

Reyburn waded into the sea to join the others heaving and pushing at the sides of the craft. They'd get it out a few yards, then a wave would promptly push it back. Reyburn kept as low a profile in the water as he could; the less of him visible the less he made himself a target. He also reckoned he would be a lot safer on the side of the boat facing out to sea instead of the beach. He had just worked his way around when a volley of bullets crashed against the steel side of the boat mere inches above his head—he'd forgotten to take into account that the Focke-Wulf 190s overhead could take a shot at any side. There was just nowhere, but nowhere, you were safe on that beach.

When they finally got the boat into deeper water they grabbed onto a rope that dangled in loops from each side and, shoulder to shoulder, were dragged along with the forward momentum of the vessel. Reyburn later remembered that his hands got so cold he had to loop his arm through the rope to prevent being cast adrift. The problem now was to climb into the boat. There was nothing to grab onto and each time he climbed up by using the rope, the steel side was so wet and slippery he slithered back down again. As he prepared to try once more, a bullet whizzed past his ear and struck the man next to him in the head. He dropped like a stone and floated away, face down in the water.

Reyburn's next effort was rewarded by a navy crewman getting hold of one of his hands and starting to pull him aboard. But with the upper half of his body on the deck and the lower half still hanging over the side the sailor couldn't budge him no matter how hard he tried. And Reyburn didn't have enough energy left to help him either. To make matters worse, someone tried to pull himself up by grabbing onto one of Reyburn's legs. Mercifully he finally let go, and between the sailor and himself Reyburn at last got up onto the deck where he lay exhausted. By the time he got his strength back and was about to join the rest of the men jammed down in the hold someone shouted, "We're sinking!"

Reyburn watched the bow of the boat dip as water started to pour into the hold. But this was not bluish-green sea water. This water was red—*blood* red. Reyburn particularly remembered the imperturbably calm manner in which the sailor who had helped him aboard took charge, keeping everyone from panicking, pointing out that there was another boat nearby, totally unruffled.

When he jumped into the water, Reyburn was astounded at how close they still were to the shoreline—no more than a few hundred feet. It had seemed like hours since they'd pushed the landing craft out of the sand.

Now came the ordeal of a repeat performance of getting into another boat. Fortunately, this time helping hands assisted him. Reyburn went to the top of the hold and dove head-first down into it—an even more impulsive, foolhardy measure than his earlier leap from the sea wall. Once again he seemed blessed by providence. Landing on his back after dropping seven feet, he was none the worse for wear. However, he no sooner began struggling to his feet than other men came tumbling down on top of him. Soon there was a massive pile-up of bodies trying to untangle themselves. Someone was lying across Reyburn's legs, making it impossible for him to move them. Then an injured soldier collapsed across his chest so that he could barely breathe. Bullets ricocheting off the deck above gave him some consolation; down in the hold he was at least sheltered.

Then the order "Lighten ship! There are too many aboard! We're sinking!" startled everyone out of their discomfort. Frantically men started jettisoning their helmets, throwing them through the opening above the hold into the sea, followed by water bottles, webbing, bayonets; then off came tunics, pants, boots, anything and everything being tossed into the water until most men were down to their underwear shorts.

Reyburn managed to disencumber himself and struggle to his feet. He looked out on deck. Men still in the water were clambering over the sides into the craft, aggravating the situation. The more people came aboard, the lower the boat sank, until the deck was almost flush with the water.

Similar to the earlier crisis when a young sailor had taken charge of a sinking ship, panic and disorder were again averted by the cheerful conduct of a youthful Royal Navy rating, still in his teens, who set an example by the cool manner in which he carried out his duties. His job was to save his boat and the men on it—who hardly relished the prospect of abandoning ship a second time—regardless of the danger of high explosive shells bursting around him. His behaviour inspired hope. Taking complete control, he calmed everybody down. Reyburn was not at a loss for words to express his admiration: "I don't know why, but watching that kid, seeing his courage and sheer guts, I felt I wanted to cry," he wrote.

The rating was standing at the end of the boat as a ship came into view heading toward the landing craft. It was a small wooden antiaircraft ship and as it came alongside, the Navy crewman tossed up a rope, allowing it to make fast so that the soldiers could scramble aboard.

As the vessel got under way, though they were shivering, soaked, and weary, many of them wounded, for the first time since getting off the beach the men felt somewhat at peace with the world and they started to relax. But not for long. Shortly after noon—a little over an hour since they had left the beach now a mile or so away—the antiaircraft ship pulled alongside a destroyer and the order came to climb aboard. Someone moaned. Not again. Nevertheless Reyburn and a lot of the others reached the deck of the ship with a sense of relief. Homeward bound at last!

But Reyburn's ordeal was far from over. He was about to live through the most harrowing, nerve-racking three hours he would ever experience.

The destroyer to which they had just transferred was HMS *Calpe*, the headquarters ship from which Major General Hamilton Roberts, in charge of the Dieppe raid, was directing the evacuation from his cabin. An officer directed Reyburn down a companionway to the ward room which, on reaching, he entered, so totally tuckered out he promptly fell on his face. A steward helped him into a large, comfortable, black leather armchair, stripped him of his wet uniform, and revived him with a couple of shots of brandy.

There were 15 all told in the room, including two wounded RN officers stretched out on blankets beside a couch. It was all very cozy and as the warmth of the Three-Star Hennessy began to take effect, Reyburn looked forward to being back in England in a couple of hours—two and a half at the most. But he was in for a rude awakening.

General Roberts had given instructions that the destroyer was to circle slowly (well within the range of the German shore batteries, dive-bombers, and fighter planes), picking up survivors, a mission that would last a frightening three hours.

Reyburn later admitted to me that he was scared every single minute. To begin with, down there in the ward room, an acute feeling of claustrophobia pervaded. All of the 15 knew that if the ship began to sink they wouldn't stand a chance of getting up on deck and jumping off before it went down. Unlike the hundreds up on deck, they were trapped. It was a totally different sensation from being in action out in the open where there was something to do, something to occupy the mind. Here, below decks, there was time to think, and lots of time—too much in fact—to be scared. The 15 could only sit there while the enemy shore batteries, dive-bombers, and fighters pounded and peppered the vessel with their artillery shells, bombs, machine guns, and cannon. They could hear the explosions and their own antiaircraft guns but could only visualize what was happening. That was the most terrifying sensation of all—that they were forced to experience what was happening through only one of the five senses—hearing. To them the battle was compressed into a series of sounds, each with its own horrific interpretation.

For example: the antiaircraft firing-control mechanism had been knocked out of action. As an alternative, to get the ship into position where the maximum amount of firepower could be directed at a dive-bomber, the engine-room telegraph had to be utilized. The control box of this mechanism was located in the ceiling of the ward room. Whenever it was turned on it emitted a series of ominous, clanging *rat-a-tats*. Every time that happened, the 15 knew it meant either that the ship was about to be dive-bombed or (wishful thinking) that the destroyer might be turning around to go home.

The latter was something that for the next three hours was just not going to happen. Instead they were forced to endure the periodic dive-bombing. First the booming 4.7-inch guns, the largest calibre aboard with the longest range, would go off. As the bomber got closer the single pom-pom would open up—*pom pom pom pom*. Then as the enemy plane came within open range, the clatter of the Orlekins could be heard. And finally, with the bomber right on top of the ship, the rattle of Lewis guns. Now everyone held their breath. An explosion—in the water. A miss, thank God! Then all the guns went off again but this time in reverse sequence as the bomber flew away—hopefully badly shot up.

The 15 knew that the bombers were diving at the ship broadside because the guns would open up on either the port or the starboard side. Each time, Reyburn involuntarily turned his back on the side of the attack then switched around to the other side as the plane passed overhead, not quite sure what he was achieving with this maneuver, an automatic reaction "like recoiling when a baseball comes flying at the netting in front of you."

Sometime around 1300 hours the noted American war correspondent Quentin Reynolds came into the ward room, having spent the past hour and a half on the bridge, and told Reyburn that the destroyer had moved in even closer to shore. He had been talking to General Roberts who said that he was not going to leave until every man who can be gotten off the beach *had* been gotten off.

Reynolds suggested they get something to eat. Since it had been nearly 12 hours since he'd had some supper on the transport crossing the Channel, Reyburn readily agreed. They helped themselves to some biscuits and cans of sardines and canned meat from a 24-hour ration box. Reyburn was lifting a biscuit with a sardine on it to his mouth when there was a terrific explosion that jolted the ship and sent his snack flying across the room. A shell from the shore batteries had struck the side of the ship and water began pouring through the door into the ward room. Reyburn's immediate reaction—his nerves were close to the breaking point—was one of doom. But his fears were soon dispelled when the ward room steward advised that the source of the gushing water was the sprinkler system, which had been punctured by a shell fragment.

As time passed and the shelling and dive-bombing continued unabated, there was no sign that HMS *Calpe* would be heading home, and the ward room soon began to fill with the wounded. Another destroyer nearby had been sunk and the headquarters ship had picked up the survivors, jamming it to the gills.

Finally, a little after 1300 hours, the ship's engineering officer appeared in the doorway to announce that the destroyer would be leaving for England immediately. It was met with snorts of derision. They'd heard that one before. But the EO assured everyone that this time it was for real. Suddenly there was a crash overhead from the ship's heavy 4.7-inch guns. A farewell blast to Dieppe.

Reyburn noted from the clock on the wall that the time was ten minutes after three (1510 hours), exactly 10 hours and 20 minutes from the time he had landed on the beach. Now he was in the last destroyer to leave, making him among the first into and the last out of Dieppe—and most probably the only war correspondent to hold that distinction.

But they were not yet out of danger. Because *Calpe* was the headquarters ship, Hamilton Roberts insisted that she lead all vessels from the battle zone. This had two consequences. It meant travelling at the speed of the slowest ship in the flotilla. And *Calpe* would pave the way through the minefields.

According to the Navigation Officer's estimates, it would be another nine hours before the ships reached port—midnight. Plenty of time for Reyburn to review and reflect upon all that had happened and might still happen. He had the material for the biggest story in his life, the biggest story of the war so far in fact. And yet ...

The events of the past ten hours were taking their toll. Reaction was setting in. Although the ship's Medical Officer had patched up the shrapnel wounds to his back, he was suffering from battle fatigue and reaching the end of his tether. He began to brood that he would never make it—never live to write his story. There was still the risk of being killed by a dive-bombing, a mine, a submarine torpedo. Later he penned his thoughts at the time: "I'm not ready to die. Right at this second I don't want to die, because this book isn't finished. When this book is finished, okay, I'll be ready to die ...

"That's what I kid myself ..."

He—and this was true of all those who survived Dieppe—had seen and been through too much, too often, in too short a span of time and it was taking its toll.

HMS *Calpe* did reach port at midnight. Reyburn's battle-dress uniform, hanging on a clothes peg on the ward room wall, was still so damp and soggy he left the ship wrapped in a blanket. He, Quentin Reynolds, and others were anxious to get back to their offices in London and file their story of the raid. But it was so late and they were so tired they checked into a local hotel and fell asleep the moment their heads hit the pillows. After breakfast next morning, they climbed into a Press car and drove up to town.

A pile of mail greeted Reyburn when he got back to his desk. He opened the envelope on top. The letter read: "Please find enclosed your income-tax assessment for the current year ..."

Postscript

In my opinion Wally Reyburn offered the most poignant assessment of the lesson learned from that costly operation in which the Canadians suffered 3367 casualties, 907 of them fatal, when he told me: "If we had tried to raid Europe without the Dieppe experience we would have been like a boxer rushing out of his corner and taking a wild slug at his opponent without first sizing him up with some sparring."

Chapter 10

LCT 6

Unlike the preceding narrative, which provides a fairly broad perspective of the Dieppe raid even though it revolves around the experiences of one individual, the following gives an isolated instance of a single platoon so beset by enemy fire and suffering such heavy casualties that their landing craft was trapped. Only the three tanks and a handful of men made it ashore. The tanks were quickly immobilized, and the men cut down unmercifully the moment they hit the beach.

"Another bloody exercise," someone grumbled disconsolately. It had been like that all the past spring into summer. On-again, off-again. But on the balmy, clear sunny afternoon of 18 August 1942, No. 3 Platoon of the Calgary Highlanders made its way by transport from battle-school to the dockyards at Portsmouth, Hampshire, on the south coast of England. Led by Lieutenant Jack Reynolds, the mortar group boarded LCT 6—officially Landing Craft Troop 163—squeezing themselves in among three tanks and a bulldozer along with some Canadian Army Service Corps types and the tank crews.

Once the landing craft, skippered by Lieutenant Thomas Andrew Cook of the Royal Navy, got under way, the men could see other LCTs equally packed with troops and equipment leaving port and they realized that this was probably the real thing at last. Reynolds confirmed it. Assembling his men around him, he announced, "We're on our way to France," then unfolded a map.

"This is the town of Dieppe. We'll land on this section of the beach, code-named 'Red,' just before sunrise." He then explained that the platoon would set up a post in the town's tobacco factory to provide covering fire for the infantry of the Essex Scottish Regiment and the Hamilton Light Infantry, as well as the tanks. Once the objectives had been attained, at 1100 hours the men were to rendezvous in a church to make their way back to the landing craft. Anyone failing to rendezvous or get off the beach would be on his own.

A slight aura of skepticism still pervaded even when the men were issued "tin hats." They'd been through the exercise before, only to see it turn into a false start. But as the twilight faded and darkness descended across the calm sea and other craft began to join the convoy, 237 vessels in all, carrying and escorting 6000 men, any doubts about the seriousness of the mission were soon dispelled. After a haversack meal of tin rations, the men tried to settle down in the evening chill—sleep eluding most everyone—cursing the army brass for failing to supply blankets on the premise that they were unnecessary for so short a voyage.

By 0200 hours the moon had gone down, and while some men had dozed off, albeit fretfully, the convoy had sailed safely through the mid-Channel corridor, cleared through the minefield by the minesweepers. Then suddenly, at 0345 hours, a star shell burst over the ships, bathing LCT 6 in daylight with dawn still over an hour away.

The advance section of the flotilla, carrying commandos, whose job was to destroy the coastal batteries before the landings took place, had unexpectedly encountered a German tanker being escorted by six E-boats. Both sides opened fire, seen and heard by the rest of the convoy. There was a tremendous explosion, and in the confusion one ship very nearly ran into the bow of LCT 6, forcing skipper Tom Cook to cut the engines and veer away to one side so violently it sent Private Red Anderson sprawling across the deck convinced that they would have to abandon ship—and he couldn't even swim! Philosophically, Sergeant Bert Pittaway pointed out that there were no life belts anyway—"Against marine regulations or something," he muttered bitterly, almost certain that they'd had it. They were also sure that the firing would have alerted the coastal defences.

In fact it had not. To the *Kriegsmarine*, it was just one more offshore nightly fracas. The firing died down as quickly as it had broken out and the German convoy, unaware that it had encountered an invasion force, sailed on toward its destination, ironically Dieppe! Once more darkness descended on the Allied convoy, which was slowly nearing the landing beaches, necessarily moving only as fast as the slowest ship in the flotilla.

Just before 0500 hours, by which time the commandos had already landed, Allied medium bombers and fighter-bombers came thundering overhead at low level to pummel the Dieppe coastal defences. Men in the troop carriers and the landing craft could hear the *whump, whump, whump* of the bomb explosions and could see flashes of gunfire from the aircraft and the antiaircraft batteries opposing them.

Tension mounted. Then, as dawn reddened the sky over Dieppe, the 4-inch guns from the destroyer escorts opened fire with an earsplitting blast. White smoke rose from the shoreline, indicating that the forward landing craft had already hit the beaches. Tom Cook put on full speed ahead. As LCT 6 surged forward, Sergeant Bill Lyster gave the order "mortar platoon load rifles." One of his men banged the butt of his rifle on the deck so solidly to steady himself, it triggered a bullet that whizzed past Lyster's ear. "You just missed my ass!" the shaken and angry sergeant hollered. "Save your ammunition for the beaches!"

As the shore batteries opened up against the landing craft, shrapnel splinters started to clang against the hull of LCT 6. Jack Reynolds, squatting beside Red Anderson, was sure the man had been hit; there was a long tear in the pants of his battle dress and a piece of metal between them. But though his leg felt numb from the shock of the explosion, Anderson didn't have even so much as a scratch. He calmly pocketed the fragment of shrapnel as a souvenir.

Now shells began landing inside the landing craft. As the boat neared the beach, Bert Pittaway shouted to those of his men helping the crew in the galley peeling potatoes to join the rest of the platoon and prepare to go ashore. They had barely left the galley when it received a direct hit that killed almost everyone inside. A close call for the mortar platoon! Then a mortar exploded on deck, knocking one of the army service corps men off his feet and into Anderson's lap. The man had been scared out of his wits and when he felt a gooey, sticky substance on his head he was sure he was going to bleed to death. But it wasn't blood he felt. It turned out to be only some potatoes that had been blown out of the galley and squashed into a pulp.

The next explosion came in the engine room, spewing smoke in all directions. From the acrid smell Pittaway was sure it was poison gas. With their respirators back in England at the battle school along with their blankets, he was certain that this time they'd really had it. But there was no real danger; the smoke had burst from a canister that had been jarred loose from its brackets and set off by the explosion.

The helmsman was so overcome by the fumes that he lost control of the craft, causing it to yaw to port. As if that wasn't bad enough, the engine room suddenly burst into flames. With the help of a few others, Anderson tried to play a hose on the fire, but it was shot so full of holes that most of the water sprayed back onto them instead of dousing the flames. Meanwhile, a new helmsman took over in the wheel house, but machine-gun fire mowed him down. Once again the LCT swerved to port, knocking a medic off his footing as he was climbing to reach a stretcher. He fell onto the point of a bayonet of an infantryman's rifle, which went right through his thigh. With the help of another medic, Bert Pittaway pulled it out.

Now a new helmsman took over the wheel, but he too was killed. A fourth man now took charge, who was luckier. He managed to steer the craft to approach the beach at a different angle away from the smokescreen caused by the wayward canister. It also allowed him to use another LCT, which was lying out of action broadside to the shore, as a shield to cross the last few yards to the beach before landing on the shale. The gates creaked open and the ramp slammed down, exposing Red Beach to full view. "Well named," Jack Reynolds said to himself as he took in the sight of the dead littering the beach after what had obviously been absolute carnage.

Some yards up the slope running from the shore was a barrier of heavy barbed wire and beyond it the sea wall guarding the promenade, at the back of which could be seen the twin spires of the Calgarys' objective, the tobacco factory. So near and yet so far.

Now the men in LCT 6 were at the mercy of enemy fire. A bullet ricocheted off one of the tanks and, if Bert Pittaway had not instinctively dodged to the left, it would have killed him—it merely grazed his shoulder patch. The man next to him was not so lucky; a shell struck his steel helmet with such force it knocked it off and blew part of his head away.

Now the vehicles got ready to move. First, the bulldozer rumbled down the ramp onto the shale, its driver exposed to enemy fire with no protection whatsoever. He had gone no more than 10 yards when a bullet killed him. Next, the turn of the tanks. The first tank turned to the left, then struck a mine which blew off its tracks, leaving it stranded. The second, after progressing a few yards from the ramp, turned right and was promptly halted by relentless machine-gun fire. The third tank made it through the barbed wire, but the wire sprang back into place instead of leaving an opening through which Jack Reynolds and his platoon had hoped to charge.

In any case, aboard LCT 6 it was chaos. The 30 men still aboard tried to help medics, most of whom had been injured themselves in their struggle to tend to the wounded. From the bridge Tom Cook did his best to maintain command of the situation, but most of his crew had either been killed or badly wounded, and the gunners of the antiaircraft pom-poms on either side of the vessel

had been taken out of action. When the tide started to go out and he gave the order, "All Ashore!" Reynolds became afraid he would lose all his men on the beach. He ordered the mortars to be set up on deck, instead. Easier said than done. The base plates wouldn't grip the sloping surface. He cursed the brass for not having the foresight to provide sandbags for just such an eventuality.

Cook pulled the craft away from the shore alongside the beached LCT that had acted as a shield on the run-in. It wasn't easy, because the steering mechanism had been damaged. A line was thrown across to take the stranded ship in tow, but that was soon shredded by enemy gunfire. The few survivors aboard swam over to LCT 6 and climbed in.

Cook steered the vessel into the central anchorage point out to sea where the large ships were directing operations, and which at this point were under severe air attack. LCT 6 joined in the battle with Lyster, Pittaway, and Anderson and the others taking turns at the pom-pom guns. Most of the wounded were now transferred to a hospital ship while a British naval crew came aboard to fix the steering mechanism. That done, the landing craft was ordered back to the beach to pick up men still there waiting to be rescued under cover of a heavy smokescreen laid down by Allied aircraft.

The Calgarians cringed at the very idea but, joined by smaller— and faster—assault boats, they plunged ahead in the face of relentless enemy fire pouring into the smokescreen, time and time again until they lost count. Finally, much to their relief, the order came to return to England. But not before they had scored a victory against the German Luftwaffe. On the last run-in to the beach, a Messerschmitt 109 fighter dived toward the landing craft, spraying cannon fire. Manning a pom-pom each, Lyster and Pittaway got the enemy plane squarely in their sights and saw their tracers plunging into its belly. Suddenly the fighter shuddered. Then, pouring smoke and flames, it plunged into the water. A cheer went up from all those aboard.

En route to Portsmouth, which they reached at dusk, they stopped to pick up a downed aviator. They had been away for just 24 hours. It was 24 hours they would never forget. After being interrogated and enduring such inane questions as "Did you see any planes?" and "What did the Germans look like?" they were given strong tots of rum and a hot meal. On their way back to their home base at Camp Halnaker, a private confided to Lyster anxiously, "Sergeant, I lost my rifle." Lyster was reassuring: "If that's all you lost, consider yourself damn lucky."

On arrival they were met by a very hostile assistant quartermaster who had been roused from his bed and demanded to know what they had done with their blankets. Pittaway blew his stack. Grabbing him by the throat he told him, "Listen buster, we've been to Dieppe and we're cold and tired and most unfriendly." That ended the discussion then and there.

"I thought you were going to hit him," Lyster said.

Very soon the camp treated them and their comrades with the respect they deserved. They had come through one of the most harrowing experiences in Canadian military history. Out of the 4936 Canadians who took part in "Operation Jubilee," the code name for the Dieppe raid, only 2210 returned to Great Britain, many of them wounded. Of the 3367 casualties, 907 lost their lives. When Lyster and Pittaway reached their quarters that night, Lyster said: "Bert, did you ever imagine we'd be back here all in one piece? We're damned lucky, all of us."

"Lucky be damned," was the reply. "It's a bloody miracle."

There was irony, too. Jack Reynolds later learned that the medic who had, while reaching for a stretcher, accidentally fallen on the bayonet that pierced his thighs, was facing a self-inflicted wound charge—a typical bureaucratic paper-pushers' balls-up. The Calgary platoon leader soon set the record straight by giving evidence in the man's defence and the charge was dropped.

Of LCT 6's adventure and contribution to the Dieppe raid, little is to be found in the history channels other than a terse statement that "after some initial difficulties the craft reached the beach ... 30 men failed to disembark and, after 15 minutes, the craft withdrew."

Chapter 11

Padre Rusty, the Front-Line Chaplain

The sun was high in the sky, and my shirt was soaked as I trudged on. Sweat ran down my face under the steel helmet I wore, and stung my eyes. I took it off and donned my khaki beret. As a truck passed headed towards the front, I slung helmet and pack over the tailgate. I never saw my helmet again, and I didn't wear one for the rest of the Italian campaign.

—Honorary Captain (The Reverend)
Russell Oliver "Rusty" Wilkes
Sicily, 10 July 1943

My introduction to the Canadian Chaplain Service in a combat zone came in May 1943 when our squadron was stationed at Redhill in Surrey. One sunny summer afternoon between sorties, the padre assigned to our squadron called a church service. We sat on the grass, our Spitfires parked nearby. For a group of young pilots far away from home and fresh from a foray into enemy territory, the sermon was not quite what we expected or wanted to hear, to say the least. It was more like a lecture. We were told that in all his experience as a padre in the armed forces, both in this war and the last, he had never encountered such vile, vulgar, obscene language from any unit—air force, army, or navy. This was our solace?

Fortunately, this sanctimonious individual was soon replaced by a padre similar to the subject of this story, Rusty Wilkes, the Hamilton-born cleric from Rainy River, Ontario, whose gallantry, care, and concern for his comrades under fire—not to mention his sense of humour—not only won him the admiration and respect of the men of his regiment (and earned him the Military Cross), but also made him a legend throughout the Canadian Chaplain Service.

When Russell Oliver Wilkes was born on 28 June 1905, Canada was a nation of churchgoers. Because his Anglican parents were poor, they were constantly on the move, looking for work from one place to another. Rusty gained early choir—and sports—experience at a variety of parishes.

He was not a dedicated student, and left school at age 16 to work at a printing firm, where his father was also employed. But Wilkes was attracted to the militia, and signed up as a reserve soldier.

During the immediate period following the Great War, the unions, particularly in the printing trade, were gaining strength and created a wide gulf between labour and management. Young Wilkes' disenchantment with his job and the labour strife grew. Still committed to the church, he went into pastoral care and took a job as a lay preacher in the Parry Sound area, determined to study theology.

In 1925 he attended Wycliffe College at the University of Toronto and completed his final year at the University of Saskatchewan's Immanuel College. During the summers he practised lay ministry in the Keewatin district on the Ontario-Manitoba border.

The summer after the stock market crash in 1929, Rusty Wilkes, along with hundreds of others of the unemployed, volunteered to help fight the forest fires raging near Winnipeg. It was there that he met Ethel McKenzie. The following year, after graduation and ordination as a deacon of the Anglican Church, he returned to the Diocese of Keewatin to take up his ministry, with headquarters in Rainy River. On 29 September 1931, he and Ethel McKenzie were married. Wilkes subsequently took up duties at Emerson on the Manitoba-Minnesota border. Their first daughter, Diane, was born two years later, only five days after Adolf Hitler became Reichschancellor of Germany on 30 January 1933. In 1935 the Wilkeses moved to Rusty's former stamping grounds of Rainy River. By this time he sensed that war was inevitable and that serving in the military was his calling.

In September 1939, shortly after World War II broke out, Ethel gave birth to a second daughter. On the 10th of the month, the date Canada declared war on Germany, Wilkes wrote a letter to the Minister of National Defence offering his services as an army chaplain. It was not until over eight months later, however, on 30 May 1940, at which time the evacuation of the British Expeditionary Force from Dunkirk had got under way, that he received a letter telling him to report for a medical examination at Fort Osborne Barracks in Winnipeg, Manitoba. This was the start of a career that he had been cut out for.

On Friday, 1 June 1940, he passed his medical exam with flying colours, signed the necessary papers, and recited the oath of allegiance to become enlisted and commissioned (as Honorary Captain Wilkes) in the Canadian army, without a single minute wasted in training. Ten days later he boarded a train for Montreal and embarked aboard the *Europa*, a Danish cargo ship designed to carry passengers in style. The draft of 50 men set sail in luxury.

The 23-day trip across the Atlantic ended at Liverpool, where the draft entrained for Aldershot, the depot to which arrivals were sent for sorting out. Wilkes reported to No. 5 General Hospital Unit, which was established on the estate of Lord and Lady Astor on the Thames at Cliveden in Buckinghamshire, 12 miles west of London.

Patients at the hospital were not battle casualties, because the Canadian army would not see action for another two years, in the raid on Dieppe. Mostly there were training injuries and a variety of illnesses and infections—including venereal disease. VD was so common that the commanding officer set up a separate VD ward;

the domineering, indomitable, irascible Lady Astor took vociferous exception to this. To mollify Lady Astor, the colonel had a sign reading "ISOLATION" mounted over the door. This was not to be Wilkes' last experience with the Canadian army's vicissitudes regarding venereal disease, however.

After a month of duty at the hospital, Wilkes was posted to the Royal Canadian Regiment (RCR) at Glove Wood on the North Downs which, although the majority of its troops were Protestants, had a Catholic padre. His days of real soldiering were about to begin.

The RCR formed part of the 1st Infantry Brigade of the First Canadian Division that comprised three regiments, the other two battalions being the Hastings and Prince Edward Regiment and the 48th Highlanders of Toronto. The First Division had been in England for six months and its early arrivals, notably the RCR, had arrived eight months earlier in December 1939.

With the fall of France—the armistice was signed on 22 June 1940—an invasion of Britain seemed imminent, the main target being the south coast between Portsmouth and Gravesend. The First Division was deployed in the southern counties of Sussex and Surrey. At first the RCR occupied a defensive position around Farnham, then later moved to Glove Wood, where it had been stationed for three weeks by the time Rusty Wilkes joined the regiment in August.

His introduction to the commanding officer, the stern Lieutenant Colonel Vern Hodson, a World War I veteran, was not one he would soon forget. Wilkes had dressed in his best service uniform for the meeting, to make a favourable impression. It didn't. He was sternly advised that whipcord was not acceptable in the RCR and was told to buy a worsted uniform to replace it. The regiment's newest chaplain was off to an unsteady start and quickly learned that despite hard living conditions under canvas, the RCR remained an outfit whose spit and polish extended to dress, discipline, and the ceremonial.

But Wilkes could not abide this pretentiousness as it applied to the regular compulsory church parade. Nor could he disguise his disdain for it. Each company would parade for the padre's arrival in full battle order, steel helmet, small pack, respirator, water bottle, webbing, rifle, and bayonet. Before the troops reached the church they were inspected, drilled, and shouted at by the sergeant majors—generally "buggered about."

One soldier got so fed up with this type of compulsory worship that he asked Wilkes to change his religion to the Jewish faith, which would exempt him from church parades. This put Wilkes somewhat on the spot; it wasn't an acceptable reason for changing religions. With characteristic Solomonic wisdom he explained that there were certain formalities that the man would have to undergo, if they had not already been carried out. In short, circumcision. The soldier leapt to his feet and, hand cupped protectively over his crotch, rushed out.

But it was these kinds of incidents that brought things to a head for Wilkes and compelled him to approach Colonel Hodson to request that church parades be made voluntary; while he did not advocate slackness in discipline, he resented the perversion of religion for its purposes. This was to be his first brush with authority, but far from his last.

When Wilkes presented his case to the commanding officer with the recommendation the church parades be made voluntary and the soldiers be allowed to attend in battle dress but not battle order and rifles, it drew a scowl from the old warrior. "Voluntary church parades?" he asked as if thunderstruck. "I've never heard of such a thing! And no guns? The men must be prepared for an emergency at all times!"

Wilkes argued that the troops were at far less risk at a half-hour church service than they were at a two-hour movie in the recreation marquee. He added: "I don't think much of men praising God by numbers." Hodson finally agreed, and at the next church parade Wilkes announced to his congregation that future services would be voluntary with the condition that if attendance dropped too much he would make the parades compulsory again.

But attendance remained high, though not entirely due to religious devotion. The officers and sergeant majors saw to it that soldiers who weren't attending church services were assigned unpleasant jobs such as garbage detail or kitchen or latrine duty.

On September 25 the RCR moved to winter quarters in Reigate, Surrey, and were billeted in civilian accommodations. One evening in the mess tent shortly before this occurred, Colonel Hodson approached Wilkes and handed him a pair of cotton shoulder flashes. Thanking the CO, as he walked away Wilkes held up the royal blue flashes with the black edging that bore the words in amber yellow thread "The Royal Canadian Regiment." It was the highest compliment he could have been paid. Although the Canadian Chaplain Service had its own distinctive ensign, it was the RCR flashes that Wilkes wore with pride, deeply honoured that, as an "outsider," he had been accepted into the regimental family.

In October, when the imminent danger of a German invasion had passed (Hitler cancelled all plans publicly on the 12th of the month), Vern Hodson was replaced by Lieutenant Colonel Murray Green, another Great War veteran, who had been the regimental CO in peacetime. Then, in early December, the 1st Brigade moved to Brighton, replacing the 2nd Brigade which was posted to Aldershot. The RCR took over some estates, hotels, and boarding schools closed for the duration. It was sheer luxury—too good to last. On the 29th of the month the Essex Scottish Regiment from Windsor took over and the RCR returned to Reigate.

When Green assumed command of the regiment, Major Eric Snow remained as second in command. Snow shrewdly calculated that he could use the padre to fill two important posts. He appointed Wilkes as canteen officer and, recognizing his interest in athletics, as regimental sports officer as well. Wilkes was delighted because the duties brought him in close contact with the men and provided an opportunity to maintain a high level of morale. This would become increasingly important as the period of absence from their homes and families lengthened.

Wilkes found that the best method of dealing with the numerous problems prevalent among young soldiers far from home was through the weekly "padre's hour," instituted by the First Division and later introduced as a policy throughout the Canadian army. Wilkes considered these sessions to be one of the most important factors in maintaining high morale. They gave the men a chance to get a lot of beefs, concerns, and doubts off their chests. To conduct them required considerable patience, understanding, and tact. It also called for sound judgment in dealing with, and solving, problems and delicate situations. A padre had access to various social services, and he could cut through red tape without concern for chain of command, which allowed him to act as a confidant rather than a superior of officer rank. The need for mature wisdom was recognized throughout the Chaplain Service: Padres had to be at least 30 years of age.

Infidelity was high on the list of problems for which the married men in the regiment sought Padre Wilkes' advice. In one case a soldier with six children wanted to divorce his wife because he had got an English girl pregnant and wanted to do "the honourable thing." Wilkes dissuaded him, reasoning that it was as much the girl's fault as his own and was certainly not sufficient reason to disrupt a large family.

Another soldier requested that Wilkes arrange for him to return to Canada because he learned his wife had been cheating on him. When the padre inquired as to just what he would do when he got home he replied, "I'll break her bloody neck." The request was denied.

Some problems solved themselves without the chaplain's help. One day Wilkes received a letter from a British WAC officer alleging that an RCR soldier was responsible for the pregnancy of one of her girls. This was a ticklish situation—Anglo-Canadian relations were on the line. Wilkes assured the WAC lieutenant that he would look into the matter. Much to his relief, and the amusement of his fellow officers, sometime later he received a telegram that read "MARY HAD MISCARRIAGE LAST NIGHT STOP THANKS FOR YOUR HELP."

In April 1941, the RCR moved to Chipstead, 15 miles east of Reigate. That July, Murray Green left the regiment to be replaced by his second-in-command Eric Snow. That was not the only change for the RCR. By this time the Canadian troops in England had become fed up with traditional routine training—route marches, digging trenches, and firing range practice had become monotonous. Moreover, based on First World War thinking, such exercises were atrociously out of step with modern combat requirements.

But the lessons of the German Blitzkrieg had not been lost on the British Imperial General Staff. "Battle drill" had been introduced into the army, a new, aggressive approach to warfare tailored to invading the continent followed up by a swift advance. It was particularly well suited to the Canadian soldier who had grown up playing team sports with emphasis on initiative. Battle drill concentrated on individual skills, the techniques of surprise and camouflage, maneuvers in small groups—platoons and sections—and tactics that allowed flexibility and initiative on the part of the individual.

Rifle sections ran obstacle courses and soldiers had to help each other scale walls and cross ditches. Each soldier learned his job and the part he would play. As the training progressed, to simulate actual combat conditions, the troops practised making their way through smoke and barbed wire while Bren and Vickers machine guns fired live ammunition over their heads. On a dead run, soldiers fired at figure targets popping up from trenches in their path and bayoneted straw dummies.

Route marches were adapted to the new-style battle training. A fitness nut, new CO Eric Snow gradually lengthened the marches to 50 miles and more. With the constant danger of air attack in combat, the troops no longer marched in step in columns of three. Rifle sections of seven or eight men moved in "ack-ack" (antiaircraft) formation on either side of the road at intervals of five yards.

In November the regiment moved again, this time to Selsey in Sussex on the south coast. One day in mid-December, Wilkes was on his way to London with a driver of an eight-hundredweight, an open-cab vehicle about the size of a jeep, to pick up canteen supplies. On a winding road north of Chichester it collided with a sixty-hundredweight lorry head on. Wilkes was thrown from the open cab and knocked unconscious as he skidded along the road for 40 yards. Several of his ribs were broken and his entire right side had been scraped raw. He woke up in the hospital swathed in bandages and with his chest taped. Although it was his closest call to being killed of the entire war, he was lucky at that; his driver later died of injuries.

After recuperating at the Canadian Officers' Convalescent Home at Garnoms Castle in Herefordshire, Wilkes returned to duty in mid-January 1942, by which time the regiment had been moved to Bognor Regis, farther west along the Sussex coast, where the officers' mess had been set up in the Russell Hotel. Then in the spring the RCR moved again, to Arundel Park 10 miles inland. Training now intensified; in May a massive 11-day exercise, TIGER, was conducted on a divisional scale in Kent and Sussex.

On August 5, the RCR moved again, this time to Possingworth Park on Waldon Downs south of Tunbridge Wells. The regiment's position at Arundel had been taken over by the Royal Hamilton Light Infantry (RHLI), a Second Canadian Division regiment that had not taken part in TIGER. The reason became clear exactly two weeks later.

Late in the afternoon of August 19, rumours of disaster on a raid at Dieppe on the French coast by the Second Division began to circulate. Wilkes' thoughts immediately flashed to his cousin Herb Poag, a captain with the RHLI, and John Foote, the regimental padre with whom he had sailed to England two years earlier. Wilkes hitched a ride to Newhaven, where he learned the RHLI had embarked, to seek them out on their return. Wilkes rushed among the soldiers asking them if they had seen Captain Poag or Padre Foote. But none would speak; the men simply looked up, shook their heads, and walked on. Later he learned that his cousin Herb had been killed and that John Foote, who had boarded a landing craft to take him back to England, opted instead to stay behind and be taken prisoner to be with his troops, an action that earned him the Victoria Cross. He would later tell me in an interview: "My job as padre was to stay with my men, not to go home."

In mid-December the regiment moved to Dukes Camp near the village of Inveraray on the rugged west coast of Scotland. Here the troops were billeted in Nissen huts and engaged in practising amphibious "Combined Operations" exercises. Clearly something was in the wind.

The first full-scale exercise—aptly named NOEL I—took place on Christmas Eve 1942. The troops embarked on landing craft in pouring rain. The boats set out in a choppy sea then ran into shore at Loch Fyne. Some of the crews manning the craft dropped the ramps down too soon, and the men, already drenched by rain, had to storm ashore, waist deep in freezing water.

It also put a chill on celebrating the Yuletide. When Wilkes, who had accompanied the men on the exercise, conducted a brief Christmas service the next morning, only a handful attended; the rest of the troops were asleep.

On the next exercise, NOEL II, held on December 27, Wilkes experienced the irony of taking over command of a company even though, technically, to conform to the rules of war, as a chaplain he could not carry arms or be directly involved in operations against the enemy. But for this exercise, Eric Snow ruled there would be no exceptions; he wanted everyone at headquarters to gain battle leadership experience. So when two of the company commanders were ruled *hors de combat* by the umpires, noncombatants Wilkes and the dental officer took charge.

On New Year's Eve, 1943, the amphibious training from Dukes Camp completed, the regiment entrained to return to

Possingworth Park south of Tunbridge Wells in the south of England. Though no one in the outfit knew it, General McNaughton, commander of First Division, had already decided that the division would be Canada's contribution to the invasion of southern Europe once the North African campaign concluded.

At the end of February, Eric Snow was replaced as CO of the RCR by Ralph Crowe, a seasoned veteran who had served with the British Army in India. He had been transferred from the Hastings and Prince Edward Regiment—the "Hasty P's." Upon assuming command, he assembled all of the officers and stressed the need to treat the men as individuals; that they weren't just bodies in battle dress. Crowe's second-in-command was Billy Pope, who, like his superior, was fated to die in battle.

By the end of April, when the regiment had moved back to Dukes Camp at Inveraray, the campaign in North Africa was drawing to a close. It was obvious that the next step would be an assault somewhere in the northern Mediterranean. When the regiment resumed amphibious operation exercises, the men had some idea why. On May 7, the regiment boarded a troop train south to the area of Cumnock 15 miles inland from Ayr on the firth of Clyde. Twelve days later the regiment entrained for Gourock further up the Clyde, where it embarked on the two-funnelled Dutch steamer *Marnix Van Sint Aldegond* from which practice landings were made, lowering the landing craft, then racing in to shore.

On the night of June 28, the vessel eased into a convoy down the Clyde and out to sea. The RCR was finally off to war; where, no one in the regiment knew. But stencilled on all kits, including the chaplain's paraphernalia, was the ominous code-name CASKET.

On the first day at sea, cotton drill shorts and brush shirts were issued, confirming that the destination was in the south. Then, on the afternoon of Dominion Day, July 1, Crowe gathered his officers and sergeant majors in the ship's dining room to announce from sealed orders, unopened until that morning, that they would be forming part of a force to invade Sicily known as Operation HUSKY.

The overall plan called for a combined Anglo-American assault by Western Task Force troops of General George Patton's 7th U.S. Army and an Eastern Force of General Bernard Montgomery's British 8th Army, which had defeated Rommel's Afrika Korps in the Libyan desert, with the 13 Corps on the right and the 30th on the left, of which First Canadian Division was to be the left-hand formation at the tip of the west side of the Pachino Peninsula. The 1st Brigade was to land on the right of the division on the shores of the Cape Paserio Peninsula, eliminate the Italian gun battery at Maucini, and then take the airfield beyond the town of Pachino. The RCR would be on the brigade's right.

When the information was passed on down the ranks, it created great excitement and distracted the troops from their discomfort below decks, with hammocks slung among pipes in every corner of the hold. Long hours were spent going over aerial reconnaissance maps, practising every detail of the first objectives to be reached in the assault.

Once through the straits of Gibraltar, the convoy sailed eastward to rendezvous off the coast of Sicily with other convoys carrying British and American troops, equipment, and supplies from North Africa, forming the largest armada assembled in the history of the world. It so awed Wilkes that it provided inspiration for the text of the sermon he preached on July 9, the evening of the landing, invoking Mark 4: 35–41, in which Jesus is said to have entered into a ship that was accompanied with "other little ships." When a storm arose He quelled the waves and rebuked those with Him for the lack of faith marked at first by their fear, then by their incredulity. Wilkes told his congregation of some 30 men crowded into the lounge that in imitation of Him they were to quell a storm and each one of them were like those "other little ships," bearing within them spiritual ammunition, a source of strength to prevail in a just war.

It was a prescient sermon. By 1500 hours, when over 1000 men had taken communion, a violent gale that had been raging most of the day was causing some concern that the landings might have to be delayed. But as Wilkes would state later: "The Gospel parallel seemed to hold as the howling wind abated that evening and a signal was received confirming the invasion for the following morning according to plan."

At 2230 hours, Ralph Crowe called his officers together for a last-minute briefing confirming instructions and asked if there were any questions. There were none, so he turned to Wilkes and said: "Perhaps we should offer a prayer. Would you lead us, Padre?" He took from his pocket a small book entitled *Divine Service Book for the Armed Forces* and indicated the text he would like read. Wilkes complied.

Into thy hands, O Lord, we commend ourselves and all we love, beseeching thee to keep us under the shadow of thy wings. Drive far from us ever in life and death, that whether we wake or sleep we may live together with thee. Through Jesus Christ our Lord. Amen.

At 2300 hours the *Marnix* reached anchorage, and for the first time since leaving Scotland the engines were silent. Hundreds of Allied aircraft thundered overhead; the sound combined with the roar of naval guns to soften up the enemy defences. Wilkes lay down, fully clothed, to take a nap.

He awoke after midnight when disembarkation from the RCR troopship should have been under way. But while ships all round them disgorged their cargoes of men and machines, a sandbar had been discovered 100 yards from the brigade's landing beach. It was feared that the landing craft from the *Marnix* would run aground. Landing Craft Tanks (LCTs) were sent for from Malta carrying DUKWs, large, amphibious, all-wheel-drive vehicles that could carry 50 men.

By 0200 hours they arrived and troops began to load into the DUKWs, and by dawn two hours later the first two companies were ashore in front of the sleepy little town of Pachino, and had cleared Maucini by 0700 hours. Two hours later the forward units were closing in on the airfield and captured a gun battery and four 6-inch guns beyond, taking 130 Italian prisoners.

By the time Wilkes got ashore, it was broad daylight. Arriving by DUKW he didn't even get his feet wet. After the rugged exercises in Scotland the invasion of Sicily seemed like a piece of cake, though far from comfortable. As he trudged inland it was hot and dusty and he soon discarded his pack and helmet.

Late in the afternoon he reached his designated destination behind the forward position just north and west of the airfield where troops were digging slit trenches and opening their rations for their first meal of the day. Wilkes went into the outbuilding in which the RCR medical officer, Captain Jack Heller, had set up a regimental aid post (RAP) to get cool and render what assistance he could in tending to the casualties that were starting to arrive. Except for three battle fatalities they were all walking wounded, sustained by "D" Company while attacking the airstrip.

During the next four days the regiment advanced steadily through Rosolini, Ragusa, and finally Giarrantana, where the troops bivouacked for the night—most of the men had had no more than eight hours' sleep since hitting the beach. Resistance was weak; the Italian troops surrendered more with a sense of relief than of defeat.

On one occasion when the MO scouted ahead for a suitable RAP spot, Wilkes followed in trucks with the rest of the medical staff. They had stopped at a village to rest when an Italian rushed up, gesticulating wildly and pointing to a house down the street. Wilkes went forward to investigate, and a dozen Italian soldiers came out holding their rifles over their heads in surrender. Wilkes took them prisoner, waiting until a rear echelon arrived to turn them over. He mused that he could just as easily have told them to start walking to the rear on their own. It wasn't really their war and they seemed to want no part of it.

Shortly afterwards General Montgomery arrived, standing in the back of his car chatting briefly in clipped tones, thanking and praising the men for the job they were doing. Wilkes was struck with "Monty's" strong, warm personality as a leader. A little later the RCR ran into his famous "Desert Rats," who were passing through cheerfully asking: "Hullo Canada! How did you leave our wives at home?"

The advance continued mostly uphill in open country through Vizzini with the Hasty P's in the vanguard. At Grammichele they met the first real resistance when they encountered the guns and tanks of the vaunted Hermann Goering Division.

At Valguarnera, the 15th Division Panzer Grenadiers held positions overlooking the junction where the road into town branches off from the main highway to Enna. The 1st Brigade was ordered to take the town while the 3rd Brigade followed the highway. On the night of July 17, the Hasty P's put up a tough fight to take the town but failed. The RCR were called forward, moving along goat trails to within half a mile of the town.

At 1030 hours, when Ralph Crowe launched the attack, Wilkes was standing on a knoll west of the town with the CO and his second-in-command Billy Pope. Pope and Crowe were discussing their ammunition situation when a soldier came up from a rifle section on the slope south of the position and told them a German tank was blocking the direction the assaulting companies were to follow. Pope immediately procured a PIAT (Projectile Infantry Anti-Tank) gun, and with two other soldiers made his way down the hill, dodging from cover to cover until they were out of sight. Suddenly there was a rattle of machine-gun fire. It was later learned that when the tank crew spotted the trio, the tank opened fire, killing all three. Pope became the first RCR officer lost in battle.

Now the attack stalled, the assaulting companies taking what cover they could, but ammunition was at a premium. Because mobile radios at this time were unreliable, there was no communication with headquarters. Crowe realized they could not hold out much longer without fresh supplies. He asked Wilkes to take a message, which he scribbled hastily, back to HQ.

The padre set off along a goat trail in full view of the enemy; there was no alternative. The Germans began lobbing mortars at the lone running figure. One landed to the right of him, then as he dived to the ground, another exploded on his left. They had him bracketed. Still another landed a mere 10 feet away but mercifully failed to go off. Wilkes scrambled to his feet and began sprinting up a slope in front of "D" Company's position, as "D" Company had been placed in reserve. Pausing only long enough to catch his breath, he continued on. Two hours later he finally reached the rear HQ, turning Crowe's message over to the regimental adjutant.

Wasting no time, the adjutant soon had a column of a dozen men loaded down with ammunition as well as water cans and rations. In late afternoon, with Wilkes guiding them, they set off along a mule track for the forward position, which they reached by nightfall. Of Wilkes' bravery, the noted historian Strome Galloway, who would later lead the RCR in battle, told me "a strictly noncombatant member of our battalion rushed into the fray and was on the objective simultaneously with Lt. Col. Crowe's command group. When a Winnipeg newspaper interviewed a Third Division officer who was in Sicily as an observer, the headline read 'THE BRAVEST MAN I EVER MET DIDN'T CARRY A GUN.'"

Brigadier Howard Graham, commander of the 1st Brigade, did not feel quite the same way. He had Ralph Crowe hauled up on the carpet and sharply rebuked him for having a chaplain up with the forward elements where he had no business being. The irony to the whole affair was that when, during Wilkes' absence, the RCR got bogged down waiting for fresh supplies, the 48th Highlanders advanced on the flank and after a brief battle the Germans pulled out of Valguarnera leaving the Canadians free to enter the town without a shot being fired.

At midnight on July 19, the division continued its advance north, passing east of Enna, which fell to the Americans. Then, after a brief fight, Monte Assaro was taken while the Second Division captured Leonforte. The next objective was Agira, the key to the German defences, which had been withdrawing to the foot of Mount Etna which, from high ground, could be seen 40 miles away to the east.

On July 22, Wilkes and "A.J." Barker, the battalion's Roman Catholic chaplain, accompanied the two assault companies on foot from a start line seven miles to the west of Agira. The platoon crossed a field in front of the village in an extended line, five yards between each man. The Germans held their fire until the last minute, then all hell broke loose as they opened up with machine guns and mortars. As Wilkes dived to the ground, the assault sections closed in on the enemy on the double. Wilkes picked himself up and started forward on the run in a crouch as bullets whizzed past him. Men were dropping left and right while stretcher-bearers went coolly about their work carrying the wounded from the battlefield.

As Wilkes ran forward he tripped on a root and went sprawling. Barker, just ahead of him, looked back, laughed uproariously, and told him that he had plowed a better furrow with his nose than any farmer; then he helped him to his feet. The pair continued on. As they neared the edge of the town, Wilkes found a soldier with a badly wounded shoulder. Pulling him behind a mound of earth, he slapped on a shell dressing he always carried with him in the combat zone and helped him to the edge of the road into Nissoria where he could be picked up by ambulance. By this time the assault had been halted outside the town, and Wilkes and Barker made their way to the RAP to help Jack Heller with the wounded.

It was during this attack that the commanding officer, Ralph Crowe, lost his life. He had lost contact with the forward companies—the mobile radios could not receive or transmit properly in the hilly terrain—so he decided to set out forward with a small party and see for himself. He had just crested a hill when he walked right into the line of fire of an enemy machine-gun post; he and two signallers were killed outright. Crowe was replaced temporarily by Tommy Powers.

That night, the forward companies remained outside Agira in a defensive role and were withdrawn the following day. The attempted assault had cost the regiment 45 officers and men. The Hasty P's and the 48th Highlanders tried their luck with no better result and the town finally fell to the Second Division, clearing the way to Regalbuto. From there, after a period of severe fighting, the RCR was withdrawn on the night of August 1. Next morning the town was found to be deserted, as the Germans were withdrawing to the mainland.

A week later First Division went into army reserve; the RCR enjoyed a three-week rest at Militello in preparation for the assault on Italy. At this time the new CO, Lieutenant Dan Spry, arrived, and Wilkes received word that he had been awarded the Military Cross for actions in which, strictly according to regulations, he should never even have taken part.

On 1 September 1943, exactly four years after the Germans had invaded Poland, the RCR was on the move to embark on landing craft that would take them across the strait of Messina to the Italian mainland, a voyage of some 17 miles. Their objective was to pass through the 3rd Brigade, which had landed earlier at Reggio di Calabria, and take the airfield beyond the town. But by the time they landed on September 3 the objective had already been taken. Italians were surrendering in droves after the fall of Mussolini and the Germans had withdrawn north to the Gulf of Salerno where they correctly guessed the main landings would take place—by General Mark Clark's 5th U.S. Army. Three days later 1st Brigade was climbing north, up 3000 feet into the Calabrian highlands.

During September, first Division met virtually no resistance; the Germans kept withdrawing as the troops drove or marched through town after town. Italy surrendered on September 8, and by then the division had swung east and was headed north along the Ionian coast toward Catanzaro and the Gulf of Taranto. A week later the 3rd Brigade moved inland as part of the strategy to link the British 8th Army with the American 5th and consolidate a line across the waist of Italy to face 18 German divisions (as opposed to the 4 the enemy had had in Sicily). But 1st Brigade continued its trek north along the coast.

In their spare time, Wilkes and his colleague A.J. Barker toured the countryside in a Volkswagen, but although they visited areas steeped in history such as Taranto, where the early Spartans had settled and Archytas, the philosopher, had taught, they failed to absorb the culture. Wilkes admitted that while he looked at a lot, he really *saw* very little. Soldiers busy making history themselves were left little time to grasp the meaning of the past.

On one of their reconnaissances they strayed from the regimental route onto a side road that led them into a village square. As they checked the map to get their bearings, they were besieged by a cheering crowd of Italian peasants swarming from their houses. They had quite by accident liberated the town.

By the end of September, the joyriding was over. The Germans were fighting a stiff rearguard action while withdrawing to their Winter Line, bisecting the peninsula along the Sangro and Garigliano Rivers. Now, once again, the regiment began to suffer casualties.

Burial of the dead was makeshift by later standards. Initially graves were dug and last rites administered where the soldiers fell. Later the Graves Registration Section (GRS) from divisional headquarters would come forward after an engagement and evacuate the dead for burial in permanent military cemeteries.

At the time the army was still struggling with the problem of identification and location of the dead. It had yet to issue fingerprint kits, for example. Except when darkness or the heat of battle prevented it, Wilkes had the burial detail wrap each body in a blanket and dig a separate grave. Before doing so he would search the clothing of a corpse and send the contents—worn wallet, creased pictures, etc.—back to battalion headquarters. He was careful to destroy pictures of girlfriends in case a man was married, engaged, or otherwise betrothed to a girl at home, in which case the photo could only add to a family's grief. At the same time he would remove the identification tags, then record in his field message pad the name, service particulars, and exact location of the burial place—identified, for the benefit of the GRS, by a crude white wooden cross, a supply of which he always carried in his jeep.

The GRS insisted that every means be exhausted to identify the dead. On one occasion Wilkes found this impossible; a body brought back from the field was mangled beyond recognition. Wilkes vainly searched the shreds of clothing imbedded in the torn flesh. There wasn't a clue as to the corpse's identity. After burial he identified it as an "unknown soldier."

But the bureaucratic GRS staff didn't accept this. Two weeks went by and Wilkes received a curt signal that there was no such thing as an "unknown soldier." He was ordered to take fingerprints with the kit he had only just received, and have the medical officer take dental impressions. In the pouring rain, he and Jack Heller had a detail dig up the corpse, which they laid out in the mud. Wilkes flattened out the grey, wrinkled fingers and took prints. But Heller couldn't get the jaws open. So, while Heller mixed the plaster compound to take his impressions, Wilkes cut away the lower jaw with his clasp knife—a grisly desecration he always regretted having to perform.

However, Wilkes recognized that there was sometimes ironic comic relief to such macabre episodes. In late September, when the regiment was marching on Motta, the troops came across the wreckage of a downed RAF aircraft. The carnage was frightful, with bits of body scattered about. Wilkes found a couple of arms so mangled he couldn't tell whether they were right and left, two lefts, or two rights. In his report he wrote that he had buried an "unknown airman or airmen." Back came a bulletin from the GRS sarcastically suggesting that he couldn't tell one body from two. He replied that if the RAF had a three-armed airman, that was probably whom he had buried.

On December 16, on the eve of the bitter struggle for Ortona when the regiment was resting just west of San Leonardo, Billy Mathews, fresh from a training command in Canada, arrived to take over from Dan Spry who had been given command of 1st Brigade. It was a poor choice. Mathews was a stickler for discipline and immediately put his stamp on the regiment by calling a battalion parade at which he announced that there would be no more slackness, no more slovenliness. Spit and polish, and clean-shaven daily. The reason so many men had been killed, he stated imperiously, was because they were not alert.

That sort of language did not sit well, coming from one who had no battle experience to a group of seasoned combat veterans, most of whom had been living in fear and danger for six months, and they resented it.

In protest, Wilkes went for two or three days without shaving, making sure that Mathews would notice in the hope that by challenging his authority the opportunity might arise to take issue with his attitude. But Mathews—perhaps wisely—refused to be intimidated or rise to the occasion.

On the following night, Dan Spry issued operation orders to take Ortona. The objective was for first Division, now under the command of Major General Chris Vokes, to skirt the city to the west and cut the highway north of it and seize the Ortona-Orsogna crossroad junction. On the morning of December 18, the regiment moved out. Wilkes, who had caught a touch of jaundice, stayed behind at the RAP. It was just as well: his help with the wounded would soon be needed. By noon the regiment had moved into a death trap officially called The Gully, a long, deep depression just south of the Ortona-Orsogna road and a highly defended position where the fighting was ferocious. All three brigades of the division being heavily engaged, the casualties mounted.

During the fighting Billy Mathews was wounded in the arm by a German sniper's bullet. He may have got off on the wrong foot with the officers and men of his regiment, but there was no denying his bravery. He continued to command after he had been wounded and would only consent to being evacuated next day at his officers' insistence. Ian Hodson, son of Vern, a former CO, assumed command, but only briefly. Laid low by jaundice and malaria, he had to turn his command over to Strome Galloway the following day, December 20. By this time, the crossroads objective had been taken and the regiment assumed a defensive stance.

Wilkes' task of identifying the dead and readying them for burial—50 graves had to be dug—took a bizarre turn. Processing had to be handled in full view of the troops marching by on their way to the final phase of the battle on December 23.

Christmas Day was a sad one for the RCR. On that day, and on its eve, 11 men were killed and 44 wounded. Wilkes did manage to get around to the companies to conduct Christmas services for those not on duty or in combat. By December 29, the battle for the city was coming to an end. The 1st Brigade was relieved by the 3rd and the RCR took time out to celebrate Christmas on New Year's Day, 1944.

As the new year got under way, the regiment continued to advance, occupying the San Tomasso and San Nicola area west of Ortona. On February 1, the 1st Brigade was pulled out of the line for a rest, the RCR to the town of San Vito Chieteno, by which time Wilkes had succumbed to laryngitis.

He had sufficiently recovered by March 2, when, along with 70 others from first Division, he was paraded before General Sir Oliver Leese, who had taken command of the 8th Army from Montgomery after the latter returned to England to prepare for the invasion of Normandy. There, in the town square, which the Canadians adopted as Dominion Square, he and the others were invested with the Military Cross. The official citation read:

On July 24, 1943, B Company of the Royal Canadian Regiment, the leading Company, was approaching the edge of Nissoria from the left-hand side of the road leading into the town when the point section came under aimed mortar and rifle fire from an enemy position 100 yards away. Honorary Captain Wilkes, Chaplain of the battalion, was moving at this time with D Company[.] [T]he Regimental Air Post was located 200 yards in the rear of the Company in a slight hollow[.] When the Company came under fire, casualties were inflicted on the leading section.

Showing no regard for his personal safety, while the area continued to be heavily mortared from the enemy position, Captain Wilkes moved up to the most forward troops with the stretcher-bearers, personally evacuating one man to the Regimental Aid Post under fire to assist in the evacuation of two more. By his example of devotion to duty and complete disregard for his own safety, although under fire at all times, he was instrumental in saving one man's life and provided an inspiration to all troops who took part in the battle.

On April 21, the St. Vito holiday came to an end and the regiment moved to a position south of the Liri Valley to take part in the offensive to capture Rome. A month later the RCR was back in the thick of the fighting to breach the Hitler Line and entered Pontecorvo. Then, on June 4, Rome fell to the Americans and the target now became the Gothic Line to the north.

On the night of August 25, the 1st and 2nd Brigades crossed the Via Flamina and advanced toward the village of Saltra, which they occupied early next morning. Although the assault companies on foot had no problem crossing the river, bridging ramps were needed for the wheeled vehicles to follow. While they were being laid, Jim Ritchie, the new CO, advanced on foot, leaving the command group vehicles to catch up. Ritchie replaced Billy Mathews after Wilkes had a chat with Dan Spry at brigade HQ, complaining that regimental morale had hit rock bottom.

Wilkes accompanied them once they got moving. Meanwhile, Ritchie had left his field headquarters with a party on a tank to make a forward reconnaissance. The command group vehicles had come within a few yards of Saltra when they were halted by a large crater, the sort of chaos the retreating Germans were creating in their wake.

A pair of soldiers went into town to collar some Italian labourers to fill it in. They began digging when suddenly there was a loud bang and one of them fell back right into the arms of the padre. His leg had been blown off by a "Shoe" land mine, and his blood splashed onto Wilkes' battle dress. Stretcher-bearers were on the spot immediately to carry him away and the project was abandoned.

While waiting for word from Strome Galloway, the second-in-command, for orders of how to move on, the men dispersed in the woods where the vehicles were parked. Wilkes was sitting on a running board when an open car pulled off the side of the road and two immaculately uniformed British staff officers stepped out. One of them asked for the CO.

Resentful of the intrusion, Wilkes replied harshly, "He's up forward with the troops."

"Then where's your second-in-command?"

"He's looking for a way around that," Wilkes answered testily, pointing to the crater.

"Who's in charge then?" the staff officer demanded.

"I am. Why?" Wilkes, by agreement with the regiment, had long ago scrapped the technicality that a chaplain had no tactical authority.

"General Alexander is here," was the crisp reply. That brought Wilkes to his feet in double-quick time. Feeling dishevelled and conscious of the blood on his battle dress, he marched forward as smartly as he could and snapped off a salute to the Commander-in-Chief 15 Army Group. General Leese, 8th Army commander, smiled and shook his hand.

"Have you met the Prime Minister?" he asked and turned toward Winston Churchill, who stood with his back to them, leaning on a cane. Churchill turned around and he and Wilkes shook hands.

Wilkes quickly explained, "I'm only the padre, but I'll get some-one for you. Captain Shuter!" he managed to bark out with some authority.

"Yes?" was the reply.

"Will you come over here and bring your map," Wilkes summoned with a soldierly air.

Ted Shuter was ambling over casually until he spotted the red and gold of Harold Alexander, which brought him to attention. As he saluted, Wilkes couldn't resist blurting out, "Have you met the Prime Minister?" Shuter's jaw dropped. Then he composed himself and gave Churchill a quick briefing indicating the crest a hundred yards in front that afforded a view of the enemy being engaged.

The Prime Minister asked one of his aides to bring up a jeep so he could go forward and take a look. Horrified, Shuter and Wilkes advised against it, pointing out that he would be in full view of the enemy and would draw fire. Churchill compromised by walking up a nearby rise where he could watch 25-pounders firing, then went back to the gun lines behind where the command group was posi-tioned and fired off a round himself. Half an hour later, German mortars fell on the exact spot where he had been standing. The incident marked the closest that Churchill had ever come to the enemy during the war.

By nightfall, the RCR were in positions halfway toward the Foglia River, the enemy having drawn back from the high ground. When the command group reached Jim Ritchie, Wilkes stuck out his hand and said: "Shake the hand that shook the hand of Churchill." Ritchie thought he was kidding until Shuter confirmed the incident.

By September 20, the RCR reached Rimini on the Adriatic. During the advance from Metauro the cost had been heavy: 7 officers and 72 men killed, 15 officers and 206 men wounded, and 2 officers and 10 men missing in action. On that date in the customary periodical processing of new arrivals and postings, after a rest had been ordered following a period of intense fighting, Major Wilkes was transferred as chaplain of No. 5 Casualty

Clearing Station (5CCS) at Cattolica, about six miles to the rear on the Adriatic.

Wilkes experienced a letdown. Since August 1940—over four years—the RCR had been family to him. Now he was leaving behind a bond of love and loyalty they had shared through hardship, death, destruction, and broken bodies and minds. War had changed his life and he was departing *his* regiment a different man. A part of his life had come to an end.

It did not help that he had little confidence in his successor, a condition bordering on an intense dislike for the man. The Honorary Captain Rockeby-Thomas was a pompous, complacent, and annoying little fellow who feigned an English accent, which Wilkes found irritating. When he tried his best to indoctrinate Rockeby-Thomas into the regiment by introducing him to the officers and men, the captain displayed disinterest and seemed distracted, insisting on regaling Wilkes with an account of his noble pedigree. He claimed to be related to royalty. When Wilkes could no longer stand it, he told him that he also had a long ancestry, adding that his great-grandfather had been hanged as a horse thief.

Wilkes had his successor figured just right. Later "Rock-a-bye," as he became dubbed, placed a pair of soldiers on charge for having their hands in their pockets. Wilkes intervened by persuading the regiment's adjutant to have the charges dropped.

As a jeep and driver took Wilkes to his new location, his mood—despondency, nostalgia, and an empty feeling that something had gone out of his life—gradually changed to one of relief and joy. He had a lot to be thankful for: he had come through it all unbroken in body or spirit; he wasn't living on the edge anymore; no more shelling, no more sweating in the dust and shivering in the mud. Already the tension was beginning to drain away.

Wilkes' duties at the 5CCS were not unlike those he had carried out on the firing line, except that here there was no firing. As he daily toured the wards, offering what cheer and hope he could to the wounded—some so badly hurt their chances of living were slim—

he often felt depressed and was tempted to question the wisdom of a God who could let this happen; but he was determined not to let it show. Every morning as he came through the door of the ward, he bolstered his spirits to project a cheerful appearance and manner.

But his time with 5CCS was brief. In December, he received word that he was being transferred back to England to take up a "senior appointment." On arrival in the U.K. he was sent to the Aldershot holding unit where he learned that the authority for a staff chaplain establishment position of Canadian Army Headquarters (CAHQ) in London had somehow got tangled in red tape and hadn't been received.

Finally Wilkes found himself at CAHQ, responsible for the well-being of four companies of the Canadian Women's Army Corps and a collection of other administrative units. To his regret he had become a member of what the fighting men contemptuously called the "Chairborne Division." His heart was still with the RCR and he continued to wear the shoulder flashes of his old regiment which, at this stage, was conducting its final triumph at Apeldoorn in Holland as World War II in Europe drew to a close.

Meanwhile, he received a telegram from Canada asking if he would stand as Kenora-Rainy River candidate at a Progressive Conservative convention in Kenora in preparation for a June 1945 federal election. Politics was not his cup of tea, so he refused at first; but he was persuaded to let his name stand at a later convention held in Fort Frances. In his absence, his wife Ethel spoke for him—so effectively that he won the candidacy.

On his return to Winnipeg in May via the bomb bay of an RCAF Lancaster, he hit the campaign trail, but it was a losing battle. He lost to the CCF (Co-operative Commonwealth Federation) candidate by 165 votes. Wilkes decided his place was with the army. He accepted a reduction in rank to captain and stayed in the service through a series of appointments beginning with that of District Chaplain, Western Command, with headquarters in Calgary, Alberta, ending in 1958 with that of Command Chaplain, Central

Command in Oakville, Ontario, where he retired with the rank of Lieutenant Colonel. He and Ethel moved to Victoria, British Columbia, where he became rector of St. Philip's Church, a post he held until 1967.

Rusty Wilkes never lost his ties with his old regiment, nor his love for it. In turn, the RCR could not have paid him a greater compliment and honour than to ask him to preach the sermon for the regiment's Centennial service at Wolseley Barracks parade ground in London, Ontario. In July 1983, almost 40 years to the day since the night he had led his comrades in prayer before the Pachino landing in Sicily, Wilkes delivered the second-most-historic message of his military career to a congregation that included the Colonel in Chief, HRH The Duke of Edinburgh, the entire regiment of three regular army battalions, and its militia 4th battalion, as well as nearly 10,000 veterans and friends of the regiment. Many an eye misted over. It had been a long march from that beach.

Chapter 12

Soldier of the Queen's

Tangmere Fighter Airfield, Sussex

Late in the afternoon of 5 June 1944, I phoned "Snack Bar," the sector controller, to ask permission to air-test my Spitfire, which had just gone through a regular inspection. The female voice answered my request in no uncertain terms: "You know you can't go up there with all those ships in the Channel!" I was flabbergasted. Whatever happened to military security? I hung up shaken, but carried out my A/T anyway. She was right, though. There were "all those ships in the Channel"—to port, to starboard, and directly south of the Isle of Wight. No question about it. This was it, the Big One!

That evening all of the pilots of our wing were assembled in the mess tent to get the word. The next day was D-Day. When we stepped outside in the dark we could hear the drone and see the exhausts and navigation lights of aircraft on their way to Normandy to drop paratroops, and gliders carrying other airborne infantry.

Early next morning found our squadron patrolling at 1000 feet above the invasion bridgehead. The 20-minute flight across the Channel took us over the endless stream of vessels steaming south toward the Baie de la Seine. It was a strange sensation. We had been accustomed to crossing the French coast at 20,000 feet to avoid enemy antiaircraft fire. Now here we were at low altitude over what was, to us in the air at least, friendly territory. Four things stand out in my memory. The crowds of landing craft and the troop and supply ships with cable balloons rising from them, the

broken gliders strewn across the fields like smashed wooden matchboxes,
the smoke rising from small fires here and there, and the lack of Luftwaffe
interference. In my log book I noted "ALLIES INVADE FRANCE!!!
Patrolled Caen area. Nothing doing at all. Weather 5/10 cloud."

Nothing doing at all! Well, that was certainly true in the air. But
directly below us at Bernières-sur-Mer (Nan Beach) the men of the
Queen's Own Rifles (QOR) were struggling to get a foothold that would
lead them seven miles inland to become the only infantry regiment to
capture and hold its assigned D-Day objective.

Among them was Charlie (Charles Cromwell) Martin, company
sergeant major, "A" Company, to me the embodiment of the bravery,
ingenuity, and selflessness of the Canadian rifleman, a soldier without
equal anywhere, in any army.

It had been a long journey from Dixie west of Toronto to the
Calvados Coast of France. In the summer of 1940, when the
Queen's Own Rifles of Canada mobilized in the Ontario capital,
Charlie Martin finished his job of clearing the ground of a 40-acre
farm on Dixie Road and arrived at the old Armoury on University
Avenue to enlist. In July of the following year, the regiment
shipped out to England where it would spend the next four years in
intensive training, anxiously waiting and hoping for the day it
would go into action. In the meantime, Charlie married an English
girl, Vi, from Newcastle-on-Tyne who joined the Auxiliary
Territorial Service (ATS) and became a radar operator with the
Royal Artillery based in London then, as the invasion of Europe
drew near, on the east coast. By that time Charlie had more than
earned his spurs, being successively promoted to corporal,
sergeant, and finally company sergeant major (CSM).

On 5 June 1944—D-Day minus one—about the same time I was
"illegally" air-testing my Spitfire, the QOR had begun boarding the
SS *Monowai* troopship from the Royal Piers at Southampton that
would carry them, along with 14,000 other Canadians, to the Nam
section of Juno Beach on the Normandy Coast.

On the following morning, reveille sounded at 0315 hours for the QOR and the men began boarding the landing craft (LCA). They were quite unprepared for the task that faced them. In training they had practised lowering themselves down the loading nets into the assault boats, but always in calm waters. On D-Day the sea was choppy and rough. This caused the LCAs to alternately swing in toward the troopship and then away from it, leaving a space of 10 to 15 feet between the hull and the landing craft. If a soldier wearing heavy boots and a steel helmet, with a 50-pound pack, and carrying a Bren or Piat (antitank) gun, mortars, ammunition, and other equipment, fell into the abyss, he would sink like a rock. If he did manage to unburden himself of the extra load, he risked being crushed when the LCA slammed against the hull. Coping with this problem ate up precious time.

Charlie Martin, in charge of one of the boatloads, was the last man to lower himself into the craft, which he executed as quickly as he could. But the landing craft cast off just as he was ready to jump for it off the net. Only the alert action of a pair of his comrades prevented him from ending up in the drink.

For a period of time the LCAs circled the mother ship, until finally the order came for them to proceed south. In the dark they could see the gun flashes and rockets on their way to pummel the enemy fortifications. As dawn loomed, the 10 LCAs, five carrying "A" Company on the right and five carrying "B" Company on the left—a total of 10 platoons—seemed very much alone. The invasion fleet behind them had disappeared from view.

As Bernières-sur-Mer became visible through a slight mist and rain, an eerie silence pervaded. The men could see the houses and buildings, and on the beach embedded obstacles and barbed wire. They knew the stretch of beach would be mined. In the middle was a 15-foot sea wall with three large, heavy cement pillboxes. The troops could see that the beach was wide open to murderous machine-gun fire sweeping a full 180 degrees.

Martin's No. 1 boat and the No. 2 boat were heading toward a breakwater and dangerous rocks on the right. Then a German gunner from one of the pillboxes opened fire, throwing up a piece of metal that cut the cheek of one of the QOR riflemen on Martin's right.

With a shout Martin told the naval lieutenant boat commander to take them in as fast as possible, on the premise that it was better to move straight at high speed than wallow about as an easy target with the danger of banging into obstacles or mines. The craft proceeded at top speed until, with a jerk, the prow of the LCA scraped the beach and the order came to put down the ramp.

Somewhere behind the sea wall, machine-gun fire erupted and mortars began exploding all over the beach. Martin shouted to Sergeant Jack Simpson, who had been sitting across from him, and all the others in the boat: "Move! Fast! Don't stop for anything. Go! Go! Go!" He and Simpson raced down the ramp side by side, the others following close behind. As they hit the beach they fanned out, heading for the sea wall.

That initial assault—across the beach, over the sea wall to the railway line running parallel to the beach—cost "A" Company dearly: ten men killed (including Jack Simpson), three wounded (one twice), all within a minute or two.

Martin had teamed up with Bert Sheppard and Bill Bettridge, racing forward at top speed, firing from the hip. To the left they spotted a small gap in the wall. An enemy belt-fed machine gun blocked the way, but there was only one man on it who was waving frantically for an accomplice to feed him the ammunition. Bettridge stopped for a moment to take out the gunner with a well-aimed short burst, then the trio reached the wall, climbed over it, and ran across the railway line. On both sides of the line there were mines, and the machine-gun and mortar fire never let up. Beyond the railway line, a field offered some grass cover, but there the troops ran into heavy barbed-wire entanglements. Martin cut the wire strands and bent them back, making an opening just wide enough to allow a man to crawl through on his belly. By this time they were joined by several others, making up a party of some 15 riflemen.

When everyone got through the barbed wire, they found themselves in a minefield. As leader, Martin gave the signal to cross, then led off. He had gone about 10 paces when he stepped on a "jumping mine," a device that vaulted five feet or so into the air, then exploded, spraying nails and buckshot over a 200-foot area. But Martin knew that by keeping his foot on it, it wouldn't go off. By the time all the others were safely across the field and over a fence into the gardens of the village houses, he leaned forward to drop to the ground when a bullet pierced his helmet and knocked it off his head. However, he was able to flatten out on the ground by the time the jumping mine exploded, leaving him bareheaded but unhurt.

The party entered Bernières-sur-Mer, where it split into two sections. Dodging intermittent machine-gun and mortar fire, they wended their respective ways through the village, one on the right flank, the other on the left, reaching their objective, the road through the village at its most southern point, by 0845 hours, less than half an hour after landing on the beach.

The small group was now joined by others from the company, some of them wounded. Within half an hour, two tanks came forward and the company, which had suffered 50 percent casualties, began to reassemble into two groups, having received orders to proceed to the next objective—Anguerny, seven miles inland.

Heading a group made up of what was left of two platoons and some headquarters troops, Martin led them across low-lying fields in full view of the enemy, with erratic dashes, stopping, flopping down on the ground, and starting again. By early afternoon "B" and "C" companies of the QOR had captured Anguerny. At the same time, "D" Company advanced to take the village of Anisy just beyond. The QOR could take pride in being the only regiment to capture and hold its assigned D-Day objective.

By nightfall the QOR had dug in, the support company—

mortars and gun carriers—taking up a defensive position in the event of a counterattack. It was just as well. Around midnight, machine-gun fire suddenly broke out; a German SS patrol had infiltrated the position. In their first night action, the regiment took four German prisoners. Two of the Canadians were wounded, one stabbed in the stomach by a bayonet.

The QOR now settled down for the night, but wide awake, alert to a repeat attack. In the darkness Martin saw someone light up a cigarette. He yelled at him to put it out. When he discovered he had been shouting at Jock Sprague, the regimental colonel, he became even more irate, rebuking him for being up at the front; as commander of the regiment, he was too important to put in jeopardy. His place was back at battalion headquarters directing the battle—not fighting it.

Five days later the QORs became engaged in an operation that at first puzzled them, and which they later learned was a sacrificial effort to halt a determined German armoured counterattack to drive to the beaches. The objective was to attack and hold the village of Le Mesnil-Patry and capture the high ground at Cheux. No reconnaissance—aerial photographs or advance patrol reports—of enemy positions was available. The plan called for Martin's "A" Company to move up on the right flank with "D" Company on the left, the men riding forward on Sherman tanks of Sixth Canadian Armoured Division.

The ensuing battle was hopelessly uneven—two companies of riflemen aboard some 30 or 40 tanks up against 70 Panzer tanks and other armoured vehicles of Brigadefuhrer Kurt Meyer's 12th Panzer Division, well entrenched and equipped with the deadly 88mm guns. When the Germans opened fire, the Shermans began twisting and turning violently, throwing the rifleman off them in the process. Some tanks caught fire, their crews, some with their clothes on fire, trying desperately to escape. It was chaos.

Within 15 minutes the Germans had knocked out 19 Sherman tanks. In effect the encounter resembled a modern Charge of the

Light Brigade. The QOR lost 87 killed or wounded including their company commander Major Elliot Dalton, who was wounded in the leg. (He ended up in the hospital bed next to his brother Major Charlie Dalton, who had been severely wounded in the head when his own company hit the beach on D-Day.) But the action succeeded in preventing a counterattack planned for the following morning; that night the Germans were ordered to withdraw. On June 12, Martin led a patrol over the battle area. There was no sign of any enemy, but the patrol came across the bodies of six of their comrades who had been taken prisoner and each killed by a pistol shot in the temple. For this crime, Kurt Meyer was sentenced by a Canadian Military Court to be shot, but the sentence was later commuted to life imprisonment.

Very little has actually been written about patrols. During the Normandy campaign, June to August 1944, Charlie Martin took part in 75 such forays. In his own words: "A patrol is as tough or tougher than any regular attack."

A patrol had one of three objectives: to gain information, take a prisoner, or simply keep the enemy off-guard. To limit casualties and provide maximum flexibility, "A" Company confined its patrols to only four volunteers. One man would station himself at the return point to keep watch. The leader and his number-two man covered the right flank. On the left the fourth man covered that flank as well as the rear. Everything depended on speed, teamwork, and timing. Most vital of all was silence. A man with a head cold would never be included; a cough or sneeze could give the show away.

On moonlit nights, communication consisted of hand and arm signals; in darkness touch signals were used—a tap on the shoulder would mean move left, a jab in the ribs might mean cover me and so on.

Armed with light weapons—garotte, knife, and Sten gun—on occasion, such as a firefight, the patrol would carry extra equipment such as a Bren gun, a stretcher, and a roll of white tape, and run a phone line back to HQ in the event of trouble to call down a smokescreen, artillery, or mortar fire.

Toughest of all were the prisoner patrols. To begin with, it meant penetrating the enemy lines. With one man standing guard at the start point, the other three would locate a slit-trench in which there were two Germans. The patrol would then wait (as long as three or four hours), until one of the enemy made a move, say to have a leak. Number-two in the patrol would take him out with a knife in the kidneys—to paralyze his vocal chords—then a quick slash across the throat. In the meantime, while the leader stood guard with a Sten gun, number-three moved into the trench, garotted the remaining German into unconsciousness then carried him back to the start point. Mission accomplished, though at tremendous risk.

The next major encounter in which the QOR became involved—along with the Royal Winnipeg Rifles supported by the armour of the Fort Garry Horse—beginning July 4, was Operation Charnwood, the capture of Carpiquet airfield. Taking the airfield was preliminary to occupying the Normandy capital of Caen, then advancing to Falaise to join up with the Americans.

Martin's "A" Company moved up on the right of the Winnipegs with the objective of taking the ground and some of the buildings in the northwest corner of the field. But the 716 German Infantry Division and the 21st Panzer Division in reserve were too well entrenched. The QORs managed to dig in along the runway and occupy part of an old hangar. Then the order came to hold and for the next five days they were subjected to relentless fire from enemy artillery—Tiger tank 88mm guns, machine guns, and mortars, and, most frightening of all, the Moaning Minnie rockets.

By the night of July 9, Caen, a heap of rubble and buried bodies as a result of two raids by RAF Lancaster heavy bombers, was in British and Canadian hands. Carpiquet fell the same day, the QOR's casualties totalling 70 men killed or wounded.

After a brief hiatus at a rest station, which was still close enough to the front line to come under enemy artillery fire, the QOR returned to battle on July 18, the start date of Operation Atlantic. Two of the initial objectives were Colombelles, an industrial suburb of Caen, and Giberville, a small village across the Orne River to the south. In both cases, "A" and "B" Companies met stiff resistance and took a number of prisoners. But at Giberville, "A" Company lost three newly arrived platoon commanders, and three out of four of their D-Day veterans were gone. By July 21, the position having been consolidated, the regiment moved forward a few miles on to Grentheville, where they came under steady enemy fire from 88mm guns, mortars, and Moaning Minnies. A week later, the regiment took up a new position on Borquebus Ridge, overlooking the road to Falaise.

The day before, Martin had had an experience he found hard to forget. He was sharing a slit-trench with another member of his company who had left to go over to headquarters. Martin was about to leave himself, to check up on the single hot meal the men were given each day, when the company stretcher-bearer arrived. He asked if he could use the trench in the CSM's absence to shelter himself from all the enemy fire. Martin readily agreed. He had gone no more than 10 yards when an 88mm shell landed in the trench, killing the stretcher-bearer. Martin was himself knocked several yards by the blast, which left him shaken in both body and spirit.

On July 31, after 56 consecutive days in action, the regiment was moved to Fontaine Henry, eight miles from the front line and out of enemy artillery range, for a week's rest. The men needed it for the battles that were to follow.

On August 8, the second phase of Operation Totalize called for the Queen's Own Rifles to capture Quesnay Woods, seven miles north of Falaise. The night before the 2nd Canadian Corps had captured Verrières Ridge. Meanwhile, Kurt Meyer had brought up two battle groups from his 12th SS Panzer Division as well as a number of assault guns and Tiger tanks.

Quesnay Woods covered 20 acres and was surrounded by bush on two sides. To the north there were grain fields and orchards divided by hedgerows of stone and dirt three feet high, with seven feet of growth on top. The entire area was well defended. The Germans had concentrated their armour in the woods where it was well protected and concealed. They had to keep the road to Falaise open as long as possible. And the hedgerows around the woods offered good defensive positions.

The assault plan was for "A" Company to take the fields to the left, "B" to the right, capture a strong point that would allow the remaining companies to move through, and take the high ground a few miles further on. Straightforward enough—if a bit ambitious—given the proper support. And that is where the trouble lay. First Polish Armoured Division south of Caen was unintentionally bombed by Flying Fortresses of the U.S. Eighth Air Force, preventing it from bringing up its tanks in support of the drive. But this was not communicated to the QOR. After a delay of some six hours, after the armour failed to arrive, close to noon the order came to advance without it. The sole support was the artillery, but the thickness of the woods made pinpointing targets virtually impossible.

"A" Company, led by Martin, carrying only a Smith and Wesson pistol with six rounds and wearing no headgear except some camouflage netting, moved forward, flushing out the enemy with Bren-gun fire and mortars, hedgerow by hedgerow. By late afternoon they had covered most of the two miles ahead of them and reached a point 250 yards from the woods where they came under concentrated and sustained enemy fire from 88mm artillery and machine guns that reminded them of the siege at Carpiquet.

Martin knew they had to keep moving or face annihilation. Also, they expected "D" Company to arrive and pass through, and take up a position ahead. And they were still under the impression that the tanks would be coming up. With a smokescreen they were able to improve their position, and Martin sent runners back to HQ to report that the company was prepared to hang on, depending on whether or not they were going to get tank, artillery, or aerial support. One of them returned to advise that the action had been halted earlier that afternoon and that they should withdraw before an artillery barrage began. Just in time. They were completely out of ammunition; Martin himself had only three pistol shots left. When they reached HQ they learned that "B" Company on the right with "C" Company in support had actually penetrated the woods, and had suffered severe losses before being forced to withdraw.

In summary, the QORs were right back where they started from, having sustained 85 casualties. However, they at least had the satisfaction in knowing that their efforts had helped break up an enemy concentration which, later, under heavy attack from artillery and air power, withdrew. This allowed the regiment to move to the village of Robert-Mesnil, two miles from Falaise, from where it would launch an attack on Maizières, its last engagement in the Battle of Normandy.

At mid-afternoon of August 14, three hours after the QORs began their advance on the village aboard Kangaroo armoured personnel carriers, they—among others—fell victim to a serious lack of communications between air and ground forces and poor reconnaissance intelligence, not to mention erroneous target pinpointing on the part of the aircrews. American Flying Fortresses and British Lancaster bombers had been assigned a "close support" role in an attack by 1st Polish Armoured Division, 3rd Canadian Infantry Division (of which the QOR was a part), and 4th Canadian Infantry Brigade.

Up to this point, aerial support usually consisted of dropping bombs well ahead of the attack line. In this case it was designed to take out defences immediately ahead. The error, although marginal, was disastrous for the attackers; the bombs fell short, bursting right into their midst. First came the missiles from the Flying Fortresses at high altitude, the bombers barely visible from the ground. Next came the Lancasters at low level, so low the troops could see the bomb bays open and the bombs drop. Yellow smoke signals set off to identify themselves were virtually ignored and in any case were too late to rescue the situation. The Allied troops on the ground were helpless.

Despite the casualties, the QOR pressed on to occupy Maizières later that afternoon. After assembling enemy prisoners and flushing out the last pockets of resistance, the regiment began digging in for the night. Martin noticed a large, expensive-looking, abandoned house and, leaving his partly finished slit-trench, he found a comfortable bedroom in which to spend the night. He fell asleep, his revolver beside him as usual—no one was going to take him prisoner, even in bed.

As if they hadn't had enough bombing for one day, that night the Luftwaffe paid the QOR's position a visit. Martin was awakened by a huge explosion. When he went outside to examine the damage, he found that a bomb had cratered his slit-trench.

By August 21, the Allied armies had slammed the door shut on the Falaise gap; the battle for Normandy was over. During the campaign the Canadians had grown accustomed to the aftermath of the fighting starting from the beaches down through the countryside and communes ravaged by war. Burnt-out artillery, cars, tanks, trucks, and buildings, the rubble clogging the streets of Caen in the wake of Allied heavy bombing, the sight of the dead and dying, not only human beings, but horses, mules, and livestock, the nauseating stench that choked the nostrils and curdled the stomach.

But all this paled in comparison to the appalling, horrifying carnage created by the massacre of the Falaise gap. Sunken roads were littered every foot of the way with corpses and burned equipment. Where the retreating Germans had been caught and shot in the open, they lay in irregular swathes in shallow ditches. Grey-clad, dust-powdered bodies were sprawled everywhere, propped up against trees, slopped over the driving seats of vehicles, or running boards. The once-crimson stains of blood on their uniforms turned quickly the colour of rust. Even from 1500 feet, pilots flying over the area were overcome with nausea from the frightful, impregnable stench. It took days to clear the roads before they were again passable. By this time the Germans were in full retreat toward the Seine, and the QOR was moved to Grand-Mesnil, 10 miles east of Falaise.

Since landing at Bernières-sur-Mer on D-Day, the regiment had lost three-quarters of its original force; less than one soldier out of four remained. Reinforcements had suffered 50 percent casualties in dead and wounded. And although the Germans had suffered a devastating defeat—more than 400,000 men lost, half of whom were taken prisoner—the war was far from over. For the Queen's Own Rifles, the immediate objective was to help clear the French Channel ports still in enemy hands.

Progress was slow; the Germans fought a skillful, well-organized rearguard action to buy as much time as possible to allow them to set up a proper defence position in the east. The regiment did not reach Lacapelle, a small village on the outskirts of Boulogne, until September 4, before moving up to the Bois de Souverain Moulin. From there they would launch an attack on the Pas-de-Calais port.

They faced a formidable task. Boulogne was well defended, making it a virtual fortress. The Germans had built deeply embedded concrete machine-gun emplacements with periscopes mounted on elevator platforms, and enjoyed an almost unrestricted line of fire. The first step for the QOR was the capture of St. Martin, an area just outside Boulogne, where there was a church and a railway station.

The Germans positioned in Boulogne were warned that the city would be subjected to severe bombing before an attack began. Civilians were allowed to evacuate. During the evacuation, from a distance the Canadians witnessed the pent-up fury of the French against women who had slept with the enemy; their heads were shorn while crowds looked on and jeered. Charlie did not share their sense of retribution; he regarded it as wanton cruelty.

On September 17, five hundred heavy bombers dropped their loads on the city and the defences surrounding it, creating enormous craters that deflected the fire from the enemy pillboxes.

With two platoons well spread out on either side of the road, "A" Company plunged ahead, moving rapidly, zigzagging and changing pace, covering between the point man in front to the end-section man in the rear a distance of 100 yards, all the while under heavy enemy machine-gun fire and shelling. When they reached a junction at the top of a hill, the Germans had the crossroads covered with machine-gun and mortar fire.

This pinned down the platoons, while tank reinforcements half a mile behind had to wait until the flail machines—vehicles with a huge fly wheel mounted 20 feet in front of them—blew up mines to clear the way. Meanwhile, the platoons were at the mercy of a German machine-gun pillbox that had to be destroyed before they were wiped out. Two men were dispatched to take it out, both of whom were killed. Martin and several others forced the enemy gunners out of the emplacement by using a smoke bomb, but not before several men in the section were wounded.

One other German machine gun had to be subdued, resulting in further casualties. "A" Company then set up HQ in the church manse where the wounded were brought in and tended to by the church nuns. It also served as a marshalling point for Germans taken prisoner.

That night, the company fought off an enemy counterattack. Next morning the unit went on the offensive again, this time with an untested platoon in the lead that hitherto had been assigned brigade and divisional HQ defence. All went well at first until the platoon surprised an enemy machine-gun carrier that opened fire, killing the unit leader. With the help of another, Martin quickly seized the Piat gun and with two shots destroyed the vehicle.

That was the QOR's last action at Boulogne. But one last piece of drama remained to be played out. Among the innumerable Germans surrendering to the Canadians was a group of submariners who came marching down the road toward the manse, displaying a large white flag of surrender led by a sailor playing "Lili Marlene" on a mouth organ. The officer in charge, carrying a neatly folded Nazi flag, marched up to Martin, saluted smartly, and in perfect English announced: "We are proud to surrender our submarine flag to the Canadians." Martin kept it as a souvenir which he brought home to Canada.

The next port of call was Calais, and its capture—surrender would better describe it—was almost pure formality. As the QOR neared the town in late September, there was a puzzling lack of response on the part of the enemy to the advance patrols. Absolute quiet—both eerie and suspect. One night, to see for himself, Charlie Martin mounted a patrol with three others that confirmed there was nothing to report or stand in the way of an advance on Calais. Next morning, "A" Company moved toward the town and although there was a flurry of machine-gun fire, there was also a curious absence of artillery or mortar shelling. Then one of the troopers noted that the machine guns were firing into the air in the direction of the sea, a clear indication that the enemy had no stomach for defending what was a lost cause, and the Germans began surrendering in droves.

As a going-away present, however, they had heavily mined the roads, which the QOR soon discovered when it entered the town. These were no ordinary mines. With typical Teutonic ingenuity, the enemy had devised explosives designed to go off from a number of causes, as the sappers—engineers—quickly learned when they began disarming them. Consisting of heavy naval shells, the mines were so designed that trip wires could set them off, as could tightening the wires themselves in an effort to defuse them. Finally, a temperature-release detonator was wired to the shell, so sensitive that the heat of one's hand could trigger it. Fortunately, there were no casualties and the area was roped off as the regiment continued with the occupation of the port.

A brief rest followed before the regiment found itself embroiled in the Battle of the Breskens Pocket. This was part of a campaign to clear the German forces guarding the north and south shores of the Scheldt Estuary and free up the Belgian port of Antwerp to Allied shipping. It involved a two-pronged attack by the First Canadian Army, an assault north across the Netherlands border, then west along the Beveland Peninsula to Walcheren Island, with a simultaneous attack south of the estuary to ford the Leopold Canal and capture the Dutch port of Breskens on the north shore of the river.

On October 9, the 9th Canadian Infantry Brigade, with a flotilla of 97 Buffalo troop and tank landing water transports, crossed the mouth of the Braakman Plaat inlet to "kick in the back door" of the Breskens Pocket. Four days later, they were joined by the Queen's Own, which crossed over from the south side of the Westerschelde River. The regiment was now about to fight over some of the most arduous and dangerous terrain it would encounter during the entire war.

The Germans had flooded the *polder*—reclaimed land. Movement was restricted to wending their way across open fields through water-filled ditches on either side of the dikes offering little cover, from farmhouse to farmhouse, where they could set up a position. The Germans offered stiff resistance from one point to the next and when forced to give up were not above deception.

On one occasion, enemy soldiers could be seen running across the open wet ground toward the Canadians in what they could only conclude was an act of surrender. However, the Germans were still carrying their rifles and, as they got closer, they opened fire. Luckily, "A" Company had two dug-in machine guns manned at the ready, and began returning the fire. One of the gunners was killed instantly with a bullet to the head. Charlie Martin grabbed the dead man's Bren gun and started shooting back. At this, those Germans still alive dropped their rifles and threw up their arms.

These were only skirmishes, but they took their toll. By the time "A" Company faced the challenge of the battles for the villages of

IJzendijke and Oostburg, it was down to half-strength, each section having only six or seven men left.

At IJzendijke, one of the platoons ran into relentless machine-gun fire from a well-sandbagged house across the town square. Charlie Martin's platoon, despite having sustained heavy casualties, was dispatched to swing around behind the enemy position and neutralize it.

As the section moved cautiously forward, using a dike for cover when possible, the other platoon, holed up in a house on the east side of the square, provided covering fire. At the same time, a third platoon on the opposite side also gave covering fire.

The advancing platoon had asked for 15 minutes of heavy mortar bombardment behind the house. Martin and six others, armed with Sten guns and hand grenades, with the help of a smokescreen they laid down, managed to get behind the house.

No firing came from it, but the platoon took no chances. One of its members threw a hand grenade through the back window. Immediately after it exploded, he and Martin barged through the opening of the blown window. Martin rolled to the left, his partner to the right, both of them spraying their Sten guns. Then two others crashed through the back door.

When the smoke cleared and the firing stopped, the Canadians were faced with only three terrified Germans shouting "*Kamerad!*" The Germans had suffered no casualties, only a few flesh wounds. Martin picked up a piece of shrapnel from the grenade, a souvenir he took home with him.

The battle for Oostburg was another matter. Its capture called for a battalion attack including artillery, mortars, and rocket-firing Typhoons, with flame throwers standing by. The subsequent assault and surrender was a masterpiece of battle experience and expertise, of coordination, timing, and courage.

The single last solid point of resistance in the Breskens Pocket was a 30-by-40-foot, heavily fortified pillbox to the north of Wescapelle. It had 3-foot-thick concrete walls topped by a 10-foot-high concertina of barbed wire a yard thick. Surrounding the pillbox was a minefield with booby traps set all around. To top it off, it was manned by diehards commanded by a dedicated SS Nazi who, in turn, was aided by a Gestapo officer. It could have been bypassed or, alternatively, blasted into rubble by a solid rain of artillery fire and Typhoon rockets. But the decision had been made to capture it.

Battalion command faced a difficult decision. From any standpoint, it was a virtual suicide mission. Although the fortification had already been subjected to some artillery shelling and Typhoon rockets, there had been no evident damage. If an attempt was made to flank the pillbox from either side, the minefield would have to be penetrated and the barbed wire either cut through or blown up. That meant exposing the demolition teams to enemy machine-gun fire for an extended period of time. There was also the added risk that the wire was probably booby-trapped. There had to be a better way. But what?

Fortunately, someone noticed that the wire gate across the roadway leading right into the position had been left open. Also, the tarmac road itself looked firm, and since it was the supply route to the pillbox, it would not be mined. It was decided to send in a section of nine of the most experienced riflemen in the company—Charlie Martin and eight others—straight down the road with a standby section in readiness as a backup in case the initial attack failed. Either way, heavy casualties could be expected.

Armed with hand grenades and smoke bombs to throw into the pillbox, the nine set off through the gate, on the run spread out on both sides of the road expecting any minute to be fired upon. Then the unexpected happened: through the pillbox slits, white flags emerged. The Germans were surrendering. The battle for Breskens was over!

For the first time in a month, the regiment could relax. During the fighting, Martin's company had been reduced to three small platoons; the survivors were cold, wet, and tired. Some were on the verge of mental and physical collapse. Once the position had been consolidated and prisoners taken care of, the Queen's Own were driven to a farm south of Knocke where they were fed their first hot meal for as long as they could remember and bedded down in warm, soft, dry hay.

The toll, the strain of five months of continuous combat, finally caught up with Charlie Martin. Utterly exhausted, the D-Day veteran fell into a deep, coma-like slumber from which, even after 12 hours, his comrades were unable to awaken him. They checked his pulse; there was no response, and they couldn't detect any breathing either. Martin's eyes remained firmly closed. In desperation, they called in a stretcher-bearer. Finally they were able to rouse him, though he was still groggy and weary, proof that no man is really indestructible. Martin certainly came close, however.

A week's rest in Ghent followed before the QORs tackled their next assignment, the Nijmegen bridgehead. On November 12, they took over a position held by the American 82nd Airborne Division, who tended to treat the rather scruffy, battle-weary Canadians with disdain. In turn, the latter were singularly unimpressed with the amateurish defences the paratroopers had built for themselves. They were weak, poorly organized, and vulnerable to enemy surveillance and attack.

The listening post to which "A" Company was assigned, for instance, had a telephone in the basement from which the wire ran openly across the field which at night could easily be cut by an enemy soldier. Nor were there any dug-in defences. To maintain security, the Americans urged utter silence to avoid alerting the enemy. Martin would have none of it. With his CO's blessing, he had slit-trenches dug all round the house and brought up a supply of hardware—Piat guns, bombs, flares, grenades, Bren guns, sandbags, and a walkie-talkie to replace the telephone along with barbed wire.

While they now had proper protection, they came under constant heavy shelling from 88mm and 75mm guns, and the dreaded, screaming Moaning Minnies. One night, about two o'clock in the morning, the warning flares went up and the dozen riflemen manning the post could hear the approach of a vehicle, which they took to be an enemy scout car. Then, for 10 minutes, mortar shells rained down followed by machine-gun fire. From the scout car, no more than 60 yards away, came a shout for the Canadians to surrender or be wiped out. Now fire was coming from everywhere, "A" Company and the Germans, creating a deafening crescendo.

Charlie Martin loaded a Piat gun and fired. The recoil struck him in the face and knocked him back through a crumbling brick wall, leaving him with a bloody nose. But his quick-thinking action had done the trick. The enemy turned tail and fled.

On November 22, the regiment moved to a position south of the Waal River to hold a 10-acre area known as the Waal flats. It was decidedly lacking in comfort. The weather had turned cold, dreary, and wet, and the river kept rising, causing the slit-trenches to fill with water. A week after their arrival, "A" Company was ordered to raid a German strongpoint at a crossroads around which the area was heavily mined.

The plan was for one platoon to take the strongpoint, another to move in from the left, and a third to stay in reserve. As soon as the lead platoon captured the crossroads and the other two units began moving in to consolidate, the Germans opened up with machine guns from another position. Then a signal came from HQ to call off the attack. But it was almost too late to save the situation. The platoons on the left and right were under heavy artillery fire and several of the men with the lead platoon were trapped in the minefield, some wounded, one severely.

The problem was to try to get everybody back. The wounded had to be carried from the field and the platoons on the left and to the rear had to be contacted. Charlie Martin, with the lead platoon who led the way in pitch-black darkness, managed to find the badly injured man, administer two shots of morphine, and carry him back, fireman's-lift style, to safety. The others followed his trail, bringing in the rest of the wounded.

Martin next went out in search of the platoon on the left to tell them the attack had been called off. By following the white tape laid down into the minefield, he was able to reach the leader's position in less than 15 minutes, when all hell broke loose—enemy flares and artillery suddenly erupted. Obeying standard procedure, Martin froze. In the eerie flashing light, to his horror he could see a dead body at his feet he thought at first was the platoon leader. Then he recognized the uniform as German.

Close to dawn all personnel had returned to the start-line, where they remained until Typhoon fighter-bombers had blasted the enemy's secondary positions, paving the way for the company's next ground attack to secure the crossroads permanently. From then on at Nijmegen, through December 1944 and January 1945, their task was simply to hold ground already won in preparation for the next Allied offensive; to break out and clear the Rhineland as a stepping stone to crossing the Rhine River into Germany.

In the north, Supreme Commander of the Allied forces Dwight Eisenhower ordered a pincer attack into the Reichswald Forest by the American, British, and Canadian armies, to begin on February 8, with the objective of breaking the Germans' vaunted Siegfried Line.

The first job for "A" Company of the Queen's Own Rifles was to capture the town of Millegen and the dikes surrounding it, one of which the enemy had blown up, resulting in the water level from the Waal River rising to such an extent that the only way to get around was by boat.

Charlie Martin had just arrived with supplies for a section that had dug in around a loading ramp for barges as well as inside a hotel, when an enemy shell exploded, knocking him through the door and down a 40-foot ramp. He was badly bruised and needed a broom handle for support to get around for the next few days. That was a foretaste of what lay in store when on February 26 the 8th Canadian Brigade, of which the QOR was a component, was assigned the task of opening up the approaches to the Calcar-Udem escarpment.

At Mooshof the regiment was to engage in the Rhineland's bitter-
est fighting against the toughest and most highly trained, well-
seasoned, and dedicated German paratroops it would ever encounter.
By 0400 hours, in driving rain, "B" and "C" Companies had consolidated the start-line under a covering artillery barrage. But even
before they reached it, "A" Company on the left and "D" Company
on the right began taking casualties from enemy artillery, mortar
shelling, 88mm guns, and the Moaning Minnies. By 0600 hours,
one of Charlie Martin's platoons had overrun a fortified building
housing an 88mm and several machine guns; however, the platoon
leader was killed and his sergeant wounded in the spleen.

A lance corporal took charge, and with several others, captured
another building with another 88mm and another machine gun.
The NCO was killed in the process and one other member of his
section was severely wounded. Martin braved machine-gun fire to
pull the injured man to safety.

By now it was daylight and the platoon had achieved two-thirds
of its objectives. By 0930 hours, it had taken all three buildings but
at a cost of losing its officer and all its NCOs. The action had taken
place so fiercely in hand-to-hand combat and so rapidly there had
been no time to release the livestock and many cows and horses
were either killed or badly shot up.

During the fighting, Martin heard the sound of the breech of a
88mm slamming shut from no more than 100 feet away. He knew
what was coming next; he dived through a doorway into a litter of
baby pigs—just in time! The shell followed him through the doorway, killing most of the pigs and splattering Charlie with their
blood. Although he was an awful mess, at least he was unhurt.

To the right, another platoon had also succeeded in capturing a
number of buildings, but it too took heavy casualties, including the
platoon leader. The last of the group of buildings held by the
enemy fell to a third platoon, so that by noon, "A" Company had
completed its objectives, but at a horrific cost in the loss of 70 men.
Only one officer and 42 other ranks had survived.

The time had now come to dig in and bring in the wounded and dead, even though there was no letup on the part of the enemy artillery, which kept up a steady barrage. Finally the commanding officer—"the Boss," Major Dick Medland—arrived in a jeep and a carrier pulled up at the same time. The carrier was sorely needed to remove the wounded. Medland called into headquarters on the wireless to report that all objectives had been secured. As he spoke, he was so overcome with emotion that tears streamed down his face.

At that moment, a cry came from a wounded man in a slit-trench. Martin and another man rushed over. One of the riflemen had taken a sniper's bullet straight between the eyes. His companion got off luckier, but only marginally. A bullet had gone through his left eye and out the back of his head. But at least he was still alive.

Martin spotted the sniper in a clump of trees some 150 yards away. Now rage took over. The artillery observer called for a barrage right down on the spot. The Boss went one better. He asked for Typhoon support also.

Martin supervised the loading of the wounded aboard the carrier; then, with Medland's sanction, he drove the mile and a half to the battalion first-aid station lickety-split through an artillery barrage. Returning to the front line, he found Medland getting ready to return to HQ for a briefing to attack the town of Steeg. While a hot meal was being prepared, the enemy prisoners were being closely guarded by two very alert riflemen. They bore careful watching; among them was a Gestapo officer under orders to shoot anyone who surrendered. These guys were fanatics; you couldn't let your guard down for one moment, as Martin well knew. But he was totally unprepared for what happened next.

One of his men found a second Gestapo officer hiding in a closet. As he emerged from the closet, the other Gestapo man seized the moment to make his move. Reaching behind him he pulled a pistol holstered between his shoulder blades and took two quick shots at Martin from 10 feet away. One bullet grazed his right ear, the other went through the camouflage netting on his head.

Martin fired off two shots from his .38, striking his assailant in each shoulder. "He was lucky I hadn't lost my temper," Martin would write ruefully.

For "A" Company, the battle for Mooshof would go down as its worst encounter of the entire war. The other companies had suffered heavily as well. Martin and his comrades now faced another immediate task, the capture of Steeg, a mile or so further on. With only 40 men in "A" Company, instead of what should have been a fighting strength of 160, it was a demanding prospect, one Dick Medland was decidedly unhappy about. However, with a hot meal in their bellies, fortified with a generous ration of rum, the survivors pressed on.

The riflemen faced a long slope of 400 to 500 feet, well protected with hidden machine guns and mortars. Not exactly a piece of cake! At least they had at their disposal the Wasps—flame throwers towed by carriers—which accompanied the advance sections. One was hit immediately by an 88mm. Another struck a mine that blew it off its track. The sergeant in charge was so badly wounded he was trapped. Two riflemen rushed to the rescue, accompanied by Martin who readied a needle of morphine. But they were unable to pull him from the vehicle, so Martin had to jab the needle through his tunic. All the while the sergeant was shouting at them to get away—the flame thrower could explode at any minute. But somehow they managed to pull him a safe distance away, 20 yards or so, before the Wasp and the vehicle blew up simultaneously, showering the area with pieces of metal. Miraculously, no one was hurt, but all four were close enough to the explosion that the heat singed their uniforms.

Now, as the lead sections continued their advance, a second phenomenon took place, at the sight of which the battle-weary riflemen could hardly believe their eyes. Although they continued to take losses, suddenly white flags began to appear everywhere as more than 200 of the toughest enemy soldiers they had ever run up against threw up their hands in surrender. The scene was unbelievable.

On March 28, the 3rd Canadian Infantry Division crossed the Rhine over a pontoon bridge at Rees. In the meantime, "A" Company of the QOR had lost the services of its CO, Dick Medland, earlier in an attack on the Hochwald-Balberger Wald Road. The target was two farm buildings at the south edge of a wooded area of tall, thick trees. Medland sent in two platoons of 15 men, which before long were pinned down by machine-gun and sniper fire. At the start-line, Medland stepped on a mine, taking a severe wound in the leg.

Martin helped a first-aid man apply a tourniquet to arrest the bleeding; then, as he worked his way forward, he spotted a sniper nest on a platform high in one of the trees. He fired off a shot, killing one of the marksmen but at the same time exposing his position and that of the others around him. Martin decided the only answer was to get out of the ambush fast with a fixed bayonet charge on the farm buildings. Martin took the Bren gun from a gunner whose right hand had been shattered and led the 40 riflemen remaining in the company through the woods, screaming at the top of their voices.

At first the enemy stood their ground and kept up steady defensive fire. But, unnerved, they soon broke and made a run for it. When Martin rushed one of the farmhouses a German soldier suddenly appeared from around a corner and stabbed him over the left eye with his bayonet. As Martin tried to fend off the weapon, he was wounded in the left hand, but he was able to fire the Bren gun, wounding the German in the left side and putting him out of action.

When the Canadians captured the farmhouses they found them full of German civilians—*terrified* civilians. The "savage" Canadians' wild, screaming attack had put the fear of God into them. Nevertheless, when hot food was brought up from the rear after the company had dug in, those same terrified civilians helped serve it.

With the loss of the commander and the appointment of a

replacement, and its number diminished to 40, the company badly needed a rest and time to regroup. One day an order came through from the newly appointed CO for a company parade. Martin considered it highly uncalled for, and unnecessary for men who needed instead to recover from months of tough combat. But it was lucky that he did not express his disapproval. He soon learned the ceremony had been ordered for the express purpose of investing him with the Distinguished Conduct Medal for his part in the QOR's engagements in Normandy, France, and Holland.

Once across the Rhine, the role of the Canadian army was to open up the supply route to the north through Arnhem, then clear the northeastern Netherlands, the coastal belt of Germany eastwards to the Elbe River, and Western Holland. By April 16, the QOR had reached an area near the village of Skeen close to the Zuider Zee where "A" Company was assigned the job of closing off a causeway to block the German retreat out of Holland.

The countryside consisted of open fields and farms and a 30-foot-high dike, across the top of which ran a 16-foot-wide road bordered by 8-foot shoulders and ditches filled with water, bordered with poplar trees. Directly ahead was a stone bridge 20 feet wide. The vicinity was stoutly defended by fanatical Hitler Youth soldiers armed with machine guns and mortars, as well as antiaircraft guns trained to fire at ground level along the dike.

The company's plan of attack was for two platoons to advance on either side of the dike along the ditches in waist-high water, protected from view by the poplars, and supported by a flame thrower and a Bren gun carrier, with a third platoon held in reserve. Because he had a bad chest cold, Charlie Martin elected to stay out of the water and take the high road—along the dike some 70 yards behind the platoon on the left. At the outset they ran into machine-gun fire which, while harassing, was ineffective. The flame thrower charged the bridge and unleashed its load before retiring but to little avail. Next the Bren gun carrier with six men aboard went into action, but accurate ack-ack fire knocked it out, killing all the occupants.

As soon as the flame thrower went into action, the men from the platoon on the left hit the deck because of the machine-gun and ack-ack fire that had also been aimed in their direction. Following behind, as soon as Martin reached the bridge, he was in trouble. As he stepped past a stone wall, to his left a German soldier let fly with his Schmeisser automatic. Dum-dum bullets struck his right leg and left arm and smashed his binoculars. Behind him, exploding ack-ack shells sent shrapnel and pieces of brick flying in all directions, some of them penetrating his back. But Martin managed to fire off a round from his .38 that hit his assailant right between the eyes.

A stretcher-bearer rushed to the scene and administered morphine. Martin figured he was a goner. "Please let me die in peace," he moaned and asked for a drink. The stretcher-bearer complied with a swig of straight rum from his flask.

Meanwhile, the third platoon in the company led by the new commanding officer took the objective and the Germans surrendered. Martin was taken to a first-aid station. Sporadically passing out and coming to, Martin remembered the regimental padre consoling him, tears streaming down his face. Last rites—now he was sure he'd had it. He was loaded aboard an ambulance, but the driver in his haste ran the vehicle off the road. Finally, it was towed out, but by the time they reached the hospital Martin was in such bad shape he was immediately taken to the operating room where the doctor began removing the bullets, patching up pieces of bone, and reattaching nerve ends. When he began working on his arm, Martin pleaded with him not to take it off. Then he passed right out. For Charlie Martin, the war was over.

In fact, it ended exactly two weeks later on May 8, the day Charlie regained consciousness. His first concern was to get in touch with his wife, Vi. She had already heard from the padre that he had been "slightly wounded." Charlie sent off a telegram but wartime security restrictions forbade identifying his whereabouts, so he sent her a letter—the only way of letting her know the name and place of the hospital in which he was recuperating.

After an arduous journey from England to the continent to reach the hospital, at the sight of a "slightly wounded" Charlie she wondered what someone suffering from *major* injuries would look like. But even with his right hip, his stomach, and his chest and left arm in a cast, and the fact that his loss of so much weight gave him a cadaverous appearance, to Vi he was still a sight for sore eyes.

At Sea

Chapter 13

The Teenage Merchant Mariner of Convoy PQ 16

One of my instructors at the Royal Air Force Operational Training Unit at Aston Down in Gloucester where I was learning to fly Spitfires in the winter of 1942–43, George Fenwick, had been a Hurricane fighter cata- pult pilot on the Murmansk run, ferrying supplies by convoy to Russia for the Red Armies. In the event of air attack, these pilots would be launched from merchant ships to fend off the raiders. There was no return. Once their job was finished, they had to bail out and hope to be picked up by one of the convoy escorts before freezing to death in the icy Arctic seas.

Fenwick didn't say much about his experiences—it wasn't fashion- able to "shoot a line" in those days—except to voice his low opinion of our Soviet allies. "When we went ashore, the Russian women working on the docks spat at us. That's the thanks we got after being under attack, often for a week at a time, to bring them the equipment they demanded from us."

But at the same time he also had the highest praise and respect for the merchant mariners, whom Canadian author James Lamb called the "bravest of the best." "While the navy acts as the shield," Fenwick went to pains to point out, "it's the merchantmen who are the targets for German U-boats and Luftwaffe bombers." One compensation: at least their rate of pay was substantially higher than that of the servicemen— if they lived to collect it!

Many of the sailors who manned the merchant ships were either too old for service with the navy or—as in the case of the teenage son of a Newfoundland fisherman from St. John's—too young. It is highly possible and most probable that Fenwick and that young mariner shared the same experiences on the Murmansk runs in the spring of 1942—the deadliest and costliest of any Russian-bound convoys.

Since the beginning of the war, St. John's harbour had buzzed with excitement. Merchants ships from all over the world, along with camouflaged warships, crammed into the harbour. Some vessels were towed in for repairs, damaged by a mine or an enemy submarine's torpedo. American and Canadian army and navy bases had sprung up rapidly. It was all very thrilling to young George Evans of St. John's, who aspired to serve his King and Country at sea. He joined the Sea Cadets, a branch of the local Church Lad's brigade.

In mid-July 1941, he entered the Royal Navy recruiting office in the King George V building on Water Street East to make application. "How old are you?" the recruiting officer asked. "I am 16," the 15-year-old replied. He was told to come back next year. Angrily, as George turned to go he said, "You won't see me next year. I'm joining the Merchant Navy or I'll stow away."

The next morning, George went fishing with his father. As they entered the harbour on returning from the fishing grounds, George saw a man aboard a ship flying the Norwegian flag waving to them. When his father pulled the fishing vessel alongside the gangway of the Norwegian merchantman, the man who had been waving introduced himself as the ship's chief steward and asked if they would sell him some fish.

While his father did business with the chief steward, George climbed aboard the ship and went aft to talk to some of the crew whom he joined for dinner. During the meal, he learned the name of the vessel—SS *Einvik*—and that a cabin boy was needed. After helping clean the mess deck, he took the pans back to the cook in the galley. George was asked if he would like to sign on as cabin boy. He was ecstatic.

He was told he could begin work at 0700 hours next day, but he would have to provide his birth certificate and a letter from his parents granting permission to join the ship's crew. When asked how old he was, George repeated the lie he had told the recruiting officer. The letter of permission presented no problem, but George would have to doctor the birth certificate he had requested from the Registrar's General Office, changing his date of birth from 1926 to 1924, which would make him 17 years old.

During his first week as part of the ship's crew, among his duties were helping the cook peel spuds and clean the galley, setting the table for the skipper and officers in the saloon, serving them their meals, making up their bunks, and cleaning their cabins.

One afternoon he was given time off to get his birth certificate. But when he tried to change the date it didn't work. It ended up looking like a spoiled ballot that would fool no one, so he decided to avoid the issue; he tore it up and threw it away. When he presented the skipper with the letter of permission from his parents, the captain again demanded the birth certificate. George stalled, saying that it had not been available when he visited the Registrar's office. That satisfied the skipper—at least temporarily. Knowing that the ship would be sailing for England in a few days, George managed to stay out of the skipper's way. Once he was at sea, lacking a birth certificate would cease to be a problem.

At 1600 hours on the afternoon of 1 September 1941, *Einvik*, along with other vessels in port, sailed through the narrows of St. John's harbour to rendezvous with convoy SC 41 from Sydney, Nova Scotia, and make up a flotilla of a total of 61 merchantmen escorted by eight warships, including three Royal Canadian Navy (RCN) corvettes: HMCS (His Majesty's Canadian Ship) *Arvida*, *Chicoutimi*, and *Matapedia*. The German navy knew of the contingent. A "Wolf Pack" comprising 15 U-boats had intercepted a signal from the convoy giving the exact time of departure.

Trying to keep up with the convoy was a struggle for the 2000-ton Norwegian freighter. The stokers did their best to keep up a sufficient head of steam but it was a losing battle. By the second day at sea *Einvik* began to straggle behind the convoy. Late in the evening the Canadian corvette *Arvida* pulled along on the port side to notify *Einvik*'s captain that the convoy had changed direction due to the detection of U-boats in its path and gave the new heading. *Einvik*'s skipper acknowledged the message and advised the corvette that he was having engine trouble.

Shortly after midnight the *Einvik*'s captain told the crew that their ship was now on its own and ordered a strict blackout. There was to be no smoking on deck, because a lighted cigarette could be seen in the darkness by an enemy ship for quite a distance and would give away their position.

By the next day, September 3, *Einvik*'s situation had worsened. The engine failed; a bearing in the crank shaft had broken. The ship was forced to heave-to while the engineers replaced the bearing and the stokers cleaned the boiler tubes.

The vessel drifted for several hours, but the ship's master could not signal an SOS for fear of radio interception by the U-boats. The engineers soon got the engine going again and the ship was able to proceed on its way at a healthy seven-and-a-half knots. But the next day in late afternoon the engine broke down again. This time a broken steam pipe had to be repaired. Suddenly *Arvida* appeared on the horizon with news that the convoy was now two days ahead. The captain advised the Norwegian skipper to watch for U-boats coming from the northwest and suggested steering a course northeast. To this the *Einvik*'s skipper replied that under the circumstances he would sail his ship on a direct course to England.

This was young George Evans' first time at sea and he accepted his ship's trials with a youthful exuberance. But when the ship got under way again, it ran into a heavy sea that tossed it around like a cork and George got seasick, a malady compounded by the lack of heat in the cabins. The coal was sorely needed to keep the engine operating at full speed instead of being used for warmth.

When the sea calmed down George soon recovered and spent his spare time playing cards for cigarettes with his crewmates and learning all he could about the ship's engine; his ambition was to become a stoker and eventually an engineer.

Next day, September 5, at 2330 hours, the ship's fireman on watch reported "something black on the water a mile or so ahead." George had retired to his cabin, which was directly over the engine room on the main deck. It was cramped—about two feet wide and six feet long, with barely enough room for a bunk, table, chair, washbasin, locker, and his trunk. Because the crew had been put on alert, George lay down on his bunk fully clothed and fell asleep.

About an hour later he was rudely awakened by a resounding bang against the side of the ship. George grabbed his lifejacket and bolted for the lifeboat deck. Someone was shouting that a torpedo had hit the starboard side. Something then struck George in the middle of the back, knocking him face down on the deck. One of the crew picked him up, carried him forward, lowering him into the starboard lifeboat ,which was bobbing in the water. As the lines were let go, the U-boat sent a salvo into the bridge of the merchant-man; the explosion set fire to the aft quarters and to a small lifeboat still on board.

The skipper called a roll of the two lifeboats. Everyone was accounted for except the radio officer. Someone had seen him racing from the radio room across the deck to the port side. The chief officer in the second boat ordered his crew to row back to the ship, but it was now under heavy fire from the German submarine. Then the *Einvik* began to sink. The lifeboats had to keep their distance.

Miraculously, however, the radio officer had managed to escape. As soon as the first torpedo had struck, he had tapped out an SOS. Then, when the submarine continued to shell the ship, he rushed from the radio shack to one side of the ship and then the other; on the starboard side he had found a small boat that he lowered into the water. He managed to row a safe distance from the ship before the suction from the sinking merchantman could drag him down too. He was sighted at dawn by the lifeboats and one of them took him aboard and let the little boat that saved him go adrift.

The skipper reckoned their position to be approximately 450 miles from the Westmann Islands (*Vestmannaeyjar*), off the south shore of Iceland. The boats set off in that direction. The boat captained by the chief officer was under sail, and it towed the second, in which George found himself, alongside the skipper of the lost *Einvik*. The sea was calm with a slight breeze from the northwest, but that evening it started to blow and a heavy sea began to run. Then the tow line broke and the boats were separated. The crew in George's boat hoisted a sail and with a strong wind were making good time until the mast snapped in two. Some of the crew took turns rowing, which kept them warm, while others repaired the mast. Once it was mended they got under way again.

On the following day the crew treated themselves to part of the rations they had managed to salvage from the ship—some food and a few ounces of water, the first nourishment they'd had since abandoning the vessel. It was cold and to keep warm they took turns rowing. Later in the day, however, the sun came out and while this was comforting, the wind died down completely, leaving them to entirely depend on rowing. George's hands became blistered and swollen, and then his feet started to swell. The skipper told him to stand up and keep the blood circulating. But he started to feel faint and drowsy, and needed to lie down. With 11 men crowded into the small boat, making room for him wasn't easy. But, with the skipper's direction, they made enough room to allow George to stretch out on the bottom of the boat, where he slept until dawn and off and on through the next day, which was sunny, calm, and warmer. However, the crew was becoming exhausted— still no wind.

That night they sighted a ship. But since they could not identify it, they silently rowed past, fearing that if it was an enemy vessel, they would be taken prisoner. Later, a heavy rain and a choppy sea added to their discomfort all that night and throughout the next day. They were down to the last of their rations—only some hard bread and a little drinking water. With his feet sore and badly swollen, George was in agony. But, mercifully, their distress was about to end.

On mid-morning, September 1941, the 11 survivors began to shout for joy and hoisted sail again as the Westmann Islands hove into view. About noon an Icelandic fishing vessel came alongside and took the lifeboat, with the Norwegian flag aft placed there by the skipper, in tow. The fishermen then fed them lunch along with hot chocolate and tea, the first warm substances they had had inside of them for over a week.

By the time they docked at the pier at the fishing village of Storhord, the word of their arrival had spread and hundreds of Icelanders were on hand to greet them. Suffering from acute edema of the arms and feet, a bad cold, and bronchitis, George was the last to be taken off the lifeboat and, with the others, got into a British army truck to be taken to the local hospital for treatment. It was two weeks before George was able to walk without a cane, and his feet still bothered him if he stayed on them for too long.

During that time he and his crewmates learned that the other lifeboat had made it safely to another port on the island. There had been a skirmish aboard when one of the crew had been caught stealing some of the rations. The chief officer had threatened to shoot the culprit (a .38 revolver is carried on board all lifeboats in case of attempted mutiny). If another member of the crew had not intervened, he might well have carried out his threat.

At the beginning of the last week of September, *Einvik*'s crew was ferried to Reykjavik on the southwest coast, Iceland's main industrial centre, to board a Norwegian troopship. At dockside the German crew of the U-boat that had torpedoed them was under British army guard.

The harbour was full of merchant vessels and warships. George and his shipmates—and most aboard all of the vessels except senior officers—were unaware that the first Allied convoy was being assembled to carry cargoes of weapons and supplies around the North Cape to the Russian ports of Murmansk and Archangel.

At this time, the destination of his troopship was Greenock, Scotland. It reached Greenock on September 30 after a four-day voyage, during which, one night, the escorts had to scare off a U-boat attack. Roused by the ship's bell, George was not so much afraid of being torpedoed again as he was distressed by the nagging pain in his feet.

While in Scotland, George, who had yet to reach his 16th birthday, began to get homesick. There was one compensating factor; his feet were giving him less trouble. But he was running out of money; ashore, at his own expense, he had to stay in a hotel because there was no naval establishment available. In desperation he signed on with a British supply ship, the SS *Daytonian*, aboard which his ambition was at last realized—he was assigned the job of stoker. He had to work in oppressive temperatures as high as 110 degrees, which made it impractical to wear a lifejacket. In any case, because the boiler room was so far below decks, chances of surviving a torpedo were virtually nil. He had at least the compensation—and relative safety—of occasionally taking his turn at watch on deck, as the ship made its way to North America.

The merchantman reached Charleston, North Carolina, safely, where it took on cargo for the United Kingdom, and then put in at Sydney, Nova Scotia, to load up with coal. There George asked the ship's master to be paid off; he'd had enough of the Merchant Navy, at least for the time being, and wanted to go home to his family for a while.

The request was denied, and George shipped out across the North Atlantic.

Fog shrouded the convoy for most of the journey, but U-boats claimed several of the merchantmen on those rare sunny days. *Daytonian* docked at Liverpool on December 13 and George wasted no time detraining for London to see the Newfoundland commissioner and arrange for passage home.

He was duly accommodated by the commissioner to join a ship departing two days' hence from Liverpool. George promptly hopped the train from Euston Station to take him back up north. But, on arrival, in anticipation of returning home at last, he got so drunk that he failed to make it to the ship, and it sailed without him. And he was broke—again.

"Maybe I wasn't ready to go home just yet," he mused later.

With only enough money in his pocket for tram fare, George had no choice but to apply to the Merchant Navy Manning Depot for reassignment. He was ordered to report to the small 1695-ton Dutch coastal vessel SS *Aurora*. Its job was to sail around the British Isles coastal ports picking up and delivering cargo, all the while looking out for enemy German aircraft. On 25 March 1942, a week after George turned 16, the ship arrived at London without incident. After three months and five days at sea George was at last paid off with orders to proceed to Hull in Yorkshire to join the SS *Pieter de Hoogh*, a British Empire ship taken over by the Dutch. Though neither he nor the crew were told of the ship's assignment, it was clear from the amount of supplies being taken aboard, and the heavy armament fore and aft manned by British army and Royal Navy gunners, that they were in for a long voyage and very likely a dangerous one.

On 27 March 1942 the ship sailed for Iceland where it joined a massive convoy designated PQ 16. The convoy's destination was the Russian port of Murmansk on the Barents Sea. The crews had been issued with long underwear, heavy woollen socks, duffel coats, leather boots, rubber boots, and floating suits to protect them from the arctic weather. To preserve the tightest security there was no shore leave granted. On May 23, under heavy escort by battleships, destroyers, antiaircraft ships, and submarines, the convoy, which also included supply tankers and Hurricane fighters that could be catapulted from the merchantmen, set sail from various Icelandic ports.

The prospect for the convoy was a scary one indeed. The stories he had heard in the pubs in Hull about convoys to Russia "frightened me," George confessed. On May 24, the convoy sailed into the Denmark Strait, and straight into thick fog. The ships became separated, but the following day, due to careful and skillful searching and shepherding on the part of the escort, all 39 merchantmen were regrouped, spread out into nine columns. Ahead, astern, and on the flanks the destroyers, corvettes, and converted trawlers, acting as rescue vessels, were constantly in motion. A cruiser squadron was positioned between the columns of merchant ships. Before dawn, all ships were in their designated places. As George Evans would later write, "Now everything was ready, whatever the enemy had to throw at us."

At 0535 hours George was standing watch when sirens sounded throughout the convoy, alerting the escort ships that a German Focke-Wulf four-engine Kondor was shadowing them to the rear, flying in circles. One of the destroyers opened fire. The enemy aircraft flew off but it had done its reconnaissance. That afternoon at 1400 hours, a British convoy returning from Murmansk and Archangel reported a U-boat several miles to starboard of the outgoing fleet. One of the destroyers gave chase, carrying out an attack with depth charges, but it was unable to determine whether the submarine had been damaged.

At 1830 hours the convoy experienced its first air attack, one of a series that would continue for the next six days. In a cloudless sky, from out of the sun, seven Heinkel III torpedo bombers and six Junkers 88 dive-bombers dropped their loads. But only one vessel was hit, an American merchantman. One of the British merchantmen launched a Hurricane fighter that shot down one of the Heinkels and badly damaged another. The Hurricane pilot, who was wounded by machine-gun fire from one of the rear gunners, was able to bail out and be picked up. Two of the destroyers also scored, bringing down one of the Junkers.

The American merchantman that had been hit was blowing smoke, and the flames could be seen for miles, George remembered. Though the crew worked tirelessly to put out the fire while the convoy was still under attack, the ship drifted behind and a trawler rescue vessel was ordered to stand by. At 2240 hours, when her skipper reported that it would take 48 hours to repair the damage, she was taken in tow by one of the destroyers to return to Iceland. An hour later, 12 JU-88s attacked but were driven off by the convoy gunners with no damage to any of the ships.

But there was no letup. Now it was the turn of the U-boats. At 0305 the next day, one of the American cargo ships took two torpedoes in its port side and sank immediately. Miraculously, 28 of the crew were rescued although seven perished in the icy waters and two others died later. Sometime afterwards an enemy submarine fired at one of the destroyers, but missed. The warship in turn dropped 10 depth charges but no hit was registered. Then, at 0557 hours, one of the destroyers sighted two U-boats off the starboard side of the convoy—the flank always in the greatest danger with the coast on its right beam—a mile apart and five miles from the convoy. The destroyer chased after one of them but it dove before the ship could take action. One of the problems plaguing the escorts was the poor Asdic detection device conditions brought on by the severe cold. This hampered their operations during the running duel between the destroyers and the U-boats that ensued over the next 10 hours. An American freighter was slightly damaged, but otherwise the battle was inconclusive.

At 1800 hours the convoy came under aerial attack once more by eight Heinkel torpedo bombers and three Junkers dive-bombers. "Hell indeed!" was the way 16-year-old George Evans described the terrifying ordeal that followed—men crouched at their posts, eyes and mouths agape looking haggard, tears rolling down their cheeks, some praying: "the air trembled with a rain of bullets, shell fragments, and the bombs would [just] miss the side of the ship." The sea heaved from the concussion of the bombs when they struck the surface and exploded. Ships were rocked by the blasts, their propellers clattering in the air as their stern rose out of the water. Then it was over—but the crews knew the respite was only temporary. At 2300 hours one of the destroyers sighted a submarine seven miles ahead and gave chase, but didn't engage.

At 0320 hours on Wednesday, May 27, the Luftwaffe returned with a vengeance. This time seven HE-IIIs and three JU-88s simultaneously rained bombs and torpedoes down on the convoy. Though the raid lasted only minutes and not a single bomb landed on target, the effect on the morale of the merchant crews was devastating. The continuous bombardment, the anticipation after one attack that another would quickly follow, stretched the sailors' nerves to the breaking point. Most of the men had been without sleep for three days and Murmansk was still three days away; they "sprawled head down on mess decks or room tables," George recalled. The only communication between them was an occasional nod to each other.

Now the convoy was plagued by another peril—large pack-ice floes, heavy and impenetrable—south of Bear Island. The armada was forced to change course continually to steer around them and avoid collision. The snow-capped majesty of Mount Misery was clearly visible from 60 miles away.

Just before noon, the Luftwaffe launched one of the most devastating aerial attacks made on any Allied convoy during the entire war. A total of 180 German dive-bombers and torpedo bombers assaulted PQ 16 for a solid eight hours with 120 missiles, escalating the convoy's total losses since leaving port to 20 percent.

Diving through broken cloud at 3000 feet, the Luftwaffe not only achieved surprise but had to its advantage an intermittent filmy haze at 1500 feet that made it difficult for the defending gunners to take proper aim. Right off the bat, the SS *Alamar*, an American vessel, was hit by two bombs that set it on fire, forcing the crew to abandon ship. A British submarine was dispatched to finish it off and get it out of the way; then, joined by a destroyer, it picked up survivors. The explosions from two near misses so badly damaged another American ship, SS *Mormacsul*, below the water line that it began filling with sea water and sank. Survivors were picked up by a destroyer and a rescue trawler.

At 1405 hours the Russian vessel SS *Stari Bolshevik* received a direct hit in the forecastle, which started a fire. The crew, which included women sailors, refused to abandon the ship and over the next 38 hours, with the help of a French corvette, they finally brought the fire under control. Though smoke billowed from her foreholds, the vessel continued to maintain her place in the convoy.

Two near misses started so bad a leak in the No. 1 and No. 2 holds of the American freighter SS *City of Joliet* that the ship had to be abandoned. The British merchantman SS *Empire Baffin*, also damaged by two near misses, was luckier: she was able to make repairs and continue in line with the convoy. By now a crisis had developed. The rescue trawlers were overloaded with the survivors they had already picked up. The merchantmen could not pick up any; it would make them too easy a target for the enemy. From then on it was up to the destroyers.

Almost simultaneously, SS *Empire Lawrence*, a British vessel with a Hurricane fighter aboard, was hit and two destroyers were ordered to stand by. Shortly after they had maneuvered into position the ship was hit by four more bombs, and by the time the smoke had cleared she had sunk. The destroyers, by this time under attack themselves, picked up the survivors.

As a stick of four bombs rained down abreast of the Polish destroyer *Garland*, the first one hit the water and exploded, triggering others. Shrapnel riddled the ship from stem to stern. The "A" and "B" guns, the starboard Oerlikon gun, and the No. 1 boiler room were knocked out of action and a fire broke out on the forecastle. It was finally brought under control, but casualties were heavy: 25 killed and 43 wounded.

The situation was so critical that a medical officer from one of the other destroyers, who was transferred to the ship to attend to the wounded, recommended making port as quickly as possible where those in the most serious condition could be hospitalized. The destroyer then proceeded to Murmansk at a hasty 24 knots.

Strapped to a 20mm Oerlikon with the ship's bosun helping him aboard SS *Pieter de Hoogh*, George Evans gathered some idea of just how frightening that type of bombing could be. Because the enemy torpedo planes were attacking from astern with the sun at their backs, George and the bosun couldn't see them for the bright glare of the sun in their eyes. George opened fire in what he hoped was the general direction of the Heinkels, then as they passed overhead swung his gun around and kept shooting. But the bomber managed to drop a stick of bombs so close to the vessel that, when they exploded, the water erupted and splashed the decks amidships.

At 1945 hours a bomb struck the British merchantman SS *Empire Purcell* on the forward deck, starting a bad fire. The ship had to be abandoned. Two destroyers under heavy attack pulled survivors from the water. Five minutes later, the crew of another British cargo carrier, SS *Lowther Castle*, was forced to abandon ship when a torpedo fired from a Heinkel III at 4000 yards' range struck her port side.

That was the last direct casualty of an air raid that had lasted all afternoon and evening. Finally, at 2130 hours, in George Evans' words, "the enemy left us in peace except for the inevitable German Blohm and Voss float-planes circling the horizon."

For convoy PQ 16 the situation was grim. In a single day, five merchantmen had been lost. Poor weather conditions made it impossible to accurately assess the damage inflicted by the ack-ack gunners on the attacking aircraft. At least five JU-88s had been seen to crash into the sea after being set on fire. From radio intercepts German aircraft returning to their bases in Norway could be heard signalling an SOS.

The worst crisis now facing the convoy was the shortage of ammunition. Orders were issued to conserve it within reason—not to exceed an expenditure of 1000 rounds. But many ships already had less than 1000 rounds available. Although George Evans' vessel, SS *Pieter de Hoogh*, carried a volatile cargo of TNT, ammunition, and other explosives, the crew had no ammunition at all— in effect, their ship was defenceless. However, they accepted this situation philosophically and went about their duties calmly, which won them the admiration of the crews of the ships immediately surrounding them.

Next night the convoy was joined by three Russian destroyers. Evans marvelled at their speed and maneuverability, and the accuracy and versatility of their gunnery. When 18 Heinkels and Junkers attacked from the rear, as the bombers passed overhead the destroyers opened up with everything they had. Then they continued to press forward, following the attackers' exact route, the gunners skipping the shells of their 37mm Bofors guns off the water so that they bounced up into the bellies of the torpedo planes. Two Heinkels caught fire and crashed into the sea. Another was damaged and flew away. Not a single ship was damaged.

Next day, May 30, the ships finally reached their destination, the port of Murmansk, the largest within the Arctic Circle, which had once been a peaceful fishing hamlet. The ships began docking to unload their precious supply cargoes, so desperately needed by the Red armies. Though PQ 16 had reached its journey's end, there was no respite. With a Luftwaffe fighter base only 50 miles away, to protect the Norway-based bombers, the port was under constant aerial siege. Though Russian Stormovik fighters, helped by a Royal Air Force Hurricane fighter wing based at Murmansk, did their best to ward off the attacks, the raids continued daily except when weather interfered. The targets were the docks and the railway cars bound for Leningrad.

When SS *Pieter de Hoogh* tried to dock, a bomb struck her forward deck. Though damage was slight, other missiles blew the wharf to pieces and the merchantman had to anchor outside while White Russian prisoners, under the watch of Russian army guards armed with machine guns and German police dogs, rebuilt the dock.

PQ 16 remained at Murmansk for nearly a month. The crews were billeted at the Arctica Hotel, adjacent to the International Club recreation centre, both of which they shared with RAF and

RN officers as well as Russian army and navy officers, some 1000 personnel in all.

During their time in Russia, George Evans and his shipmates had several opportunities to talk to the men and women working around Murmansk—always under guard. Contrary to my Spitfire instructor Paul Fenwick's experience, they found the Russians to be cordial though understandably wary. They were also subjected to Communist Russian propaganda films, which as an interpreter translated, glorified the Russian Revolution and praised the heroic Red armies in the field. The underlying message was not lost on George and his shipmates: "The Russians were very anxious to rule the world," he commented later. "We truly felt sorry for the Russian people. They were hard working and were treated like animals."

The convoy crews' accommodation was comfortable enough by local standards; the only real discomfort was the constant bombing raids, some of them alarmingly close to the hotel. In fact it was that very factor that precipitated the convoy's eventual departure.

At a Big Three meeting on June 24, it was decided jointly by the Americans, British, and Russians that all ships at Murmansk should be ready to leave the port as soon as possible due to the bombing by the enemy.

Three days later PQ 16 set sail to rendezvous next day, June 28, with another convoy from Archangel. Compared to the outward voyage—though the convoys were twice sighted by German aircraft but never came under attack either from the air or by submarine—the trip home was like a holiday cruise. By the first week of July all ships reached port safely in Iceland.

That was one of the last of the convoy PQ series. The loss of so many merchantmen resulted in their being discontinued temporarily. At issue also was the harsh treatment of Allied seamen by the Russians, to which Paul Fenwick and George Evans, each in their own way, had alluded, and the Russians' refusal to allow the British to send in a hospital unit to Murmansk. Once these problems had been thrashed out at the highest level—

between British prime minister Winston Churchill and Soviet premier Joseph Stalin—the convoys to northern Russia were resumed the following spring after the ice went out.

George Evans, by this time a "mature" 17 years old, was among those aboard the merchantmen who made some of those subsequent perilous voyages and later served in the Middle East and the Indian Ocean. But nothing rivalled the baptism of fire he had experienced with convoy PQ 16. After the war, becoming a Canadian citizen after Newfoundland joined the Dominion in 1948, he was employed in the Customs Service. He wrote this epitaph:

The only remembrance of the convoys is a graveyard overlooking the Kola Inlet in Murmansk. A large globe-shaped monument outside the Merchant Seaman's Club recalls the common fight of the countries of the Anti-Hitler coalition, [as does] a textbook in the Russian schools of Murmansk.

Chapter 14

Three-and-a-Half Unforgettable Hours Before Dawn

Following a two-week dive-bombing course, in mid-April of 1944 our squadron was posted to Tangmere fighter field on the south coast of Sussex where, along with the rest of our wing, we engaged in bombing No-Ball targets—the concrete launching pads for the German V-1 flying bombs. At the same time we bombed bridges, and attacked trains, transports, and any enemy aircraft we could find across the breadth of northern France, from Cherbourg to the Pas de Calais. Clearly this was a softening-up for the inevitable invasion of Europe. Isolated as we were in our fighter pilots' world, we remained unaware of the buildup of the Allied armies (well camouflaged) and the naval preparation to clear the sea lanes. But, in the English Channel, there was plenty of action, as the following story reveals.

On Friday evening, 28 April 1944, two of the Royal Canadian Navy's four Tribal Class destroyers, *Athabaskan* and *Haida*, set off from Plymouth, England, for the French coast, as part of naval operations to clear the English Channel of German shipping in the months before the invasion of Europe. These destroyers were well equipped for the task. Unlike the Canadian destroyers and corvettes assigned to carry out convoy duty and protect the merchant marine from U-boats, the Tribals were designed and equipped to attack surface vessels. They had a top speed of 36 knots and were heavily armed with 4.7-inch guns, Oerlikons, pom-poms, torpedoes, and depth charges. Both of these two particular Tribals were skippered by veteran commanders and manned by battle-hardened crews.

John Stubbs, captain of *Athabaskan*, had distinguished himself in 1942 while on convoy duty as commander of the destroyer *Assiniboine*, which sank a German submarine by ramming it. Harry DeWolf, captain of *Haida*, first saw action in June 1940 as skipper of *Restigouche*, evacuating British personnel from France and later in the year supervising the rescue of survivors from the *Aranadora Star* troopship.

On 26 April 1944, only two nights before their joint foray off the French coast, the two Tribals had formed part of a flotilla that included sister-Tribal *Huron*, a British destroyer and cruiser that intercepted three Elbing-class German destroyers northeast of Île de Bas, off the north coast of Brittany. A firefight ensued, and one of the enemy was sent to the bottom without an Allied loss. But on this night *Athabaskan* and *Haida* were on their own.

Their first job was to cover British minelayers laying their charges 10 miles east off the Île de Bas, scene of the action two nights earlier. By 0200 hours on April 29 they were in position to carry out their routine task, allowing the crews to catch up on their sleep. At 0300 they were all through, ready to set sail back to Plymouth, when British radar picked up a German force hugging the French coast, steaming westward toward the mouth of the Morlaix River.

The two Tribals veered in a southerly direction. DeWolf, in charge, hoped to cut the Germans off before they could round the Brittany coast and make for Brest. The moon had gone down and a slight haze made visibility difficult. When radar showed the enemy within 7000 yards' range, DeWolf gave the order "Ignite." Three star shells illuminated the enemy force: two Elbing-class destroyers T-24 and T-27 that had escaped the Tribals' attack two nights before, and an E-boat. The destroyers discharged smoke and began to make a run for it. But DeWolf had already given the order to fire and the guns of *Haida* and *Athabaskan* opened up at the same time as they turned their bows directly at the destroyers to present as little silhouette as possible to avoid enemy torpedoes.

But their action was too late. The Germans put star shells over the Tribals and furiously began returning their fire. A torpedo struck *Athabaskan* near the stern. John Stubbs reported from the bridge, "I'm hit and losing power." DeWolf laid down a smoke-screen to give the consort ship protection, and at the same time chased after the enemy.

Aboard *Athabaskan* there was feverish activity but no panic. All the guns were out of action and fires burned above and below decks. The propeller shaft was smashed. *Athabaskan* was adrift, her stern beginning to settle. Stubbs gave the order for all hands to "stand by their abandon-ship stations." The crew started to file off the bridge when one of the magazines exploded and with a roar a spire of flame shot skyward. Able Seaman Roy Westaway, whose job was to pipe hands to abandon-ship stations, was told, "You'd better get over the side yourself."

The rear of the ship was a mass of fire and smoke. Then the deck collapsed. The only survivor in that area, Chief Petty Officer Charlie Burgess, was thrown forward by the explosion, and had his arm broken in two places. Helpless and unable to hang onto anything, he slid under the railing into the sea. Globs of burning oil were falling everywhere. Some men took refuge in the lifeboats and others jumped into the water. As the crew watched *Athabaskan* sinking stern-first, they had to struggle in the thick sludge of oil that was spreading over the surface of the water. Fifteen of the men gradually formed a group and managed to find a Carley float. Luckily the crew had been issued with new self-inflatable lifesaving vests two weeks earlier that had a cord with a snap-hook at the end to attach to the floats. The vests doubtless saved a lot of lives, but the hooks became a problem when the Carley float, which was full of holes, began to sink. Unhooking themselves proved difficult for the men; their hands were numb from the cold.

Meanwhile, as the survivors of *Athabaskan* watched their ship go down, *Haida* exacted revenge, returning the fire of the German destroyers and scoring a direct hit on one of the Elbings. Flames burst amidships, then in the confusion of darkness, flames, and smoke, the two German ships began firing on one another while *Haida* continued her assault. One of the Elbings broke off; the other, realizing escape was impossible so close to shore, deliberately ran aground on a reef.

Haida wheeled away to quickly pluck as many of *Athabaskan*'s crew as possible from the sea. DeWolf gave the order to stop engines and fired off star shells to light up the ocean—a panorama of men in groups, some clinging to rafts, others drifting about in their lifejackets. *Haida* lowered her power launch with Bill Maclure at the helm. He first picked up two of his shipmates who had been swept into the water while manning the scramble-nets. As *Haida* pulled alongside the Carley float, Leading Seaman Jim L'Esperance grabbed the scramble-net with one arm and held onto the float with the other. In the meantime, one sailor who'd already been rescued came to help him, because he kept drifting away from the ship. So L'Esperance sat on one end and his shipmate hung on to the other while survivors climbed up the scramble-net.

It was getting close to dawn and DeWolf realized they could not stay in the area much longer; as soon as it got light they would be at the mercy of enemy bombers. From the water, DeWolf heard *Athabaskan*'s skipper, John Stubbs, shout "Get away! Get clear!" Those were the last words he would ever speak.

Reluctantly DeWolf gave the order to proceed. As the ship began to pull away, L'Esperance, who was still hooked to the float, lost his grip on the scramble-net. He unhooked himself from the float and swam after it. He was just one hand's-length away from it when a seaman on the net tried to reach him. But although their fingers touched, L'Esperance simply couldn't make it.

Eventually, however, L'Esperance got to another float and climbed into it. It was still pitch black. He could hear people yelling all around him, one repeatedly shouting for help. L'Esperance abandoned the float and swam toward the voice, grabbed the sailor and pulled him back onto the float. He was in terrible shape. In the explosion he'd injured his back, and was paralyzed and badly burnt. L'Esperance recalled that his skin "was hanging from his face, and his hands were like gloves hanging from his fingernails ... I got him into the float and made him as comfortable as he could get."

Despite his broken arm, Charles Burgess, a strong swimmer, managed with the help of a shipmate to drag several of the survivors onto a Carley float. Two of them were sure they could reach *Haida*'s scramble-nets. But a young seaman they had rescued cried out, "Don't leave me!" Burgess and the other man knew what they had to do. They climbed back onto the raft. Luckily, all three were soon picked up by the motor launch.

Jim L'Esperance and his mates were not so lucky. They sat on their float until daylight when they were spotted by a German minesweeper, which picked them up.

Once aboard, the Germans ordered the survivors to strip off all their clothes, because they were covered in fuel oil. They were taken two at a time into a shower room and given detergent soap to try to scrub down. It worked only partially; it took weeks before they were able to wash it all off.

As *Haida* vanished over the horizon, the men in the motor launch were beset with problems; the engine kept conking out. Then three German minesweepers appeared, but they were too busy pulling *Athabaskan* survivors from the sea to pay the whaler boat any attention, one of them taking the seamen aboard, the others guarding the flanks. For the survivors the voyage to Brest in the hold of the ship was highly uncomfortable and frightening as the German ships were bombed twice by British planes.

At sea around 0900 hours, Maclure and the men in the motor launch suddenly saw two fighter planes flying low toward them from the north. In the mistaken belief they were friendly, the crew got to their feet and waved and shouted furiously. Maclure even fired off a red flare. Then somebody spotted black crosses on the wings of the planes, and shouted that they were enemy. Everyone ducked. But for a second time they'd got lucky. The Messerschmitt fighters paid them no attention and simply flew on toward the French coast.

At about this same time the German minesweeper with *Athabaskan* survivors on board landed at Brest. The Germans loaded the men, still naked, into trucks, then drove through the town to a naval barracks. There, in front of the building, a guard of a dozen sailors armed with rifles marched forward and told them to stand up. The officer in charge stood before them waving his sword and shouting instructions in German, which the prisoners could not understand. Then the guards aimed their rifles at the Canadian seamen. The officer's next order was clear enough. In plain English he blurted that if they tried to escape they would be shot.

They were then issued French naval clothing and taken inside the barracks where they were told to lie on the floor. Anyone caught talking earned a rifle butt across the side of the head. However, conditions improved dramatically that evening when soldiers from the German army took charge. The prisoners were given cigarettes and permission to talk to each other.

Maclure and his crew fared better. Around noon that day, the engine in the motor launch again conked out, but Maclure soon had it going once more and it ran steadily as they cruised slowly toward England. Then at 1830 hours some fighters appeared on the horizon and the men ducked to avoid being spotted by the enemy. This time the fighters turned out to be Royal Canadian Air Force Spitfires who signalled the Air Sea Rescue service to send out a motor launch to pick up the whaler crew.

One hundred twenty-seven *Athabaskan* crew had perished along with their skipper, John Stubbs. The 85 survivors taken captive were imprisoned at Wetstertimke, a POW camp between Bremen and Hamburg. During their confinement, Hec Cooper remembered that around Christmas 1944 a lot of new prisoners started arriving at the camp. In particular, he recalled a group of French internees who were in bad shape. They had been treated very roughly by their captors. "I have to admit, the Germans always respected a prisoner of war," Cooper alleged. "This is an odd thing about their thinking. They respected what they called 'the fighting man,' but they wouldn't respect the civilian that refused to become a loyal German."

Significantly, in addition to the *Athabaskan* survivors, only 14 other Royal Canadian Navy personnel were made prisoners-of-war during the entire conflict.

Chapter 15

And the Sea Shall Give Up Her Dead

Two thousand miles away to the west of the sinking of the Athabaskan, *and two weeks later, another sea disaster took place, this time in home waters. It was a tragedy fraught with irony. As I look back, had I and some of my buddies known of it at the time, we would have probably been indifferent. For those of us stationed in England, Europe was the battleground—not the waters off the coast of Newfoundland.*

Members of a Royal Canadian Navy court of inquiry convened on 10 May 1944 at St. John's, Newfoundland, to "inquire into the loss of HMCS *Valleyfield* and the death and injuries of certain officers and ratings on board the said ship at the time." They were acutely aware that the evidence they were about to hear and upon which they were compelled to pronounce judgment, represented as bizarre a proliferation of confusion, delay, indecision, uncertainty, lack of judgment, indifference, and ineptitude as had ever been brought forward before a formal military inquest. They would learn too of the unprecedented acts of valour and sacrifice also surrounding that horrific incident which had occurred at midnight four days earlier.

Ironically, on that Monday, May 6, the iceberg- and ice-floe-infested seas upon which this tragic turbulence and misery would be played out in bright moonlight, were as serenely calm and unruffled as an inland lake. Fate, however, was about to lay a heavy hand on the serenity.

Slightly awash—its conning tower partially penetrating the surface—south of St. Mary's Bay off the Avalon Peninsula, Unterseeboat *U-548*, commanded by Kapitanleutnant Eberhard Zimmermann, prowled the sea in search of enemy shipping. His was no ordinary submarine. It was one of the later type of U-boats now in service with the *Kriegsmarine*, larger and faster and designed to attack from the surface as well as underwater. With torpedo tubes both astern and in the bow, among the 23 missiles it carried were some of the new "Gnat" acoustic torpedoes that could be fired in the general direction of the enemy ship and would home in on it from the noise of the ship's propellers. As an undersea predator, *U-548* represented a lethal menace to Allied shipping indeed. Captained by a seasoned veteran of U-boat warfare, its crew was eagerly intent on finding and destroying enemy shipping, a mission that had eluded it for the past six weeks.

To the south, the crews of Escort C-1, comprising five Royal Canadian Naval vessels spread 300 yards apart out in line abreast—the frigate *Valleyfield* in the centre with two corvettes on either beam, *Halifax* and *Frontenac* to port, *Giffard* and *Edmunston* to starboard—having turned their convoy escort duties over to a relief group, were returning home. They were sailing north to St. John's after an arduous escort duty across the Atlantic. The crews were happily in the grip of "Channel Fever"—looking forward to savouring the delights of a stint of shore leave.

Unknown to the chief protagonist of this unfolding drama, Zimmermann's movements had not gone undetected. His signals back and forth from his operational headquarters in Germany were being monitored by the British Admiralty and decoded through the Ultra Secret device, the more memorable of them being a message on the evening of May 6: "Zimmermann, for Commander: Daughter born May 4. Mother and daughter well. Congratulations. Admiral Commanding U-boats." Earlier, that afternoon, a general signal had been sent out to all ships warning of the presence of a U-boat in the vicinity of Cape Race and giving its approximate position to two corvettes from Escort Group W-32, *Timmins* and *Agassiz*, which had been dispatched to hunt *U-548* down.

Crews of Escort C-1 accepted the U-boat bulletin laconically as nothing more than a routine message to be entered into the signal log, certainly nothing to get excited about. Such communications were regularly issued to ships at sea, a drill one got accustomed to and thought no more of. And, after all, hadn't another group been assigned the search duty? There was, however, a single exception to this otherwise indifferent attitude. Because of the extraordinarily clear conditions prevailing, the standard procedure of zigzagging to make a U-boat attack difficult had been put into effect. But maintaining this pattern was complicated by the need to quickly change and correct direction to avoid collision with the icebergs and floes all about. It was therefore with some relief that at 2030 hours the nervous, weary watch-keepers learned that the senior officer, Royal Navy Commander James "the Brain" Byron, aboard *Valleyfield*, had ordered the zigzagging discontinued; that a clear, straight-ahead course could be steered. Among other things, this cut the time needed to reach St. John's; but, with the sea so clear and mirror-like and the moon so high and bright, conditions could not have been better for a submarine to pick off a target at will!

And that wasn't the only invitation to Zimmermann to try his luck. Aboard the frigate there was a radar hang-up. The operators hadn't completely got the hang of the new RX/C equipment that had recently been installed in their ship. When Lieutenant Ian Tate, standing watch on the bridge, failed to receive a radar report of a huge iceberg he had sighted dead ahead, he called down the voice-pipe for a bearing. In frustration, the operator replied that his screen was so cluttered with echoes from the many ice floes about the ship it was impossible to distinguish one object from another. In disgust Tate ordered the operator to switch off the newfangled machine and turn on the original SW1C set. But, while the operators were thoroughly familiar with the older mechanism, it was too antiquated and limited in range to be of any practical use. Detection of surface objects—not to mention enemy submarines—meanwhile had to depend on the lookouts. And *Valleyfield* wasn't the only ship with radar problems. *Frontenac*'s set had been unserviceable for some days. So now, on this lovely clear, vulnerable night, two of the ships at the heart of the formation were without radar protection. Chalk up another point for Kapitanleutnant Zimmermann and his *U-548* crew.

Though he didn't know it, Zimmermann had something else going for him as well. Ever since the introduction of the German acoustic torpedo, RCN escort vessels had been equipped with a counter-device called the Cat Gear. This was a rudimentary contrivance consisting of a pair of metal pipes joined together streaming out at the end of a wire bridle and towed astern to attract the homing missile toward it and away from its intended target, the ship's propellers. But on this night, because the noise of the Cat Gear interfered with radar reception, the Cats on all five C-1 ships had been secured inboard, rendering them inoperative and at the same time leaving the vessels vulnerable to acoustic torpedo— *Zaukonig*—attack.

Some of the radar vigilance among the group was still effective at least, though it proved to be of little consequence. At 2100 hours *Edmunston*, on the extreme right flank, had picked up echoes to starboard at a distance of three miles. It was a false alarm, however; the sources turned out to be the corvettes *Timmins* and *Agassiz* steaming from the opposite direction in their sweep for the reported U-boat. All clear—or so it seemed.

By 2315 hours, 150 miles southeast of St. Mary's Bay, the key figures in the drama were closing to within 3200 yards of each other on a collision course at 20 miles an hour. On the bridge of *Valleyfield*, it was bitterly cold. Lieutenants Ian Tate, the antisubmarine officer, and Cashman Mason, the gunnery officer, along with the ship's signal men and lookouts muffled in sheepskin-lined coats or hooded parkas, stamped their feet to keep warm while scanning the surface of the sea, a job now made more difficult by a gathering mist.

But in the conning tower of *U-548* Zimmermann suddenly noticed something shadowy off his port bow which, in the bright moonlight, he quickly identified as an enemy ship. Alarmed at the speed with which he was approaching it, he quickly put the submarine into a crash-dive. Setting a course parallel to his target, he studied it through his periscope and became satisfied that it was "clearly recognizable as a United States destroyer escort."

This misinterpretation was typical of the faulty intelligence throughout Admiral Karl Doenitz's U-boat high command. Incredibly, high command was completely ignorant of the shipping routes off the Atlantic coast of North America. In fact, *U-548* had been ordered to patrol the east coast off Newfoundland at the height of the iceberg season to seek out merchant shipping—which never operated within 100 miles of the area. Worse still, Zimmermann had been specifically assigned to conduct his quest in the vicinity of St. John's, avoided by merchant shipping and which ironically was the main base for antisubmarine ships and aircraft. After a number of close shaves, Zimmermann noted in his ship's log that "St. John's is probably a destroyer escort base." But this realization did not extend to recognition of the nationality of enemy warships or antisubmarine aircraft. Even after five years of U-boat warfare, the German submarine captains were still identifying British and Canadian ships and planes as those of the United States. Zimmermann's encounter with HMCS *Valleyfield* was certainly no exception, though it made no difference to the outcome.

All of *U-548*'s torpedo tubes were ready for underwater firing. Zimmermann estimated his quarry's speed to be approximately 14 knots and his range three nautical miles. The periscope, barely awash, was all but undetectable. Though he was quite unaware of it, he could have taken comfort in the fact that C-1 Group's sonar range of 3000 yards meant the U-boat was at that moment beyond the limits of underwater Asdic detection. Now on a slightly converging course, Zimmermann was in perfect attacking position—one on one, or so he thought. Suddenly his hydrophone operator reported high-speed propeller sounds to port and starboard. *U-548* was right in the middle of an enemy formation. Startled, Zimmermann rotated his periscope round the horizon but its limited range revealed nothing. Keeping his cool he concentrated on his objective and closed in on the target. At 1500 metres he fired a single *Zaukonig* set to run at a depth of four metres and aimed at *Valleyfield*'s port bow. The time was 2332 hours.

Above and below decks, the crews aboard the frigate routinely went about their duties. Allowing for the usual half-hour's notice, ratings scheduled for the next watch were fully dressed except for their boots and coats, in case of emergency. Yeoman Irving Kaplan, the senior signal rating, in readiness for any call that might summon him to the bridge, was asleep on the cushioned locker top that ran down the side of the mess deck, warmly dressed in a padded zip-up "zoot suit" with his lifejacket worn over it. Coder Ed Munro, half asleep, wearing only his underwear shorts, was fumbling with his shirt and pants. Others, still asleep, were also clad only in their underwear shorts—"shoreside fashion."

In the engine room the watch-keeping petty officer's artificers were busy checking bearings and oil levels, looking forward to going off watch and getting some sleep before docking at St. John's two hours hence, while the stokers kept an eye on the pressure and temperature gauges.

On the bridge the lookouts continued to scan the surroundings through their binoculars, more concerned with dodging ice floes and sighting icebergs than worrying about U-boats. Ian Tate noticed that the "captain's pointer" on the compass, which indicated the direction in which the Asdic was transmitting, had locked onto a "Red 60" bearing—broad on the port bow. Obviously the operator was concentrating on something in that area. Tate switched on the bridge loudspeaker, which amplified the sounds the operator was listening to so that everyone could hear what was going on. Then the operator stopped the set's transmission to concentrate on the faint noise emanating off *Valleyfield*'s port bow. Everyone on the bridge now pricked up their ears. It was a curious, eerie sort of noise, like the ticking of a watch, but much faster, a kind of muffled drone. Tate reacted immediately. "Investigate from 250 to 290 degrees," he ordered through the Asdic voice-pipe. But before the operator could respond all hell broke loose!

The torpedo struck and exploded on the port side to the rear of the bridge, sending a huge cloud of flame, water, and steam skyward. The shock reverberated through the ship from stem to stern. Its impact knocked some men off their feet and sent others tumbling out of their bunks and hammocks. Yet it failed to shatter that fabric that is the tradition of Canada's navy—the ingrained discipline of its officers and crew to react and act instinctively as they had been trained to do in the event of emergency. That was not enough, however, to save the mortally stricken frigate nor most of its sailors.

On the bridge Cashman Mason pushed the emergency button to set off the alarm bells that would summon all hands to their stations. Ian Tate shouted into the engine room voice-pipe hoping to alert the stokers and artificers and clear everyone out of the lower decks. But it was too late. The damage was fatal. The ship's power failed. The lights went out. The bells stopped ringing. *Valleyfield* was doomed.

In less than a minute the frigate began to break apart. The main-mast toppled into the water as the forecastle and bridge separated from the aft section of the ship, listing to starboard, the lower areas filling with water. When the torpedo exploded in No. 2 boiler room, killing all the stokers, it burst open the main fuel tank, releasing the bunker fuel that spilled out into the freezing-cold sea, turning it into a viscous tar-like scum that spread over the surface. All this calamity to the accompaniment of the screech of tearing metal and the hissing and shrieking of escaping steam.

Standing by his bunk getting ready to go on watch in the wireless room, coder Ed Munro, clad only in his shorts when the torpedo exploded, suddenly found himself in total darkness, the deck tilting sharply below him and icy water splashing around his feet. Buckling on his lifejacket he climbed through the hatch above him onto the deck, by which time half the ship had been swallowed by the sea, and jumped into the freezing sea.

Irving Kaplan, the signal yeoman, rudely awakened from his slumber, had also hastily climbed out on deck through a safety hatch—from the flooding petty officer's mess—and made his way along the side of the heavily listing ship to the gun deck where he and three others tried to launch a Carley float. But the list of the ship made that impossible. Kaplan scrambled onto the shield of the forward four-inch gun, the platform by then completely awash. Like Munro, he jumped into the water without a second thought. But, unlike Munro, he was protected from the chill by his thick "zoot suit."

Those on the bridge tried their best to maintain order out of disaster. Rushing up from the chart-room on the deck below, the ship's captain, Lieutenant Commander Dermot English, shouted to the men scrambling up the boat deck: "Man boats and Carley floats!" and tossed his lifebelt to one frightened crewman who was frantic without one. As a substitute Tate tried to loosen one of the life preservers that hung on a bracket, but it wouldn't budge. He soon gave up and told his skipper, "Better swim for it!" English needed no further urging and slipped into the water from the now fully exposed bilge keel. Tate soon joined him.

By this time the ship's bows were standing on end and, as the mass of metal sank into the sea, the vortex dragged Tate down with it. But the buoyancy of his lifejacket saved him, and he was able to struggle to the surface within yards of a floater net which, with others, he reached and clung onto. Finally they maneuvered it over to a Carley float, but it was so overloaded with men that they could only latch onto it.

From there they watched the stern half of their ship begin to sink. First the rudder appeared, then the propellers, then finally in its death throes—bursting bulkhead, exploding boilers, and screaming crewmen—it vanished below the surface taking those who never had a chance to abandon ship with it.

It had all happened so quickly.

According to James Lamb, author of *On the Triangle Run*, those in the water owed their existence to three of their shipmates trapped inside who went down with the ship. Immediately the torpedo exploded, Leading Seaman Donald Brown, Ordinary Seaman David Brown, and Able Seaman Mervyn Woods had made their way to the stern of the vessel clutching at anything they could get their hands on in an uphill battle as the hull continued to tilt more sharply with every step. On reaching the quarterdeck they stopped to set the cluster of 10 depth charges, kept in readiness for instant detonation, from "fire" to "Safe." In so doing they had sacrificed their own safety; that selfless deed ate up precious time and cost them their lives. But had the charges detonated when their firing pistols filled with water—as they were set to do—the stern section of the ship would have been blown to smithereens, killing all those struggling in the water.

Suddenly a calcium flare—attached to a lifesaver ring and designed to ignite on contact with the water—illuminated the Dantesque scene of shipwrecked men fighting for their lives in a calm, moonlit, freezing sea that reeked with slimy bunker oil. Some were aboard the three Carley floats so overburdened they were in water up to their waists, some clinging to the floats, others buoyed by their lifejackets, and still others holding onto each other or to pieces of wreckage. By then *Valleyfield* had disappeared into the depths leaving behind an aura of eerie melancholy, a despair broken by a seaman on one of the rafts who started singing "For she's a jolly good fellow, for she's a jolly good fellow ..." Others quickly joined in.

As soon as he fired his torpedo, Zimmermann put *U-548* into a diving turn to starboard placing it right under his target. At a safe depth he shut off his electric engines and waited to hear the results of his attack. At exactly three minutes and 12 seconds, as he noted in his log, "a very loud, hollow-sounding detonation" was heard followed by "violent break-up and cracking noises." The frigate's bulkheads were giving way. The noise kept coming closer and the impact of a large piece of debris could be heard striking the seabed nearby—*Valleyfield*'s bow section filled with the dying and dead of her crew. Fearful that the debris would damage his U-boat, Zimmermann restarted the engines and got under way. Once clear of the wreckage, he throttled back to dead slow and, running silently, stole away from the area.

Aboard the corvette *Giffard*, on *Valleyfield*'s starboard beam, its skipper, Lieutenant Commander Charles Petersen, was asleep in his bunk when the sound of the explosion awakened him and sent him scurrying to the bridge. Those on watch reported that the blast had sent up a huge column of white spray that dissipated into a shimmering cloud. Petersen was mystified. What had happened? Had the lead ship sustained an engine room or boiler explosion? Or had a depth charge accidentally been dropped? There was no visible evidence to go on. At 2343 hours, three minutes after the explosion, he became alarmed. He called *Valleyfield* on the ultra-high-frequency radio telephone but there was no answer. His radar operator reported that the frigate's blip was diminishing and seconds later had disappeared. Petersen then ordered his yeoman to signal the vessel by light projector directed at her estimated position. There was no answering flash.

Petersen then steered his ship toward *Valleyfield*'s last reported position. Those on the bridge intently scanned the sea through their binoculars. Suddenly a bobbing light came into view—a calcium flare. *Giffard* headed straight for it, no doubt now in Petersen's mind that *Valleyfield* had met with misfortune. But he had already committed the first of several errors, the result of which would plague him the rest of his life. He had failed to notify the rest of

Group C-1 that he had broken formation to determine the lead ship's fate. In the meantime, the rest of the corvettes had continued on their way to St. John's, their radar operators so concerned with looking out for ice floes and other objects that they were completely unaware of the disappearance of two of their group.

Ironically, Group C-1 corvettes were well positioned to destroy *U-548* had they only known the submarine was lying on the seabed close to the port side of the group. Had a square search pattern been ordered, with *Halifax* on the extreme left and particularly well placed, the corvettes would certainly have detected the submarine and destroyed her. The survivors of *Valleyfield* could have been pulled from the sea. The onus was on Petersen to initiate such a measure but he hesitated, still uncertain as to what fate had befallen the doomed frigate and what course of action he should take.

Had it been a mine or internal explosion, Petersen could stop his ship and pick up the survivors without any danger to his ship. On the other hand, if a U-boat had caused the disaster and was still on the loose, his corvette would present an ideal submarine target during the half-hour or more it would take to complete a rescue. He had to determine what had actually happened before he could reach a decision.

When *Giffard* reached the spot where the men were struggling in the water, the corvette slowed almost to a stop and over the ship's loud hailer, a voice thundered "HAVE YOU BEEN TORPEDOED?" To the survivors the question seemed so absurd it brought an angry, equally inane, response: "No, you stupid bastard, we just thought it seemed like a nice night for a swim!" followed by a stream of curses and invective. But the vituperative responses gave Petersen the answer he needed—*Valleyfield* had indeed been torpedoed. And, he also knew that the U-boat had to be close by. From his Asdic operator's report that he had heard nothing, the torpedo must have had a very short run, so that the submarine must have fired at very close range.

He now faced the agonizing dilemma of whether to hunt down

the U-boat, which was his prime responsibility, or risk being torpedoed by picking up survivors. Petersen decided on a compromise, one that tragically would cost many more lives. He would not bring *Giffard* to an absolute stop, but he wouldn't entirely abandon the men in the sea, either. He would slow down as safely as he dared and proceed to search for the submarine, picking up as many survivors as he could on the way. It somewhat satisfied his conscience that he was rendering what aid he could, at the same time fulfilling his duty as a warship captain. But it created a no-win situation.

Sailors lowered *Giffard*'s scramble-nets on both sides of the ship, while others cast rope-heaving lines to the survivors. But the momentum of the vessel, slow as it was, proved too fast for even the strongest swimmers who, numbed by the cold, could not grasp or hold onto the nets and ropes.

The men on one of the Carley floats did manage to catch one of the heaving lines and fasten it to the raft. But as the raft drew alongside the ship, the weight of the survivors crowded aboard forced the forward part of the float to dip further and further under the surface until finally it capsized, spilling the occupants into the water. The half-naked Ed Munro, hanging onto a line he'd got hold of, saw the seaman who had been seated next to him on the float sucked astern under the corvette toward the propeller. Munro clung on in the hope of rescuing the unfortunate individual, but it was impossible, the current from the ship being too strong. Munro had to let go, then swam to the safety of another Carley float, so exhausted that when he pulled himself onto it he collapsed.

At a minute past midnight, 23 minutes after *Valleyfield* had been torpedoed, Petersen finally acted as he should have in the first place. He signalled the other three ships in the group "CLOSE ME" with the intention of conducting a proper U-boat search and a bona-fide rescue operation. But the naked bulletin left those on the watch and the skippers aboard *Edmunston*, *Frontenac*, and *Halifax* both baffled and irate. What the hell for? Who was Petersen to be giving orders? What was this all about? Eight minutes later they had their answer in a second message "VALLEYFIELD TORPE- DOED," an entire ominous half-hour after the attack.

By this time Petersen had completely abandoned those who had survived and was bent on pursuing the submarine. He had even streamed out his Cat Gear to prevent an acoustic torpedo strike, though ironically this had alerted his quarry, which was much closer than he could have imagined.

Zimmermann had listened to *Edmunston*, *Frontenac*, and *Halifax* passing to the north and then heard the shrill of *Giffard*'s Cat Gear which alerted him to the fact that *U-548* was directly underneath. Under the impression that he was now the object of a submarine hunt and in danger, he shut down his engines and laid low, only two fathoms above the ocean bed, to wait it out. He need not have worried. Group C-1 was very disorganized and precious time, always a key factor in any submarine search, had already been lost. *Giffard*, the only ship anywhere near the enemy vessel, was simply going through the motions, a drill Petersen felt it his duty to carry out. Zimmermann listened as the "pings" from the corvette's Asdic transmissions through his hydrophones grew fainter and fainter, then disappeared altogether.

As the other three ships hove into view, Petersen turned over the search to them and brought *Giffard* about to return to *Valleyfield*'s survivors and devote the ship's energies to rescuing them from the sea. They had been in the icy water for about an hour but it seemed more like a lifetime—endless and without hope—and their ranks were thinning by the minute, the men succumbing to the bitterly cold ocean.

Coder Ed Munro was so weakened from his exertions that he was slipping in and out of consciousness. As he wakened from one of those comas he realized that the men around him on the Carley float were strangely quiet and immobile. When an attempt at conversation with the one closest to him failed he leaned over and peered into the man's face. It was eerie. The eyes were shut, the mouth hung open. He'd been talking to a corpse. When he tried to rouse the others and there was no response, before he again lapsed into unconsciousness, he realized that all those about him were dead. He was the sole living soul on the "death float."

Lieutenant Ian Tate owed his life to quick thinking and acting on the part of Able Seaman Rene Baulne. Like many others clinging to the three Carley floats, Tate had clipped his lifejacket lanyard to the raft's life-ring. As more and more men made their way to the floats, the rafts became increasingly overburdened and this pulled them lower and lower into the water. Most of the men managed to unclip their lanyards. But Tate was dragged down so quickly that he was unable to reach the clip and he was in desperate danger of drowning. When he cried out in alarm, Rene Baulne, sitting high in the centre of the raft, quickly pulled out his hip knife from its sheath, reached over, and sliced the lanyard, saving Tate's life.

Petersen brought his corvette carefully into the midst of the floats and wreckage, positioning it facing the moon to present as small a silhouette as possible to a U-boat attack, but with the engines still idling. Rescue was difficult. Most of the men were so worn out and numbed from the cold they were unable to help themselves and had to be assisted or carried aboard by *Giffard*'s crew who went down the scramble-nets to fetch them. At the same time Petersen launched the vessel's sea-boat (a pulling craft) to pick up survivors. *Edmunston*, though busy searching for the U-boat, sent out her sea-boat as well.

Many of those rescued had reached the very limits of their endurance. Understandably, one of these was *Valleyfield*'s skipper, Lieutenant Commander Dermot English, who had braved the water without benefit of a lifejacket. He had tried to grab onto the scramble-net but was so weak that he couldn't make it. Rescuers proffered willing hands but he wasn't able to grasp those either. One of *Giffard*'s crew seized him by the back of his uniform in an effort to lift him up. But the water-sodden material ripped and English tumbled back overboard. He was last seen disappearing

below the icy, oily depths, a gallant sea captain who had forfeited his own life by giving his lifejacket to save another.

Irving Kaplan, the signal yeoman, very nearly didn't make it either. When he reached the side of the corvette his lifejacket lanyard was still clipped to the lifeline of the Carley float that was dragging him under. In a panic he shouted "Somebody give me a dirk! Give me a dirk! Give me a dirk!" calling for a seaman's hip-knife. One of *Giffard*'s seamen drew his knife and passed it down to Kaplan, who hurriedly slashed at the lanyard, finally cutting himself free to clamber aboard.

Ian Tate was hoisted aboard with the aid of a fire hose, lowered from *Giffard*'s forecastle. Tate wrapped it around and under him and was hauled up to safety without a hitch.

The Carley float bearing the dead and the unconscious Munro was caught with a boathook and pulled alongside the ship. The first two bodies hauled aboard were laid out of the way for the time being. Munro's inert form was the third to be brought aboard. He was unceremoniously dumped alongside the two stiffs. With many live survivors needing attention, the harried, overworked *Giffard* crewmen decided not to waste any more time heaving corpses onto the deck and shunted the "death raft" aside. On deck Munro was virtually in his death throes and would have been given up for dead had not an engine room artificer chanced by and noticed a slight twitch from the coder's bare right leg. "Hey!" the artificer bellowed. "This guy's still alive. Give us a hand!"

Munro was picked up and carried to the mess deck where he was given a vigorous towelling-down, wrapped in a warm blanket, and sustained with a few warm drinks, which literally brought him back from the dead. The irony of his agony and rescue is that, had he been even partially clad instead of just in his underwear shorts, the spasm that saved him would have gone unnoticed.

Petersen kept his ship idling in the area until he concluded that the very last survivor had been rescued. Then he ordered full speed ahead; with so many wounded—and dying—aboard, it was essential to reach St. John's as quickly as possible. The journey was not without incident, however. At 0530 hours the bells rang, signalling "action stations," but it turned out to be a false alarm. The radar had picked up a "growler," a small iceberg, which at first had been mistaken for a surfaced U-boat.

Giffard proceeded without further incident, reaching port early that afternoon. *Valleyfield's* survivors were taken to the RCN hospital. Next day, five of the dead were buried with full military honours.

In the meantime, the search for *U-548* had continued, inconclusively but with a bizarre, macabre ending. When *Giffard* sailed for St. John's, the remaining trio of C-1 corvettes, led by *Edmunston*, had reorganized themselves into an effective, efficient hunting team. Spread out in line abreast they began a methodical sweep— "Operation Observant"—probing for the U-boat they knew could not be far away. At 0100 hours they dropped the first depth charges on a suspicious echo. But it was not *U-548*.

Zimmermann, a safe distance from where he had torpedoed *Valleyfield*, had taken his submarine to the bottom of the sea, resting it on the ocean bed. As the surface ships came closer he could hear their Cat Gears screeching, but he was confident that he was deep enough to be out of depth-charge range. In fact none were dropped nor were there any Asdic contacts on the part of the corvettes. At approximately 0400 hours the German submarine commander considered it safe enough to sneak away from the area and conduct a patrol in the vicinity of Halifax.

As soon as the RCN authorities in St. John's received *Giffard's* signal that *Valleyfield* had been torpedoed, the frigate *New Glasgow* was dispatched to the scene to join Escort W-2—*Agassiz* and *Timmins*. Teamed up with the three corvettes from Force C-1, this resulted in a much wider, more intensive search for *U-548*. After some hours the patrol was rewarded by a firm Asdic echo that indicated a submarine was lying doggo below. *U-548!* *Edmunston* began the attack, dropping her depth charges with unerring precision that produced a tremendous explosion.

Once it subsided, wreckage appeared and oil began to spread over the water. A strike! the searchers thought. Then, suddenly, dead ahead in the oil slick, an object bobbed to the surface. It had an eerie familiarity about it: the letters in English, the shape, the size, the colour. On closer inspection it soon became obvious—it was unmistakably a Canadian naval lifejacket, a distinctive design unlike any other. It was equally obvious that it had come from the battered wreck of *Valleyfield*, now a tomb for those who had gone to the bottom with her. A sad epitaph to its fate and that of the 125 sailors who had lost their lives.

At nightfall on the third day of the search, after scouring the seas for 70 hours without result, the hunt was finally abandoned.

Perhaps it was fortunate that one of *Valleyfield*'s victims had been Escort Group C-1's senior officer, Commander James Byron, who had gone down with the ship. At the formal court of inquiry, held only four days after the tragedy, the blame for the disaster was placed squarely on his shoulders.

On a clear, calm, moonlit night, ideal for a U-boat attack, under perfect Asdic operating conditions, his antisubmarine group, with no escort responsibilities and which had been alerted that a submarine was lurking in the vicinity, did not have its CAT gears streaming to protect it from acoustic torpedoes, and had been ordered to alter its zigzagging to a straight course. On the face of it, this was a clear case of neglect and poor judgment—and an open invitation to disaster.

But the board of inquiry was made up of experienced naval officers who empathized with those in command on the sea under battle conditions. This case, like many others, could not simply be viewed or dismissed in black-and-white terms. The circumstances of decisions made under the pressure of war had to be given proper, fair, and just consideration.

The order to secure the CAT gears aboard, for example, was

acceptable and understandable, since it interfered with radar efficiency crucial to safety while sailing through waters heavy with ice. The directive to discontinue zigzagging was not so easily dismissed. Steering a straight course increased the danger of colliding with icebergs and at the same time presented the ships as targets for submarine attack. But again the circumstances had to be considered. After their arduous escort duties, the officers and men of every vessel in the group were anxious to reach port as quickly as possible.

Lieutenant Commander Charles Petersen's role in the events was quite another matter. His conduct throughout was beset with indecision, procrastination, and downright dithering. He had been unable to accept the fact that the *Valleyfield* had been sunk, despite obvious evidence—visual sighting by those on watch and a disappearing Asdic echo. By the time he signalled the other ships in the group to close in after seeing the survivors in the water, 18 minutes had elapsed. Worse still, by the time he reported the torpedoing, half an hour had been lost. This the board could not condone.

Petersen had dilly-dallied too long in deciding whether to carry out a rescue or go after the U-boat. The compromise of combining both—sailing into the midst of the survivors first in the hope that some might be saved proved to be as completely ineffectual as the subsequent, perfunctory submarine search was totally unfruitful, the latter costing precious minutes during which many of *Valleyfield*'s survivors succumbed to the cold and died. But idling in the water when *Giffard* returned to the scene to stay on readiness in case of a torpedo attack was commendable in a way (Petersen's first duty after all was to his ship and his own crew), but in doing so survivors were sucked under from the propeller wash, while others, such as the frigate's captain, lost their lives when they could not be pulled over the side onto the ship.

A terrible indictment. It left no question that delay and indecision on Petersen's part were responsible for the death toll among those of *Valleyfield*'s survivors drifting in the water. Once again, however, the board weighed heavily the mitigating circumstances. A terrible responsibility had suddenly been thrust upon *Giffard*'s captain, and he lacked both preparation and experience. He had never commanded a group operation—a role with which he was unexpectedly faced. Under the circumstances he had, to the utmost of his ability and limited experience, done the very best he could. Accordingly the board did not censure him in its report.

In fact the entire *Valleyfield* tragedy—the last Canadian frigate to be sunk by a German U-boat—was, and had to be, accepted as one more instance of the wages of war at sea. Meanwhile, for the survivors, the memories would gradually fade away.

But there was one regrettable exception. Charles Petersen never overcame the memories of the ordeal or the responsibilities with which he had been forced to cope. Lamentably, he tried to drown these in alcohol and died at an early age.

Chapter 16

The Luck of the Irish!

I almost felt guilty writing this chapter. I had already been discharged from the RCAF when the following event took place. Lying on the beach at the Surf Club in Miami, the war to me was a million miles away. But in fact there was still a lot of fighting going on. The saga of Lieutenant Frank McCormick's ordeal when he was cast adrift in the Atlantic after his ship, HMCS Guysborough, *was torpedoed by a German U-boat certainly bears this out.*

Friday, 17 March 1945—a *special date for the wearin' of the green!* In the HMCS *Guysborough*'s wardroom, the minesweeper's communications officer, Frank McCormick, had just finished supper. Because he wasn't scheduled to take his turn at watch for another two hours, he decided to go below decks and do some sketching, a pastime he enjoyed during his time off duty.

At 1900 hours, comfortably seated on the bunk in his cabin, his feet resting on a chair with a sketchpad on his lap, he was happily drawing away when a blast threw him flying in the air. He hit the ceiling (the deckhead above him). Knocked unconscious, his limp body was thrown stomach-first on the chair, his upper torso dangling head-down over the seat, his lower half hanging loosely from behind with his feet dangling inches from the deck (floor). Happy St. Patrick's Day!

Up until that moment, McCormick had had little to complain

about. His duty at sea had been pretty tame by most standards. Routine really. After quitting his job with Canadian Industries Limited (C-I-L) in Montreal, Quebec, where he was born in the suburb of Ville St. Pierre, at age 18 he had enlisted in the Royal Canadian Navy in the fall of 1942. After training at Montreal, Toronto, and St. Hyacinthe, Quebec, he served aboard the minesweeper HMCS *Comox* as visual signalman, then on the corvette, HMCS *The Pas*, before joining the minesweeper HMCS *Guysborough*.

In early 1945, the ship put into Lunenburg, Nova Scotia, for a refit. She then sailed for Halifax to stock up on supplies for a complement of 90 officers and men—most of whom had never been to sea before. She then left port for Plymouth Harbour, England, to rejoin the minesweeping fleet to which she had been assigned a year earlier.

En route *Guysborough* stopped in at the Azores, a cluster of islands 800 miles west of Portugal, to replenish her supplies. Only the captain and a handful of others were given permission to go ashore, so McCormick and his fellow officers pooled their financial resources and assigned one of their group, who was allowed off the ship, to stock up on wine. (They had such an ample supply of liquor bought in Halifax that there was no storage space left in the wardroom; the wine had to be put away in their cabin lockers.)

On that St. Patrick's Day evening of 1945 when McCormick recovered from the explosion that had temporarily knocked him unconscious, although all he had on were his socks, underwear, grey slacks, and shirt, he didn't bother to pick anything up—not even his lifebelt. He ran to the gangway to climb up on deck but found Stan Slope, the ship's Asdic operator who had been standing watch in his sheepskin coat, blocking his path. Obviously stunned by the explosion, he had temporarily lost his bearings and was climbing down. "I had a hell of a time trying to get Sam to turn around and go up rather than down," McCormick recalled.

By the time the pair reached the deck, they found the entire ship's company, including the captain, standing around wondering what had happened. In any case, the explosion had been treated as an emergency; the ship's whaler and the small motor launch had been lowered into the water.

At first glance a heap of twisted metal piled up haphazardly at the bow suggested the ship had struck a mine; but closer examination revealed that the minesweeper had taken a torpedo in the propellers and the entire quarterdeck had been blown up over the mast and landed on the bow. After studying the extent of the damage, the captain, the ship's engineer, and the coxswain agreed that by shoring up aft of the ship she could be saved and they decided to continue on course.

As McCormick pondered why the torpedo hadn't sent *Guys-borough* to the bottom when so many other Canadian minesweepers that had been torpedoed at this stage of the war had sunk in a matter of minutes, a seaman with a name as Irish as his own sidled up to him and smirked: "Those bloody Jerries has a nerve pickin' this day of all days to put a fish into us!"

The ship's gunnery officer, Junior Sub-Lieutenant Harry Potter, another descendant from the Auld Sod, took exception to that irony with style; he retrieved an armful of wine bottles from his locker and brought them up on deck grinning from ear to ear. But the skipper soon wiped the smug smile from his face; he reached over and, one by one, tossed each bottle over the railing into the sea.

Meanwhile, orders were given to secure the motor launch and whaler craft alongside the minesweeper. As communications officer, McCormick was instructed by the captain to immediately fix the ship's position and get a wireless message off to any and all ships in the vicinity. McCormick made a quick calculation (which turned out to be remarkably accurate), then drafted a message jointly with the captain for transmission. McCormick took his two telegraphers down to the wireless cabin and, while he stood in the doorway, they tapped out the communication. "How many times they repeated the message I can't recall," he wrote later. "But we never did receive an acknowledgement."

It had been only half an hour since the torpedo had smashed into the ship's propellers. Then at 1930 hours another "fish" struck the minesweeper. This time it hit the starboard bow, only 10 feet from where McCormick was standing. And for the second time that evening he was knocked unconscious. "I felt this tremendous pressure surround me," he remembered, "worse than the first time and ... I seemed to be falling through space."

McCormick imagined he was going right through the bottom of the ship and into the sea below. When he came to, he found himself in complete darkness groping around until finally he felt the steps to the companionway leading to the upper deck. When he reached it the only people still on deck were the captain, standing on the starboard side, Harry Potter, lying on his back behind him, and two seamen at the stern awaiting orders from the skipper. Everybody else was in the water on both sides of the vessel.

Potter was badly hurt and couldn't move. McCormick picked him up—not an easy task, because the gunnery officer was a big, heavy fellow—and, as gently as he could, dropped him over the side onto a five-man Carley float that had drifted close to the hull. The captain meanwhile ordered the two seamen to abandon ship and told McCormick to do likewise. McCormick jumped into the water followed by the skipper only a second or two behind him.

The Carley float carrying Potter had begun drifting toward the gaping hole the torpedo had made in the side of the ship. With the help of a Royal Air Force pilot officer who had come aboard *Guysborough* as a passenger in Halifax, the pair swam over and pulled the raft away from the ship to prevent it from being sucked down under.

Incredibly the sturdy old minesweeper stayed afloat for as long as half an hour before being swallowed up in the depths. Just as astounding was the fact that not a single crewman went down with the ship. McCormick and his two telegraphers had come closest to such a fate. They were the only ones below decks when the torpedo struck and all three had escaped.

Because both the whaler and the motor launch had been destroyed by the second torpedo—thanks to the misguided order to tie them alongside the ship instead of lifting them back up to the deck where they would have been safe—there remained only three ten-man Carley floats and one five-man raft to hold 90 men in the water. The ten-man float on the port side, with 36 men sitting on the raft or clinging to the sides, drifted out of reach of the rest of the survivors.

Using their ingenuity the crew on the starboard side lashed their three floats together to make one large raft. Some of the 54 men were lucky enough to climb up on to the float, while others clung to the sides up to their necks in the water.

Midway through that miserably long, dark night, a bitterly cold breeze sprang up, chilling the survivors to the marrow. Waves sloshed across the floats, adding to their discomfort. Many of those in the water hanging onto the sides of the float kept drifting off to sleep, periodically pulling their heads up to prevent from slipping away and drowning. But many simply gave up. "I guess they figured we would never be rescued," McCormick reckoned after the war. "They swam off a distance and put their heads under."

It was not until mid-afternoon next day—Saturday, March 18, around 1500 hours—that those still alive—half of the men who had abandoned ship had drowned or died from exposure—were picked up by a Royal Navy destroyer that had come all the way from Plymouth. McCormick's wireless messages had gotten through after all. His Irish luck had held. Those who had survived the ordeal could be thankful—*and proud, sure and all*—perhaps that part of it had rubbed off on them. They held the distinction of having been afloat as castaways for 19 hours—a wartime record in the Atlantic Ocean.

Ironically this incident is absent in histories of Canada's navy. In fact it was not even in the files at the Department of National Defence Directory of History when that operation was still in existence. But in my opinion it remains a remarkable piece of heartrending Canadian marine history and is worthy of the recognition I have tried to give it.

Following his discharge from the navy, McCormick went back to work for his old employer, C-I-L, where he rose to become sales promotion manager of the Ammunitions Division.

He was also active in sports, serving with many national, provincial, and local sports organizations including the Canadian Pan-American Games Association. In 1983, suffering from arthritis, he became an outpatient of the Liaison Veteran's Day Centre in Ste. Anne de Bellevue, Quebec. In 1987 he founded the Liaison Association of War Veterans, of which he was elected Treasurer.

In the Hands
of the Enemy

Chapter 17

The Big Canadian

I was still in school at the time, six months away from being eligible to enlist in the Royal Canadian Air Force, when Germany was forced to come to the rescue of its ally, Italy, whose forces were floundering against the British army in North Africa. At this stage in the war, Canada had no significant part in the struggle against the Axis' weak sister with the exception of an extraordinary Canadian who, in his own way, took up arms against the Fascist state. This is his story.

A Roman holiday? Not exactly.

But it was a welcome, however brief, diversion from working as a collaborator with the Italian Underground to help escaping Allied prisoners of war to freedom across the Swiss border. So, when in late January of 1944, the Marino family who were sheltering him in Milan, invited Lieutenant George "Pat" Paterson, a Canadian paratrooper with the British No. 11 Special Air Service (SAS) Battalion, to spend the weekend at their villa on the south shore of Lake Como in northern Italy, he jumped at the opportunity. Although he would still be on call, he had learned to savour and take advantage of such rare periods of respite. Ironically, Paterson was himself an escaped POW who, in September of 1943 after the fall of Mussolini, had jumped from a train carrying him and his fellow inmates from an Italian internment compound to a prison camp in Germany.

While he had intended to make for neutral Switzerland, he had been persuaded by the Italian Underground, who had given him shelter, to join their organization. When Italy surrendered, in the aftermath of Il Duce's demise and the ensuing confusion as the Germans moved to take over, hundreds of Allied captives left unguarded prison camps and disappeared. They found refuge in farms and other dwellings of sympathetic Italians who were opposed to the Fascist regime, while they looked for the chance, with the help of partisans, to make their way across the Swiss border to freedom. Because the Italian Underground needed a British liaison, they appealed to Paterson's strong sense of duty to take on the job. Under the circumstances it was an offer he could hardly refuse.

On the Monday following the weekend at Lake Como, Paterson had been summoned back to Milan for a freedom operation getting under way. Elsa, the Marinos' daughter, who often accompanied him on missions, agreed to travel with him as a safety precaution. She could buy the tickets and, because his knowledge of the Italian language was limited, if he was drawn into a conversation she could butt in and do most of the talking.

The trip was a short one, no more than 30 miles, and usually nonstop. But on this occasion the train unexpectedly ground to a halt at Monza, halfway to Milan. On the platform a company of fanatical black-shirted Fascist youths waited to board the train to conduct an identity check. Because Paterson had no identity card—he had decided that if he was recaptured he would rather be taken as an escaped prisoner than as a spy with a forged document—he whispered to Elsa: "I think the game's up. I'm going into the next carriage and remember, if I'm taken, you don't know me." He got as far as the next car when one of the Blackshirt thugs halted him. "Your card," he demanded. Paterson decided to bluff it out. "I showed it to the man back there," he told him. "Let me pass—I'm in a hurry."

Then, from behind him an authoritative voice announced: "I'm an officer of the *Questura* [Fascist secret police], and you must show your identification card." Game over.

"All right," Paterson confessed, "I haven't got one, I'm an escaped British officer." In seconds the Blackshirts set upon him like a pack of hungry wolves—*Inglesi! Inglesi! Inglesi!*—the *Questura* agent brandishing a revolver, egging them on. He was beaten, dragged from the train, marched to the local barracks, and handcuffed, then driven to San Vittore prison in Milan where a pair of German SS men threw him into a cell. End of the line.

Disgusted, distraught, despondent, and forlorn, Paterson lay down on the bunk hanging from the wall by chains and pulled the single blanket around himself to try and get warm. He had come a long way from his family's fruit farm in Kelowna in the Okanagan Valley of British Columbia, which he had left before the war to study engineering at the University of Edinburgh. At the outbreak of hostilities, he had enlisted in the British army as an engineer then transferred to the parachute corps. Now as he pondered his fate, his mind went back to what he had already been through and wondered whether it had all been worth it.

On the night of 10 February 1941, Paterson was one of 36 volunteer paratroopers from No. 11 SAS Battalion who took off from Malta aboard four twin-engine Armstrong Whitley bomber/transports to be parachuted into the heart of Mussolini's Italy. Their sabotage target was a large aqueduct near the village of Calitri that supplied water to the major cities in the south. Once its destruction had been accomplished, the plan was to break up into small teams and trek 60 miles across mountainous country to the mouth of the Sele River on the west coast, where they would be picked up by submarine. But the mission was jinxed.

A snafu developed at the very outset when one of the Whitleys was unable to take off due to engine trouble, thereby reducing the force by a quarter. It also put a heavy onus on Paterson. His demolition expert partner in the party was in the grounded plane, so that as far as destroying the aqueduct was concerned, Paterson would be on his own. Then, over the drop zone, in the transport carrying the "Big" Canadian—his nickname differentiated the tall, blond-headed, six-foot-three Paterson from his fellow countryman in the group, the short, stocky Corporal Geoff Jowett from Montreal—the release mechanism to drop the small arms, ammunition, and explosives refused to budge. That meant the party would have to depend on equipment from the other two aircraft.

All three sections of the paratroopers landed intact. Paterson's section and one other assembled at the aqueduct while the others went in search of the equipment dropped by the aircraft. On examining the structure, Paterson found the piers that supported the pipe to be strongly reinforced with steel. The limited amount of explosive he had might not be sufficient to blow up the entire structure. The others then arrived with the explosives and firearms—plus some prisoners, a motley collection of scruffy peasants and badly frightened *carabinieri*—military police—along with the village stationmaster. The paratroopers put them to work carrying the heavy 40-pound guncotton canisters to the aqueduct.

Paterson decided to concentrate on a single pier, hoping it would pull the aqueduct down and the rest of the piers with it. When he had the guncotton in place and had inserted the detonators, he connected the long length of fuse and ordered everyone to get back 200 yards. He then lit the fuse and waited. Sixty seconds later there was a tremendous explosion and when the smoke and debris cleared, one pier was completely gone. Another angled over awkwardly. The aqueduct itself had been sliced and torrents of water gushed down the ravine and into the valley beyond it. Mission accomplished. Now to get clear; not a minute to lose. They knew that the detonation, which would have been heard for miles around, would have alerted the authorities.

The group split into three parties. After tying up the prisoners and leaving them in a hut, then destroying all surplus equipment, the paratroopers set off. They estimated they had five nights to cover the 60 miles to the Sele River and rendezvous with the submarine.

That night Paterson's team covered 16 arduous miles over a mountain and then through muddy, freshly plowed fields. But as the crow flies they had made no more than six miles' progress. At dawn they took refuge in a ravine and were sheltered by trees. They fell asleep, exhausted. But the cold soaked through their clothing and made sleep impossible.

At first light, Paterson could hear voices in the distance; it turned out to be two boys herding some goats. However, overhead a spotting plane appeared, flying slowly back and forth, and the paratroopers were forced to lie doggo, remaining hidden for the rest of the day, cold and uncomfortable, with conversation limited to a whisper here and there. That night, tired and weak from lack of food, they made another torturous hike up and down a mountain slope and by dawn reckoned that so far they had still only travelled about 17 or 18 miles of the 60 needed to reach the coast. They decided that, despite the risk of running into enemy patrols, their only recourse to make the rendezvous with the submarine was to take to the roads. If stopped, they would have to try their best to bluff their way through.

That night, in the first two hours, they had marched six miles with solid ground under their feet. What a relief! This was more like it. On to the coast! After a short rest, they carried on and were halfway across a bridge when they came face to face with a squad of *carabinieri*, rifles at the ready. The paratroopers readied to engage them, but out of the darkness an angry gaggle loomed, made up of at least 100 men, women, and children armed with shotguns, axes, and shovels, in support of the police only too anxious to vent their venom on the *Inglesi* intruders. The paratroopers had no choice but to surrender.

While the mob spat and jeered at them, the prisoners were taken to a small village where they were prodded into a basement and searched. They were then handcuffed and herded into mule wagons and taken to a much larger town where they were imprisoned in the local jail, already occupied by another party of the sabotage group.

Later the third party joined them, led by Paterson's smaller countryman Geoff Jowett who reported: "We killed three of the bastards." Now the entire SAS party was captured.

Moments later, the cell door opened and an Italian army officer backed by several *carabinieri* entered and told them that all officers in the group were to accompany him. Paterson wondered whether they were being taken out to be shot as a reprisal for Jowett's action, which had included armed civilians as well as soldiers.

Paraded down a hall into a smaller cell, they were told to wait. No sooner had they settled onto a wooden bench than a short, ostentatious individual wearing a uniform heavy with braid entered and, standing imperiously before them, proceeded to angrily berate them in Italian, leaving them bewildered and, to put it mildly, antagonistic toward the officious little son-of-a-bitch. One of the paratroopers, who had been assigned to the group as interpreter, explained that the man was a general who expected them to stand up when he entered the room. This was correct procedure even as prisoners, and as they rose to their feet, the mood changed dramatically.

To their astonishment the Italian general told them that Italian officers admire gallant enemies and that they would be treated with honour. Although they were rewarded with a bully beef dinner and bread, their first meal in two days, they soon learned Italian promises, even from generals, were cheap.

Next morning they were handcuffed and put aboard a train for a military prison in Naples. Paterson found himself wedged in between two guards who passed the time spitting on the floor. When he could no longer stand it, as one of the escorts started to clear his throat Paterson pointed to the "NON SPUTTER" sign on the carriage wall and bluntly told him to knock it off.

On arrival at the prison, which to Paterson seemed like a medieval dungeon, they were locked in individual cells, each containing a wooden bench covered by a damp, dirty straw mattress and a slit high on the wall for a window. Before slamming the heavy steel door shut, the rough-looking guard who had escorted him to his "dungeon" snorted in broken English, "You goddamn son of a bitch. You pretty soon be shot."

Next morning the Big Canadian heard the welcome sound of a key rattling in the lock. But though he had not eaten since being fed on the train, the guard was not bringing him the breakfast he had anticipated. Instead he was marched into an office in which a pair of civilians, who identified themselves as the *Questura* secret police, invited him to sit down. That civility quickly faded. He was put through a gruelling interrogation. However, despite the persuasion, cajoling, and threats, he refused to reveal anything except his name, rank, and serial number. After half an hour his interrogators gave up with the warning that he would regret it if he didn't learn to cooperate.

Following the grilling, Paterson was led back not to his cell, but to a much larger one where he joined his fellow officers and learned that they too had been interrogated. Now things quickly changed. First they were fed and given a ration of wine. Then a young officer advised them that since they had arrived by plane they would be considered to be air force prisoners and were moved to an air base—at least temporarily. This turned out to be a big improvement. Though they were still heavily guarded, they were treated more like guests than captives. The meals were first-class. They were given baths every second day, were provided with such necessities as soap, towels, toothbrushes, and razors, and were allowed to exercise.

But the *Questura* were not yet through with them. They insisted on finger-printing and photographing the captives, who took immediate umbrage, protesting that they were prisoners of war, not common criminals. Their objections were shared by the base commandant who screamed at the Secret Service representatives: "Swine! Pigs! How dare you interfere with prisoners of the Royal Italian Air Force without my permission?" and promptly threw them out. Next day he told the captives they were being transferred to a proper prison camp at Sulmona in the mountains 60 miles northeast of Rome. He painted a rosy picture: beautiful scenery, excellent food, wine, and cigarettes, plenty of recreation—but regretted that they would not be allowed women.

Sulmona prison camp, where the paratroopers joined the ranks of hundreds of other British POWs, was far from luxurious, but the food was passable and the accommodation bearable. The SAS party quickly melded into the dull monotony of prison life and its attendant boredom with one thing uppermost in their minds—escape!

It was not an easy prospect. The 10-to-12-acre rectangular camp was surrounded by a high brick wall outside of which were three fences of barbed wire. All about the perimeter were guard towers from which spotlights glared down at night. The compound was divided into several units, each with its own facilities—mess hall, kitchen, living quarters—all locked off from one another. An omen of what to expect had greeted the paratroopers at the gate when an Italian officer, whom they nicknamed "Fish Eyes" because his eyes were so far apart, addressed them as "criminals," and warned that if they tried to escape they would be shot. Though they treated the warning with the contempt it deserved, the message was clear enough. Any escape attempt would be a risky business and anyone caught would be severely dealt with.

Nevertheless, some months later, when Garrard Cole, an RAF fighter pilot with whom Paterson had struck up a friendship, asked him if he would like to come in on an escape attempt, his reply was an enthusiastic affirmative.

Cole outlined the plan. The scheme was to break out through a tunnel being dug under the wall and wire fences from a broom closet off the washroom. The soil was being passed to the prisoners to dribble from their pockets. But one morning a squad of *carabinieri* burst into the washroom as the men were shaving and uncovered the tiles hiding the tunnel's opening. The tunnellers suspected there must be an informant, but in reality a heavily laden mule carrying supplies from the local market was the culprit.

When the path outside the wall had suddenly given way, the beast had disappeared into the tunnel.

This was a terrible letdown. Then, as six of the POWs, including Paterson and Cole, were drowning their sorrows in wine, someone came up with the suggestion of taking advantage of the guarded weekly country walks to make a break for it. At one point of the walk, drainage ditches cut across a field. The ditches would be dry at this time of year (September) and, once in them, the escapers would be safe from rifle fire; in any case, it was hoped that in the confusion the guards would be too surprised to shoot straight.

On the chosen day, as some 50 POWs plodded along with an escort of a dozen *carabinieri* led by Fish Eyes, the signal was given to start running just as the group reached a point where they could see the ditches 60 to 70 yards ahead of them. The six made a dash for it, Cole to the left of Paterson, the other four on his right. They had run 40 yards before the first shot rang out, off to the left. Then another came, followed by a volley that spattered earth in front of the Big Canadian; to his right one of the escapers crumpled to the ground. Finally Paterson reached the ditch and Cole came tumbling in after him. Behind them they could hear angry Italian shouts and more gunfire. The pair kept running for another 100 yards until they had to stop to catch their breath.

Ahead, where the ditch ended, they could see olive trees and some men working in the field beyond. They decided to take a chance and keep going, hoping that the workers were too busy or frightened—or even too stupid—to challenge them. It was a forlorn hope.

When they started toward the grove, they were suddenly startled by a high-pitched shout of *"Alta! Alta!"* They swung around to face a huge, heavy-set farmer levelling a shotgun at them. Labourers in the fields hurried forward, brandishing shovels and pitchforks. Paterson and Cole were returned to the waiting column and a tirade of abuse from Fish Eyes.

For their efforts they were awarded 30 days of isolation in the cooler. At that, they were luckier than the man Paterson had seen fall; he had received several bullet wounds, while another of the escaping party was executed by firing squad as a traitor when the authorities learned that, despite the fact he had been a British subject for most of his life, he was Italian by birth.

In February of 1942, Paterson, Cole, and the SAS officers and a couple of others were singled out as troublemakers responsible for hatching escape plots and transferred to a prison camp farther north at San Romano on the banks of the Arno River between Florence and Pisa. An ancient monastery, it still housed monks and 50 Greek army officers, who were prisoners.

From the moment of their arrival, the Britishers began exploring means of escape. The building was well guarded. Every possible exit was covered by machine guns and rifles. But they focused their attention on the monks' side of the building, which was completely unguarded, though sealed off from the prison sector by brick walls blocking all the corridors. One of the paratroopers, proclaiming himself a staunch Roman Catholic, obtained permission to attend chapel services. After many weeks of observation he reported to Paterson, who used his engineering talents to map out a chart of the entire structure. The POWs were able to concentrate on one particular corridor that led, were it not for the brick wall, to a little-used cloister.

Their plan was to disassemble a few bricks in the wall to make a hole large enough to crawl through at night when the monks were asleep and walk through the monastery and out the gate. Meanwhile, there was plenty of work to do. Clothes had to be altered to give a civilian appearance. Identity cards had to be forged. Routes had to be plotted. Everything was hush-hush; they had learned there were collaborators among the Greeks. To cover their escape while two men worked away at loosening the bricks, the rest would play party-host to the Greeks with rations from their Red Cross parcels to prevent anyone using the corridor.

On the given date, things were well under way when one of the monks heard a brick drop and reported it to the guards. The POWs hustled off to their beds to pretend they were sleeping and knew nothing about an attempt to escape. The *carabinieri* wasted no time rushing in to jostle them awake. Paterson protested his innocence, but a guard discovered his set of plans under the linoleum covering his bedside table. Thirty days in the cooler for the lot.

Later, one of their number did manage to escape by feigning illness so that he was taken to a military hospital in Florence where he slipped past the guards at night and made his way to Switzerland by train and on foot. This venture and the failed attempt angered the Italian officers more out of fear than recrimination. They knew that a successful escape from San Romano would mean instant exile for them to the Russian front. They became surly, disagreeable, and suspicious, so much so that Paterson and his fellow POWs were eventually transferred to an "escape-proof" prisoner-of-war camp at Giva, 20 miles north of Genoa.

It was well characterized. A walled fortress high on the side of a mountain, the camp could only be reached by a single winding road from a valley below. The walls bristled with machine guns and sentries on patrol, and on every side were precipitous drops. Escape was completely out of the question—a grim prospect that, after 18 months in captivity and two failed escape attempts, Paterson was reluctantly forced to accept.

The POWs faced day after endless day of boredom, broken only by exercise and reading and pastimes such as a dramatic club, and a casino—poker, bridge, roulette, faro, and other games. The seasons passed from one to another, and from freshly arriving prisoners they learned of the British victory over the Afrika Korps in Egypt, the Anglo-American landings in North Africa, and, in July 1943, the Allied landings in Sicily. The war was going in the right direction at last.

Then one day, at the end of July 1943, news arrived of the fall of Mussolini and a new government that was suing for peace. The

Italian guards were jubilant, deserting their posts and joining in celebration and wine toasts with their prisoners. In fact, the POWs could have walked out of the camp, and would have done so had it not been for instructions through secret channels that, in the event of a capitulation, they were to remain together in one place for ease of repatriation.

Their joy and that of their captors was premature. Overnight, a German regiment moved into Giva and sent the Italians back to their posts with the threat that if they released any prisoners they would be shot.

Early in September, the Germans dismissed the Italian garrison and took over the camp. Next morning the prisoners were told they were being moved to a camp in Germany. Paterson decided to try and escape before the move got under way by hiding in the rafters of a small coal shed behind the cookhouse. It might have worked except that 100 others had the same idea and they were soon discovered. This postponed the move for a day then finally they were taken by trucks to the Mantua marshalling yards and herded with hundreds of other POWs into freight cars.

That night Paterson and four others, with the aid of a penknife and a pair of dental pliers, managed to pry a hole in the wooden side of the freight car large enough to wiggle through and leap from the train as it slowed going up a grade onto the gravel track— every man for himself. Hearing shots from the direction of the train as it sped off, Paterson ran into the woods bordering the rail line and kept on going. Reaching a river, he decided to swim across, first stripping off all his clothes and shoes which he bundled and pushed ahead of him. But when he reached the middle of the river, the current became so strong he lost his clothes bundle. When he reached the far bank he realized that here he was, a fugitive in enemy territory without a stitch of clothing on.

Wending his way across country and through vineyards to put as much distance between himself and the river as possible, he finally came upon a farmhouse into which he lowered himself through an open window to the basement. Finding a pile of sacks, he wrapped them around him and lay down on the floor to rest. As dawn appeared, he could hear footsteps on the floor above him. Gambling on the hope that those in the house might help him— he really had no other option—he climbed back out the window. From a clothesline behind the house he took a sheet, clothed himself as best he could, went to the front door, and knocked.

Coming face to face with *la signorina* of the house, in what Italian he could muster he quickly introduced himself as an escaped Canadian officer who needed clothes and help. Sympathetic but frightened, the woman replied that her daughter would take him to the village priest, who would know what to do.

At the priest's house he was told that it would be unsafe for him to stay. The Germans were in the next village and they were bound to find him, but the priest agreed to go and search for some clothes he could wear. While he was gone, the priest's house women fed Paterson. Soon the priest returned with some clothing, and Paterson was steered in the direction of a range of hills beyond which lay Lake Garda; around the lake to the north he would find passes leading through the mountains to Switzerland.

By evening, as he made his way down from the high ground into a small valley—after trudging all day in the September heat, tired and hungry, his feet burning from the walk and the worn, under-sized shoes with which the priest had furnished him—he could see a congregation leaving church. When their priest emerged from the church, Paterson boldly confronted him, announcing that he was a Canadian officer escaping from the Germans and asked for his help and some food. But the cleric, his eyes cold and unfriendly, refused him and told him to leave at once.

Sensing that the priest might summon the police, Paterson quickly left the area. That night he slept under a clump of bushes, utterly famished and exhausted. Next morning he continued on, his feet killing him. But in the afternoon a shepherd's wife took pity on him and gave him some bread and milk. That night he again slept out in the open, not daring to take off his shoes; his feet had swollen so badly he knew he would never get them back on.

Next morning, he decided that it would be easier on his feet if he took to the road. The going was much easier and along the way he helped himself to grapes from the vineyards to help quench his thirst and ease his hunger. He was still dead tired and his feet ached miserably but he kept moving, knowing that if he sat down he would draw attention to himself from the men and women working in the fields and the German traffic passing along the road. Finally he reached a large, dry culvert into which he crawled and stretched out where he would be unseen.

After sleeping for several hours, late that afternoon he climbed out and started walking again. A sign ahead read "Brescia—15 km"—an industrial city in the Alps. As he progressed, the fields gave way to squalid rows of houses and dirty-looking warehouses. There were crossroads and much more traffic and he was conscious that people were noticing him. His appearance was shabby, he was unshaven, and his sore feet made him lurch as though he was drunk. He was desperate to find food and shelter and looked for a church or a monastery that might harbour him.

Suddenly a cyclist rode by, stopped a short distance ahead and looked back. Paterson kept walking and when he reached him the small dark man asked in a whisper: "*Inglese?*" Paterson nodded.

"I have helped another *Inglese*," the man said. "You follow me and I'll help you."

From 40 yards behind, Paterson followed the Italian through streets and alleys into a noisy courtyard where the cyclist stopped in front of one of the doorways, introduced himself as Luigi, and beckoned him inside. "My home," he announced.

It was like a homecoming. As Paterson collapsed into a chair, Luigi's wife and mother-in-law pulled the ill-fitting shoes from his feet, swathed the feet in bandages, and brought him a plate of spaghetti, some bread, and a bottle of wine. Word of his arrival spread and neighbours gathered round to stare in awe as Luigi told him: "You are a hero, and we who also hate the German pigs are your friends. You can have anything you wish." With an accumulated thirst that no amount of wine could satisfy, Paterson asked for some beer. Though there was none in the house, Luigi quickly procured two bottles. To Paterson, a drink had never tasted so good.

Seeing how fatigued Paterson was, Luigi took him to his sister-in-law's house next door where he could sleep. Her husband was away in the army, he explained. When he led him into the bedroom they were confronted with a very naked sister-in-law and a very naked man—the other "*Inglese*," Corporal Jack Harris. Harris, who had been sheltered in the house for five days, said that he had been well looked after. Paterson grinned and nodded.

After five days of recovering from his trek across country, Paterson began to give serious consideration to the situation in which he and his newfound companion had landed. He didn't like it. While he appreciated Luigi's help and sentiments, he feared that his garrulousness might spread the word of their presence too far afield and lead to their being discovered by the Germans.

He and Harris agreed they might be better off out in the country with the Italian partisans whom they could help with their raids. Luigi consented to make all arrangements and led them to a small pasture some miles from the city, surrounded by beechwood trees with a roughly built stone barn off to one side that served as the partisans' headquarters. After being informally inducted into the band over much wine, they found the group resembled nothing much more than a group of schoolboys playing high-risk adventure. There was a lack of planning; although they often talked of daring raids far into the night, after sleeping off the effects of too much wine by next morning their grandiose schemes were apparently forgotten. Worse still was a shortage of weapons. The two POWs calculated that if the Germans attacked the encampment such as it existed, it would easily be overrun. They also despaired at the lack of security. Villagers seemed to come and go as they pleased and often the partisans themselves took leave when they felt like it; as one of them put it to Paterson, he wanted to see if his wife was behaving herself.

Matters came to a head when the guerrillas captured Luigi, whom they accused of betraying them. Had it not been for Harris' intervention—he pleaded that it was Luigi who had saved him and Paterson from the Germans—he would have been shot. All this was too much for the POWs. They asked Luigi to help them get to Milan, 50 miles west of Brescia, from which they could get across the border into Switzerland.

Luigi introduced them to a young girl who guided them to a prosperous farmhouse outside Brescia owned by the Riccini family, where they were assured they were welcome to stay as long as they wished. They were provided with smart-looking clothes that passed them off as cultured, well-to-do businessmen. Several days later, Roberto Ostre arrived to take them to Milan by train. On arrival he escorted them to the apartment of a Spaniard named Pedro. Pedro had worked out a plan for their escape. They were introduced to Maria Resta, who had friends in Lecco on Lake Como to the north and that afternoon the four of them—the two POWs, Maria, and Roberto—boarded a train to the small resort town. However, it turned out to be a wild goose chase. Maria's friends were nowhere to be found, so they journeyed back to Milan where they spent the night in Maria's apartment.

Next day, through Maria and Roberto, they met an engineer— *Signor* Rossi, who, because his wife was English, spoke the language fluently. Rossi told them that his organization could get them out of the country in a couple of days. However, in the same breath he asked them to consider joining his organization. When Italy surrendered, he explained, thousands of Allied prisoners-of-war, working on farms and doing other nonmilitary work, disappeared. Scattered about the countryside, Rossi's organization had trouble finding them, and once found, of convincing them that they were friends. This is where Harris and Paterson might help him—particularly in the Brescia area where Rossi had no representation and where they could make their headquarters with the Riccinis.

At first they were reluctant to accept. Besides, how would the Riccinis react to the idea of harbouring two fugitives engaged in undercover work? In the end, they decided to join Rossi's group, and they need not have worried about the Riccinis, who welcomed them back with open arms, only too happy to render what help they could against the hated Fascists.

Over the next few weeks, Harris and Paterson, working with Roberto, were busy tracking down escaped prisoners. As expected, they were initially treated with suspicion by the Italians sheltering the POWs, who took no chances that they might be the *Questura*. Some of the ex-prisoners were reluctant to abandon the comfortable existence with the hospitable local families.

One night there was a knock on the door from one of Rossi's agents who reported that he had just returned from north of Lake Garda where a battle between the partisans and the Germans involving some *Inglese* had taken place. Next morning Paterson and Roberto set off for the area but although there were signs of a shootout—abandoned weapons—the place was deserted. Before making the return trek back to the Riccinis, they spent the night at a lodge. The following evening, when they reached their destination, they sensed trouble; the lights in the front room weren't on. Suspecting a trap, Roberto volunteered to investigate while Paterson hid in the bushes. Roberto knocked on the door and waited. When it opened a man with a flashlight in one hand and a gun in the other pushed him roughly inside.

After a while the door again opened and this time Roberto was pushed out. Staying hidden, Paterson waited until Roberto was a safe distance from the house and asked what had happened. It was the *Questura*, but Roberto had told them he was a boyfriend of the Riccinis' daughter Gabi and they let him go. The Riccinis had been imprisoned but Gabi must have got away because the secret police asked him where she was and who her friends were. But there was no word of Harris.

The pair visited the Riccinis' aunt in Brescia and learned that their arrest had been part of a general roundup in the area. Harris had taken Gabi to the aunt's, then she had taken a train to Milan to stay with some cousins. Harris had disappeared. Paterson and Roberto decided to leave the vicinity as quickly as possible and took the first train they could to Milan.

On arrival, Rossi told them he doubted that the Riccinis were in any danger. The only evidence the *Questura* would have had against them were Paterson and Harris. All agreed that the Brescia area had to be abandoned as a "hunting ground" for the moment, and Paterson and Roberto asked to be assigned to the Milan region.

Roberto went to stay with some friends while Paterson moved in with an elderly couple employed as caretakers in an abandoned factory. He also met the Marino family with whose daughter Elsa he enjoyed evenings wining, dining, and dancing, getting a big kick out of the fact that he was sharing all this night life with German officers and their lady friends sitting at the next tables.

In between assignments, which were so few that Paterson was becoming bored, Roberto showed him the sights of the city: the Gothic Cathedral, the renowned La Scala Opera House, scarred by Allied bombing, the Ambrosian Library, the Piazza del Duomo—and the notorious San Vittore prison, a huge pile of interconnected buildings surrounded by a high rampart wall. "Stay away from there," the Italian joked. "If they get you in there, you've had it."

Paterson shuddered. "Let's get the hell out of here," he said. "It gives me the creeps."

That evening, the Marinos invited him to spend the weekend at their villa at Lake Como. There he was arrested and taken to the San Vittore prison. On his first night there, as he tried to sleep he was disturbed by two things: the light bulb dangling above him and

Roberto's words, "If they get you in there, you've had it." What would become of him now?

Paterson was kept in solitary for five days, a hardship broken only on the third day when he was taken from his cell to Gestapo headquarters in Alberto Regina where he was interrogated and accused of spying. Paterson denied the allegations and maintained that he was just an escaped prisoner-of-war wandering about the countryside trying to find a way to the Swiss border. Whether they believed him or not, or were simply tired of his evasiveness, they released him and returned him to San Vittore.

Finally he was moved into a larger cell, which he shared with another prisoner and assigned to orderly duty, cleaning out vacated cells and replacing dirty, lice-ridden blankets with clean ones from the storeroom. Now he had a chance to survey the opportunities for escape. But it was pretty hopeless. The prison was shaped like a star, with six separate cellblocks each housing 500 prisoners; courtyards closed by a tall wall separated each block. Outside, a road encircled the entire structure and there was an even higher outer wall studded with guard towers and machine-gun posts.

Inside, the jailers were Italian, not entirely hostile unless there was provocation. But supervising them were two sadistic German guards who took delight in brutalizing the prisoners, particularly any Jews taken captive and destined for the Matthausen death camp in Austria. One morning, in a fit of rage, Corporal Franz snatched a crying baby from the hands of its mother and smashed its head against the cement wall, then threw the dead infant back into the arms of the distraught woman.

As the months rolled on and winter passed into the spring of 1944, Paterson gave up hope of escape and concentrated on simply staying alive until the war ended. Then one afternoon in early June, while taking a load of dirty blankets to the laundry, which was in the next cellblock, he almost ran headlong into Rossi, the Italian Underground organizer who was being herded into an isolation cell.

A collaborator had turned him in, and although the Gestapo could pin nothing on him they had arrested him on suspicion. After successfully resisting days of intense interrogation during which he was constantly threatened with torture and being shot, he revealed nothing and pleaded total innocence, and was finally released from solitary confinement and assigned to work with the same gang of orderlies as Paterson. When Paterson told him that escape was virtually impossible, Rossi assured him that anything was possible if you paid for it; he had already bribed a prison turnkey to plan an escape for himself, the Canadian, and three others.

It had been carefully worked out and timed to take place at 2:40 in the afternoon on a given date following the midday meal, when the guards felt drowsy and took a siesta on benches near their posts. Walking 10 minutes apart, the orderlies were to carry blankets for laundering through the side door of the cellblock, across the yard into the next block, drop the blankets in a corner, and go out the far side door into the courtyard, where there was a gate between the two walls, always open and unguarded, used by trucks to bring in supplies to the storeroom.

Once outside the gate, the escapees would be between the two walls. Fifty yards to the right against the outer wall was a toolshed to which the orderlies were allowed access to pick up and return shovels, wheelbarrows, and the like. Inside the lean-to they were to exchange their prison overalls for the civilian clothes they were wearing upon their arrest. The final step of the escape was a locked door through the wall, and the turnkey had supplied Rossi with a key.

When Paterson's turn came, he walked past the row of cells, out the side door, crossed the courtyards, and entered the building, where a guard slouched in a chair smoking a cigar looked up momentarily from the magazine he was reading but didn't give the Canadian a second glance. It was a tense moment that sent his heart racing. Finally he reached the gate and went into the toolshed. Quickly changing his clothes, he opened the door, stepped outside, and pulled it shut. He was free! Now he had to get away—quickly, before the escape was discovered.

Outside the wall there were trolley tracks in the road. In the distance he could hear a tram rattling toward a pickup stop at the corner 50 yards along the wall to the right. As he began walking in that direction, suddenly a burly figure in the green uniform of the SS emerged from around the corner headed in his direction. Paterson's heart skipped a beat. If he turned around, his action would be a dead giveaway. If he tried to run for it, he would be cut down by machine-gun fire from the sentry posts at the top of the wall. He had no choice but to bluff. Pulling down the brim of his black fedora, he kept on walking looking straight ahead. The German ignored him—just another Italian civilian. As the tram pulled to a halt, Paterson hopped aboard, bought a ticket with the money Rossi had given him, and took a seat, soaked in nervous sweat from the ordeal.

By evening, Paterson reached the apartment of Maria and Fortunato Resta, who welcomed him with open arms. They were anxious to know what had happened to him. Over and over he recounted the details of his imprisonment punctuated by much eating and drinking late into the night. His frame too long for the chesterfield, Paterson found it hard to sleep—plus too much good food and wine after the starvation rations at San Vittore. Restlessly he pondered the fate of Rossi and the others. He wondered if Milan had become the scene of a mass manhunt as a result of their escape.

Next morning every noise outside the house, a car drawing up, or footsteps down the corridors, startled him. Was it the Gestapo or the *Questura*? His nerves jangled. Maria tried to soothe his fears, assured him that with them he was safe. That afternoon, when she went shopping, he gave her a phone number to call where Rossi had told him he could be reached.

On her return, Maria had good news: Rossi and the others were safe. To avoid capture, Rossi had decided to go to Switzerland and advised Paterson to do the same. He gave Maria the name of a fireman, Orlando, who could arrange to get him across the border.

Two days later, Maria took Paterson to the Milan Fire Station—a man and woman walking together on the street would arouse little suspicion, even if there was a dragnet out—where he met Orlando. In a fireman's garb, Paterson rode in the back of a pumper truck, which Orlando drove to Como to return it to that city's fire brigade.

When they reached the outskirts of the city, Orlando drove the pumper to a farmhouse where he turned him over to Francesco, a smuggler by trade, who would guide Paterson across the border into Switzerland. After Paterson changed into his civilian clothes, Francesco led him some miles from the house through rocky countryside and woods until they reached the top of a small bush-covered bluff looking down on a path, patrolled by the Germans. There was a high fence at the bottom—the Swiss border. A patrol went by and they waited. Then Francesco told him to move—to get under the fence and keep going on the other side.

Paterson made his way under the fence, and he was almost immediately confronted with a squad of soldiers in green uniforms. Startled, he at first took them for a German patrol like the one he had watched go by earlier. But that was impossible. The border was clearly marked by the high fence. He asked if they were Swiss. They were indeed. When Paterson explained that he was an escaped Canadian officer, they ushered him to a guardhouse where they fed him and put him up for the night. Next day, he was taken by train to a quarantine centre at Bad Lostorf. There he renewed acquaintance with Jack Watson, a former member of the 11th Special Air Service Battalion with whom he had parachuted into Italy three-and-a-half years earlier. Watson had escaped from a POW camp after the fall of Mussolini and had been on the run ever since. Like Paterson, he was a newcomer to Switzerland, having crossed the border only a week earlier.

At the centre, Paterson was given a thorough medical checkup. His clothes were deloused, he was debriefed, and 10 days later was on his way to a life of relaxation and comfort at Montreux on the shore of Lake Geneva. It was a luxury few people could afford even in peacetime. There he met a beautiful Swiss girl, Karen, with whom it was love at first sight. But it was a romance destined to be short-lived.

Some days later, Paterson was summoned to the British Press Office in Bern. On arrival he was met by a Mr. McTavish, who took him into his confidence to explain that the BPO was really a front for the Special Operations Executive branch of the secret service. SOE wanted Paterson to go back into Italy as a liaison officer with the partisans who were growing stronger by the day. It was hoped that with SOE support—supplying arms, munitions, and supplies by air drop—they could foster a rebellion in northern Italy that would occupy that area of the country, cut the German army's supply line, and force a surrender. A long shot, but not out of the realm of possibility—everything, anything in wartime was a calculated try—and Allied high command was showing an intense interest. They wanted firsthand details from one of their own rather than take the word of the partisans.

The initial task was to survey the situation—the partisans were a mixed bag of some 3000 Democrats, Socialists, Royalists, and Communists—and assess their effectiveness and potential. Paterson was not entirely enthusiastic at the prospect. After all, he had already been through a very rough time and this might be even tougher. To top it all off he was in love with Karen and had in fact asked her to marry him. Yet there was no doubt in his mind that with his experience he was the logical choice for the job. His sense of duty won out, and he agreed to take on the assignment, with the proviso that Jack Watson was to go with him if he was willing (which he was) as his bodyguard and wireless operator. He also negotiated a weekend with Karen at Locarno on Lake Maggiore, the jumping-off point from where he and Watson would reenter Italy.

After much last-minute preparation and planning, during which Paterson, due to the suspicion he had been under with the Gestapo at San Vittore, was given a new identity—Major George Robertson of the Royal Engineers, captured in North Africa, escaped from the POW camp at Padua—he and Watson were driven to an isolated spot five miles south of Locarno. They walked across a small bridge over a ravine and were greeted by partisans, who welcomed them to "Free Italy."

They travelled on foot for two miles west along the road to Malesco where Paterson was introduced to three of the four partisan leaders—brigadiers. The fourth, Moscatelli, a Communist, was absent. The others explained that he was probably too busy, trying to turn the peasants into Reds, indicating there was no love lost between him and the other brigadiers.

Paterson accompanied the partisans on their march west through the Toce River valley, mopping up scattered German detachments, the final objective being the main garrison in the area at the town of Domodossola. Luckily, the Germans they encountered were a sorry, frightened lot, only too happy to surrender. In fact, at Domodossola, 60 Ukrainians who had been conscripted into the Wehrmacht willingly joined the partisans in exchange for being fed properly. Paterson realized that this lack of opposition was as potentially dangerous as it had been fortuitous. The partisans, though hospitable and kind, and resolute and determined to rid the country of the hated "Tedeschi," hadn't the faintest idea what war was all about. Poorly organized, they lacked even the most fundamental knowledge of tactics or planning.

The exception was Moscatelli, both a soldier and politician, who had been trained by the Russians in guerrilla warfare. With by far the largest of the bands under his command—2000 as opposed to 500 in each of the other three—he seemed to know where he was going. He assured Paterson that after the war Italy would have a Communist government, the "party of the future."

But now that Domodossola had been overcome, to Paterson's chagrin the guerrilla leaders, even Moscatelli, seemed content to sit back and guard what they had captured. To Paterson, this was inviting disaster. With only 3000 lightly armed, untrained, undisciplined men, they would never be able to stand up against an organized enemy attack. They should keep on moving, harassing the enemy at times and places of their own choosing, keeping him constantly off guard. But as an advisor, he was in no position to impress his views too strongly on his hosts.

When news of the successful march through the Toce River valley reached the Allied-controlled government in Rome via Switzerland, a representative arrived to set up an administration made up of a delegation of a half-partisan and a half-local population. This embryo government faced a raft of problems. The partisans were running woefully short of ammunition. There was also a serious lack of money with which to buy food. The partisans requisitioned local cattle and supplies, which did not sit well with the civilian members of the council. The government representative had his hands full trying to keep peace among the various factions.

Paterson, named "Giorgio" by the partisans, suggested he take a quick trip to Locarno where he could deal with the crisis in person. In Switzerland he reported the problems to the authorities, who agreed to arrange for ammunition and supply drops and to provide him with the funds he needed. That evening Paterson phoned Karen in Montreux. It was a reunion both happy and tearful. Karen was overjoyed that he was back safely, but distressed that they would not be able to see each other because Paterson was returning to Italy the next day.

The following afternoon Paterson met with the SOE representative and a guide, Carlo, who was to take him across the border. He was given a schedule of the airdrops and 20 million *lire* (the equivalent at the time of $200,000). At the border they were stopped by a Swiss guard. Paterson pondered that 20 million Italian *lire* would take a lot of explaining. Carlo explained to the guard that Paterson was an Italian refugee whose wife was dying in Malesco and that he was escorting him back to be near her.

When he reached Domodossola and told the partisans that ammunition and supplies would be forthcoming by airdrop, and handed over the money, he was welcomed like a conquering hero. But three nights later when the first airdrop failed to materialize, he and the dozen partisans awaiting the consignment returned at dawn to the town, had breakfast, and fell into bed. Late in the afternoon Paterson was awakened by reports that the Communist partisans, dug in some 15 miles south of the town, had been beating off German attacks by several tanks and dive-bombers. The other partisans were not unduly concerned, but Paterson knew that it was a series of preliminary feints preparatory to a large-scale assault. Only Moscatelli appeared to appreciate the situation. He had pulled back all his forward patrols in hopes of being able to hold back the enemy. If that failed, he intended to withdraw still further and fight in the mountains.

Late that night, Paterson was again awakened, this time to learn that a battalion of German Alpine troops and some Fascist infantry had crossed Lake Maggiore and landed near Cannobio to the east of Malesco. This meant the partisans were being squeezed from both south and east. The Royalist brigade had a patrol in the area and blew the bridge leading through the pass to slow down the German advance. DiDio, their chief, was marshalling his brigade at Malesco and intended to move forward at dawn and halt the enemy. Paterson surmised that if the Royalists could not stop the enemy at the point where the bridge was blown, they could never hold off a force that size in open country. The question in his mind was whether DiDio could assemble his brigade before the Germans arrived. He decided to see for himself and drove to Malesco, taking Jack Watson and Monetta, the partisan liaison officer, with him. Arriving just before dawn, they left Watson in the town, then proceeded some miles farther on past the column of Royalists reinforced by some of the Democrats (Green flames) where they found DiDio surveying the ground ahead.

The Royalist chieftain told them that he and his entourage of seven partisans were about to reconnoiter the bridge they had blown and, if it was not too badly damaged, planned to get his brigade across. Paterson and Monetta joined them and at the entrance to the pass, left their cars and walked the rest of the 600 yards to the bridge on foot. Surveying the wreckage, Paterson advised against trying to cross it. His assessment was that what remained could come down at any minute.

DiDio agreed and decided to dig in on the ridge above and catch the enemy as they came along. With that, he and Paterson walked over to the retaining wall on the side of the bridge where they were soon joined by Monetta. All three lit up cigarettes. In the distance, they could see the brigade column approaching. After a minute, they planned to drive back and halt the march and assign the men to positions on the ridge. Then suddenly the world went crazy.

From up on the ridge, machine-gun fire blazed down into the valley. The brigade column broke, the partisans diving for cover. More gunfire erupted from another hill on the other side of the bridge. The 10 men caught in the crossfire sheltered themselves against the wall with one thought in mind: get to the two cars and get the hell out of there. Meanwhile, across the valley the partisans began to answer back with fire of their own. Then the Germans brought up their heavy guns.

Half crawling along the ground, the trapped 10 inched forward toward the vehicles. It took half an hour and just when they thought they were within reach, tracer bullets slammed into the cars, setting the fuel tanks on fire. Their only chance now was to make for a large cement storm culvert on the side of the road and hope for the best.

Some of the partisans succeeded, though one was cut down as he ran across the open ground. Monetta and the others intended to sprint across the open space to a spot where the German fire could not reach—dead ground—before making for the culvert. Monetta went first and only just made it, bullets kicking up dirt all around him as he dove to safety. Now it was Paterson's turn and behind him DiDio, then the latter's courier.

Paterson had to wait until the firing eased, but every time he got ready to start, it opened up again. Finally it let up altogether and, grabbing his Tommy gun, he dashed forward expecting at any moment to be struck down. Miraculously he made it to right beside Monetta, who was waiting for him.

DiDio's turn came next. But as he got to his feet, machine-gun fire ripped into his left knee. As he hit the ground, Peterson and the others watched as the Germans cut him to ribbons. Unnerved, DiDio's courier shouted that he was staying put rather than risk crossing the open space. With a temporary lull in the firing, Paterson and Monetta rushed out and joined the other five in the temporary safety of the culvert. But they knew they were trapped. Monetta viewed the situation fatalistically; the best they could do was to take some Germans with them.

The Germans now brought up the dreaded 88mm guns, but while they could not actually bring them to bear on the culvert, the shelling shattered the rock formation above it, sending chunks of rock crashing down at the entrance to the culvert. The siege lasted over two hours and the partisans were losing all hope. They knew they were doomed; documents, letters, money were destroyed. But they were determined to go down fighting, and they checked their weapons and what ammunition remained.

Then the shelling stopped, followed by an eerie silence. Suddenly they heard sounds of rocks falling and pebbles rattling down. This was it; the Germans were closing in for the kill. Monetta and another partisan moved slowly to the entrance, then charged out firing their guns in all directions. The rest followed. They would fight to the death. When Paterson emerged, two grenades exploded almost in his face, but he was only slightly wounded in the wrist. He ignored the wound, positioning himself behind a giant boulder where he saw two of his partisan comrades dashing down the hill, stopping only to let off a volley of fire before continuing on. When a German soldier suddenly appeared to take aim on the pair, killing one of them, Paterson felled him with a short burst from his Tommy gun. Then he spotted another enemy creeping from boulder to boulder, and with another well-aimed burst caught him in the chest.

Monetta, unluckily, was killed by a machine-gun burst that sent him crumpling into a shallow pool of water. Seconds later Paterson shot the German man who had killed him in the head.

Paterson began shooting at everything in sight, when he saw a German in full view on his right. He raised his gun and squeezed the trigger, but nothing happened. He was out of ammunition. The partisans around him had been killed. He threw away his Tommy gun and stood ready to face the inevitable. The Germans were on him instantly, kicking and punching him; then a rifle butt sent him reeling into unconsciousness.

When he came to, a pair of German soldiers standing over him cocked their rifles, ready to shoot. Just in time, a warrant officer intervened with the admonishment that prisoners were not to be shot—they were needed for interrogation. Paterson was pulled to his feet and prodded toward a road leading to the German camp. As they passed Monetta's body, one of the soldiers pulled out his Luger and emptied three shots into the lifeless head. He then frisked his pockets and, finding nothing, yanked off the dead man's boots and walked away. Along the road other Germans brought in DiDio's courier, who had wisely remained at the mouth of the culvert. He and Paterson were the only survivors of the battle.

When they reached the bivouac, one of the Germans addressed Paterson by name. It was a guard from the San Vittore prison, who recognized him as one of his former prisoners. So much for his Major George Robertson cover. He needed to get rid of his false identity card at the first opportunity.

As a result of the encounter, Paterson was singled out and interrogated by an SS sergeant. Identifying himself as George Paterson who had escaped from a POW camp, he admitted only to having hidden out with the partisans, carefully avoiding any reference to having crossed the border, which might label him as a spy. He and DiDio's courier were then taken by truck to the dreary town of

Cannobio on the lakeshore where they were herded into a shed housing other partisan prisoners. That night Paterson tore up his false identity card and shoved the pieces down between the cracks in the floorboards.

Next morning, after being fed some bread and black coffee they were loaded into two trucks and driven 25 miles south to Novara, on the same parallel as Milan, another 25 miles to the east. There they were ushered into a drab, grey stone prison that housed other partisan prisoners. Paterson learned it was only a transit camp; they were going to be either sent to Germany as forced labour or shot.

Paterson was again singled out for an interview with the SS. He told the same story he had related to the previous interrogator. But this officer wanted names and advised him that if he cooperated, it would help him at his trial. Trial? Paterson lied that the reason he laid low with the partisans was to await the inevitable arrival of the Allied armies. Normally such an answer sent the Germans into a rage. To his surprise, this individual agreed with him and with that, he was dismissed.

Weeks followed in the uncomfortable, overcrowded cell. The food was even worse than at San Vittore. On Armistice Day, 11 November 1944, after the evening meal one of the guards read out a list of those to be deported to Germany. Paterson's name was not among them, but that of an 18-year-old partisan was on the list. This young partisan was determined to escape en route. Paterson gave him a letter he had written to the SOE representative in Locarno, which he asked him to deliver if he escaped. No trouble at all, the youngster assured him; he had been across the border several times. Good as done.

Three weeks later, Paterson was told by one of the jailers to get his things together because he was being moved. His things? He had nothing to get, not even a razor or a toothbrush. Outside the cell, two burly SS men carrying machine guns escorted him to a car, which carried them to the Novara railway station where they boarded a train for Milan. On arrival, another car picked them up and drove through the all-too-familiar streets. Paterson did not need to ask their destination. Looming ahead was the forbidding, formidable outer wall of San Vittore.

To his horror, the first visitor to his cell was the brutal Corporal—now Sergeant—Franz. Paterson steeled himself for the worst. He expected a harsh reprisal for his escape from the prison; at the very least he was sure they would put the boots to him. To his surprise Franz smiled, looked him over, then began to laugh uproariously at his shoddy, unshaven, half-starved appearance. "Guess you've come back for some kindness," he grinned.

"I've missed all of you too," Paterson shot back in the same jocular vein.

Franz's mood abruptly changed, more curious than serious. He wanted to know how on earth Paterson and his friends were ever able to escape. Paterson decided to come clean, relating the whole plan, but omitting the part about the turnkey supplying a key; instead he said that by pure chance the door through the wall had been left open. With that Franz, as amused as he was dumbfounded, left with instructions that Paterson was to be kept in solitary.

A week later, the Gestapo arrived to take him to their headquarters in the Alberto Regina. Just like old times. Now the grilling began in earnest. Who had helped him after his escape from San Vittore? Paterson recited his well-rehearsed, oft-told story that he had been hiding out as a fugitive, until he had thrown in his lot with the partisans. The Gestapo officers were adamant. They called him a liar, threatened that if he didn't reveal names he would be shot. The interrogation went on for hours. Although he could take satisfaction that the bastards had failed to get anything out of him, the experience left him drained and distraught. Next day he was put through another grilling, during which he was threatened with torture and finally told that he would be reported for his lack of cooperation and shot as a spy.

That night, commiserating over what his fate held in store—a concentration camp or death from a bullet to the head—he was distracted by an itchy wrist. He rubbed it. It was rough and red. Scabies of course. The prison was rife with it. Next morning his hands, wrists, and stomach were inflamed and itchy. He demanded to see the prison doctor.

Taken to the dispensary, he found the young Italian doctor to be sympathetic and understanding, particularly when he learned Paterson was a Canadian. He had a cousin living in Toronto and thought about moving there himself when the war was over. Paterson concurred it would probably be a good idea; there wouldn't be much worthwhile left in Italy after what Mussolini's Fascists had done to it. Right off the bat they had established an empathy. After several visits in which the scabies seemed to be clearing up, the doctor asked Paterson if he would like to escape. The sooner the better his patient replied; the Gestapo was making up its mind whether to shoot him.

The doctor then devised a scheme to have him transferred to the prison infirmary located right by the outer wall where the gate for the ambulances was always open and seldom guarded. To get Paterson admitted, he gave him some pills that would turn his skin yellow, as if he had contracted jaundice. On his next visit the doctor told Paterson he had been able to bribe an orderly to help him escape; he had also contacted a partisan friend who knew all about Paterson and, once he was on the outside the partisans would provide him with money and hide him until they could get him across the Swiss border.

Paterson's spirits soared, but a week later the pills hadn't taken effect. The doctor gave him something stronger which, although it made him groggy, did the trick. He was a sure candidate for the infirmary—and freedom. Then the house caved in.

Shortly after Christmas 1944, Sergeant Franz appeared at the door to his cell, entered and cheerfully informed him that all charges by the Gestapo against him had been dropped and he was being transferred to the Wehrmacht wing of the prison to await a court-martial. Goodbye, Operation Infirmary-Escape. The German army had jurisdiction over the wing that housed offenders charged with military crimes such as desertion, cowardice, rape, or robbery awaiting their fate—execution or incarceration in a slave labour camp.

Paterson was put in a cell on the main floor and given the limited amount of daytime freedom allowed all inmates. That was about the only amenity. Food was in short supply and the result was near-starvation rations. As the months rolled by—January, February, March—the war dragged on to its inevitable conclusion, leaving Paterson wondering when he would be summoned for trial before it ended. Then one morning in the latter part of April, the distant crackle of rifle fire and the rattle of machine guns could be heard. It could mean only one thing. The partisans were rising in the city. That being the case, the Allies couldn't be far away. What now?

Later in the day, all prisoners were moved to the second floor of the prison wing and Paterson found himself in a cell with eight others, among them a major who had been decorated several times for bravery and was charged with homosexuality. The major, who had the inside track, gave them the grim news that as so-called political prisoners, they were going to be evacuated to Germany. In Paterson's case, being an enemy of Germany, he could possibly be held for ransom. In any case the situation called for drastic measures no matter how risky.

He and the major huddled together to work out a plan for a mass escape. Next morning when the two orderlies (prisoners like themselves) brought in their rations, the major took them aside and spoke in a whisper so the guard couldn't overhear him. Their role in the scheme was crucial to its success.

In the course of their rounds from cell to cell, the orderlies alerted all of the inmates to get ready for a mass breakout. When they reached the last cell, which was opposite their own, with the help of the six or seven prisoners inside, they overcame the guard, took his keys, then dashed back down the catwalk, opening all the cell doors. All of the prisoners made as much noise as possible, shouting and banging on the doors to surprise and confuse the soldiers guarding the prison.

A mob of 300 to 400 prisoners surged onto the main floor yelling and screaming at the top of their lungs, which so unnerved the two machine-gunners positioned behind sandbags at the end of the building that they simply looked on in horror. The major motioned to one of the prisoners to go down and order the gunners to open the outside door or be torn to bits. After a brief conversation, one of the gunners opened the door to a roar of triumph from the crowd stampeding through it to freedom.

Paterson found his way through the streets of Milan to the Restas. The city was in an excited state of confusion. It appeared the partisans were at least in partial control, but no one could offer any information on the situation in general. In any case, the Restas were celebrating the fall of Fascism, and Paterson, after so many months of imprisonment and meagre rations, happily joined in. Next day he made his way to police headquarters to meet the new chief, who had taken over control of the city except for a few pockets of German resistance. He was told Mussolini and his entourage had garrisoned themselves in the prefecture guarded by Fascist troops. Paterson was provided with a car and driver in which he toured the city. Everywhere, everyone was celebrating. The following day, a victory parade was held, prominent among which was the Communist guerrilla leader, Moscatelli, who persuaded Paterson to join him in his vehicle.

Later in the day he learned that American artillery observation planes had landed at the airport to survey the situation. They were anxious to obtain firsthand information, which Paterson, happily sated on whiskey and steak, did his best to supply from his own recent experiences.

The next afternoon he drove to Como, where he tried to reach Karen by telephone. He could not get a call through, so he decided to cross the border. However, he was politely refused entry by the Swiss guards unless he obtained permission from Bern. And for that he would need official clearance. He returned to Milan to learn that British paratroops had landed at the airport and had commandeered the luxurious villa once occupied by Mussolini's henchman Alessandro Pavolini. He soon learned that the paratroop unit was No. 11 Special Force—his own!

Paterson was introduced to Colonel Salvadori, a British officer of Italian descent, who had for some months been working with the resistance in Milan and was familiar with Paterson and his adventures. He and his associates had earmarked five million *lire* for anyone who could arrange his release from San Vittore, and they had also been behind the doctor's attempt to free him through the infirmary.

Paterson was given Pavolini's sumptuous quarters for accommodation. After lunch he went upstairs to lie down and read. But the hectic pace of escaping from the prison and the excitement of the last few days finally caught up with him and he fell asleep. He awoke to the noise of the telephone ringing. A voice from the other end in Italian barked "Get Pavolini on the line and hurry."

The voice had a familiar sound to it. He'd heard it often in speeches broadcast over the radio.

"Pavolini?" he replied.

That voice again: "Yes, and hurry, you fool."

"One moment, Excellency, and I will get him," Paterson assured the caller and rushed downstairs to the colonel's office.

"I swear I've got Mussolini on the line," he said. Salvadori told him to advise Mussolini that Pavolini had been sent for and try and keep him talking. But when Paterson picked up the phone, the line had gone dead. He and Salvadori looked at each other wondering whether they had missed a historic opportunity to persuade Mussolini to surrender to them.

Next day they learned that Il Duce, on that very afternoon of the phone call, had gone to Cardinal Schuster's palace to confer with the National Committee of Liberation to arrange a surrender. But that evening after returning to the prefecture he suddenly left

Milan with his mistress, Claretta Petacci, and a handful of his closest associates, driving through the city unnoticed in all the confusion. The reason for the phone call soon became clear. It was rumoured that Pavolini, who was still in Milan, was rounding up 3000 to 4000 diehard Fascists to join Mussolini in the mountains for a last-ditch stand.

Salvadori introduced Paterson to the unit's commanding officer, to whom Paterson appealed for some leave and his help to get him across the border into Switzerland to be reunited with his fiancée. The colonel, though sympathetic, explained that until the situation stabilized, it was out of the question and advised him to bide his time.

Several days later, the SOE liaison officer who had made the arrangements for Paterson and his sidekick Jack Watson to cross the border into Italy from Locarno arrived in Milan to join his old unit, and delivered a bombshell to Paterson in person. Karen was calling off the engagement, which on reflection she considered to have been hasty and ill-advised, and she was going to marry another man she had known for some time with whom she had fallen in love. Paterson was crestfallen. After all he'd been through, he was left with a bleak outlook for the future.

Next afternoon, a young policeman whom he had met earlier suggested the Canadian try to forget his troubles for the moment and join him in a drive around the city. As they neared the Piazzale Loreto, renamed the Square of Fifteen Martyrs in honour of a group of partisans executed there by the Germans some months earlier, their way was blocked by a delirious, cheering mob. They abandoned their vehicle and with the help of a policeman on either side of them, pushed into the centre of the plaza where the pavement was littered with 14 corpses.

One of them, Paterson noticed, was a beautiful young woman whose lustrous black eyes stared lifelessly and vacantly at the sky. "His mistress," a woman beside Paterson scowled. "His whore." The head of Benito Mussolini, one side of which had been kicked in, lay across her breast. They had been captured and shot by Communist partisans the day before.

A cry went up: "String them up. String them up so that we can all see." A picture of the hanging bodies was printed on the front pages of newspapers around the world.

For his remarkable bravery working with the partisans, George Paterson was awarded the Military Cross and two bars and made a Freeman of the City of Milan. After the war he remained in Italy to work with the Allied authorities in restoring order in the northern area before returning to the University of Edinburgh to complete his degree in forestry.

After graduation, he took a government post in Tanganyika, East Africa, where he married. After a number of years, he, his wife Oojie, and their two children moved to British Columbia, where he became a partner in a forestry management firm.

Chapter 18

Le Commandant Guy

Kindly indulge me while I do a little namedropping. It has a purpose, as you'll see. When I arrived in England as a freshly graduated RCAF Pilot Officer, in September 1942, I was granted five days' leave from the aircrew assembly depot at Bournemouth to visit my father, who was staying at Claridges Hotel in London. One evening he hosted a reception in his suite for the wartime bigwigs and luminaries, among them Generals Dwight Eisenhower, Mark Clark, Tooey Spaatz, and Jimmy Doolittle, as well as actress Merle Oberon and her movie-director husband, Alexander Korda, who had just been knighted at Buckingham Palace that very afternoon. In one corner a short, nondescript man wearing a dark blue suit was talking to Air Marshal Sholto Douglas, chief of Royal Air Force Fighter Command. Later that evening, I asked my father who the civilian was among all that senior military brass.

"Civilian?" he exploded. "Bill Stephenson! He's Winston's closest confidant!" For my benefit he added, "And he was a damned fine fighter pilot in the last war, too!"

Indeed! William Stephenson, otherwise known as "the Man called Intrepid," was the mastermind behind Allied intelligence and espionage in Europe during World War II and the proponent of fighting the conflict with "gloves off, the knee to the groin, the stab in the dark"— what Churchill called the "Ungentlemanly War." Link number one to my interest in the subject.

Link number two. Many years after the war, my school friend Lord

Shaughnessy introduced me to Colin Gubbins, the chief Baker Street Irregular, the organization responsible for training saboteurs and spies and conducting clandestine operations in enemy-controlled territory. It was Gubbins who headed the operation into Poland in 1939 to steal a copy of the German coding machine known as Enigma that allowed the Allies to listen in on enemy directives—some directly from Hitler himself.

Very little has been written about individual Canadians who participated in all this intrigue, though "Intrepid" was himself a Canadian, born in Manitoba near Winnipeg. As my interest in the subject grew I started to scout about for sources on the subject. They were few and far between, but one individual who stood out among all my research was Gustave "Guy" Bieler, a French-born, naturalized Canadian citizen from Montreal. His story is one of such unmatched heroism, devotion to duty, and self-sacrifice that it needs to be remembered—indelibly.

An ominous squeal of tires against the cobblestones and the screech of brakes suddenly shattered the evening serenity and silence of the quiet side street leading to the St. Quentin canal. Leaping from a pair of Mercedes-Benz staff cars, a dozen black-uniformed German Gestapo burst through the doors of the drab red-brick Café du Moulin Brûlé, and at pistol-point confronted the four occupants who were enjoying an aperitif. "On your feet," they ordered gruffly. "You're under arrest."

There was no need to ask why.

By 15 January 1944, the Gestapo had been hot on the trail of the Allied saboteur, *le Commandant Guy*, the only name by which the French Resistance knew him, as well as his wireless operator, code-named "Mariette." Though the other two occupants in the cafe, the proprietor and his wife, could scarcely be called collaborators, they knew full well the risk they were taking, simply catering to anyone abetting the Underground. Like so many brave French sympathizers, they were caught in the web.

After more than a year conducting sabotage activities in northern France, Major Guy Bieler, British Special Operations (SOE) agent, and Yolande Beekman, a member of the Women's Auxiliary Air Force, accepted the fact that this was the end. Not just *finis* to their clandestine operations, but the end of the road, period. Now they faced certain torture, incarceration in a concentration camp, and eventual execution. Gestapo Chief Heinrich Himmler's dictum that all such "terrorists" should be murdered "but not before torture, indignity, and interrogation had drained from them that last scintilla of evidence which should lead to the arrest of others," was well known to all undercover agents.

For Gustave Daniel Alfred Bieler, it had been a long journey and a physically demanding one since the bitterly cold winter night of 18 November 1942 when, along with two other agents, he had parachuted into some woods near Montargis, 65 miles southwest of Paris. It turned out to be an inauspicious start for the man whom his SOE instructors rated the best student they had ever had—"the most brilliant of all the Canadians"—as well as being the first Canadian army volunteer to be parachuted into France.

Bieler landed roughly on some rocky ground and severely injured his back. For some hours he lay helpless, but one of the other agents, Englishman Captain Michael Trotobas, who had been assigned as his radio operator, managed to help him to the nearby village of Auxy-Iuranville and took him by train to Paris. There he was sheltered in a "safe house," home of Mademoiselle Marie-Louise Monnet, on the Boulevard de Suffern. There he was put in contact with his brother, René-Maurice, a French army veteran and member of the French Resistance, whom he had not seen since emigrating to Montreal, Quebec, at the suggestion of his uncle, a teacher at McGill University.

Born in France of Swiss parents, Bieler was educated at Lausanne and Geneva. Fluently bilingual, he taught school at Pointe-aux-Trembles, near Montreal, before joining the head office of the Sun Life Assurance Company where he became chief translator. In 1934 he took out Canadian citizenship and in 1939 volunteered for duty with the University of Montreal Canadian Officers'

Training Corps contingent. The following year he was given a commission in the Régiment de Maisonneuve. In July 1940 he sailed for Great Britain aboard a troopship, leaving his wife, Marguerite, and their two children in Montreal.

By the spring of 1942, Bieler had become the battalion's intelligence officer. But, like other Canadian Army personnel stationed in the south of England, he had become disenchanted and restless while waiting for the day when the Allies would invade Europe, something that seemed—and was—in the far-distant future. Fortuitously, his intelligence work had put him in contact with the British War Office, where he met Colonel Maurice Buckmaster, the head of SOE's French "F" Section, who took an immediate liking to the Canadian and saw in him a potential undercover agent. The fact that he spoke the French vernacular was a big asset. Over some drinks Buckmaster outlined the work of his organization—coordinating Resistance operations with Allied strategic needs and plans, sabotage, training, and arming French patriots to strike when the invasion came. Basically its broad objective was best delivered by Winston Churchill's blatant decree: "Set Europe ablaze."

Bieler needed little persuasion to make application. After an interview by a selection board he was accepted, and at the beginning of June he began an intense period of training before being given an assignment. At 38, Bieler was by far the oldest in his class and known affectionately as "Granddad" to the other agent trainees. He took to the routine like a duck to water and passed every test with flying colours—"Very conscientious, keen and intelligent ... sound judge of character; good natured; even tempered; absolutely reliable; outstandingly thorough and painstaking; a born organizer." It was as if espionage was a career specifically cut out for him and one that he, in turn, had been born for. An affable man, short and sturdy with dark hair and a thick moustache, who had a good sense of humour, he was highly popular with—and respected by—his instructors and fellow students alike.

A fatalist, Bieler became a determined and dedicated potential agent, highly conscious of what the Germans were doing to his native land, to his brother as well as his friends. "I am a soldier," he said, "and I am here because I want to help save people from being pushed around."

Ever since arriving in England, Bieler had been a frequent visitor of his sister Madelaine Dale and her husband, who lived in a red-brick house in the London suburb of Ewell. On the evening of 10 November 1942, having completed his training, Bieler turned up for dinner wearing civilian clothes instead of his uniform as he usually did. Madelaine had guessed for some time that her brother must have some sort of secret undercover job, because he had repeatedly told her and her husband that he wasn't allowed to talk about it. This night when Madelaine looked inside his "civvie" over-coat and could find no label identifying the manufacturer, she was certain he was being sent to occupied France. "We guessed this was his last visit," she said.

"See you soon," Bieler said. But that was the last time Madelaine would ever see him.

Two weeks later, in France, René-Maurice arranged for Bieler to be admitted to a Paris hospital under the assumed name of Guy Morin so that he could be treated for the spinal injury he sustained after his parachute jump. This was followed by three months of recuperation in a flat run by the Resistance near the Eiffel Tower.

Although his back injury still gave him pain and made it difficult for him to walk, Bieler adamantly rejected an offer from SOE head-quarters to be flown out of France and back to England. He was determined to complete the job he had been trained for and assigned to: organizing sabotage operations in the St. Quentin area northeast of Paris.

By the first week of April 1943, though still in pain, Bieler finally felt strong enough to travel. On the seventh of the month, he boarded a train to St. Quentin. Eugène Cordelette, a land surveyor and leader of the local Underground, who had received word by wireless from London that an Allied officer would soon arrive to assist them with their sabotage activities, met Bieler at the railway station. He was shocked at the Canadian officer's appearance. Stooped and wan-looking, he had barely enough strength to walk the eight miles to Cordelette's house in the village of Fonsomme to the east of St. Quentin. By leaning heavily on the Frenchman's arm and limping badly as he stumbled along, Bieler eventually made it. But nearly a week passed before he recovered sufficiently from his journey to venture outside. Even then he was unable to stand on his feet for longer than a few hours a day. However, dressed in blue trousers and the grey jacket of a labourer and seated at a table beneath a tree at the back of Cordelette's house, he began recruiting men for his sabotage network (*réseau*), coded "Musician." (Bieler was an accomplished pianist.)

Bieler chose his workers carefully and wisely: mostly railway men with an expert knowledge of the local rail system. He soon had a knowledgeable, aggressive group of saboteurs at his disposal. A strong rapport quickly developed between them. *Le Commandant Guy* was one of them, a native-born Frenchman, a patriot willing to risk his neck in the most dangerous business of them all.

Their objective, along with other sabotage networks in the same region (25 in all), was to play havoc with the St.-Quentin-Lille-area railway system. This was a vital communications link connecting the Pas de Calais, where the Germans were concentrating their forces in preparation for an Allied invasion, to the main European industrial centres. Its continual disruption, destruction of railway equipment and the rail lines themselves, was of paramount importance to the Allied war effort. It called for proper planning, training, and skill in the use of ammunition, explosives, and weapons that the Royal Air Force dropped into designated fields at night, and above all, daring. Bieler was in his element. This on-the-ground sabotage was not only more accurate and effective than aerial bombing, it also spared civilian casualties that inevitably resulted during air attacks. It was an unceasing battle, because as fast as the saboteurs blew up a rail line the Germans repaired it; but it kept the enemy off-balance, diverting manpower from the front.

A novel development for this particular type of work had been introduced by SOE: a seemingly ordinary grease containing a highly abrasive substance that when applied to mechanical parts as a lubricant rapidly corroded them. With this untraceable substance at their disposal, French railways' employees working for the Underground put 31 locomotives out of action, in addition to destroying an engine repair shop.

In addition to rail targets, Bieler's teams also diversified their activities by destroying bridges and petroleum storage tanks. Another of their objectives was canal traffic. Among the Germans' supplies essential to the war effort were submarine components being manufactured in Rouen and loaded onto the canal barges. St. Quentin formed an important link in the waterway system stretching from northeast France south to the Mediterranean. It was crucial, therefore, that the canal locks there be put out of commission, even though it would only be temporary. RAF bombing, while inflicting serious damage on the locks, failed to destroy them and they were easily and quickly repaired. The lot now fell to Bieler's saboteurs to put them out of business.

Limpet underwater time-bombs, designed to cling to underwater surfaces such as a vessel or a canal lock, encased in canisters, were parachuted to the saboteurs. Two nights later, armed with the explosives, Bieler and two assistants stealthily climbed into a punt, shoved it away from the side of the canal in the direction of the main lock gate and, lying prone in the bottom of the punt, let it drift up against the lock. Then, as quickly and as quietly as possible, they affixed the time-bombs below the waterline. Then they paddled a safe distance away before a massive explosion blew the lock gate apart. But that was only part of the operation that Bieler had planned.

With the collaboration of a junior clerk in the canal's administration office—a member of the Resistance who provided the shipping schedules—Bieler's saboteurs destroyed 40 fully loaded barges by affixing limpet bombs to them. The damage caused by the resultant explosions along with the earlier destruction of the lock gate created such chaos and confusion that canal traffic was blocked for several weeks.

As the "Underground war" progressed and the date for the invasion of Europe drew nearer, the assignments for the French Resistance, both local and overall, had become increasingly complex. Equipment was more advanced and sophisticated, techniques more complicated and ingenious, and the agents more professional. The objectives, however, remained the same—to keep the enemy on guard, compel him to disperse his forces, play on his nerves, and outwit him at every turn. But, at the same time, great care had to be taken to avoid putting the population in danger. No one practised active Underground resistance within that parameter more diligently or more successfully than *le Commandant Guy*. When he learned that an ammunition train, targeted for demolition, had been side-railed dangerously close to a group of houses, to avoid loss of life he cancelled the operation. To make up for it, he ordered a large ammunition convoy, a far more appetizing and rewarding target passing through uninhabited countryside, to be destroyed instead.

Despite crippling pain, one shoulder hunched, his head to one side, Bieler had proven to be a gifted leader who put risk and duty ahead of his own discomfort. He often put his talents to use above and beyond his mandate as an operative to help his fellow countrymen. On one occasion, to provide his workers and fugitives with food, he organized a burglary on the town hall of Vaux-en-Digny and distributed food coupons to those who were most in need.

For the first six months of his operations, Bieler had worked without his own wireless operator, relying on the telegraphers of two other Underground networks to send and receive his coded messages for him. Then, in October, his own wireless operator, Yolande Unternahrer Beekman, a bilingual Anglo-Swiss member of the Women's Auxiliary Air Force (WAAF) who had been educated in both Paris and London, was assigned to him. Beekman had been landed in France near Angers by Lysander on September 17 and had made her way across country carrying her heavy transmitter disguised as a suitcase, to join Bieler in St. Quentin where she set up shop in Mademoiselle Odette Gobeaux's house under the code name "Mariette."

Ironically, while the addition of a wireless operator to his network expedited Bieler's sabotage operations, increased their efficiency, and provided him with greater flexibility, it also placed him and his colleagues in greater danger of discovery, a risk already grave enough as it was. Although even those working closely with him, including Yolande Beekman, never knew his true identity other than that he was a Canadian and married—a family man who on rare occasions talked longingly and lovingly of the wife, son, and daughter he had left back home—there was still the ever-present danger of betrayal on the part of *provocateurs*, collaborators, and infiltrators. And there existed other factors that could lead to discovery as well.

Late in November, an agent from the network at Lille operated by Michael Trotobas, the Englishman who had parachuted into France with Bieler a year earlier, through sheer carelessness and incompetence on his own part was picked up by the Gestapo and, under torture, revealed his commander's hiding place. Trotobas fought it out with the Germans, but was killed in the firefight. However, all his fellow workers were taken alive, tortured, and executed, virtually eliminating Trotobas' Underground cell. This put a heavy onus on Bieler to salvage what he could of the sabotage activities in the Lille area.

For Bieler, the entire affair might have been an omen. But if it was, he chose to ignore it. Under the pressure of husbanding his resources in readiness for the coming Allied invasion of the Continent and at the same time stepping up harassment of the Germans through his sabotage operations, he was too busy to worry about the jeopardy in which his increased activities were placing him. His successes, in fact, were becoming an albatross around his neck that inevitably attracted closer and closer attention from the Germans who over the past year had improved their techniques in tracking down the Resistance. The most notable advancement was the increasingly sophisticated electronic detection devices used to locate wireless operations.

Early in December, one of Bieler's operatives spotted a German vehicle equipped with a radio direction-finding apparatus a few streets from Mlle. Gobeaux's house. The Gestapo were getting closer, tightening the noose around the Musician network. Bieler hurriedly moved Mariette's wireless equipment to the home of a local pharmacist and member of the Resistance, Camille Boury, and his wife. There at Yuletide for a brief interval the cares, dangers, and responsibilities of Underground work were forgotten. On Christmas Day Bieler, Yolande, and Camille and his wife celebrated the festive holiday *chez Boury*. It was an occasion their hostess would long remember.

Dressed in workman's clothes as usual, Mme. Boury would later recall fondly, Bieler arrived, a cheerful smile on his face, bearing two Santa Claus gifts stuffed with candies for their hosts' two children, who had already been sent to bed, and several bottles of wine tucked under each arm. The Bourys had arranged a truly festive atmosphere with a traditional pine Christmas tree and candle setting. After dinner the two SOE agents and the Frenchman and his wife listened to the British Broadcasting Corporation messages (forbidden by the Germans on penalty of arrest and imprisonment) and Christmas music. At midnight, after singing English and French carols followed by Bieler's reading some of Victor Hugo's poetry, *le Commandant* suddenly became pensive, overcome with emotion, eyes closed, holding his head in his hands. He rose from his seat and asked for a pencil. Then on the back of a photograph he wrote out his former business address: Chief, French Dept., Sun Life Assurance Company, Dominion Square, Montreal, and asked the Bourys that in case anything happened to him to write to his wife at that address telling her how much he had enjoyed this Christmas party, and that she and the children were constantly in his thoughts.

Mme. Boury remembered that Bieler often spoke of his children and that it helped remind him of them when he looked in on her own little boy and girl at night in their bedroom. He always made certain to visit the Bourys only when the children were asleep ("We had to take so many precautions against the accursed Gestapo," Mme. Boury said), so that they never saw him and therefore couldn't accidentally say anything about him.

Meanwhile, every one of Yolande's wireless transmissions drew the Gestapo closer. Bieler sensed that his wireless operator's days were numbered. His fears were well founded. Though they decided to send no more messages in the hope the danger would pass, it was too late. Four days later, only three weeks after Yolande and Bieler had celebrated Christmas with the Bourys, came the arrest in the Café du Moulin Brûlé.

They were not the only fish caught in the Gestapo net, though Bieler was the big one. That night and during the days to follow, 50 other members of his network were systematically arrested— rounded up without warning in a meticulously planned operation designed to break up the cornerstone of his carefully constructed organization. However, the organization, though badly reduced in number, remained intact, a tribute to Bieler's inspired exam- ple, leadership, and administrative ability. Six months later, when the Allies invaded France, the network's ambush and sabo- tage teams were instrumental in obstructing the movement of German troop reinforcements being transferred from Norway to the Normandy battlefield.

Among those caught in the Gestapo roundup web was Eugène Cordelette, in whose house at Fonsomme Bieler had first set up headquarters to organize his *réseau* 10 months earlier. On the night of their arrest, Cordelette saw Bieler, chained hand and foot, being taken along a corridor in the St. Quentin prison to a small cell for the first of the many brutal interrogations by the Gestapo that he would be forced to endure. "His face was horribly swollen, but I could read in his eyes this order: 'Whatever happens don't talk!' … In spite of all torments he showed no weakness."

For Bieler there followed three months of being shuffled from prison to prison during which he was subject to the most barbaric interrogation under torture. But he courageously refused to divulge the names of his associates or the location of his network's cache of arms. Finally, in September, his back injury so painful he could hardly stand, weak, and suffering from malnutrition, along with 14 British officers, Bieler was shipped by cattle car to a concentration camp at Flossenburg in Bavaria. There they were confined to tiny, windowless concrete cells cut off from each other, barely sustained on a sparse diet of black ersatz coffee in the morning, watery soup at noon, and a soppy spongy substance passed off as bread in the evening. But at least these so-called meals served as the prisoners' indicator of the passing of day into night. Through a prison official, a Danish army officer, Captain Nords Lunding—one of the few inmates to survive the atrocities meted out at Flossenburg—learned that Bieler, starved and frail, was a complete physical wreck. Providentially, at the time, his wife in Montreal was spared those gruesome, lurid details. She only knew from a cryptic War Office message that her husband was missing following an operation "somewhere in Europe."

Most prisoners executed at the Bavarian concentration camp were either marched or dragged from their cells and summarily shot or shoved into a gas chamber. But Bieler's courage and dignity under the most inhumane conditions and treatment had so impressed his captors that—on direct order from Berlin—they provided a black-uniformed SS *Schutzstaffeln* (Protection Squad) guard of honour for his execution, affording him a last shred of dignity. On the morning of September 9, gaunt, stooped, and limping painfully, *le Commandant* stumbled bravely forward toward the concrete wall in the prison courtyard, did an about-turn and, in a

final gesture of defiance, refused a blindfold to face the firing squad. He was executed as a heroic resistance fighter.

Colonel Maurice Buckmaster, head of the SOE "F" Section, later put on record: "This is the only instance known to us of an officer being executed in such circumstances by a firing squad with a Guard of Honour." For his "determination and courage," Gustave "Guy" Bieler received the posthumous award of the Distinguished Service Order.

Chapter 19

Niigata

On Sunday, 7 December 1941, exactly four months since I had been accepted for pilot training in the Royal Canadian Air Force, I was halfway through my Initial Training School course (Navigation, Armament, Aircraft Appreciation, and so forth) at Belleville, Ontario. Late that night I had returned from a weekend leave—a "48"—in Montreal. Next morning we learned of the Japanese attack on the American Fleet at Pearl Harbor. This action was damned by the Americans who were on course with us. But to us all, one way or another, it was an exciting and welcome development of bringing the United States onto our side. In his memoirs Churchill wrote simply: "So we had won after all!"

For some Canadian soldiers it meant tragedy, however. During an uneven 18-day battle for Hong Kong against the Japanese in December, two Canadian regiments, the Winnipeg Grenadiers and the Royal Rifles of Canada, as part of the defence force under the command of the British garrison, suffered 1975 casualties, among them 290 killed and 493 wounded who, along with the rest, were taken prisoner and confined under the most appalling, barbarous conditions.

Prisoner-of-war Private Ken Cambon wrote, "I did feel cheated. At 18 there was so much that I had yet to taste, and it seemed a shame to miss it all. I would like to say that I thought of all the great books I had not read, classical music I had no chance to appreciate, etc., but that was not really the case. I primarily thought of how few girls I had laid and *regretted not having been more aggressive with some that came to mind recalling several missed and bungled opportunities."*

Just before dawn on 8 December 1941 (December 7 by the western dateline) three battle-hardened regiments of the Japanese Sano force (named after the division commander) smashed across the New Territories frontier under air support that knocked out the meagre British air defences and bombed the key gun emplacements. In five days they had captured the mainland. It took less than two weeks more to overrun Hong Kong island in what was little more than a mopping-up exercise. On Christmas Day 1941 the battered defenders surrendered to the superior numbers of the Japanese forces.

The Canadian contingent, which consisted of the Winnipeg Grenadiers and the Royal Rifles of Canada, lost 290 killed and 493 wounded, leaving 1418 survivors to face nearly four years of captivity under the most barbarous, inhumane conditions imaginable, 267 of whom died as prisoners. One of the survivors was Ken Cambon, who in 1940 had quit his job as a soda jerk in Quebec City when his weekly pay of ten dollars was cut in half over an issue of a broken coffee percolator. He had to lie about his age to join the army (he was 17).

At the Stanley Garrison on the southeastern tip of Hong Kong island, on the day after formally surrendering, Ken Cambon and the remnants of the Royal Rifles, who had lost 130 men killed and 227 wounded in the brief 18 days of fighting, sat down to enjoy their first hot meal in peace since the battle began. It would be their very last solid repast for more than three-and-a-half years.

That momentary luxury did nothing to assuage their anxiety about what lay in store. Rumours, wishful thinking, misleading reports abounded. Chiang Kai-shek's Nationalist Chinese forces were closing in on Kowloon—relief was thought to be only days away. Rescue by the Americans and the British from the sea was imminent. Surely the Japanese officers in charge were going to be courteous and respectful of their prisoners of war.

Nothing could have been further from the truth.

The fate of Hong Kong had been a foregone conclusion as early as 1940—sacrifice would be a more appropriate designation—when the British joint chiefs of staff on the Far East declared that "Hong Kong is not a vital interest and the garrison could not long withstand a Japanese attack."

Assurances of consideration and kindness on the part of the Imperial Nipponese Army fell on deaf ears. First-hand accounts of prisoners who had escaped from St. Stephen's Hospital told of the wounded being bayoneted in their beds, 60 of them to their death, by the Japanese enemy. Medical officers who protested were executed, and five Canadian nurses were raped repeatedly before being taken to Stanley Garrison where more indignity awaited them.

On December 30, the 500 remaining Royal Rifles who were still able to walk were marched under guard to a prison compound at North Point on the Hong Kong waterfront across the bay from Kowloon. Here they were incarcerated along with Indian Army troops and some British. Originally a refuge for Chinese fleeing the mainland, the compound had been badly damaged in the fighting. There was no water and nothing to eat for two days. Three hundred men were packed into huts built to accommodate 30. There was no glass in the windows, no furniture of any kind; prisoners had to sleep on the cold concrete floor, most without blankets.

Plumbing was nonexistent; the sea wall acted as an open latrine where the tide washed up Chinese bodies along the perimeter of the breakwater. Nearby, a dump served a dual purpose for the Japanese who emptied all their refuse there and got rid of the bodies of the Chinese they killed. Jointly the receptacles produced a breeding ground for flies, lice, and fleas—not to mention bedbugs—that swarmed over everything, including the meagre servings of food. An outbreak of bacillary dysentery resulted, of which Ken Cambon was one of the first to fall victim. Relieving himself at the sea wall, he was holding on to the fence, very weak with fever, nauseous, and racked with cramps. When he glanced down he saw a bloated body drift by.

He was fortunate that an Indian medical officer had given him some sulfa pills for his discomfort before the surrender. Cambon credited the pills with having saved his life. Dysentery was indeed a killer. Only six days after the end of the battle, on New Year's Day 1942, the disease claimed its first Canadian victim—the first of 21 Canadians to die of various causes during the nine months spent at North Point.

Avitaminosis—various kinds of vitamin deficiency—caused by the limited food rations, however, was the major cause of ailments that plagued the prisoners. Among them: beriberi, a wretched blend of swollen feet and ankles, shortage of breath, and cardiac failure; pellagra, commonly known as "Strawberry Balls," a rash and itching in the scrotum area; "Electric Feet," a neuritis resulting in extreme pain in the legs; a sense of loss of balance in which some sufferers were unable to walk even with the help of a cane; partial and permanent loss of vision.

Major Gordon Gray of the Royal Canadian Army Medical Corps (RCAMC) later stated: "The sudden change in diet from meat, potatoes, and vegetables to one of 90 percent rice and some unrecognizable green things in it, and little unrecognizable pieces of fish—it's quite a shock. I was lucky in that I could eat a lot of rice."

A typical daily diet consisted of a handful of rice (usually crawling with maggots) for breakfast, two buns for lunch, and rice and watery soup for dinner. One prisoner, William Ashton, described the food as "so awful, I wouldn't feed it to my dog!"

Hunger reduced men to the lowest levels of depravity simply to stay alive. One survivor said that he couldn't believe he could be so hungry. He chewed grass, weeds, anything he could find:

We all had diarrhea or dysentery or both a good deal of the time and knew that rice and barley could go through you practically untouched. I was in such bad shape that—I'm going to tell this as quickly as I can to get it over with—I cupped my hands under a man squatting with diarrhea, caught the barley coming through, washed it off as best I could and ate it. Later I saw some other men doing this now and then but it didn't make me feel less ashamed. I didn't feel ashamed while I was doing it though. I was too hungry to feel anything but hunger.

After six months' imprisonment the Japanese organized work parties to lengthen the runways at Kai Tek Airport. Any ineptitude such as the inability to balance the two Coolie baskets at either end of a pole angled across the shoulders for carrying loads was duly rewarded with face slappings and head beatings for "sabotage," though the beatings were mild in contrast to the punishment meted out later at the Niigata work camp in Japan.

The Japanese never did discover one true act of sabotage of which Cambon and some of his buddies were guilty. When mixing concrete and sand they deliberately made sure that they put as little concrete into the mix as possible in the hope of weakening the runway surface and damaging planes as a consequence.

They knew full well the risk they were taking and the penalty they would suffer if caught: they had been witness to the inhumane cruelty of their captors, not to the prisoners themselves but to the Hong Kong populace. Just outside the camp fence bordering the street, the Chinese civilians daily passed by in full view. Without cause, the prison guards would tie a Coolie to a post and bayonet him while other guards looked on shrieking with laughter. Cambon wrote: "I still painfully remember them killing a Chinese woman and her baby when she went down to the seawall beside the camp."

Toward the end of his captivity at North Point, Cambon was assigned as an orderly to the Bowen Road Military Hospital under the command of Colonel Donald Bowie of the British Royal Army Medical Corps (RAMC). The move would save his life.

The transfer was like being transformed into another world. After sleeping on the cold concrete floor of the prison hut, he had a bed with sheets and mosquito netting, and clean clothes and washing facilities. But although the food was a marked improvement, it wasn't sufficient to prevent malnutrition. During his first week at the hospital, Cambon contracted a bad bout of his old nemesis, dysentery.

About that time the Japanese closed the North Point Camp and moved the prisoners to Shamshuipo at Kowloon on the mainland. Coincidentally, an epidemic of diphtheria broke out, which might have been prevented had all the Royal Rifles been inoculated before leaving Canada. Most of them had not, Cambon among them, and although he nursed many advanced cases, he was fortunate enough not to contract the disease himself. At first the Japanese refused to supply antitoxin and many men died. The prisoners were not allowed to put down the proper cause of death on the death certificates issued by the Red Cross. Instead they assigned the Cause of Death as laryngeal croup, which any medical person would recognize as diphtheria.

In July 1943, Cambon's hiatus as a hospital orderly came to an end when he was returned to prison camp life. But he found conditions at Shamshuipo vastly improved over the North Point Camp and the food even more nourishing than the hospital facility. His stay was short; after a few weeks, the Royal Rifles and the Winnipeg Grenadiers found themselves herded into the hold of a filthy coal transport vessel, the *Manryu Muru*, on their way to the infamous Camp 5-B in Niigata, 200 miles northwest of Tokyo, far enough from the Japanese capital to allow the successive camp commanders an inalienable control over the fate and lives of their prisoners. By far the most sadistic was the psychopathic Lieutenant Masato Yoshida, who was judged the most brutal of all the prison camp bosses in Japan. He welcomed the arrivals to his camp with the greeting: "You are prisoners of the Imperial Nipponese Army. The war will last a hundred years and you will be here forever." Then brandishing his sword he slashed it through the air with the promise: "This is the punishment for disobedience."

It was no idle threat. During his six-month tenure, until 5 February 1944, 69 of the 267 Canadians under his control died of deliberate neglect, disease, overwork, and starvation.

The camp was a temporary one, pitifully inadequate to accommodate nearly 300 prisoners. It consisted of a two-storey building divided into 10 rooms separated by paper walls. Thirty people were crowded into a single room, each one with barely enough space in which to lie down. But at least the POWs were provided with a cotton blanket and a small, hard pillow. Outside at one end was a single outdoor pump for water but no washing facilities. At the other end one lone outdoor toilet—a "benjo"—hardly enough to serve the needs of that many men particularly when most of them were afflicted with chronic diarrhea.

The prisoners were divided into three different slave groups. "Rinko" was the group that worked on the docks where coal brought by boat from Manchuria was unloaded into small cars carrying half-ton loads. Each car had to be pushed by a prisoner along rails mounted on a trestle 30 feet from the ground and dumped onto different storage areas around the docks. Another group, "Shintetsu," laboured in an iron foundry, while the third, "Marutsu," worked as stevedores on a general cargo dock. By far the toughest assignment was Rinko, and it was Cambon's misfortune to be picked for that work gang.

The POWs were roused at five in the morning and given a potato and some greens for breakfast before setting out on the two-mile trek to the docks. On the first day they were confronted with another welcoming harangue, this time from the work boss of the Rinko Coal Company, Ichsaku "Rasputin" Kojima, a tough taskmaster, who was later found guilty by the War Crimes Trials of causing the death of a Canadian prisoner-of-war, Leo Bottie, by beating him so badly he could hardly walk, then forcing him to go to work.

The foremen, or *fuo*-men, under him known as "Honchos" carried long, heavy sticks, worn like swords, which on the slightest provocation or excuse they used to beat a prisoner across the head and back. By far the worst of them was Sato "Satan" Katsuyasu, who on one occasion locked Canadian Private Ernest Heuft, a prisoner ill with diarrhea, in a latrine overnight to die of freezing.

Lunch for the slave labourers was brought from the camp and consisted of some grain cereal, radish soup, and a small piece of fish. The workday ended at five o'clock in the afternoon when the prisoners were marched back to the barracks. Before lying down for the night amid bedbugs and lice, they were fed a potato and a handful of rice for dinner. Tired and dirty, underfed, weak from diarrhea, badgered and beaten consistently, Cambon was soon down to 90 pounds and could barely drag himself to and from work. He knew he couldn't last much longer on the coal detail.

The numbers of sick and dying soon became so numerous that one of the barrack rooms was converted into a makeshift hospital and Cambon applied for a job as orderly. At first his request was refused; but out of necessity, as the number of ill became overwhelming, it was accepted. It was a losing battle: lack of doctors and trained medical personnel was compounded by the absence of medicinal supplies. Camphor had to be used to treat pneumonia, bismuth subnitrate for dysentery, neither of them effective.

In desperation, fearing possible consequences from his superiors over the spreading sickness and disease in his camp, the commandant brought in a pair of priests to administer acupuncture and its cousin moxibustion, but without significant results. Finally, a British medical officer, Major Bill Stewart of the RAMC, was allowed into the camp; even though drugs were scarce, the fact that a specialist had arrived to take charge gave morale a much-needed lift.

But without proper supplies and qualified assistance Stewart was powerless to correct the appalling situation in which 150 men were unable to work, suffering from a variety of ailments without enough hospital facilities to accommodate and care for them. "All this," he reported later, "obviously indicated gross, callous neglect on the part of the Japanese."

When he confronted Lieutenant Masato Yoshida to complain that the men needed rest from work, relief from exposure until adequate clothing and housing could be provided, and better food and proper medication, the camp commandant was singularly unmoved. "He informed me in the toughest of tones," Stewart wrote, "that these men had been sent here to work, and work they would or die."

Stewart did what he could. He separated those most likely to die from the rest. He inaugurated a daily examination of those reporting sick and took men off work, to rest up for three to four days—which saved many a life. But when news of the sick reached Tokyo, a warrant officer from the Japanese Medical Corps was sent to Niigata to investigate and take necessary steps as he saw fit. One, Sergeant Major Fugi, ordered everyone back to work except those in the hospital and 20 others who were obviously too ill to make it. The situation rapidly became even more of a nightmare than before.

On 24 December 1943, the prisoners were moved from the temporary camp to the newly built one. Conditions there were even worse. The buildings had not been completed. There was no kitchen, food was cooked two miles away, and by the time it arrived it was cold. There were no windows. The spaces were boarded up, leaving cracks through which rain and snow found their way into the buildings. There was no water supply—it had to be brought in by barrels—and no heating. Then on New Year's Day one of the buildings housing 50 men collapsed in the middle of the night, killing eight and severely injuring 12 others.

Four of the men with pelvic injuries were moved into a small cottage in the city. Cambon was assigned to look after them. The Japanese staff were surprisingly friendly, especially the women who even brought their "enemies" small gifts of food. While crowded, the house was comfortable with a small kitchen and full toilet facilities. Cambon treated himself to a hot bath, his first in three years. The respite ended all too soon and after a few weeks the patients and their orderly were returned to Camp 5-B, which had been split up and moved to new quarters. Disturbed over the increasing death rate—but not on merciful grounds, as the Japanese were only concerned with the number of bodies available for slave labour—they knew the only way to keep the POWs alive was to improve living conditions. The camp was divided into two—the foundry workers in one camp, and the coal workers and dock loaders in another in a building near the docks.

The Rinko and Marutsu camps, though still cramped, were a decided improvement, with stoves in the buildings. Every prisoner was given a weekly bath and provided with toilet paper, soap, and more clothing. At this time the first Red Cross parcels began arriving in Japan. Best of all was the departure of the vicious sadist, Masato Yoshida. But before he left he was responsible for one of the worst cases of brutality in any of the Japanese prisoner-of-war camps.

On 4 March 1943, James Mortimer, a rifleman with the Royal Rifles, and an American prisoner stole a can of salmon from the bicycle of a Japanese worker. The theft was discovered when a guard found the empty tin in their hut while the prisoners were asleep. One of Yoshida's subalterns, presumably on direct orders of the camp commandant, flew into a rage and beat both men with the flat of his sword, then had them strung up by their thumbs over a rafter, their toes barely touching the floor. They were then taken outside in the snow and freezing weather and tied to a gate post, where they were left for an entire day despite pleas and protestations from Dr. Bill Stewart. Mortimer was wearing only cotton pants and worn footwear with no socks and no shirt. The American was dressed no more warmly. Finally, when the guards cut them loose, Cambon with the help of others carried them into the hospital. The American died 15 minutes later.

Although Mortimer's upper body was only superficially frozen and he had the use of his arms, his lower limbs were frozen beyond repair and became gangrenous. He died two days later on 7 March 1944. At the war crimes trial, George Dixon of the U.S. navy, a fellow prisoner, testified, "His feet were so badly frostbitten that all his toes had to be removed to prevent further infection. ... I attribute his death to exposure, malnutrition and lack of medical attention." Cambon paid him this tribute: "Mortimer showed incredible courage and tenacity, knowing he had almost no chance of survival." Another observer, John R. Stroud stated, "He is officially listed as dying of frostbite and exposure but in my opinion he was murdered."

Yoshida, a former school teacher who had served in China with the army in 1937–38 where he was wounded, was brought before the War Crime Trials and charged with murder, torture, and other crimes, to which he pleaded insanity. Later he was declared sane, and as the evidence against him mounted on 16 June 1948, he hanged himself in his cell. He had been responsible for more ill-treatment of Canadians in Japan than any other war criminal.

The Japanese medical corporal in charge, who was named Takashi, took a perverse delight in neglecting proper treatment and care for patients and refusing medication. For withholding medicine. which resulted in the death from dysentery of three Quebec soldiers, as well as other war crimes, Takashi was convicted and sentenced to 15 years' imprisonment.

Early in December 1944, somehow the POWs working in the prison hospital acquired a microscope which was to mark a fortunate change in conditions. Dr. Stewart immediately began conducting tests of prisoners' stools, which revealed that amoebic dysentery was rampant in the camp. When the new camp commandant, Lieutenant Jiroshi Takeuchi, learned of this result he went into a frenzy, beating up the hospital staff and blaming them for inadequate medical care.

He must have had second thoughts, however, because next day a professor and a group of students arrived from the University of Niigata Medical School armed with microscopes of their own and stools-testing equipment. Work parties were suspended and tests were conducted on everyone. The early results confirmed Bill Stewart's findings. To make sure the Japanese were presented with the worst possible picture of the dysentery situation, one of the prisoners, John Stroud, who suffered from an acute attack of the disease, provided the more healthy prisoners with samples of his own stools to submit as their own. The ruse apparently had the desired effect. The Japanese professor recommended a mass quarantine, mass treatment, and a general improvement of sanitation facilities. All this could not have come about at a better time. Niigata was besieged by one of the worst winters of snow and wind in its history, with drifts 20 feet high. The moratorium on work schedules doubtless saved countless lives.

By spring when the work schedule was resumed, there was little work to be done. Not much coal from Manchuria was reaching the Honshu harbour. American submarines and aircraft attacks had all but eliminated Japanese merchant shipping and Niigata port was blocked by mines dropped from the air.

At this time news reached the camp of the Axis surrender and American victories in the Philippines, Okinawa, and Iwo Jima. The Japanese, aware that an invasion of their homeland was imminent, began softening the treatment of POWs.

Though the harsh treatment from their captors eased, the outlook for the prisoners remained gloomy. To the half-starved captives it seemed the war would go on for a long time. Food was scarce and coal was in short supply—it would be a bleak winter. A large pit had been dug outside the camp which the prisoners were told was an air-raid shelter but they suspected (quite rightly as it turned out) that it was to be a mass grave for them when the Americans landed. In fact, Field Marshal Hisaichi Terauchi, a chief of the Imperial Army staff, had issued the edict: "At the moment the enemy lands on Honshu, all prisoners are to be killed."

Ken Cambon expressed the despondency that was catching up to him after three-and-a-half years of imprisonment in a diary he kept. Here are some excerpts:

I can think of nothing but the futility of this narrow, cramped existence. I wonder if it is worth fighting [for]. Is the cause a hopeless one? Is life outside just another prison, where your dearest desires, thoughts, ambitions are crushed by reality? Is there such a thing as happiness?

Somehow or other some mysterious power urges me onward, telling me that there is just one more hill to climb to reach the peak. I fear that I am losing my grip as each successive hill comes into view ... yet I know I will never give up. What drives me on I do not know.

... [I]s death such an important thing? I think I have seen too many die to really fear it. In fact it is one concrete thing we can be sure of. One merely fears the unknown. Yet I know death, what I do not know is life and sometimes I find myself very much afraid indeed.

Early in August, without explanation, on several successive nights the prisoners were made to stand outside the barracks. Then, on the 15th of the month, the entire Japanese prison guard detachment lined up in single file outside the guardhouse, the commandant emerging with a small table radio under his arm that was hooked up to an electrical outlet by the gate. Standing in front of the guards he shouted a command and they all, including the commandant himself, bowed dutifully toward the radio as a dull, monotonous voice droned from the set. As the voice ended to be replaced by the blare of martial music, the guards snapped back to attention, bowed once more then perfunctorily trooped back into the guardhouse.

Arthur Rance, the only prisoner fluent in Japanese, hastily and happily explained. The voice had been that of the Emperor Hirohito announcing the Japanese surrender, including in his proclamation the understatement: "The War situation has not developed necessarily to Japan's advantage." In fact that war was over!

The end had been a close call for the prisoners of Camp 5-B. The United States Air Force orders to the B-29 bomber *Enola Gay* carrying the atomic bomb read: "In the event of Hiroshima being clouded over, proceed to Niigata."

Yes! The Second World War had come to an end. But for the Canadian prisoners-of-war captured at Hong Kong and elsewhere, the ordeal never ended, the scars could never be erased physically or mentally.

In a final diary entry, Cambon wrote:

> I have literally grown up in a prison camp. Most of all my experience has been on the more unpleasant side of life—starvation, sickness, cruelty, robbery, torture, depravity—all overshadowed by death.
>
> I must make every effort to remove myself from the intense hatred and disrespect I have toward my captors. I must banish from memory the pangs of hunger, the cruelty, the sadism, the torture, the smell of death of the last few years.

Not all the ex-POWs felt that way. In 1985 on a visit to Tokyo, Leonard Birchall met a Japanese historian who had been a prison camp guard during the war:

> I looked at the guy and the minute he said he had been a policeman I could just picture that guy with the hat on shouting and hollering and beating the prisoners. You just want to take him around the corner and beat the hell out of him. You'll never lose that feeling. At least I won't.

Kay Christie, a nursing sister attached to the military at Hong Kong said:

> The fear remains. It took years to find the courage to go back. I always had excuses. I couldn't go at that time of year. I couldn't

afford it, or I couldn't take holidays then. Finally, I realized I had been caught there once and I was afraid to get caught again.

Wilf Queen-Hughes, a Winnipeg Grenadiers veteran, did not disguise his bitterness when he told Dave McIntosh, author of *Hell on Earth*:

... [T]he government—never really wanted to know what happened after sending us stupidly to Hong Kong in the first place. They might have to do something about it, like providing a decent pension, or asking Japan for compensation.

Most never recovered physically or psychologically. Harold Atkinson:

For five or six years afterwards I would have nightmares. I would wake up crying and fighting. Sometimes even now I wake up and my feet are kicking involuntarily.

Joseph Gurski:

It has affected both my physical and mental health. I feel nervous. I feel scared. It takes me a long time to articulate answers—I'm not as sharp in my thoughts. My memory is very poor.

John Vilbert:

I was unable to work for years afterwards and the pension they gave me was twenty dollars a month. I'll never forget, I couldn't sleep for nights with shooting pains—nerves. Couldn't mix with people, church or any crowded place. When I did work, after breakfast, I'd throw up part of it when I stooped. All the tissues in my fingers, hands, the veins, and nerves all dried up. Still my hands and the tips of my fingers have no feeling. ... [My feet] are so tender I can't walk in my bare feet, socks or slippers.

Ken Cambon seems to have been one notable exception. Aside from a gastrointestinal problem that cleared up, his imprisonment in no way handicapped his return to civilian life. The very first Hong Kong veteran to be discharged from the army, on his return to Canada he enrolled in medicine at McGill University in Montreal, where he married a fellow medical student, Eileen Nason. On graduation the Cambons moved to Vancouver, where they set up practices, both highly successful. Eventually Ken became Professor Emeritus (Surgery) at the University of British Columbia.

Though on leaving Japan after three-and-a-half years as a prisoner he had vowed "I shall never return," 40 years later he and Eileen flew to Hong Kong, where they visited the War Cemetery at Saiwan, then on to Tokyo, from which they took a train to Niigata.

It was a far cry from his prison camp days of thatched-roof houses, narrow streets, and ox-drawn carts, women in long bloomers and men in army-style uniforms with the inevitable peaked hats—of beatings and other abuse and mistreatment. This time, as the Cambons stepped from the train into the station, which opened up onto a square surrounded by shining steel and glass buildings, they were given the full VIP treatment. Greeted by representatives from the Japanese Foreign Affairs Section, they were taken to the mayor's office, where Ken was given the keys to the city, honouring him as the first member of Prison Camp 5-B to return.

But there was no trace of the prison camp sites. The area had given way to the modern expansion of Japan's fastest-growing city. At the Rinko coal yards where the prisoners had slaved to load coal onto one-ton rail cars, huge automated cranes now stood on the docks with scarcely a worker to be seen.

For Ken the memories flooded back: that New Year's Day when the building collapsed, the sick and the dying comrades. But they were fleeting memories best forgotten. He would later write: "In the plane winging home I was reminded of the words of Confucius: 'A man came to me with hostility and I let him keep his gift.'"

Compassion

Chapter 20

One Helluva Guy

Wally Floody of 401 RCAF Spitfire squadron was shot down over German-occupied France on 27 October 1941 by a German Messerschmitt 109, a year and a half before I also joined 401. We did not meet each other until a dozen years after World War II ended. By that time Wally had become legendary as the tunneller of the Great Escape from the German prisoner-of-war camp Stalag III. He and I worked together on several commercial enterprises and became the closest of friends. At the time he was the leading force in the Canadian Prisoners-of-War Association. He was known to his fellow ex-POWs as a warm, loyal, and compassionate comrade and friend, a description that fit him to a T. But I never realized or fully understood how deep that humanitarianism lay until after he died, when I uncovered the tale that follows.

This is not a story about Wally Floody the war hero, for that has been told many times. It is the account of his relationship with one of his closest friends—ironically a confessed teenage murderer.

His name was George Rutherford Harsh, and he was the son of a millionaire shoe manufacturer in Atlanta, Georgia. In 1928, only 18 years old, he was convicted of the "thrill killing" of a shoe clerk in that city, during one of a series of armed robberies by a gang of wealthy college kids out for kicks. Harsh was given the death penalty, a sentence that was later commuted to life imprisonment.

Although by his own admission he was "guilty as hell," he was spared because he came from a wealthy white family with considerable influence.

As a convict, Harsh spent six years' hard labour on a chain gang before he was given a job as an orderly in the prison hospital. One night in 1939, during an ice storm when the prison doctor couldn't make it to the hospital, Harsh saved a fellow convict's life by removing his ruptured appendix. In November 1940, the governor of Georgia granted him a pardon.

Free at last. However, on the outside Harsh was haunted by his past. He tried his hand at newspaper reporting but found that people didn't trust him. In desperation he considered taking a job with ex-convicts as a gunman in the numbers racket. But when he learned the Royal Canadian Air Force was recruiting Americans for aircrew, he hopped a train to Montreal, where he enrolled and was accepted as an air gunner.

A year later, at about the same time Wally Floody was shot down, George Harsh was commissioned as an officer and sent overseas where, after operational training, he joined a bomber squadron. In the fall of 1942, Harsh's bomber was shot down on a raid over Germany. Harsh was wounded but managed to bail out. He was soon captured, stitched up, and sent to Stalag III, where he met Wally Floody. A close friendship grew from the time Floody offered to use the monthly letter from the camp to his wife Betty to let Harsh's family know that he was alive; they received word two weeks before the official notice arrived.

Before the war, Floody had been a rock miner at Kirkland Lake, Ontario, so the prison escape committee put him in charge of digging three tunnels, at least one of which, they hoped, would elude detection, allowing for a mass breakout. It was an ambitious undertaking and Floody placed Harsh, whom he regarded as a "southern gentleman" despite the latter's admission that he'd been a convict and his admonition that "You crazy bastards are going to get the lot of us shot," in charge of security.

While Floody led a team of tunnellers underground digging their way through sand and clay, above ground Harsh played watchdog with a team of 200 *Kriegies* (prisoners) on constant alert for German "ferrets" who prowled the camp in search of tunnel operations. Two of the tunnels were discovered, so all efforts were directed to finishing the third.

By 14 March 1944 "Harry," the code name given the third and as yet undiscovered tunnel, was finished. However, 10 days earlier the Germans had singled out 19 of the prisoners and, without telling them why, marched them off to another prison camp. Floody and Harsh were among them. They later learned how lucky they'd been. On the night of March 24, 76 *Kriegies* broke out of Stalag III through "Harry," but only three actually escaped, and of the others rounded up, 50 were brutally murdered by the Gestapo.

In January 1945, the Germans began marching thousands of POWs west as Russian troops advanced from the east. The prisoners were put on a train to a prison camp near Berlin. There they were liberated by the Russians and their ordeal ended.

Floody went into business in Toronto running trade associations and kept the friendship among the *Kriegies* very much alive. Once a year he and Betty visited George Harsh at his home in New Jersey where he worked in the trucking business. But Harsh had trouble adjusting to civilian life. His days as a convict and war prisoner had left their scars; he began drinking heavily and his wife left him.

In 1971, Harsh published his memoirs, in which he paid tribute to those whom he had shared his days with as a POW, and at the same time expressed his sorrow over the murder he had committed as a youth. He deplored capital punishment as a "law zeroed in on the poor, the underprivileged, the friendless, the uneducated, the ignorant." He stated he was living proof that "You can't hang a million dollars," and maintained that capital punishment represents a sickness of the human spirit, drawn from the worst of motives: revenge.

In 1973 his estranged wife fell fatally ill with cancer and he was at her bedside when she died. Thoroughly disillusioned, on Christmas Eve of the following year he shot himself in the head. He survived the suicide attempt but a subsequent stroke left him partially paralyzed. He was unable to talk and he needed help to walk. Wally and Betty Floody took him into their home in Toronto. That he lived another five years was solely due to their devotion.

Harsh stayed with them for a year and a half, but became worried that he was becoming too much of a burden on the Floodys. They moved him into a nursing home. However, he found that so depressing that Wally arranged to get him into K Wing, the veterans' section of Sunnybrook Medical Centre in Toronto. Wally and Betty encouraged other ex-POWs to visit him regularly and took him home for weekends.

His final visit lasted 10 days at Christmas 1979. Early in the new year, George Harsh died peacefully in his sleep. Of the care and kindness that he and his wife had shown the man, Wally would only say, "I loved him. He was one helluva guy."

The same endearment could be applied to the selfless compassion of Wally and Betty Floody.

Bibliography

Bashow, David. *All the Fine Young Eagles.* Don Mills, Ontario: Stoddart Publishing Co. Limited, 1996.

Bercuson, David J. *Maple Leaf Against the Axis: Canada's Second World War.* Don Mills, Ontario: Stoddart Publishing Co. Limited, 1995.

Bishop, Arthur. *Canada's Glory: Battlefields That Forged a Nation.* Whitby, Ontario: McGraw-Hill Ryerson Limited, 1996.

Bishop, Arthur. *Courage in the Air.* Whitby, Ontario: McGraw-Hill Ryerson Limited, 1992.

Bishop, Arthur. *Courage on the Battlefield.* Whitby, Ontario: McGraw-Hill Ryerson Limited, 1993.

Bishop, Arthur. *Courage at Sea.* Whitby, Ontario: McGraw-Hill Ryerson Limited, 1995.

Blackburn, George G. *The Guns of Normandy: A Soldier's Eye View—France 1944.* Toronto: McClelland & Stewart, 1997.

Blackburn, George G. *Where the Hell Are the Guns?* Toronto: McClelland & Stewart, 1997.

Blakely, Tom. *Corvette Cobourg: The Role of a Canadian Warship in the Longest Sea Battle in History.* Cobourg, Ont.: Cobourg Branch of The Royal Canadian Legion, 1990.

Brodsky, G. W. Stephen. *God's Dodger: The Story of a Front Line Chaplain 1905.* Sidney, B.C.: Elysium Publishing, 1993.

Buch, Mary Hawkins and Carolyn Gossage. *Props on Her Sleeve: The Wartime Letters of a Canadian Airwoman.* Toronto: Dundurn Press, 1997.

Calvocoressi, Peter and Guy Wint. *Total War: Causes and Courses of the Second World War*. London, England: Allen Lane the Penguin Press, 1972.

Cambon, Ken. *Guest of Hirohito*. Vancouver: P.W. Press, 1990.

Christie, Carl A. *Ocean Bridge: The History of RAF Ferry Command*. Toronto: University of Toronto Press, 1995.

Churchill, Winston S. *The Second World War: The Grand Alliance*. Boston: Houghton Mifflin Company, 1953.

Cosgrove, Edmund. *The Evaders*. Toronto: Clarke, Irwin & Company Limited, 1970.

Dancocks, Daniel G. *In Enemy Hands: Canadian Prisoners of War 1939–45*. Edmonton: Hurtig Press, 1990.

Dancocks, Daniel G. *The D-Day Dodgers: The Canadians in Italy, 1943–1945*. Toronto: McClelland & Stewart, 1941.

Dearborn, Dorothy. *True Stories: New Brunswickers at War*. Hampton, N.B.: Neptune Publishing Company, 1994.

Dewar, Jane, ed. *True Canadian Stories*. Selected from *Legion Magazine*. Toronto: Lester & Orpen Dennys, 1986.

Donaldson-Yarmey, Joan. *50 Personal WW II Stories*. Edmonton: Jomet, 1995.

Dunmore, Spencer. *Above and Beyond: The Canadians' War in the Air*. Toronto: McClelland & Stewart, 1996.

Evans, George H. *Through the Corridors of Hell*. Antigonish, N.S.: Formon Publishing Company Limited, 1980.

Frazer, William Wallace. *Trepid Aviator*. Burnstown, Ontario: General Store Publishing House, 1995.

Gilbert, Martin. *Second World War*. Don Mills, Ontario: Stoddart Publishing Co. Limited, 1989.

Gossage, Carolyn. *Greatcoats and Glamour Boots: Canadian Women at War (1939–1945)*. Toronto: Dundurn Press, 1991.

Granatstein, J. L. *Canada's War: The Politics of the Mackenzie King Government, 1939–1945*. Toronto: Oxford University Press, 1977.

Hoare, John. *Tumult in the Clouds*. London, England: Michael Joseph, 1976.

Hobbs, Charlie. *Past Tense: Charlie's Story*. Burnstown, Ontario: General Store Publishing House, 1994.

Lamb, James B. *On the Triangle Run*. Toronto: Macmillan of Canada, 1986.

Legion Magazine. *True Canadian War Stories*. Toronto: Lester & Orpen Dennys, 1986.

Liddel Hart, Basil Henry, Sir. *History of the Second World War*. New York: G. P. Putnam's Sons, 1970.

Maclaren, Roy. *Canadians Behind Enemy Lines, 1939–1945*. Vancouver: University of British Columbia Press, 1981.

Martin, Charles Cromwell with Roy Whitsed. *Battle Diary: From D-Day and Normandy to the Zuider Zee*. Toronto: Dundurn Press, 1994.

McIntosh, Dave. *Terror in the Starboard Seat*. Don Mills, Ontario: General Publishing Co. Limited, 1980.

McIntosh, Dave. *High Blue Battle*. Toronto: Stoddart, 1990.

McIntosh, Dave. *Hell on Earth*. Whitby, Ontario: McGraw-Hill Ryerson Limited, 1997.

McVicar, Don. *Ferry Command*. Shrewsbury, U.K.: Airlife, 1981.

McVicar, Don. *North Atlantic Cat*. Shrewsbury, U.K.: Airlife, 1983.

Peden, Murray. *A Thousand Must Fall: Canada's Wings*. Stittsville, Ontario: 1976.

Porter, Bob. *The Long Return*. Burnaby, B.C.: B. Porter, 1997.

Pudney, John. *Atlantic Bridge*. London: HMSO, 1945.

Reader's Digest. *The Canadians at War 1939/45*. Commemorative edition. Montreal: 1969.

Reyburn, Wallace. *Glorious Chapter: The Canadians at Dieppe*. Toronto: Oxford University Press, 1943.

Saunders, Hilary St. George. *Royal Air Force, 1939–1945; Volume III: The Fight Is Won*. London, England: Her Majesty's Stationery Office, 1954.

Slessor, Sir John. *The Central Blue*. London, England: Cassel, 1956.

Swettenham, John. *D-Day*. Ottawa: Canadian War Museum, 1971.

Churchhill, Winston S. *The Second World War: Triumph and Tragedy.* Boston: Houghton Mifflin Company, 1953.

Toland, John. *The Rising Sun, Volume 2.* New York: Random House, 1970.

Tute, Warren, John Costello, and Terry Hughes. *D-Day.* London and Sydney: Pan Books Ltd., 1974.

Watt, Sholto. *I'll Take the High Road.* Fredericton: Brunswick Press, 1968.

Windsor, John. *The Mouth of the Wolf.* Sidney, B.C.: Gray's Publishing Ltd., 1967.

Index